Write to Read
Read to Write

Write to Read
Read to Write

Kathleen T. McWhorter
Niagara County Community College

Candalene J. McCombs
Canisius College

Little, Brown and Company
Boston   Toronto

Library of Congress Cataloging in Publication Data

McWhorter, Kathleen T.
    Write to read, read to write.

    Includes index.
    1. English language—Rhetoric.   2. College readers.
I. McCombs, Candalene J.   II. Title.
PE1408.M398   1983   808'.042   82-22838
ISBN 0-316-56403-6

Library of Congress Catalog Card No. 82-22838

ISBN 0-316-56403-6

9 8 7 6 5 4 3 2 1

MV

Published simultaneously in Canada
by Little, Brown & Company (Canada) Limited

Printed in the United States of America

ACKNOWLEDGMENTS

The authors wish to thank the following authors and publishers for
permission to reprint their material in this text.

UNIT ONE READING SELECTIONS

1. Dru Scott, from *How to Put More Time in Your Life*. Copyright
   ©1980 Dru Scott. Reprinted with the permission of Rawson-
   Wade Publishers, Inc.
2. "The Other You," reprinted by permission of *American Way*,
   inflight magazine of American Airlines. Copyright ©1975 by
   American Airlines.
3. Charles Garfinkel, from *Racquetball the Easy Way*. Copyright
   ©1978 by Charles Garfinkel. A Sport Marketing, Inc. Book.
   Reprinted with the permission of Atheneum Publishers.
4. "To Lie or Not to Lie," ©1978 by The New York Times
   Company. Reprinted by permission.
5. From Ian Robertson, *Sociology*, pp. 327–329. Copyright ©1977 by
   World Publishers, Inc.
6. Robert C. Yeager, *Seasons of Shame*, pages 7–8, copyright ©1980,
   published by McGraw-Hill Book Company. Reprinted by
   permission of the publisher.

UNIT TWO READING SELECTIONS

7. "Kids' Country," Copyright 1972 by Newsweek, Inc. All Rights
   Reserved. Reprinted by Permission.
8. "Angels on a Pin," *Saturday Review*, December 21, 1968, reprinted
   by permission of *Saturday Review*.
9. "Thermography—A Fabulous New Way of Seeing," reprinted
   with permission from the January 1975 Reader's Digest.
   Copyright ©1975 by The Reader's Digest Assn., Inc.
10. "The New (and Still Hidden) Persuaders" reprinted by
    permission of the author, Vance Packard.
11. "What You See Is the Real You," ©1977 by The New York
    Times Company. Reprinted by permission.
12. LIFE SCIENCE LIBRARY/Time, by Samuel A. Goudsmit, Robert
    Claiborne, and the Editors of Life. Time-Life Books Inc.
    Publisher. ©1966 Time Inc.

UNIT THREE READING SELECTIONS

13. "Dazzled in Disneyland" reprinted from *Holiday Magazine*, Vol.
    34, July 1963, pp. 68–70. Curtis Publishing Company.

Introduction to the Student

A basic premise expressed throughout this text is that writers should write to be read. That is, as you write you should always keep your reader in mind and remember that you are writing to be understood. Furthermore, as you read, you often read in order to write. Many situations require you to write about what you have read—reacting, evaluating, or summarizing.

Each chapter will begin by discussing communication from the reader's point of view. In the first part of the chapter you will learn the basic patterns and structures commonly used in effective writing. In the remainder you will use what you have learned to write more effectively. However, as you develop skill in writing, you will find that you are also acquiring the skills to become a more effective reader.

The text begins by organizing the most important features of the reading and writing into parallel step-by-step procedures. These steps provide an overall structure for the text. Unit One provides a general overview of the reading and writing processes. Chapter 1 introduces you to a step-by-step method for effective reading and writing. Chapter 2 emphasizes audience and purpose in both writing and reading. You will see how your purpose affects how you approach each task, and you will see how a writer's intended audience determines what is said and how it is said in any particular piece of writing.

Unit Two focuses on developing skill in reading and writing various types of sentences. You will learn about the various ways sentences can be written, and you will practice writing sentences that express your ideas in clear, effective ways. Specifically, you will learn how ideas can be combined within a single sentence and how you can show the relationship among ideas using particular sentence patterns. By learning these sentence patterns you will be able to understand complicated sentences more easily and to select what is important in a long or difficult sentence.

In Unit Three you will learn how paragraphs are structured, and then you will learn how to develop and arrange your ideas in paragraphs that more effectively explain and communicate your ideas. Unit Four of the text develops your ability to comprehend longer selections and to organize groups of ideas into an essay.

Throughout each unit you will continue to apply the Steps to Effective Reading and Writing presented in Chapter 1. In addition to practice exercises for each skill presented in a chapter, there will be a chance for you to apply the skills you are learning to a wide range of reading materials in the reading selections at the end of each unit. Then, by completing the corresponding writing exercises, you will have a chance to react to what you read using the writing techniques presented in the unit.

Overall, this text provides a systematic approach to developing the writing skills needed in college and on the job. Through the combined instruction you will be able to see the relationship between writing and reading skills and to develop both skills at the same time. Through systematic use of step-by-step procedures and the benefit of guided practice in applying each technique as it is presented, you will find that you are able to express your ideas accurately and clearly in writing and to comprehend reading assignments easily.

K.T.M.
C.J.M.

Contents

Contents

Write to Read
Read to Write

Unit One
A Systematic Approach to Reading and Writing

You have probably always thought of reading and writing as opposite skills. Reading is a process you use to get information from printed sources. For example, in order to get specific information you desire from want ads, TV listings, telephone directories, and textbooks, you have to read. On the other hand, to give or communicate information to someone else, or to record information for yourself, you write it down. You jot down a phone number, you address an envelope, you leave a note for a friend, you fill out a job application. Each of these activities involves writing. You have been accurate in thinking of reading and writing as opposite skills in the sense that each skill has a different purpose or result. In reading your purpose is to get information, whereas in writing your purpose is to give information. However, if you think of reading and writing as parts of a total communication process, you will see that the two skills have much in common. In fact, you may think of them as mirror images of each other.

Let's consider any communication process as a trading and sharing of information, ideas, and feelings. You can express your ideas and feelings to someone else by speaking, writing, or using such nonverbal cues as facial expressions, gestures, body posture, and tone of voice. Also, you can derive information by listening to a person's speech, watching his or her behavior, or reading something he or she has written.

Throughout this text, as we discuss reading and writing as parts of the communication or information-sharing process, you will discover how closely the two skills are related. Reading and writing are both means of communication, so they both involve sharing information. A writer has information he or she wishes to share with someone, and a reader wants to get information from something another person has written. In writing you must express ideas accurately and clearly so that they can be understood. In reading you must be careful to get the information the writer has recorded.

As part of the communication process, reading and writing have much in common. First, each skill relies on a general knowledge of common language patterns and structures. For example, to read or to write a paragraph you must be familiar with the basic structure of a paragraph. Similarly, reading or writing a sentence involves a knowledge of how a sentence is put together. Second, to be effective, both reading and writing depend on organization. When you write, you arrange and organize your ideas; when you read, you must recognize and follow the structure and logical progression of ideas. Third, reading and writing are mental processes in which you translate ideas and feelings to or from written words. Finally, both reading and writing depend on a common language system, including vocabulary and grammar, which provides the vehicle for communication.

As you can see, there are numerous similarities and parallels between reading and writing. For this book we have attempted to create an appreciation of the similarities and parallels between the skills required for reading and writing. They provide a solid base for the development of habits that will result in effective reading and writing habits.

This unit will present an overview of the reading and writing processes, and Chapter 1 will outline steps that can lead to reading and writing more effectively. These steps will be introduced here, but they will be built on and emphasized throughout this book. In Chapter 2 we will discuss two factors—audience and purpose—that are important to both reading and writing. You will see how both audience and purpose influence how you read and how you write.

1. Effective Reading and Writing

Reading and writing are essential skills for every college student. To be successful in your courses, you must understand and remember what you read and communicate your ideas effectively in writing.

What do reading and writing have in common? Your first response to this question may be "nothing" or "very little." However, if you think of reading and writing as ways of exchanging or sharing information, you may realize that they have much in common. You use reading to get information from printed sources, whereas you use writing to record information or ideas. You may read a bus schedule, a magazine article, a movie review, or a final exam. If, for example, you address an envelope, you expect that someone else will read that information to send your letter to its correct destination. Or, if you are reading a movie review in a newspaper, you can be sure that the film critic wrote it to offer information about the film to those who read the paper. Both the reader and the writer, then, are involved in exchanging information. A reader and a writer have a common purpose—the exchange of ideas. You read to learn about someone's thoughts or ideas, and someone reads your writing to learn about your ideas and feelings.

Since reading and writing are both forms of communication, an effective way to develop both skills is to consider them together as the exchange of ideas between a reader and a writer. Since reading and writing are parallel skills, as you are learning one you also develop skills in the other. Learning to write more effectively can help you to read more effectively. Similarly, carefully applied effective reading techniques can contribute to writing skills. The following demonstration emphasizes the parallel features of reading and writing.

The following sample paragraph describes how a student felt about college after the first day of classes. Read this paragraph and then write the answers to the two questions that follow.

My first class today was at 8:00 in American history, and the instructor has already assigned a term paper. I think this will be my worst class for the semester. My next class was at 10:00. It's a sociology class, and it seems pretty interesting. The only other class I had scheduled for today was math, but there aren't enough students, so the class might be cancelled. This means I'll have to schedule a different class. I hope I can get it at a good time so I can stay in *my car pool. I didn't have time to talk with anyone today because I had to get my books, and the lines in the bookstore were long. It seems like college is going to be a lot of work, and it might not be as much fun as I thought it would be.*

1. How did this student feel?

   _____

2. What happened that made him or her feel this way?

   _____

Now, write a few statements on how you felt about college after your first day of classes. Try to describe what happened that made you feel that way. Write these statements before continuing with the rest of the chapter.

_____

_____

_____

_____

_____

_____

_____

_____

Next, write the answers to the following questions.

1. Before you started to write did you think about or remember how you felt?

   _____

   _____

2. After you decided how you felt, did you try to remember things that happened that day that explain why you felt that way?

   _____

   _____

Finally, reread the sample paragraph and then look at the statements you wrote. You will see that both pieces of writing do the same thing: they describe how someone felt about college after the first day.

Let's consider the skills you used to read the student's paragraph and to write your statements. In reading the sample paragraph you had to identify what happened to make the person feel a certain way. In the statements you wrote you had to describe how you felt and tell why you felt that way.

In your statements you expressed and explained your ideas. You decided what to write about and how to explain it; then you wrote it so that someone else could understand it. In reading the paragraph written by someone else you had to do just the reverse. You had to understand the ideas expressed by someone else.

From this example you can see that reading and writing involve similar skills and approaches. To further understand the relationship between reading and writing, let's look at what is involved in the communication process from the point of view of the reader and of the writer.

Read the following sample selection, "The Jeaning of America," trying to remember as much as you can about the selection. This sample selection will be used later on in the chapter to show more clearly how reading and writing are similar skills.

The Jeaning of America—and the World

Carin C. Quinn

This is the story of a sturdy American symbol which has now spread throughout most of the world. The symbol is not the dollar. It is not even Coca-Cola. It is a simple pair of pants called blue jeans, and what the pants symbolize is what Alexis de Tocqueville called "a manly and legitimate passion for equality. . . ." Blue jeans are favored equally by bureaucrats and cowboys; bankers and deadbeats; fashion designers and beer drinkers. They draw no distinctions and recognize no classes; they are merely American. Yet they are sought after almost everywhere in the world—including Russia, where authorities recently broke up a teen-aged gang that was selling them on the black market for two hundred dollars a pair. They have been around for a long time, and it seems likely that they will outlive even the necktie.

This ubiquitous American symbol was the invention of a Bavarian-born Jew. His name was Levi Strauss.

He was born in Bad Ocheim, Germany, in 1829, and during the European political turmoil of 1848 decided to take his chances in New York, to which his two brothers already had emigrated. Upon arrival, Levi soon found that his two brothers had exaggerated their tales of an easy life in the land of the main chance. They were landowners, they had told him; instead, he found them pushing needles, thread, pots, pans, ribbons, yarn, scissors, and buttons to housewives. For two years he was a lowly peddler, hauling some 180 pounds of sundries door-to-door to eke out a marginal living. When a married sister in San Francisco offered to pay his way West in 1850, he jumped at the opportunity, taking with him bolts of canvas he hoped to sell for tenting.

It was the wrong kind of canvas for that purpose, but while talking with a miner down from the mother lode, he learned that pants—sturdy pants that would stand up to the rigors of the diggings—were almost impossible to find. Opportunity beckoned. On the spot, Strauss measured the man's girth and inseam with a piece of string and, for six dollars in gold dust, had them tailored into a pair of stiff but rugged pants. The miner was delighted with the result, word got around about "those pants of Levi's," and Strauss was in business. The company has been in business ever since.

When Strauss ran out of canvas, he wrote his two brothers to send more. He received instead a tough, brown cotton cloth made in Nimes, France—called *serge de Nimes* and swiftly shortened to "denim" (the word "jeans" derives from *Gênes*, the French word for Genoa, where a similar cloth was produced). Almost from the first, Strauss had his cloth dyed the distinctive indigo that gave blue jeans their name, but it was not until the 1870s that he added the copper rivets which have long since become a company trademark. The rivets were the idea of a Virginia City, Nevada, tailor, Jacob W. Davis, who added them to pacify a mean-tempered miner called Alkali Ike. Alkali, the story goes, complained that the pockets of his jeans always tore when he stuffed them with ore samples and demanded that Davis do something about it. As a kind of joke, Davis took the pants to a blacksmith and had the pockets riveted; once again, the idea worked so well that word got around; in 1873 Strauss appropriated and patented the gimmick—and hired Davis as a regional manager.

By this time, Strauss had taken both his brothers and two brothers-in-law into the company and was ready for his third San Francisco store. Over the ensuing years the company prospered locally, and by the time of his death in 1902, Strauss had become a man of prominence in California. For three decades thereafter the business remained profitable though small, with sales largely confined to the working people of the West—cowboys, lumberjacks, railroad workers, and the like. Levi's jeans were first introduced to the East, apparently, during the dude-ranch craze of the 1930s, when vacationing Easterners returned and spread the word about the wonderful pants with rivets. Another boost came in World War II, when blue jeans were declared an essential commodity and were sold only to people engaged in defense work. From a company with fifteen salespeople, two plants, and almost no business east of the Mississippi in 1946, the organization grew in thirty years to include a sales force of more than twenty-two thousand, with fifty plants and offices in thirty-five countries. Each year, more than 250,000,000 items of Levi's clothing are sold—including more than 83,000,000 pairs of riveted blue jeans. They have become, through marketing, word of mouth, and demonstrable reliability, the common pants of America. They can be purchased pre-washed, pre-faded, and pre-shrunk for the suitably proletarian look. They adapt themselves to any sort of idiosyncratic use; women slit them at the inseams and convert them into long skirts, men chop them off above the knees and turn them into something to be worn while challenging the surf. Decorations and ornamentations abound.

The pants have become a tradition, and along the way have acquired a history of their own—so much so that the company has opened a museum in San Francisco. There was, for example, the turn-of-the-century trainman who replaced a faulty coupling with a pair of jeans; the Wyoming man who used his jeans as a towrope to haul his car out of a ditch; the Californian who found several pairs in an abandoned mine, wore them, then discovered they were sixty-three years old and still as good as new and turned them over to the Smithsonian as a tribute to their toughness. And then there is the particularly terrifying story of the careless construction worker who dangled fifty-two stories above the street until rescued, his sole support the Levi's belt loop through which his rope was hooked.

STEPS TO EFFECTIVE READING

Now that you have read "The Jeaning of America," take a moment to think about the skills you had to use to read the selection. What did you have to do to understand what Quinn was saying? You used a variety of skills: you recognized letters, associated sounds with letters, and identified words. Other, more difficult skills involved knowing the meaning of difficult vocabulary and recognizing complex relationships. Most readers are not completely aware of all the skills they use. Usually they cannot describe or list them step by step. Although you have developed many skills over the years, you might not have developed the *most* effective ways to use and connect them. Here are a few questions that will help you to discover whether you read in the most efficient way. Read through the following list and think about how you would answer each question.

1. Did you do anything *before* you began reading the selection to enable you to read it more easily, better, or faster?
2. Did you have specific information in mind that you wanted to find as you read?
3. As you read each paragraph, did you notice how it was organized? Did you identify what each paragraph was about? Did you notice how everything else in the paragraph related to that idea?
4. As you read each sentence, did you look for the connections and relationships between ideas?
5. Did you notice how the paragraphs were connected?
6. Did you notice how the entire selection was organized?
7. Did you do anything when you finished reading to help you remember what you read?
8. Did you react to and think about what you read?

Unless you were able to answer yes to each question, you are not reading at peak efficiency. These questions were designed to suggest to you the kinds of activities that are involved in reading to retain what you read. These useful activities are organized into an effective, step-by-step approach to reading that can improve your efficiency:

1.   Prereading
2.   Establishing a purpose for reading
3.   Reading
4.   Reviewing
5.   Reacting

The procedure involves very specific activities before, during, and after reading. After you learn more about these steps, you will have a chance to try them out on a sample selection, and by the time you have completed this course, the step-by-step approach will be a matter of habit. In a later portion of this chapter, you will see that a similar set of steps is involved in producing effective writing.

Prereading

If you have read an article or essay previously, you will find it easier to read the second time, even if the first reading occurred several years ago. Also, if your instructor tells you what an assignment is about before you read it, it will usually be easier to understand and remember. Reading is always easier if you are familiar with the content or if you can easily follow the author's train of thought.

You do not usually have the advantage of previous reading, however, and instructors do not always give you an introduction or over-view of a reading assignment. In fact, some instructors avoid doing this because they feel that whatever they say will in some way limit or direct your thinking about the content. They might want you to approach the reading with an open mind.

Fortunately, there is a technique that you can use before you read nonfiction that will give you the same familiarity with and confidence toward a reading assignment that you get from previous reading or from an instructor's overview. The technique is called *prereading*, and it pro-vides you with some ideas of what the material is about. Prereading enables you to become familiar with what you are going to read before you begin to read it, providing you with an overview, or a mental outline, of the material. You develop some ideas about what you expect to learn from a particular reading assignment.

In prereading you will look at the parts of the material that will give you the most information about what you will read. Here are the steps to follow:

1.   *Read the title.* In many cases the title will tell you the general subject of the material. It may also help you to identify the author's approach or point of view toward the subject. For example, if a selec-tion is titled "In Defense of Contact Sports," you know it is about contact sports and that the author will argue in favor of contact sports.
2.   *Check the author(s).* If the author is identified, be sure to notice the name. If you recognize the author, you may know the type, general subject, and style of writing to expect. For instance, if the author of an article is Bill Cosby, you might expect it to be informative but also

light and humorous. On the other hand, you would expect something written by former president Jimmy Carter to be fairly straightforward, serious, and probably about politics.

3. *Check the source and date of publication.* Unless you are reading a text-book assignment or a current magazine or newspaper article, always check to see when and where the article was originally published. In many subject areas it is important to know how up-to-date your information is.

4. *Read the first paragraph completely.* The first paragraph frequently serves as an introduction or lead-in. Often in the first paragraph an author tells what the material will be about and what he or she will say about the topic.

5. *Read any dark print (boldface) headings.* If an article has headings that divide it, read them. Together the headings make up a very brief outline of the topics or main ideas. Many articles and selections do not contain headings. For reading material without headings, read the first sentence of each paragraph

6. *Read the first sentence of each paragraph.* The first sentence often explains more fully what is stated in the heading. It also states what is important to know about the topic or main idea identified in the heading. Frequently this sentence states what the whole paragraph is about. If the material is longer than one or two pages, reading the first sentence of each paragraph might be too time-consuming. Instead, you might read one or two first sentences per page.

7. *Glance at the remainder of each paragraph.* By glancing at the remainder of each paragraph, you might notice names, dates, or italicized words. You will get a general impression of the difficulty and organization of the rest of the article.

8. *Notice any maps, graphs, charts, or pictures.* Graphic aids such as maps, graphs, charts, or pictures are used to emphasize or further explain important ideas and concepts. Notice the subject of each graphic aid, and you will discover the concepts that deserve emphasis.

9. *Read the last paragraph.* In many types of writing the last paragraph serves as a summary (restating the most important ideas) or a conclusion (often making a new statement that is drawn from the ideas presented in the reading). Reading this paragraph will often give you a clear statement of the most important ideas in the selection.

10. *Look at end-of-chapter aids.* When prereading textbook chapters, quickly read through any study aids at the end of the chapter. Review questions, lists of important vocabulary, chapter outlines, or questions for discussion will help you to identify what is important and what to look for as you read.

Adapting Prereading to Suit the Material

Because various reading materials are organized differently, you may need to adapt the prereading technique to fit what you are reading. Because of the content and organization of what you are reading, you may not be able to follow each step listed above. Some types of reading assignments may lack introductions; others may not include summary statements. In general, try to notice all features of the material to provide yourself with an overview of the material.

Now, go back to "The Jeaning of America" on pages 5–7 and try out prereading. Although you have already read this article, it will be useful to preread it now so that you can easily see how prereading does acquaint you with the main ideas of the selection. Follow each step that applies to this selection. After you have preread, turn back to this page and continue reading from this point.

In "The Jeaning of America" the title suggests the topic. In the first paragraph Quinn introduces the topic that is discussed throughout the selection—blue jeans. The first sentence of the third paragraph confirms that the article will trace the history of the invention of blue jeans. The remaining first sentences point to further developments in the growth in popularity of blue jeans. The last paragraph discusses how jeans have become a tradition and have acquired a history of their own.

Establishing a Purpose for Reading

Many students complain that they cannot remember what they read. Almost all people, at one time or another, have read a whole page and found that they cannot remember anything they have read. You may have found that when your instructor makes an assignment and tells you what to look for, you have less difficulty recalling what you read. The reason is that you have something specific to look for, and searching for information as you read helps you to concentrate. Unfortunately, in most reading situations, specific purposes for reading are not provided.

However, you can develop your own purpose for reading. The easiest way to do this is to form questions that you will try to answer as you read. By developing your own questions, you will produce results that are similar to those provided by an instructor's assigned purpose for reading. Looking for the answers to specific questions will also make it easier for you to concentrate and to understand the material.

Setting up your own purpose for reading should be based on your prereading of the material. From your prereading, you have a general idea of what a selection is about and how the author approaches and develops the subject. You have an idea of what to expect. Relying on this information, you can form questions that are important to answer as you read. For "The Jeaning of America," you might ask questions like this:

1. What does the "Jeaning of America" mean?
2. Why did Strauss invent blue jeans?
3. Why did blue jeans become popular?

If you go back and reread the selection using these purpose questions as a guide, you will find that they help you keep your mind on what you are reading. You will find that you are actively searching for information as you read.

Reading the Material

Many people think of reading as simply a matter of moving their eyes across a line of print and recognizing the words. Actually, reading is a complex activity that involves numerous physical and mental processes. Of course, you have mastered most of these processes and are now at the point of developing and polishing skills that contribute to your comprehension and retention of reading assignments. For example, you have already developed a core vocabulary consisting of tens of thousands of words that you recognize automatically. Now you are ready to expand that core vocabulary to include specialized words and terms that apply to the courses you are taking.

In some of your college courses you may encounter long and difficult reading assignments. To handle these you need to develop skills to make reading these assignments easier and to help you remember more of what you read. Maybe you feel you read too slowly, but at this point you should not be overly concerned about your reading rate. Many students who read slowly feel that a slow reading rate is the reason they do not understand what they read. These students think they need to be taught to read faster. Actually, most students who read slowly do so because they are having difficulty understanding and remembering what they are reading. In fact, they do not need to learn to read faster, but they *do* need to learn how to comprehend and remember difficult material.

To read effectively you must be able to understand the ideas the writer expresses. This requires a knowledge of word meaning as well as the structure of sentences, paragraphs, and passages or selections. Once you understand how each is "put together," you will be able to read each more easily. For example, a sentence is made up of a number of pieces, some of which are more important than others. Also, ideas are combined into a sentence in a variety of ways, and these patterns affect its meaning. Once you are familiar with the parts and patterns used in sentences, you will be able to read them more accurately and more easily. Paragraphs, passages, and articles and selections have similar pieces and organizations. The three remaining units of this text will concentrate on skills for more accurately comprehending sentences, paragraphs, and selections, but to begin, one essential key to word meaning is the dictionary.

Types of Information to Find in the Dictionary

An essential aid to effective reading is the dictionary. Although the dictionary, of course, is a source for definitions of words, it also contains a variety of other types of useful information that can significantly expand your vocabulary. Here is a list of some types of information it contains.

1. *Multiple word meaning.* Many words have more than one meaning, some of which are appropriate for certain contexts and not for others. When you are looking up a particular word, be sure to choose a meaning that makes sense in the sentence in which the word is used.

2. *Word pronunciation.* Have you ever been unsure of how to pronounce a word? This situation most commonly arises when you attempt to use a word from your reading vocabulary in your speaking vocabulary. Rather than to guess at the pronunciation of a word or to avoid using it because you are unsure of its pronunciation, take a moment to look it up. Immediately following the word entry, you will find a pronunciation key. At first, this key may not appear very useful. Suppose you are trying to figure out how to pronounce the word "deign," meaning to agree in a condescending manner. After the word you would find the following: (dān). Although this phonetic spelling may not translate immediately into an easily

pronounceable word or phrase, the key at the bottom of the page provides an easy way to interpret the phonetic symbols. For instance, the *American Heritage Desk Dictionary* lists the following key

ă pat ā pay â care ä father ĕ pet ē be hw **which** ĭ pit ī tie î pier
ŏ pot ō **toe** ô **paw,** for oi noise o͞o took o͞o b**oo**t ou **out** th **thin** th **this**
ŭ cut û **urge** zh vision ə about, item, edible, gall**o**p, circus

From the key you learn that the "a" sound in "deign" rhymes with the word "pay," and an accent mark (´), for words with two or more syllables, is included to indicate which part of the word should receive the greatest emphasis.

3. *Key to spelling.* The common complaint about using a dictionary as a spelling aid goes as follows: If I cannot spell it, how can I locate it in the dictionary? Generally, most spelling errors do not occur at the beginnings of words anyway (with the exception of words beginning with ph, mn, or ch-sh). Thus, it is possible to locate a particular word in a dictionary. In addition to the basic spelling of a word, the dictionary often shows how spellings change when the word becomes plural or an -ing ending is added to the word.

4. *Useful tables and charts.* Many dictionaries contain numerous tables and charts that make the dictionary a handy general reference book rather than just an alphabetic list of words and meanings. Commonly included among a dictionary's tables and charts are tables of weights and measures with metric equivalents; lists of abbreviations; lists of signs and symbols; a guide to punctuation, mechanics, and manuscript form (also called a style manual); a table of periodic elements used in chemistry; and lists of famous people (dead and alive), and what they are noted for.

5. *Information on language history.* Actually, the dictionary functions as a brief history of the English language. For each word entry, information is given about the origin of the word. This etymological information tells you the language or languages from which the word evolved. In the following entry you can see that the word *establish* is derived from Middle English, Old French, and Latin.

es·tab·lish (ĕ-stăb′lĭsh, ĭ-stăb′-) *tr.v.* **-lished, -lishing, -lishes.** Also *archaic* **stab·lish** (stăb′lĭsh). **1.** To make firm or secure; fix in a stable condition. **2.** To settle securely in a position or condition; install: *"he established me in the firm which thereafter bore my name"* (Louis Auchincloss). **3.** To cause to be recognized and accepted without question: *His flight established Lindbergh as a national hero.* **4.** To originate on a firm, lasting basis; to found. **5.** To create a state institution of (a church or religion). **6.** To introduce as a permanent entity; promulgate: *ordinances established by the king.* **7.** To prove the validity or truth of. **8.** *Card Games.* To gain control of (a suit) so that all remaining tricks can be won. —See Synonyms at **confirm.** [Middle English *establissen,* from Old French *establir* (stem *establiss-*), from Latin *stabilīre,* to make firm, from *stabilis,* firm. See **stā-** in Appendix.*] —**es·tab′lish·er** *n.*

6. *Foreign expressions used in English.* Certain expressions from other languages have become widely used in the English language. These phrases often express an idea or feeling more accurately than do the English translations. The French expression *faux pas* is a good example, translated to mean a social blunder. Most dictionaries list foreign phrases alphabetically along with English words, although in some dictionaries you may find a separate list of foreign expressions. A few more examples of commonly used foreign expressions

that are listed in most dictionaries are: *ad hoc, non sequitur, de facto, tête-à-tête,* and *bona fide.* Throughout this text, exercises are included to give you practice in reading dictionary entries and in choosing appropriate word meanings for words used in the reading selections.

Reviewing

As soon as you have finished reading an article or assignment, you probably close the book with a sigh of relief and the satisfaction that you have completed a task. However, there are several steps to follow before calling a reading task complete. If you want to remember more of what you read, spend a few minutes reviewing what you have read right after you finish reading it. In fact, reviewing immediately after you finish reading is much more valuable than reviewing later on. Immediate review will make what you read "stick" in your mind and enable you to recall it later. You will find that reviewing will improve your comprehension and increase the amount of material you are able to remember. It will also help you learn to look for organization in a piece of writing. This will prepare you for the revision process in writing. The procedure to use for review will vary according to what you are reading and how it is organized. However, you can use the following steps as a guide:

1. Look at the title and try to recall the important points the author made.
2. Reread the introduction and summary. These paragraphs will give you a quick review of how the selection began and how it ended.
3. Reread each heading or the first sentence of each paragraph and try to remember the important ideas presented in each section. If you cannot remember, then reread that section.
4. In textbooks read through any end-of-chapter aids such as review questions, questions for further discussion, outlines, or vocabulary lists. These items will also help you to recall the content of the chapter.

In reviewing "The Jeaning of America," you might reread the title, the first paragraph, the first sentence of each paragraph, and the last paragraph. Try reviewing "The Jeaning of America" now to see what this procedure brings back to mind about the content of the article.

Reacting

Reading is primarily concerned with understanding what the author said, or getting a message from a printed page. To be an effective reader, however, you must also react to, evaluate, and interpret this message. Not only should you know what the writer said, but you should also have your own thoughts and ideas about what was said. This type of reading is often called interpretive or critical reading. Although the focus of the reading portions of this text is on techniques for understanding and remembering what you read, you should be aware that interpretation is also important. To begin thinking about and reacting to what you read, you might ask yourself some of the following questions:

1. Do I agree or disagree with what was said? Why?
2. Does the writer explain or support his ideas sufficiently? How?

3. How do these ideas compare or connect with my previous knowledge and experience?

You may find that some of these questions also are useful when you are asked to write about something you have read. Two additional questions you could ask are:

1. For whom was this written?
2. Why did the author write this?

In thinking about and reading "The Jeaning of America" you might ask the following questions:

1. What evidence does the author give that supports the popularity of the blue jeans?
2. For whom was this passage written?
3. Why did the author write about blue jeans?

Now that you have read through an overview of the steps to follow to read more effectively and to remember more, test out these steps by completing the following exercise.

EXERCISE 1–1

Directions: *Select* one *of the selections at the end of the unit and read it using these steps:*

1. Preread the selection. Underline or highlight the material you used to preread.
2. Using the information you learned by prereading, write three questions you expect to be able to answer after you have thoroughly read the selection.

   a. _____

   b. _____

   c. _____

3. Read the selection. As you read, list the information that answers your questions.

   a. _____

   b. _____

   c. _____

4. Review the selection. Write a list of the parts of the article that you used to review.

   a. _____

   b. _____

   c. _____

5. React and think about what you have read. Then answer the following questions:
    a. Do you agree or disagree with what was said? Why?

    _____

    b. Does the writer explain or support the ideas sufficiently? How?

    _____

    c. How do these ideas compare or connect with your previous knowledge or experience with the topic?

    _____

STEPS TO EFFECTIVE WRITING

"The Jeaning of America" (see pages 5–7) is written in clear, correct language, and it is well organized, but this did not happen automatically. The selection is the result of many steps involving planning and organizing ideas, writing, revising or rewriting, and finally rereading the material and correcting errors. Each step will be briefly introduced and described in this section and discussed in detail in later chapters. Together these steps work as a framework or system for producing effective writing. They are:

1. Prewriting
2. Composing
3. Checking the content and organization
4. Revising
5. Proofreading

Prewriting

Have you ever sat down to write a paper and felt as if you have nothing to say or found that you could not get started? You might have stared at a blank page for a long time and not written a single word. Fortunately, there are prewriting strategies to help you overcome these problems and generate ideas to write about. Prewriting is the first step in producing a piece of writing, and it will also help you to establish your train of thought and to prepare you to continue with the other steps in the writing process.

There are two strategies involved in prewriting. Each helps you to develop ideas to write about. The first strategy, *narrowing your subject,* helps you to find a topic. The second, *developing ideas about your topic,* can be accomplished using a technique called free writing, or an alternative approach called questioning.

Narrow the Subject to a Manageable Topic

Choosing your subject and narrowing your focus to a specific topic are crucial to producing a good paper. If you begin with an unmanageable topic, regardless of how hard you work, you will not be able to produce an acceptable paper. Also, your task can be made much easier if you decide on a topic that you know something about or for which information is readily available.

The most important consideration in deciding on a topic is to develop one that is neither too broad nor too narrow. If you write about a topic that is too broad, it will be impossible for you to adequately cover all its aspects. On the other hand, if the topic is too specific, you may have difficulty finding enough to write about. For most students, the tendency is to select a topic that is too general.

Suppose that you have been taking a course in sociology and have been asked to write a two-page paper on your impression of college life. If you simply wrote down "College Life" as a title and started writing, you would find yourself struggling with too much to say.

There are many aspects of college life, and it would be impossible to cover them all in a two-page paper. For instance, you could narrow the subject of college life to meeting new friends, living in a dormitory, finding classes different than you expected, or the social activities that are available.

It is often necessary to narrow your subject two or three times. The process of narrowing a subject might be diagrammed as follows:

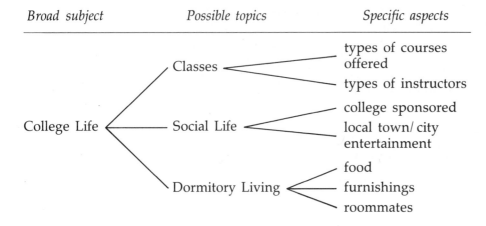

Broad subject	Possible topics	Specific aspects

Here the broad subject is college life, but within that very broad subject other more manageable topics, such as classes, social life, and dormitory living, can be developed. Notice, too, that very specific aspects of the three subdivisions of college life are also listed. For example, it would be possible to write about just the food in the dormitory, but the development of this topic would require a very narrow focus. To some extent the process of narrowing your subject will be affected by your purpose for writing, which will be discussed in detail in Chapter 2.

To narrow a subject to a manageable topic, try to think of ways the subject could be subdivided. Start by listing all possible topics that fall under that subject. For example, suppose your subject were pollution. You might list the following topics, or particular aspects, of pollution.

SUBJECT: Pollution

POSSIBLE TOPICS: long-range effects   air pollution
short-term effects   soil pollution
radiation   water pollution
chemical land fills   environmental pollution
damage to wildlife   causes of pollution

Some of your topics may be too specific, others too broad, depending on the purpose and length of your paper. Cross out those which are too specific and those which you know little or nothing about. Then, with those that remain, select a topic that would be manageable for you; using the same process, narrow one that is still too broad to a more manageable topic.

Until you have written numerous papers, you may find that you still select topics that are too broad or too narrow. Do not hesitate, once you have begun writing, to stop and further narrow or broaden your topic. It will save you time in the long run.

EXERCISE 1–2

Directions: *Assume that one of your instructors assigned a paper on one of the following subjects. Choose one and narrow it to a topic that you could write about in a three-page paper. Use a format like the one shown below:*

SUBJECTS: 1. Sports
2. Salesmanship
3. Mate Selection

FORMAT:

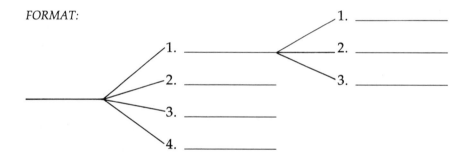

Free Writing to Develop Ideas

Once you have chosen a manageable topic, you may experience difficulty in deciding what to say about the topic. A technique called *free writing* can help you to develop ideas. Free writing involves two steps. First, begin by writing whatever comes to mind and do not stop writing until a preestablished time period has elapsed. For example, you might choose to free write for five minutes, so you write for five minutes without stopping, not worrying about grammar or punctuation or organization. Write down any idea that comes to mind, whether it relates to the topic or not. The result will be a confusion of many ideas, some related to each other and some, perhaps, irrelevant, but you will have ideas that you can use in writing your paper.

Next, read through what you have written and cross out sentences that contain unimportant ideas or do not fit in with your topic. Look at the following example of free writing on the development of designer jeans. This sample is the result of three minutes of free writing.

I like designer jeans. I think they fit better than ordinary jeans. Unfortunately, I can't afford them though. Some people have their designer jeans dry cleaned. I really couldn't afford that! My mother said that when she was in high school only the really poor kids wore jeans. It's funny how things change. My sister said she never wore jeans until she went to college. She went in the sixties. She also bought an Army fatigue jacket and the more faded and torn the jeans were the better it was. I see older women wearing designer jeans in supermarkets. I heard from a friend that a whole bunch of girls wore jeans to job interviews. Designer jeans only fit people who are thin. Especially thighs. Designer jeans are always tight in the thighs. I wonder who the first designer was who put his name on jeans. I suppose it's just the name. They probably don't fit any different from Levis. I don't really know much about how designer jeans developed, but it was probably just for money. I'd put my name on jeans, too, if I made a lot of money off it. What a rip-off.

This sample of free writing helped the writer realize that the topic was not manageable. After considerable rambling, the writer finally stated, "I don't really know much about how designer jeans developed. . . ." However, this free writing exercise did provide a context for some further thought. Look at the development of ideas that followed in a second attempt at free writing on a revised topic—characteristics of designer jeans.

The first designer who put his name on a pair of jeans must have made a lot of money. I'm sure it was a man, too. Probably Calvin Klein. That would explain why jeans have become such a status symbol. I wonder who Jordache jeans were named after. Their commercials are really sexy. No wonder they sell. Designer jeans do seem to fit better, but probably that's because they're made to fit specific body types *and they're not meant for the same purpose. Jeans used to be work clothes. Now they're worn everywhere. I am really having trouble thinking of something else to say. I wish I could buy a pair of stretch jeans. But they're so expensive. They're not worth it. Although maybe the fabric is better. They don't fade. They shrink though.*

Notice that there are a number of ideas, and the order is jumbled and irregular. There are incomplete sentences and other errors, but they are not important for now. The point is, there are ideas here that can be developed. Some of the ideas are clearly not relevant, and they will be left out of the final copy.

Look at the same sample again and notice the ideas crossed out by the writer because they were not important, or they did not seem to relate to any of the other ideas.

The first designer who put his name on a pair of jeans must have made a lot of money. ~~I'm sure it was a man, too.~~ Probably Calvin Klein. That would explain why jeans have become such a status symbol. ~~I wonder who Jordache jeans were named after.~~ Their commercials are really sexy. No wonder they sell. Designer jeans do seem to fit better, but probably that's because they're made to fit specific body types and they're not meant for the same purpose. Jeans used to be work clothes. Now they're worn everywhere. ~~I am really having trouble thinking of something else to say. I wish I could buy a pair of stretch jeans. But they're so expensive. They're not worth it.~~ Although maybe the fabric is better. They don't fade. They shrink though.

The writer crossed out some statements because they did not directly apply to the topic. Other ideas seemed to be related, but they still needed to be expanded and organized.

Free writing is a useful technique because it provides an opportunity for you to explore and record your thoughts as they occur. Some writers complain that they have nothing to write about, but if they draw on their own experience and memory, or their ideas and feelings about something they have read, they find that they have many ideas.

Using Questions to Generate Ideas

As an alternative to free writing, the technique of questioning is also helpful in developing ideas to write about. For example, when you have a topic in mind but cannot get started, questions can often help you think of ideas to write about. Essentially questions are used as a means of developing ideas. You start by thinking of questions that could be asked about the topic; then you write down the questions and consider how you would answer them. You may want to write an answer to each question. Consider, for example, the questions a student developed on the topic "Jeans as a Fashion Fad."

1. Why do people wear jeans?
2. Are all jeans of the same quality?
3. Why are designer jeans twice as expensive as others?
4. What does it "say" when you wear designer jeans?
5. Are jeans comfortable?
6. Are they attractive?

Each question provides a source of ideas that can be further developed, expanded, or explained. Of course, you might not use all the questions you have written, but that doesn't matter. You may eliminate some of the questions in the same way you eliminate irrelevant ideas in a free-writing exercise.

Free writing and the use of questions are both effective techniques for generating ideas about a topic, but most students eventually develop a preference for one of the two techniques. Experiment with each method several times before you decide on the approach you prefer, but keep in mind that the topic might influence your approach, so you should be able to use both techniques. After trying each technique several times, you will probably be able to decide when each will be more helpful.

EXERCISE 1–3

Directions: *Select one of the subjects listed below. First, narrow it to a manageable topic. Next free-write about that topic for five minutes. Then cross out any ideas or statements that you probably would not use in a paper. Write a list of the ideas you could use in developing a paper on the topic.*

SUBJECTS: Time Management
Doctor–Patient Relationships
Skill in Sports

EXERCISE 1–4

Directions: *Select one of the subjects listed below. First, narrow it to a manageable topic. List at least ten questions about the topic. Then read through your questions about the topic. Select one, and list several pieces of information that might be used to answer the questions.*

> SUBJECTS: Genetic Research
> Health and Fitness
> Male–Female Relationships

EXERCISE 1–5

Directions: *This exercise will give you additional practice in the prewriting techniques. Three subjects are listed below. Use a different subject for each part of this exercise.*

> SUBJECTS: Test-Tube Reproduction
> Medical Ethics
> Morality in Sports

1. *Narrowing a subject.* Select one of the subjects and write a list of possible topics.

   SUBJECT: _____   _____

   TOPICS: _____   _____

   _____   _____

   _____   _____

2. *Free writing.* Select another subject. First, narrow it to a topic, and then write about that topic for five minutes. Find three main ideas after you have finished writing and circle them. Cross out any irrelevant ideas.
3. *Using questions to generate ideas.* Narrow the remaining subject to a topic. Write a list of at least five questions about that topic. Choose one question and explain several details that would appear in an answer.

Composing

Composing is the process of expressing ideas in an organized, understandable form. Although composing is a different experience for everyone, it involves explaining your ideas and combining them in some logical sequence. Your ideas should be written in complete sentences, and they should be related to each other. However, do not be concerned with exact wording or grammatical correctness at this point. Instead, concentrate on expressing your ideas clearly in an organized, understandable way. You will go back later and correct grammar or choose a more appropriate word or expression when you revise.

Your sentences should be grouped into paragraphs. However, these paragraphs may need to be expanded or perhaps divided later, depending on the way the organization develops. The paragraphs in most essays and papers form a pattern suggesting an introduction, a body, and a conclusion. The *introduction* states the topic that will be discussed. The *body* develops the main ideas about the topic, and the *conclusion* summarizes the most important details or makes a final statement about the main ideas and supporting details. You will learn more about the organizational pattern of paragraphs and essays throughout the text.

All pieces of writing, regardless of their length, are focused on a single subject. Also, there is a single, most important idea that is developed throughout the essay called the *unifying idea.* All of the other ideas and details in the essay, then, explain or support that idea. Each paragraph of the body should explain a separate but related aspect or feature of the unifying idea. These supporting paragraphs, too, are arranged in a logical or sequential order, with one idea leading to the next. Generally, the introduction leads up to and states the unifying idea, the body explains and supports this idea, and the conclusion or summary makes a final statement about the subject and unifying idea. In the last unit of the text, specific techniques for structuring essays to follow this pattern will be presented.

The following example of a piece of writing in the composing process was developed from the free-writing exercise on pages 17–19. The development is not complete, but notice how each idea leads to another. You can see paragraphs that need further work, but there is an introduction of the topic and some discussion and a conclusion.

The most important thing about designer jeans is a label with a designer's name on it. The label gives the jeans a status that separates them from ordinary jeans. Calvin Klein was one of the first designers to permit his name to be used on jeans. Since his clothing designs were well respected in the fashion world, the jeans became a new status symbol.

Designer jeans seem to fit better than ordinary work jeans. This may be the result of a difference in purpose. Designer jeans are supposed to look good while work jeans are supposed to hold up under heavy abuse. Designer jeans are cut differently, and the fabrics are also different.

Jeans used to be work clothes, but now everyone wears jeans, and they are worn everywhere. The old faded baggy pants that used to last forever have been replaced by *sleek and tight-fitting pants that are not appropriate for hard wear. The fabric looks nicer, but it's softer and less durable. Most important of all though, the label suggests money and success.*

You can see that the writer chose one unifying idea, or centered his or her ideas on one concern—the differences between designer and ordinary jeans. Then the writer explained and discussed these differences. Specifically, fit, purpose, cut, fabric, and durability are discussed.

When you have finished writing, or composing your piece of writing, you should plan on changing, correcting, and improving it later in the revision process. Many students assume, mistakenly, that their first attempt at writing will produce a finished, acceptable paper. Most writing, even that done by professional writers, needs revision—restating, reorganizing, and adding and deleting ideas.

EXERCISE 1-6

Directions: *This exercise is intended to give you some practice in composing. Use one of the topics you have already developed for either the free-writing exercise or for the exercise on formulating questions to generate ideas.*

If you choose to work from your free-writing exercise, cross out any irrelevant ideas you wrote and select three main ideas that can be developed into three paragraphs by adding more details. Next, decide what these three ideas have in common or how they relate to your topic. Write a statement that connects them. This statement can serve as your unifying idea. Write several statements about each idea and develop the ideas into a short paper on the topic.

If you prefer to work with the questions you formulated, choose a question, write out possible answers, and develop some ideas for a short paper on a topic. Your answers to the questions should provide details about the idea that is generated by the question.

Checking the Content and Organization

After you have produced your first draft, you need to reread your writing to determine if you have included sufficient and appropriate detail to support your ideas. Also, you need to check the order in which you express your ideas to be certain that the relationship of the ideas is clear and easy to understand. Although some accomplished writers outline their ideas before they begin to write, many others find that they have difficulty planning ahead, or they find themselves too restricted in following an outline. In this approach to writing you will be outlining as an aid to rewriting and revising your rough draft, rather than as a starting point.

To use outlining in this manner, write a series of brief statements that list ideas in the order they appear in your rough draft. Once you have written the outline, you will be able to see where more detail is needed and where there is too much. The outline will also show whether your ideas follow one another in a clear, logical way. In other words, outlining will help you to organize your ideas and to see how they fit together. Look at this outline format:

I. Introduction	Statement of what the paper is about
II. Body	
A.	
B.	Discussion of the topic and supporting details
C.	
D.	
III. Conclusion	Summary or concluding statement

Try to divide your outline into an introduction, the body, and the conclusion. These parts can then be further divided to show how the ideas are developed in each. The introduction should tell what the paper will be about; the body should present your ideas along with supporting facts and statements. The conclusion should restate your major ideas, or make a final statement concerning the topic. Usually such a concluding statement is an inference, which means that all of the ideas discussed in the paper lead up to the concluding statement.

The following sample outline shows the organization of the writing sample on pages 22–23. Look at the outline then check back to the writing.

I. Introduction of topic: Characteristics of Designer Jeans
   A. Prominent names on labels
   B. Jeans as status symbols
II. Body: Designer versus Work Jeans
   A. Change in purpose of jeans
   B. Changes in the construction of jeans
III. Conclusion: Designer Jeans Imply Money
   A. Jeans are not restricted to one class
   B. Jeans are not restricted to specific occasions
   C. Jeans are a high-fashion item

This outline shows the organization of the piece of writing developed on the topic "Characteristics of Designer Jeans." The writer discovered some problems in the paper, particularly in the progression of ideas. The final paragraph changes the focus slightly, and the result is a discussion about "jeans" rather than "designer jeans." The writer has made a generalization; the word "jeans" is assumed to mean designer jeans. The writer felt it necessary to make a distinction between designer jeans and "regular jeans," so the last paragraph still needs work. You will see the changes the writer made when you read the section of this chapter that covers the revision process.

Outlining is one way to check your organization; prereading is another effective way. If you preread what you have written, you will be able to see how clearly organized it is. Use these steps:

1.   *Read the title.* If you have titled your paper, does the title not only reflect what your topic is, but does it also give clues to your reader on how you will present it? Could your readers see from it how you feel about your topic or what special views you propose?

2.   *Read the first paragraph.* Does your first paragraph clearly establish your topic and introduce your overall approach? Does it introduce your topic in a clear and interesting way?

3. *Read the first sentence of each paragraph.* Does the first sentence introduce a new aspect or feature of the unifying idea? Is each idea clearly related to the unifying idea?
4. *Read the last paragraph.* Does the last paragraph "wrap up" or conclude your paper? Does it in some way indicate that this is the final paragraph?

Either outlining or prereading will help you to evaluate the overall organization of your ideas to decide whether they are clearly presented. You may find that your ideas are not expressed as clearly as possible or that they could be more effectively organized. Then you can begin to change or rewrite certain statements or ideas. This need for change leads directly to the next step in writing effectively—revising.

EXERCISE 1–7

Directions: *This exercise is intended to give you some experience in checking the content and organization of your writing. Look at the order of the ideas you developed in exercise 1–6. Make a brief outline, deciding what should be mentioned first, second, third, etc. Decide which main idea should be in the first, second, and third paragraphs. Look for ideas that do not belong and for ideas that need further explanation. If necessary, write a new outline of the paper showing a more effective order of ideas.*

Revising

Most writers have difficulty writing at one time or another, and most professional writers will tell you that they constantly revise, or change, what they have written. Writers often revise as they write as well as afterward. If you observed a good writer as he or she were writing, you would see that the writer might write a sentence and then cross part of it out and rewrite it. A writer might also find it necessary to add a sentence or two in a paragraph when he or she discovers that there is a need to explain an idea further or to introduce an idea earlier. The writer might go back and add a sentence or two of explanation in the margin or between the lines.

The revision process begins when you discover you should have stated something differently. If, in the middle of a sentence, you decide to cross out what you have written and start over, this is revision. Usually if a writer cannot think of what to write in the next sentence, he or she reads over what is already on paper and in doing so may discover that a word or phrase needs to be changed. Revision can actually begin in the very early stages of writing. Look at the following sample revision. Notice the changes the writer made to make the essay read better. Some new elements were introduced, and some sentences were moved or left out.

The ~~most important thing about~~ distinctive feature of designer jeans is ~~a~~ the label with a designer's name on it, ~~the label~~ giving the jeans a status that separates them from ordinary jeans. Calvin Klein was one of the first designers to permit his name

to be used on jeans. Since his ~~clothing~~ designs
were well respected in the fashion world, the
jeans became a new status symbol.

Designer jeans ~~seem to~~ fit better than
ordinary work jeans. This may be the result
of a difference in purpose. Designer jeans are
supposed to look good while work jeans are
supposed to hold up under heavy abuse.
Designer jeans are ^also^ cut differently, and the
fabrics are also different.

Jeans used to be ^worn only as^ work clothes, but now
everyone wears jeans, and they are worn
everywhere. ¶ The old, faded baggy pants that
used to last forever have been replaced by
sleek and tight-fitting pants that are not
appropriate for hard wear. ~~The fabric looks
nicer, but it's softer and less durable. Most
important of all though,~~ ^a Calvin Klein or Jordache^ ~~the~~ label suggests
money and success, not to mention sex appeal.
By lending their names, designers have made
jeans acceptable everywhere. However, there
are some jeans that are more acceptable than
others, and they are distinguished by their labels.

You can see that the writer's revision clearly distinguishes the
designer jeans from ordinary jeans. The introduction of a new element,
sex, completes the image projected by designer jeans. This conclusion is
not a summary; instead, it makes a final statement—designer jeans mean
"money, success, and sex."

If possible, you should revise your writing the next day, when you
can approach the paper more objectively. It is easier then to see the
changes you should make. It also helps to have someone else read your
essay. Sometimes another person can offer new ideas or suggestions on
how the writing could be improved. Use these questions as a general
guide for the revision process:

1. Read the title and the first paragraph. Do they prepare the reader
   for the remainder of the essay? If not, what needs to be added?
2. Read the first sentence in each paragraph. Does each sentence provide a new part in the discussion? Is the sequence of events or
   organization of ideas accurate? If not, what needs to be changed?

3. Look through the remainder of the paragraph. Are there words that connect your ideas? If not, where could they be added?
4. Consider the terminology. Is the word choice appropriate for your audience? Can any words be replaced with more accurate or more descriptive words?
5. Read the last paragraph. Does it leave the reader with a clear impression of main points or your conclusions? If not, what changes are needed?

Your goal in revising your essay is to bring it to the point where you can answer yes to each of these questions. Throughout the text you will learn skills and techniques that will allow you to do so.

EXERCISE 1–8

Directions: *This exercise is intended to give you some experience in revision. Carefully reread the paper you composed in exercises 1–4 and 1–5. Then answer each of the following questions. If you answer no or if you are unsure of the answer to any question, revise that section.*

1. Does the title announce or suggest the topic of your paper?
2. Does the first paragraph state what your paper is about?
3. Do the remaining paragraphs explain and support what your paper is about?
4. Did you provide sufficient detail and information to make your ideas clear and understandable to someone who is unfamiliar with your topic?
5. Do the paragraphs connect to one another?
6. Does the last paragraph draw your ideas together or make a final statement?

Proofreading

Proofreading is the final step in which you make sure your paper is grammatically correct and free of errors. Specifically you should check for errors in spelling, punctuation, and grammar. Also check for mechanical errors, such as leaving out a word, or accidentally miscopying a word or phrase. If you have typed your paper, also check for typing errors.

To proofread, read your paper critically, specifically looking for errors. Read each sentence as though it appeared by itself to see if each is clear and grammatically correct. It may be necessary to proofread your paper several times. You might read it through once, checking for misspelled words (be sure to check in the dictionary any that you are not sure of or those that "look wrong"). Then you might read the paper again to check that your punctuation is correct.

Proofreading is the last step in the writing process, so it should be the easiest. The errors corrected during proofreading are often really a matter of oversight or carelessness. Proofreading is not a time for rearranging ideas, so if you find that you need to rearrange ideas and rewrite a number of sentences, you need to spend more time on revision.

Once you think you have found all your errors, read your paper aloud. If you find yourself reading in a halting, stumbling fashion, check your punctuation and the way you have arranged words in the sentence. Make changes so that you can read the paper smoothly. Finally, you may find it useful to ask someone else to read your paper and point out any errors you might have missed. Compare the final copy of the essay with the revision on pages 25–26.

Final Copy

From Levi's to Calvin's

The distinctive feature of designer jeans is the label with a designer's name on it, giving the jeans a status that separates them from ordinary jeans. Calvin Klein was one of the first designers to permit his name to be used on jeans. Since his designs were well respected in the fashion world, the jeans became a new status symbol.

Designer jeans fit better than ordinary work jeans. This may be the result of a difference in purpose. Designer jeans are supposed to look good whereas work jeans are supposed to hold up under heavy abuse. Designer jeans are also cut differently, and the fabrics are also different.

The old, faded baggy pants that used to last forever have been replaced by sleek and tight-fitting pants that are not appropriate for hard wear. Jeans used to be worn only as work clothes, but now everyone wears jeans, and they are worn everywhere. By lending their names, designers have made jeans acceptable everywhere. However, there are some jeans that are more acceptable than others, and they are distinguished by their labels. A Calvin Klein or Jordache label suggests money and success, not to mention sex appeal.

The following checklist will be provided at the end of each chapter. At this point you may not be able to recognize all your errors, but try to check each item on the list. As you proceed chapter by chapter, indicate how many times you made the error in the column labeled "Frequency" and describe, whenever possible, the exact type of error you made. For example, suppose that you found two verb tense errors. After putting a 2 in the Frequency column, you should record each verb (wrong and corrected) in the Description column. In the section labeled "Spelling Errors" write the correct spelling of each word that you misspelled.

As you progress through the text, you probably will begin to see a pattern in the type of errors that you make. Some students notice, for instance, that they have problems with subject-verb agreement and the use of commas. Others find they have a tendency to write run-on sentences. Once you discover and are conscious of your pattern of error, you can try to avoid making these errors as you write and revise.

Because the text discusses only the most common types of errors and does not provide a comprehensive review of grammar, mechanics, and punctuation, it is advisable to consult a writer's handbook for more information on specific types of errors.

PROOFREADING CHECKLIST

Essay Title _____

Date _____

TYPE	✔	ERROR	FREQUENCY	DESCRIPTION
GRAMMAR		Run-on Sentence Sentence Fragment Subject/Verb Agreement Verb Tense Pronoun Agreement		
MECHANICS		Capitalization Italics Abbreviation		
PUNCTUATION		, (Comma) ; (Semicolon) ' (Apostrophe) " (Quotation Marks) . (Period) ! (Exclamation Point) ? (Question Mark) : (Colon) — (Dash) ( ) (Parentheses) - (Hyphen)		

		ERROR	CORRECTION	
SPELLING ERRORS				

EXERCISE 1-9

Directions: *This exercise is intended to give you some experience in proof-reading. Read over the final copy of the paper you revised for exercise 1–7 on page 25. Use the preceding checklist as a guide. Then, ask another student to proofread and suggest corrections on your paper before you submit it to your instructor.*

SUMMARY

This chapter explained similarities in reading and writing that involve parallel skills and approaches. Effective, step-by-step approaches for both reading and writing were presented. Steps leading to efficient reading are prereading, establishing a purpose for reading, reading, reviewing, and reacting. Effective writing involves the following steps: prewriting, composing, checking the content and organization, revising, and proofreading. The steps in each process contribute to more effective reading and writing.

2. Audience and Purpose

Effective, productive reading and writing depend on an awareness of audience and purpose. An essential part of planning what to write and how to write it depends on your purpose and the nature of the audience for whom you are writing. By the same token, an alert reader is aware of an author's purpose in writing and has some ideas about the type of audience for whom the message was intended. Understanding the relation of audience and purpose in both reading and writing is central to developing reading and writing habits that produce good results.

Audience refers to the person or group for whom something is written or intended. In reading you should consider the person or group the writer had in mind when the material was written, and in writing you should keep in mind the types of people for whom you are writing. *Purpose* is concerned with the reason or reasons for reading and for writing. In writing your purpose affects what you say and how you say it, but as a reader you need to be alert to the author's purpose for writing and be aware of your goal in reading.

UNDERSTANDING AUDIENCE AND PURPOSE

Understanding Audience

If you go to see a movie, you are part of the audience. If you attend a concert or go to a football game, you are part of the audience. If you read an article in the college newspaper, then you are part of the writer's audience. Audience affects how a piece of material is written, what is said, and how it is said. Often the same essential message can be written in different ways to appeal to various kinds of readers. For example, an article that would appear in a child's encyclopedia is written differently than it would be if it were to appear in an encyclopedia intended for an adult. Similarly, a letter from a friend would be written differently than a letter from an insurance company. In each of these cases, the audience is responsible for the necessary differences in the written material.

The following advertisement was written in three different ways to appeal to three different types of people, or audiences. As you read, consider the type of audience for whom each ad was intended.

Advertisement 1
Mrs. Roberts, a graduate of the International Culinary Arts Institute and founder of the famous New York gourmet restaurant, Le Taste, has finally released her secret recipe. Her famous chocolate cream pecan pie, the most popular dessert at Le Taste for the past ten years, is now available

in the frozen-food section at your supermarket. Only the finest imported German chocolate and the best pecans from Georgia are used to produce this superb gourmet treat.

Advertisement 2

A new item is now available in the frozen-food section of your supermarket. Try Mrs. Roberts' chocolate cream pecan pie, and you'll be surprised to find such a delightful dessert at such an economical price. The large economy size, which serves nine people, is priced at $2.99. At 34 cents a slice, you would have difficulty making the same pie at home for the same price. And, of course, homemade quality is assured at the lowest possible price.

Advertisement 3

A new convenience item is now available in the frozen-food section of your supermarket—Mrs. Roberts' chocolate cream pecan pie. Of course, you would like to do all your own baking, but with the pressure of a full-time job and a family, you don't always have the time. This pie contains only the finest ingredients and tastes homemade, and it takes only 20 minutes to defrost at room temperature. And remember—the best part is that your family will never know that it wasn't homemade.

Now, look back at each ad and decide the group or type of person the writer had in mind as he or she wrote the ad. In the space provided, describe the type of person for whom each ad was written.

1. _____

2. _____

3. _____

Ad 1 was written for gourmets—people who are interested in the quality and taste of food. Ad 2 was directed toward budget-minded shoppers and was written to show that Mrs. Roberts' pie is an economical purchase. Ad 3 was intended to capture the interest of shoppers looking for convenience. The writer here tried to appeal to people who are short on time but looking for quality items.

A writer can develop a topic in a number of ways, depending on whom it is written for. Intended audience may even determine how a writer develops and explains his or her ideas. The ad for the chocolate pecan pie was written three different ways because each advertisement was directed toward a different audience or group of people. Advertising is a business that is necessarily cautious in saying the right thing to the right people, so the audience was fairly easy to predict. Even topics involving scientific facts are written for an intended audience with specific characteristics.

Now read the following passages. You will see that each passage discusses the composition of the earth's interior but each presents the material in a different manner. Each one is written for a different audience.

Passage 1

A shell of hard rock covers the whole earth. We call this shell the earth's crust. In some places the crust shows. Rock sticks out of the ground. It forms hills, cliffs, and mountains. But most of the crust is hidden.

The earth's hard crust varies in thickness, and no one really knows just what is under it. As men go down into deep mines, they find the earth becomes hotter and hotter. Way down, it must be hot enough to melt rock. Probably that's what is inside the earth—melted rock.

The deepest hole made so far is an oil well. It goes down about five miles. Five miles is only a small part of the way to the earth's center. From the outside to the center is 4,000 miles.[1]

Passage 2

Because these shock waves travel at different speeds as they move through different substances, scientists have been able to get a rough idea of what is inside the earth. They have learned, for example, that the earth's crust is an average of 20 miles thick beneath the continents. Under the oceans, however, the crust is only about three miles thick.

The next layer toward the earth's center is known as the mantle. Where the crust ends and the mantle begins, the shock waves from earthquakes suddenly speed up. This increase in speed grows as the waves travel ever deeper into the mantle. But at a point 1,800 miles below the surface of the earth, another abrupt change takes place. The faster P waves speed up even more, and the S waves simply disappear. This is the region known as the core, and scientists believe it consists of liquid iron.[2]

Passage 1 explains the earth's interior on a very basic, simple level and seems to be intended for audiences without scientific backgrounds. Passage 2, on the other hand, explains the same topic in a more detailed, scientific way. This passage is written for an audience with some knowledge of scientific principles and terminology.

You can see from these examples that audience can influence what a writer says and how he or she says it. A writer manipulates many factors to make his or her writing appropriate for the intended audience, including the level of complexity, completeness, amount of detail, choice of words, number of examples, amount of repetition, background information, and implications and related ideas. For example, the author of an advanced college textbook on child psychology would *not* include a thorough explanation of childhood fears. The author would expect his audience to be completely familiar with this concept and would not include a definition, details, examples, or background on this topic. On the other hand, if an article on family life appeared in *Family Circle,* you would expect to find the topic of childhood fears to be fully detailed because the reader would not be expected to have formal training in child psychology. Definitions would be given, reasons for fears would be explained, and numerous examples would be included.

In reading, a specific awareness of audience is not crucial to understanding the basic message that the author is communicating, but a sense of the intended audience is necessary when you begin to react to and evaluate what you have read. Often an awareness of audience will help you to establish the author's purpose and to assess the writer's attitude toward the subject. A sense of audience may help you to determine whether a writer is objective or biased, whether both sides of an issue are presented, or whether the author favors one side.

Awareness of audience is also useful when you are researching a topic or collecting information. In a research paper, for example, it is particularly important that your sources be appropriate, which means that the material should have been written with the appropriate audience in mind. Suppose you are collecting information for a term paper in a sociology class. You would want to be sure the materials and sources you are using contain sufficient detail, explanation, research, and so forth. A social studies textbook written for junior high school would be too basic; it would not contain enough information and detail. However, a reference book written for sociologists and psychologists would probably be too technical.

Here are a few ways to tell if a source or reference is appropriate.

1. Check the preface of the book. In the preface the writer often states for whom the book was written.
2. Read through a few paragraphs in the first chapter. (a) Can you understand what is being said? (b) Did you find so many difficult words that you found yourself losing meaning?
3. Select a chapter on a topic that you know something about. Preread the chapter, using the techniques described in Chapter 1. This prereading will give you an idea of the level of difficulty, amount of detail, etc.

Understanding Purpose

Basically, the word "purpose" means the reason or goal for doing something. In reading you should consider two types of purposes. First, you should be aware of the author's purpose for writing; that is, you should try to understand why the author wrote what you are reading. Second, you should know your own purpose or purposes for reading various types of material because your purpose in reading influences *how* you read.

Identifying the Author's Purpose

Authors write for a variety of reasons. The author of a front page newspaper story is writing to inform, or to present information. The author of an advertisement is writing to make consumers aware of a product and to encourage them to buy it. Authors of comic strips are writing primarily to entertain, whereas people who write questions to Ann Landers or one of the other advice columnists are writing to get help with their problems. The author of an editorial may be writing to explain a controversial issue and to give his or her opinion about the issue.

Suppose you are reading an advertisement describing a new car that you are thinking of buying. The writer's main purpose in writing is to convince you to buy the car. You should not expect, then, a completely objective report of the car's construction and performance. Instead, only facts that will help sell the car will be included. If the car's gas mileage is poor, for example, you would not expect that fact to be included in the ad. If, on the other hand, the car's gas mileage is high, the writer would be sure to include it. Think of some situations affecting you in which the author's purpose would influence what would be said, how it would be said, and what might be omitted. Here are a few examples to think about: your college catalog, your car insurance policy, credit card agreements, the student or campus newspaper. To further illustrate how purpose can affect style (the way something is written) and content (what is said) three paragraphs follow. Notice that each is written on the same topic—abortion. Also notice that each paragraph is written differently and contains different information. After you have read them, decide the writer's purpose for each paragraph and write it in the space provided.

PARAGRAPH 1:   Abortion is the ending of a pregnancy before the embryo or fetus can live outside the female body. An abortion results in the death of the fetus and may either be spontaneous or induced. In a spontaneous abortion, also called a miscarriage, the fetus passes from the woman's body. Many spontaneous abortions result from natural causes. In an induced abortion, the fetus is removed by artificial—usually medical—means.[3]

AUTHOR'S PURPOSE: _____

PARAGRAPH 2:   An abortion results in the death of a fetus and may be natural or induced. A natural abortion is called a miscarriage. An induced abortion— one caused by medical means—destroys a living fetus and is morally wrong. An induced abortion is the unjustified killing of an unborn child.

AUTHOR'S PURPOSE: _____

PARAGRAPH 3:   Abortion is the termination of a pregnancy before the fetus is born. Abortions may be natural or induced. A natural abortion is called a miscarriage. An induced abortion—one caused by medical means—is often necessary to protect the mother's physical or emotional health. Induced abortions are also used in situations when the child may be born with severe mental or physical handicaps.

AUTHOR'S PURPOSE: _____

Because an author's purpose affects not only what is said but also what is not said, it is important that you distinguish facts and information from ideas and opinions. In a textbook you already know the author's overall purpose in writing was to provide information on a subject. However, you do want to be alert for special features within the text and the purposes they serve. For example, textbook chapters often include such items as a case study, an excerpt from a novel, a report of an experiment or research study, a first-person description of an event or incident, or a related true story. For these types of material, it will be necessary to determine how the special feature relates to the content of the chapter. Also, pay attention to typographical aids such as pictures, maps, charts, and graphs and think about the author's purpose for including them.

Focusing Your Own Purpose in Reading

A reader must also establish his or her own purpose for reading because a reader's purpose directly affects how he or she handles the material. Depending on purpose, a reader might read rapidly or slowly, very carefully, or perhaps even casually, skipping some portions of the material. For example, imagine you are in a dentist's office flipping through a magazine, and you find an article that looks somewhat interesting. You decide to use the waiting time by reading the article to find out what the article is about, but you might not want to remember everything you read. Because you do not need a high level of comprehension and recall, you could read the article rapidly. You might even skip portions of it. In this instance you can see the extent to which purpose affects how you read.

On the other hand, suppose you are reading an assignment from one of your textbooks, and you know that your next exam will cover that chapter. Your purpose in reading, this time, is to retain as much as possible. It would be necessary, then, to read slowly and carefully and to review the material thoroughly in order to ensure that you remember most of what you have read. Again you can see that your purpose affects how you read, but of course there are many situations that lie between the two extremes mentioned here. The following list suggests other possible situations, possible purposes, and suggestions for how to read in each situation.

Type of material	Purpose	How to read it
movie review	decide whether to see the movie	read through quickly
insurance contract	decide whether to sign	carefully, word by word
letter from friend	find out what the friend is doing and how he or she is feeling	casual reading; details not important for recall
encyclopedia article	find pertinent facts	read and skip, then read certain parts carefully
menu in restaurant	locate items to order	read parts, skip parts
_____	_____	_____
_____	_____	_____
_____	_____	_____

Complete the list by adding several types of material you have read lately and indicate your purpose for reading each.

Identifying Audience and Purpose

To provide a better understanding of the function of audience and purpose in the reading process, we will discuss each in reference to the following sample selection titled "The Campaign." Preread the selection, establish purposes for reading before you begin to read, and then read the selection.

The Campaign

Fred R. Harris

The phone rings jarringly. For a moment, she cannot remember where the phone is—or even where *she* is. It is still dark outside. But months ago, she started leaving the light on in the bathroom of each motel she stayed in, so tht she could quickly get her bearings when, like this morning, she woke up disoriented.

"Yes?" she asks raspingly into the mouthpiece, her voice slightly hoarse from too many speeches.

"Time to get moving, boss," an aide's voice says, adding with an attempt at humor, "If you hadn't wanted to work, you shouldn't have hired out."

She ignores the humor, but she does get moving. She has to. There is an important breakfast meeting this morning with a classroom teachers' group, and she desperately needs their support.

Since she announced her candidacy for governor, a year and a half before the election, she has logged thousands of miles, using virtually every kind of transportation and sleeping in hundreds of strange beds. She has answered the dozen or so usual questions so often that she can now do it by rote. She has delivered "the speech," the basic statement of her campaign, so many times that even her husband, sitting next to her at countless public functions, has to work at looking interested. She has eaten enough tough roast beef and cold peas to deserve a medal for bravery and has consumed enough coffee to cause a rise in world coffee prices.

She has also learned to travel light and dress quickly, so she is ready when the aide knocks on her motel door, just thirty minutes after the wake-up call.

At the breakfast, the eggs are cold and the bacon is greasy, but she eats them anyway while she thinks about what she will say to this group. She's been trying to eat more lately because in the closing weeks of the campaign, she has been losing weight. She has even taken to drinking a milkshake every day to keep her face from looking thin and haggard on television. Her major campaign promise is a cut in property taxes, but she assures the teachers that savings in expenditures will allow for a cost-of-living increase in teachers' salaries.

After the breakfast and an on-the-spot radio interview, she is driven to a shopping center for some handshaking. She is preceded by a sound truck and three campaign aides who pass out literature while "Come meet your next governor" blares out over the loudspeaker. She wonders if shaking hands with prospective voters makes any real difference, but she feels better on this misty morning when a local television crew shows up to film her campaign activity for the evening news. "I love it," she says during the interview. "You get a chance to talk to people personally and find out what's on their minds."

There is a ten o'clock press conference at the local press club. A reporter rides with her to the press conference. He is doing a story about her family life. "But don't you feel bad about having to be away from your children so much?" he asks. It is a question she has fielded a hundred times before. "My husband is very good with them," she says, "and then Betsy, who's eleven, and Henry, who's fourteen, are very much involved in the campaign themselves, and they feel that what we are all doing together is very important."

The press conference goes smoothly. She reads the prepared statement, which explains how much the proposed property tax cut will mean for the average family. She and her staff write many of her press statements long before they are to be used. During the last two weeks of the campaign, she will issue two such statements each day, one in the morning and one in the afternoon. The statements are aimed at making news twice a day—in both the morning and evening newspapers—but the main hope is that one of them will get a minute segment on the nightly television news broadcasts. She knows that television is the key to a successful statewide campaign, and she has planned her campaign accordingly.

At noon, she visits a senior citizens' center, where hot lunches are served to about sixty older people each day. She prefers to call them "older people," and they appreciate her frankness and support.

After lunch, she goes back to her motel room for some urgent fund raising, the aspect of the campaign that she likes least. But it has to be done. Today, on the way to the motel, she learns that she could lose the right to buy some vital last-week TV advertising spots; they will be offered to other candidates unless she can come up with $12,000 to pay them before the day ends. At the motel, two wealthy friends are waiting. She has another cup of coffee, pours them a beer, and makes the pitch. "I know you've given more than you should be asked to give," she says sincerely, "but we've just got to raise the money for these spots." She always finds it a little demeaning to ask for money, and she wonders what kinds of implied commitments she may be making. One of the men she is soliciting for an additional contribution is a wholesale beer distributor. The other is an architect. What will they want when she becomes governor?

Establishing Your Purposes for Reading

First, let's consider your purpose for reading "The Campaign." Of course, you read it because you were directed to do so, but beyond that primary purpose, you should have developed questions based on your prereading of the selection to guide you as you read. You might have asked:

1. What campaign is this selection about?
2. What does this writer want me to know about campaigns?
3. Who is the person described in this article?

Of course, your purpose may vary depending on the context in which you are reading the material. If this selection were assigned by an American government or political science instructor, you might read with purposes such as:

1. What does this article say about the American political system?
2. What skills are required of a political candidate?

Identifying the Intended Audience

To identify the intended audience, ask these questions:

1. For whom does this type of writing seem to be written?
2. Who would be interested in this?
3. For whom does this type of writing seem appropriate?

Think about the manner in which the article is written, what it says, and how the ideas are supported and developed. In this article the language is direct and straightforward. Ideas are expressed primarily through a detailed description of a day in the life of a woman running for governor. You might conclude, then, that this selection is written for an audience that falls into one or more of the following categories:

1. Readers who are basically unaware of the factors that influence national/state elections.
2. Readers who are generally unfamiliar with the specifics of life in political campaigns.
3. Readers who are unfamiliar with the "try to please everyone" aspect of political campaigns.

Identifying the Author's Purpose

To identify the author's purpose, ask yourself why the author wrote the article or what he was trying to prove or establish about the candidate's campaign. Also consider the author's attitude toward the subject. In general, this author feels that life on the campaign trail is difficult and stressful. Your first clue comes in the first sentence of the selection. The phone rings "jarringly"; the candidate awakens and for a moment does not remember where she is. Immediately, you know something is wrong. Then in the fourth paragraph you learn that this situation has been going on for a year and a half.

As you read through this selection, you pick up more and more clues that this woman is, at least on the surface, unhappy with her life. She doesn't feel like getting up but she has to. At breakfast, the eggs are cold and the bacon is greasy. For dinner she eats tough roast beef and cold peas. Although it is not directly stated, you begin to realize that the life on the campaign trail is causing this person's unhappiness and discomfort. Taking this situation one step further, you begin to realize the writer is trying to make a statement about the lives of political candidates. That is, the writer's purpose here is to offer an observation or comment on the skills, stresses, and sacrifices required of someone running for political office. You should notice that no *one* sentence directly states that political candidacy is stressful and demanding. However, when you add all the facts together, you begin to realize that the author's intent is to provide an insight or perspective into the lives of political candidates.

EXERCISE 2–1

Directions: *Choose one of the reading selections at the end of Unit One. Read the selection using the following steps.*

1. Prereading. Underline or highlight the portions of the selection you used to preread.
2. Using the information you learned from prereading, write three questions you expect to be able to answer as you read.

   a. _____

   b. _____

   c. _____

3. Read the selection. As you read, look for the information that answers your questions.
4. Review the selection.
5. React and think about what you read. The exercise at the end of the writing section of this chapter will give you an opportunity to write about the subject of this selection, so take this time to begin preparing for a writing assignment. Write down your immediate reaction to the article.

   _____

   _____

After you have read the selection, answer the following questions:

1. For whom did the selection seem to be written?

   _____

2. What do you think the author's purpose was for writing the selection?

   _____

AUDIENCE AND PURPOSE: THE WRITER'S STARTING POINT

Many factors influence how effectively a writer is able to express ideas so they will be understood by the reader. These include how you arrange and combine your ideas within sentences, how you organize and connect sentences within paragraphs, how you structure the paragraphs, and how you connect paragraphs within a piece of writing. All these factors contribute to the writer's general purpose of communicating ideas or information to other people.

Before beginning to focus on these specific aspects of writing effectively, you should keep in mind two general factors. These two factors—audience and purpose—influence and shape everything in the writing process. *Audience* refers to your awareness of the person for whom you are writing, and *purpose* refers to your reason for writing. Your audience and your purpose affect what you say and how you say it. It is important to be aware of audience and purpose before beginning to focus on specific writing skills.

Developing an Awareness of Audience

You saw from the sample advertisement for Mrs. Roberts' pies (pages 31–32) that audience greatly affects how prose is written, and it also influences the type of information included in written materials. A writer has to make conscious choices about such variables as vocabulary, sentence structure, and organization so the message will communicate the thought most effectively for the intended audience.

Aspects of Writing Affected by Audience

Levels of Language. A writer uses several levels of language. You speak differently to different people, and you should write differently for different people, too. For example, you probably speak differently to a friend than you do to your employer, so you also need to write differently to a friend than you would to an employer.

The four basic levels of language are slang, colloquial, informal, and formal. *Slang* refers to words that are used by a particular group of people and are not commonly understood by others. It is a type of specialized vocabulary that is meaningful only to group members and often involves newly invented words and phrases. *Colloquial* and *informal* writing use common speech patterns, and those patterns use language that any of us might also use in conversation. *Formal* writing, found mostly in textbooks, reports, research articles, essays, and business and career writing often involves sophisticated vocabulary and complicated sentences. It also maintains a distance between the reader and the writer. The following examples demonstrate how a message might be communicated through each of these levels of language.

EXAMPLES:	Slang:	I really bombed the test.
	Colloquial:	I flunked the test.
	Informal:	I didn't pass the test
	Formal:	I failed the examination.

Since slang and colloquial levels are usually reserved for speech, you need to be concerned only with the formal and informal levels in writing. However, there is not a systematic set of rules to follow in distinguishing between the two levels. Further, language is constantly changing, new words become acceptable and other words become outdated. Therefore you have to use your judgment and natural sense of the language to find a level suitable to your audience. Regardless of your audience, try to use language that is comfortable. You should not try to be strictly formal, nor should you attempt to make your writing exactly like everyday speech. As you read and revise your writing, look for words and expressions that do not seem to "fit" with what you have written. For example, in the following paragraph written by a student to his academic adviser, notice that the italicized words do not seem consistent with the level of formality used in the rest of the paragraph.

> EXAMPLE: I am enrolled in Mr. Higgin's American history course, and *I got a "D."* I completed all my assignments, and I thought I was *doing okay.*

Notice, for example, that "enrolled" is a more formal word than "okay." Also the expression, ". . . I got a D" is informal. Changing the words to "I received a D grade" would make a statement that is consistent with the level of language established by the word "enrolled." In this situation it would be better to assume that the audience and purpose demand a formal rather than colloquial level of writing.

The author of "The Campaign," however, uses both colloquial and informal language. The conversations that are included use everyday language. Expressions such as "Time to get moving, boss," are colloquial. In general, an informal level of language is used because the author's audience is probably the average man or woman, and the author's purpose is to point out that political candidates do not lead glamorous lives. The author's purpose is to relate closely to the audience, so the language has to appeal to the members of the audience on a fairly personal level.

Idea Complexity and Amount of Detail. In adapting a piece of writing to suit a particular audience, a writer has to consider the reader's background knowledge. If the reader's knowledge of the subject is limited, ideas will have to be explained in a simple, straightforward way. Numerous details and examples might be needed. If a reader is completely familiar with the subject, basic explanations will be unnecessary. The amount of detail included, the types and number of examples, and the difficulty of the words can be adjusted for a knowledgeable reader. In "The Campaign" a large amount of detail is included to present a clear picture of the hectic but routine life of a political candidate to readers who are unfamiliar with political campaigns.

Sentence Length and Complexity. The length of sentences and the relationships they express may also be varied to suit particular audiences. You can combine and expand ideas by using various sentence patterns and arrange them to show the relationship among your ideas.

Sentence structure can be used to adapt your writing to suit your audience. For example, if you need to express ideas as simply and clearly as possible, shorter sentences can be more effective than longer ones. On the other hand, if you are writing to a fairly knowledgeable, sophisticated audience, longer sentences that combine ideas and make the information more compact may be more appropriate.

"The Campaign" uses both extremely short sentences as well as longer, complicated ones. The short sentences seem written for emphasis; for example, the sentence "She has to" (line 11) or "It is still dark outside" (line 2) emphasizes unpleasant aspects of the political life. Other sentences that provide background information or explain relationships are longer and more complex.

Tone. Tone is the attitude a writer expresses toward the subject. You communicate this attitude primarily through your choice of words and your phrasing of ideas. Depending on the audience, you may need to select fairly direct and obvious words that reflect your feelings. However, when writing for readers who have prior knowledge of your attitude and the various meanings a word can suggest in a given context, you can afford to use subtle language. For example, if you attended a party you didn't enjoy, you could say it was boring, or you could be subtle and say it was quiet and not exciting. By using more subtle language, the tone of the message becomes less negative.

In "The Campaign" the author's overall tone is sympathetic. He seems to understand that life is difficult, but he also seems to suggest that the candidate deliberately chose such a life.

The Importance of Word Choice to Audience

If you were answering a question on an essay exam, you would try to choose words that indicate your awareness of the subject matter and the context. If you were writing a letter to a friend you would choose more casual, informal words because you would expect a friend to understand what you mean. Words can have more than one meaning, so it is important for a writer to consider how the audience will react to vocabulary.

Denotation and Connotation. There are often two levels of meaning for a word: denotative and connotative. The denotative meaning is the literal meaning of the word as stated in the dictionary, whereas the connotative meaning consists of additional meanings a word may take on in the culture. For example, both the words "cheap" and "inexpensive" have the same denotative meaning; both mean low in price. However, the word "cheap" has a connotative meaning that suggests inferior quality or value, whereas "inexpensive" does not. Here is another example: which of these terms meaning underweight would be favorable and which would be unfavorable?

thin, skinny, slim

Although each word has the same denotative meaning each has a different connotative meaning. The word "skinny" is somewhat negative, whereas "thin" is more positive; the word "slim" is even more positive because being slim is fashionable in our culture. As you can see some words have positive connotations, and others have negative connotations. Here are a few more groups of words that are similar in meaning but carry different connotations:

cry, weep, snivel

walk, stroll, lumber

compliment, flatter, praise

As you write, be sure to choose words carefully, selecting those with the appropriate connotative meaning to suit your audience and purpose.

Often a thesaurus can help you find words that have similar meanings. The following entry from a thesaurus shows how the information about terms is listed.

ENTRY WORD:	**fight** *n* **1** *syn* BRAWL 2, affray, broil, donnybrook, fracas, fray, knock-down-and-drag-out, row, scrap, scuffle **2** *syn* QUARREL, altercation, beef, bickering, brawl, feud, hassle, row, squabble, word(s) **3** *syn* ATTACK 2, aggression, aggressiveness, belligerence, combativeness, pugnacity **fighter** *n syn* SOLDIER, fighting man, GI, man-at-arms, serviceman, swad, || swaddy, || sweat, warrior **fighting man** *n syn* SOLDIER, fighter, GI, man-at-arms, serviceman, swad, || swaddy, || sweat, warrior
GENERAL EXPLANATORY *INFORMATION:*	*syn* synonym(s) *rel* related word(s) *idiom* idiomatic equivalent(s) *con* contrasted word(s) *ant* antonym(s) *vulgar || use limited; if in doubt, see a dictionary The first word in a synonym list when printed in SMALL CAPITALS shows where there is more information about the group. For a more efficient use of this book see Explanatory Notes.

Notice that the entry for the term "fight" includes synonyms; however, the brief notes located at the bottom of the page in the thesaurus show other types of information that may be available in an entry. A statement is included that directs the reader to the Explanatory Notes, which are located in the beginning of the thesaurus, for a more detailed discussion. Similar notes are also found in the beginning of dictionaries, and these notes can help you use these reference books more effectively.

From this entry a writer could find a variety of terms that have the same denotative meaning of "fight" but a different connotative meaning. Look at the following sentences and notice how the connotative meanings differ.

The fight resulted in several arrests.

The brawl resulted in several arrests.

The fray resulted in several arrests.

A brawl sounds worse than a fight, and a fight sounds worse than a fray. The use of any one of the terms would depend on the purpose of your writing and the impression you would want to make on your audience.

The general explanatory information in the thesaurus includes symbols that are used for labeling other types of information. For example, you could find idiomatic equivalents, or expressions that are used in the culture to mean the same thing. You could also look for antonyms (words that are the opposite in meaning), and you could find words that relate to the same meaning as well as words that contrast with the word. An asterisk (*) marks a word as vulgar (popular, everyday speech that is inappropriate in written form) and two bars (\| \|) show that the word has limited use, which means it is appropriate only in certain contexts.

EXERCISE 2-2

Directions: *For each of the following words write a word that is similar in meaning but has a negative connotation, then write another word that is similar in meaning but has a positive connotation. If you have difficulty thinking of words, check a thesaurus and if necessary a dictionary.*

		Negative	*Positive*
EXAMPLE:	quiet	passive	calm

She is a very passive person.

She is a very calm person.

		Negative	*Positive*
1.	shy	_____	_____
2.	speak	_____	_____
3.	drink	_____	_____
4.	nervous	_____	_____
5.	quiet	_____	_____
6.	overweight	_____	_____
7.	young	_____	_____
8.	unattractive	_____	_____
9.	unproductive	_____	_____
10.	intelligent	_____	_____

General and Specific. Words and phrases may be either general or specific. A general term refers to a category or group of things, whereas a specific term more carefully names a particular part of that group or category. The word "tree" is a general term and includes many different types of trees, whereas "oaks," "elms," and "maples" are more specific terms that describe a particular type of tree. Here is another example. Suppose you are describing a film you have just seen. Which of the following comments would give your reader the most information about a film?

"The film was great."

"The film was fantastic."

"The film was an exciting horror movie."

Although "great" and "fantastic" indicate that you liked the film, they are general terms and provide very little information. "An exciting horror movie," on the other hand, tells your reader or listener something about the film. As a general rule, try to choose words that are as specific as possible. Usually specific words provide your reader with more accurate or descriptive information, as well as make your writing more interesting.

EXERCISE 2–3

Directions: *Revise each sentence so the underlined general term is replaced by terms that provide more specific information.*

EXAMPLE: The restaurant serves ~~good food~~ *spicy Mexican food*.

1. The movie was okay.
2. Nobody makes you attend classes.
3. I just heard a terrible thing.
4. My sister is a good person.
5. I really feel bad about my father's accident.
6. The play was wonderful.
7. The exam was terrible.
8. That day is bad for me.
9. The weather prevented us from going on our trip.
10. The animal caused an accident on the freeway.
11. The parent gave permission for the child to go to the museum.

Concrete and Abstract. Words can also be abstract or concrete. Concrete words refer to real objects, actions, or places that you perceive through your senses. New Orleans, your sociology class, the Niagara River, and ice skating are all concrete terms. Abstract words refer to ideas or qualities, rather than real objects. Here are a few examples of abstract words: cities, education, love, government, pleasure, fun. Of course, each of these words has meaning, but there is room for interpretation that can lead to confusion. Suppose you decide to write a paper on modern education. Education can mean many different things to many people. A reader cannot know whether you mean college education, nursery school education, education in America or in foreign countries, or adult education classes at the YMCA. You can see, then, that abstract words need further explanation; they can either be replaced with more concrete terms during revision or fully explained by additional details.

The following paragraph contains abstract words or expressions that give the reader only a vague sense of what the topic of the paragraph is about. Notice each underlined word or expression.

One of the worst things about living at home while you go to school is your social life. You don't do the same things that the other kids at school do because you're still tied to your past. You probably don't get the most out of school.

Now look at the paragraph after it was rewritten with concrete words in place of the abstract words.

One disadvantage of living at home while you go to college is that you don't meet as many new friends as you might if you lived in a dorm. You don't become involved in the same activities as the resident students because you still spend most of your time with old friends or new friends who are from your old high school. You probably miss the opportunity of learning through discussions with people from other cities and social and ethnic backgrounds.

The paragraph now provides some concrete ideas about the differences between commuting and living on campus. It not only provides specific information, but it is also much more interesting to read. The use of abstract language often makes your reader think you are unfamiliar with your topic or that you have not thought it through carefully. Make sure that the nouns and verbs in your writing convey precise meaning.

Establishing a Purpose for Writing

Much of the writing that you do as a student is related to participation in a classroom situation. You might write notes from a lecture, answer essay questions, or write term papers, reviews, lab reports, or reaction papers. In each of these situations the instructor generally provides the overall purpose in writing. That is, your overall purpose in writing would be to complete the assignment. However, in writing other than for academic classroom assignments, your purpose is established by your need to communicate for specific reasons. For instance, you may write to explain something, to describe something, to request information or action, to agree or disagree with someone, or to express your feelings.

Just as your purpose for reading affects *how* you read, so does your purpose for writing affect *how* you write. Purpose influences both the style and content of your writing. Assume that you were involved in an automobile accident and your insurance company has asked you to complete a form requiring that you describe how the accident occurred. Your purpose, in this situation, is to explain what happened as clearly and accurately as possible; that purpose would control how you write your explanation. The task requires you to be highly factual and to be as accurate and detailed as possible. You would probably organize the information chronologically, the order in which the events occurred. Finally, this situation would require precise wording and careful language so as to suggest or not to suggest (again, depending on your purpose) who was at fault in causing the accident. In this example the purpose would affect content, amount of detail, organization, and choice of words.

Now let's consider another example involving a different purpose. Suppose you are writing a letter of application for a summer job as a counselor with a resident camp for children. You are writing to inform the camp director that you are interested in working at the camp next summer, and to do this you must describe the skills, abilities, and training that qualify you for the job. You would also want to convince the director that you are the best candidate for the job. Since it is a letter of application to someone you do not know, the language would be somewhat formal, but you would want to indicate that you can communicate on more than one level.

Aspects of Writing Affected by Purpose

Earlier in this chapter you learned how audience influences the style and content of your writing. In a similar way, your purpose in writing shapes various other features of your writing. You will find that many of the same aspects of writing that are influenced by audience are also shaped by purpose.

Topic Selection. Often a broad or complicated subject can be narrowed down or focused as you establish your purpose for writing. Let us presume the subject you are going to write about is city life. This is a very broad subject, and there are many aspects of city life. If you decide to describe features of city life you might choose topics such as "The Sense of Neighborhood" or "Everybody on the Block Knows What I'm Doing." Now read each of the following statements of purpose and notice how the topics are consistent with the purpose.

PURPOSE: to discuss problems of city life

TOPICS: 1. Street Gangs
 2. The Need for Urban Development
 3. The Increasing Crime Rate

PURPOSE: to persuade someone to live in the city

TOPICS: 1. The Social Advantages of City Life
 2. The Many Conveniences of City Living
 3. The Educational Opportunities of City Living

Types of Supporting Details. The ideas you choose to write about and the types of details and examples you select to support the ideas are affected by your reason for writing. Suppose you are writing an essay about violence on television. If your purpose is to suggest that violence on TV has caused an increase in crime and violence in society, you would choose a particular set of facts and details. You might include examples, statistics, and arguments that link crime and violence with TV watching. On the other hand, if your purpose is to suggest that violence on television has little to do with increased crime and violence, you would choose a different set of facts and details.

Levels of Language. Whether you use slang, colloquial, or formal language is determined in part by your reason for writing. If your purpose in writing is to communicate with a friend you might use some slang words. However, if you were writing to apply for a job, you would use a more formal level of language.

Tone. Tone, the writer's attitude toward the subject, is also related to purpose. If your purpose in writing is to amuse or entertain, then the tone of your writing will reflect this purpose. The tone might be light and humorous, or it might be sarcastic and cutting. However, if your purpose in writing is to inform, then your tone might be objective and factual. If your purpose is to persuade or convince someone about something, then the tone could be subjective and biased.

Word Choice. The words you choose to express your ideas are also shaped by your overall purpose in writing. If your purpose is to define a term or concept, then you would choose very precise, accurate words. However, if your purpose were to describe an object, then you would choose words that create a mental picture of the object. If you were writing to convince someone to vote against a political candidate, you might choose words with negative connotations, but if you were writing to convince someone to vote for a candidate, then you would choose words with a positive connotation.

EXERCISE 2–4

Directions: *In this exercise you will follow all the steps involved in writing while you keep audience and purpose in mind to guide you. First, select one of each of the following subjects, purposes, and audiences and write your choices in the spaces provided.*

Subjects	Purposes	Audiences
Cloning	To explain information on the subject	A friend
Truth in Medicine	To describe a personal experience	A college instructor
Mate Selection	To relate your beliefs on the subject	The student newspaper

SUBJECT: _____

PURPOSE: _____

AUDIENCE: _____

Step 1: Prewriting.

a. Narrow the subject you selected by dividing it into three possible topics.

TOPICS: _____

_____

_____

b. To generate ideas about your topic free-write for five minutes; do not stop writing once you have begun; or if you already have some ideas about your topic, make a list of some questions that are related to your views, your purpose, and your audience.

Step 2: Composing. Read over your free-writing exercise or your questions. Look for several related main ideas and list them below. Next, write one statement that ties them all together. Now, go back to the main ideas you underlined and develop each. Look at your free writing or your questions for details to support them. List the details below.

UNIFYING IDEA: _____

SUPPORT: a. _____

                b. _____

                c. _____

Develop the unifying idea into a paper that has an introduction, body, and conclusion. Include the supporting ideas along with any additional information needed to explain them.

Step 3: Checking the Content and Organization. Read over the rough draft you have written, considering the sequence or order of your ideas. Write a brief outline that describes the order of your ideas. Decide whether you should change the order of the ideas, and, if so, rewrite the outline so it shows how your ideas will progress.

Step 4: Revision. Use the five questions on pages 26–27 to help you revise your paper. Answer each question and note the changes you need to make. Then read your paper aloud to see if there are places where the wording is awkward, and if the pronunciation of words, or phrases, might cause your reader to read in a halting fashion. Look carefully at your choice of words and decide whether there is other vocabulary you could use that would be more suitable for your audience. Specifically check each of the following: (1) appropriateness of language, (2) amount of detail, (3) idea complexity, and (4) word choice. Use a dictionary or thesaurus, if necessary. Next, rewrite sentences or paragraphs, making the ideas progress in the same order you decided on when you checked the organization of your paper. Ask a fellow student to read over the changes you have made and to tell you if your topic, purpose, and audience are identifiable. Wherever necessary, rewrite sentences or paragraphs. Then make a final copy of the paper.

Step 5: Proofreading. Refer to the following proofreading checklist. Proofread your paper carefully, checking for each item on the list. At this time you might not be able to recognize all the errors, but make an effort to look for each one. Place a check next to each item on the list you correct. In the column on the right, write each error you corrected, showing how you corrected it. Always review these errors and corrections before you begin revising your next paper.

SUMMARY

In this chapter we discussed the importance of an *awareness* of audience and purpose to effective reading and writing. Audience refers to the person or group for whom something is written. A reader should be conscious of the intended audience, and a writer must adjust various features of his or her writing to suit the audience. Purpose refers to the reason or reasons for reading and for writing. A reader must be concerned with the writer's purpose for writing as well as his or her own purposes for reading. A writer must recognize that his or her purpose determines what is said and how it is said.

PROOFREADING CHECKLIST

Essay Title _____

Date _____

TYPE	✔	ERROR	FREQUENCY	DESCRIPTION
GRAMMAR		Run-on Sentence Sentence Fragment Subject/Verb Agreement Verb Tense Pronoun Agreement		
MECHANICS		Capitalization Italics Abbreviation		
PUNCTUATION		, (Comma) ; (Semicolon) ' (Apostrophe) " (Quotation Marks) . (Period) ! (Exclamation Point) ? (Question Mark) : (Colon) — (Dash) ( ) (Parentheses) - (Hyphen)		

		ERROR	CORRECTION	
SPELLING ERRORS				

Unit One Reading Selections

Difficulty level: A

1. The Secret Pleasures of Mismanaging Time

Dru Scott

You may be all too familiar with the many problems that mismanaging time can stir up. Did you ever realize that it offers secret pleasures as well? Without being aware of it, you may already have a clue to what they are. You may even have experienced some of them yourself.

Have you ever put off an important project until the last minute—even when you could have done it earlier? Ever made a wild and frantic dash to get to an appointment you could have left for earlier? Have you ever known an activity was off target and heading you straight for a time crunch—and you still kept at it? Those last-minute time crunches are charged with electricity and excitement, aren't they?

Mismanaging time can pay off in some rarely revealed ways that many of us unconsciously take advantage of. Some of us mismanage time to get attention or gain a sense of power. Mismanaging time also can serve as a way to avoid unpleasant tasks or shirk personal responsibility. It can be used to resist change, sidestep new feelings, avoid feeling close to others, and deal with that age-old fear of feeling "too good."

However, don't make a blanket indictment of the time mismanagement practices this chapter will reveal. We all gain something from our use of time, even when we mismanage it. But it is important to understand what the secret payoffs are. Uncovering hidden or conflicting motivations gives you a handle on this information. When you understand motivations, you work more effectively with the people around you. You are also equipped to make wiser decisions about your own time. You don't have to change your behavior just because you've learned about these secret payoffs, but if you decide you want to, you can do it faster and more easily.

GETTING ATTENTION—"LOOK, MA! NO HANDS!"

In today's crowded, rushed, and anonymous world, it's hard to dream up any sure-fire techniques for being noticed. Time mismanagement has emerged as one of the few proven attention-getters.

Picture the people in your life who don't handle their time well. It's highly probable that this behavior gets them a lot of attention. Relatives nag them, co-workers chide them, friends schedule plans around them. People kid them about it. Sometimes the attention leaves a bad taste in their mouths; it's not always complimentary or admiring. But it *is* attention. Mismanaging their time gets them noticed.

Sally R. makes herself the center of attention at all staff meetings—regularly scheduled meetings, special project meetings, even emergency meetings. She always arrives late, bursting in with breathless apologies. She drops a load of charts and notes on the table, and pushes past everyone to get to the coatrack in the back of the room. She rattles the metal coathangers, apologizing again for the interruption. Then she offers a string of loudly whispered "Excuse me's" as she wriggles through the group to get to her seat. Although the other staff members are familiar with her antics, she is always noticed. She captures everyone's attention—and their time.

The late-arrival technique has many variations, but it's always an attention-getter. Surely you've run into someone who arrives late at every party to make a "grand entrance." What about the dinner guest who is chronically late? All the other guests have been there for an hour. They've munched through the hors d'oeuvres, had a couple of drinks, made inroads on the salted peanuts. They want to sit down to dinner. Delicious aromas waft from the kitchen, and the hostess is beginning to worry that the veal will be overcooked. The host wonders if he should offer another round of drinks. Then in sails the latecomer, full of excuses. Everyone is so happy they can finally eat that, instead of being greeted angrily, he or she is welcomed with enthusiasm and relief.

Arriving late is an old and common way to get attention. Those who make it a practice may be reluctant to give it up until they find something that works just as well. In subsequent chapters, you'll discover a variety of ways that such people can learn to get the recognition they want and deserve without imposing unfairly on others.

SECRET POWER—"I'LL SHOW YOU WHO'S BOSS!"

Many people feel powerless to control their own destiny in our modern mass society. Some react by trying to gain control in a variety of everyday situations. For example, on her way out to lunch with a group of friends, Myra decides that she must redo her makeup. The others shift around in the hall waiting for her, looking at their watches, and calculating whether they will get to the restaurant on time. Myra gains control by making them wait.

A major aspect of control is determining *when*. If the data-processing department delays the start of a marketing campaign because forecasts are late, data processing is in control. If a subordinate holds up the new project plans because he hasn't finished the graphics, unconsciously he is showing everyone who's boss. He also may risk planting the suspicion that he's inefficient, but for the moment, he gains a sense of control. If a low-ranking civilian guard on a military base stops every entering vehicle to make a maddeningly meticulous examination of passes, he's in control. A long line of colonels and captains may fume as they sit in their cars, but the guard controls the slow-moving line. This kind of control may only offer a *false* sense of power, but it is one of the ways mismanaging time can pay off.

COMPREHENSION

1. This article is mainly about
    a. why mismanaging time is not necessarily bad
    b. how to enjoy mismanaging your time
    c. how to avoid mismanaging your time
    d. the reasons why some people mismanage their time
2. The author feels that it is important to
    a. gain a sense of power
    b. use your time more efficiently
    c. gain a feeling of satisfaction
    d. understand conflicting motivations that cause time mismanagement
3. Some people mismanage time to
    a. control their motivations
    b. reduce negative attitudes
    c. get attention
    d. control their lives
4. According to the article, a major aspect of controlling a situation is determining
    a. when an event will occur
    b. where a meeting is conducted
    c. how a situation is handled
    d. why an action has been taken
5. People who arrive late for an event are always
    a. respected
    b. perceived as out of control
    c. resented
    d. noticed

VOCABULARY

Directions: *The meaning of the following terms from selection 1 cannot be clearly determined from the context. Using the dictionary entries, select the appropriate definition of the term as it is used in the reading selection.*

1. shirk (par. 3)
    a. discharge
    b. scoundrel
    c. parasite
    d. avoid

    shirk (shûrk) *v.* **shirked, shirking, shirks.** —*tr.* To put off or avoid discharging: "*A number of high civil servants shirked their duty to preserve their jobs.*" (Nevil Shute). —*intr.* To put off or avoid work or duty. —*n.* A person who avoids work or duty. Also called "shirker." [From obsolete *shirk,* parasite, rogue, probably from German *Schurke,* scoundrel, perhaps from Old High German *(fiur)-scurgo,* "fire stirrer," stoker, hence devil (as an infernal stoker), from *scurigen,* to poke. See **skeu-** in Appendix.*]

2. indictment (par. 4)
    a. crime
    b. accusation
    c. written statement
    d. law

    in·dict·ment \in-'dīt-mənt\ *n* **1 a :** the action or the legal process of indicting **b :** the state of being indicted **2 :** a formal written statement framed by a prosecuting authority and found by a jury (as a grand jury) charging a person with an offense

3. anonymous (par. 5)
   a. authorship
   b. agency
   c. unknown
   d. unaware

a·non·y·mous (ə-nŏn'ə-məs) *adj. Abbr.* a., anon. 1. Having an unknown or unacknowledged name. 2. Having an unknown or withheld authorship or agency. [Late Latin *anōnymus*, from Greek *anōnumos*, nameless : AN- (without) + *onoma*, name (see nomen- in Appendix*).] —an'o·nym'i·ty (ăn'ə-nĭm'ə-tē), a·non'y·mous·ness *n.* —a·non'y·mous·ly *adv.*

4. chide (par. 6)
   a. reprimand
   b. impel
   c. state
   d. goad

chide (chīd) *v.* chided or chid (chĭd), chided or chid or chidden (chĭd'n), chiding, chides. —*intr.* To scold; rebuke; reprimand. —*tr.* 1. To state one's disapproval of. 2. To goad; impel. [Middle English *chiden*, Old English *cīdan*, from *cīd†*, strife.] —chid'er *n.* —chid'ing·ly *adv.*

5. chronically (par. 8)
   a. acutely
   b. prolonged
   c. lingering
   d. constantly

chron·ic (krŏn'ĭk) *adj.* 1. Of long duration; continuing; constant. 2. Prolonged; lingering, as certain diseases. Compare acute. 3. Subject to a disease or habit for a long time; inveterate. [French *chronique*, from Latin *chronicus*, from Greek *khronikos*, pertaining to time, from *khronos†*, time.] —chron'i·cal·ly *adv.* —chro·nic'i·ty (krŏ-nĭs'ə-tē) *n.*

6. hors d'oeuvres (par. 8)
   a. cocktails
   b. main dishes
   c. workday meals
   d. appetizers

hors d'oeuvre (ôr dûrv'; *French* ôr dœ'vr') *pl.* hors d'oeuvres (ôr dûrvz') or hors d'oeuvre. An appetizer or canapé served with cocktails or before a meal. [French, outside of the ordinary meal, side dish, "outside of work" : *hors*, outside, from Latin *foris* (see dhwer- in Appendix*) + *de*, of + *oeuvre*, work, from Latin *opera*, from *opus* (stem *oper-*), work, OPUS.]

7. waft (par. 8)
   a. convey
   b. float
   c. carry
   d. flag

waft (wäft, wăft) *v.* wafted, wafting, wafts. —*tr.* 1. To carry or cause to go gently and smoothly through the air or over water. 2. To convey or send floating through the air or over water: *"flowers brighter than love wafting the odour of spices"* (Ronald Firbank). —*intr.* To float easily and gently, as on the air; to drift. —*n.* 1. Something, as an odor, carried through the air. 2. A light breeze; rush of air. 3. The act of wafting or waving. 4. *Nautical.* a. A flag used for signaling or indicating wind direction. b. A signal with a flag. [Originally "to convoy (ships)," back-formation from obsolete *wafter*, a convoy, Middle English *waughter*, from Middle Dutch *wachter*, a guard, from *wachten*, to watch, guard. See weg-² in Appendix.*]

DISCUSSION

1. Consider your time management habits. Do you enjoy crises that involve deadlines or do you always get everything done ahead of time?
2. How do you feel about people who are consistently late? Do they intrude on your schedule? What do you do about it?
3. The article stated that many people feel powerless to control their own destiny, so they try to gain control in everyday situations. How much control do you think you have over your destiny? How does your view affect your behavior in everyday situations?

Difficulty level: A

2. The Other You

Isaac Asimov

What if our society uses new-found technologies of "genetic engineering" to interfere with the biological nature of human beings? Might that not be disastrous? 1

What about cloning, for instance? 2

Cloning is a term originally used in connection with nonsexual reproduction of plants and very simple animals. Now it is coming into use in connection with higher animals, 3 since biologists are finding ways of starting with an individual cell of a grown animal and inducing it to multiply into another grown animal.

4   Each cell in your body, you see, has a full complement of all the genes that control your inherited characteristics. It has everything of this sort that there was in the original fertilized egg-cell out of which you developed. The cells in your body now devote themselves to specialized activities and no longer grow and differentiate—but what if such a cell, from skin or liver, could be restored to the environment of the egg-cell? Would it not begin to grow and differentiate once more, and finally form a second individual with your genes? Another you, so to speak? It has been done in frogs and can undoubtedly be done in human beings.

5   But is cloning a safe thing to unleash on society? Might it not be used for destructive purposes? For instance, might not some ruling group decide to clone their submissive, downtrodden peasantry, and thus produce endless hordes of semi-robots who will slave to keep a few in luxury and who may even serve as endless ranks of soldiers designed to conquer the rest of the world?

6   A dreadful thought, but an unnecessary fear. For one thing, there is no need to clone for the purpose. The ordinary method of reproduction produces all the human beings that are needed and as rapidly as is needed. Right now, the ordinary method is producing so many people as to put civilization in danger of imminent destruction. What more can cloning do?

7   Secondly, unskilled semi-robots cannot be successfully pitted against the skilled users of machines, either on farms, in factories or in armies. Any nation depending on downtrodden masses will find itself an easy mark for exploitation by a less populous but more skilled and versatile society. This has happened in the past often enough.

8   But even if we forget about slave-hordes, what about the cloning of a relatively few individuals? There are rich people who could afford the expense, or politicians who could have the influence for it, or the gifted who could undergo it by popular demand. There can then be two of a particular banker or governor or scientist—or three—or a thousand. Might this not create a kind of privileged caste, who would reproduce themselves in greater and greater numbers, and who would gradually take over the world?

9   Before we grow concerned about this, we must ask whether there will really be any great demand for cloning. Would *you* want to be cloned? The new individual formed from your cell will have your genes and therefore your appearance and, possibly, talents, but *he will not be you*. The clone will be, at best, merely your identical twin. Identical twins share the same genetic pattern, but they each have their own individuality and are separate persons.

10   Cloning is *not* a pathway to immortality, then, because *your* consciousness does *not* survive in your clone, any more than it would in your identical twin if you had one.

In fact, your clone would be far less than your identical 11
twin. What shapes and forms a personality is not genes alone,
but all the environment to which it is exposed. Identical twins
grow up in identical surroundings, in the same family, and
under each other's influence. A clone of yourself, perhaps
thirty or forty years younger, would grow up in a different
world altogether and would be shaped by influences that
would be sure to make him less and less like you as he grows
older.

He may even earn your jealousy. After all, you are old and 12
he is young. You may once have been poor and struggled to
become well-to-do, but he will be well-to-do from the start. The
mere fact that you won't be able to view it as a child, but as
another competing and better-advantaged *you*, may accentuate
the jealousy.

No! I imagine that, after some initial experiments, the 13
demand for cloning will be virtually nonexistent.

But suppose it isn't a matter of your desires, but of 14
society's demands? I, for instance, have published 158 books
so far, but I am growing old. If there were a desperate world
demand for me to write 500 more books, I would have to be
cloned. The other me, or group of me's, could continue. Or
could they?

The clones will not grow up my way. They won't be 15
driven to write, as I was, out of a need to escape from the
slums—unless you provide each with slums to escape from.
Unlike me, they will all have a mark to shoot at—the original
me. I could do as I please, but they will be doomed to imitate
me and they may very well refuse. How many of my clones will
have to be supported and fed and kept out of trouble in order
to find one who will be able to write like me, and will want to?

It won't be worth society's trouble, I assure you. 16

COMPREHENSION

1. The main idea of this essay is that
    a. genetic engineering will result in hordes of semi-robots
    b. genetic engineering does not pose a threat to society
    c. genetic engineering works only on plants and animals
    d. genetic engineering will lead to privileged classes
2. Cloning is
    a. a form of nonsexual reproduction
    b. a pathway to immortality
    c. capable of reproducing a person's consciousness
    d. likely to replace ordinary reproduction
3. Each cell in the human body
    a. can be fertilized
    b. carries all the genes that control inherited characteristics
    c. can become an egg-cell
    d. grows and differentiates

4. The ordinary method of reproduction
   a. produced submissive, downtrodden peasants
   b. produces all the human beings that are needed
   c. results in downtrodden masses that are subject to exploitation
   d. will destroy civilization
5. A cloned human being
   a. would live the same life as its donor
   b. would grow up in a different environment than its donor
   c. will be jealous of its donor
   d. is the same person as its donor

VOCABULARY

Directions: *The meaning of the following terms from selection 2 cannot be determined from the context. Using the dictionary entries, select the appropriate definition of the term as it is used in the reading selection.*

1. imminent (par. 6)
   a. perilous
   b. projecting
   c. overhanging
   d. about to occur immediately

2. exploitation (par. 7)
   a. heroic act
   b. display
   c. unfair use
   d. profit

3. caste (par. 8)
   a. class in a society
   b. heredity
   c. Brahman
   d. system

4. accentuate (par. 12)
   a. emphasize
   b. syllabic accent
   c. quantitative
   d. voice

im·mi·nent \'im-ə-nənt\ *adj* [L *imminent-, imminens*, prp. of *imminēre* to project, threaten, fr. *in-* + *-minēre* (akin to L *mont-, mons* mountain) — more at MOUNT] **1** : ready to take place; *esp* : hanging threateningly over one's head <was in ~ danger of being run over> **2** : IMMANENT — **im·mi·nent·ly** *adv* — **im·mi·nent·ness** *n*

¹**ex·ploit** \'ek-ˌsplȯit, ik-'\ *n* [ME, outcome, success, fr. OF, fr. L *explicitum*, neut. of *explicitus*, pp.] : DEED. ACT: *esp* : a notable or heroic act *syn* see FEAT
²**ex·ploit** \ik-'splȯit, 'ek-ˌ\ *vt* **1 a** : to turn to economic account <~ a mine> **b** : to take advantage of : UTILIZE <~ing the qualities of the material> **2** : to make use of meanly or unjustly for one's own advantage <~s his friends> — **ex·ploit·able** \-ə-bəl\ *adj* — **ex·ploit·er** *n*
ex·ploi·ta·tion \ˌek-ˌsplȯi-'tā-shən\ *n* **1** : an act of exploiting: as **a** : utilization or working of a natural resource **b** : an unjust or improper use of another person for one's own profit or advantage **c** : coaction between organisms in which one is benefited at the expense of the other **2** : PUBLICITY. ADVERTISING — **ex·ploit·ative** \ik-'splȯit-ət-iv\ *adj* — **ex·ploit·ative·ly** *adv*

caste \'kast\ *n* [Pg *casta*, lit., race, lineage, fr. fem. of *casto* pure, chaste, fr. L *castus*; akin to L *carēre* to be without, Gk *keazein* to split, Skt *śasati* he cuts to pieces] **1** : one of the hereditary social classes in Hinduism that restrict the occupation of their members and their association with the members of other castes **2 a** : a division of society based on differences of wealth, inherited rank or privilege, profession, or occupation **b** : the position conferred by caste standing : PRESTIGE **3** : a system of rigid social stratification characterized by hereditary status, endogamy, and social barriers sanctioned by custom, law, or religion **4** : a specialized form (as the soldier or worker of an ant) of a polymorphic social insect that carries out a particular function in the colony — **caste·ism** \'kas-ˌtiz-əm\ *n*

²**ac·cent** \'ak-ˌsent, ak-'\ *vt* **1 a** : to pronounce with accent : STRESS **b** : to mark with a written or printed accent **2** : to give prominence to : make more prominent
ac·cen·tu·ate \ak-'sen-chə-ˌwāt, ik-'\ *vt* **-at·ed;** **-at·ing** [ML *accentuatus*, pp. of *accentuare*, fr. L *accentus*] : ACCENT. EMPHASIZE — **ac·cen·tu·a·tion** \(ˌ)ak-ˌsen-chə-'wā-shən, ik-\ *n*

DISCUSSION

1. Should cloning of human beings be permitted? Why?
2. Explain why you would or would not want to be cloned.
3. What important factors in your environment would be impossible to reproduce for your clone?

Difficulty level: B

3. Fun from the Start

Charles Garfinkel

Racquetball is this country's fastest-growing sport. 1

Eight years ago there were about fifty thousand racquet- 2
ball players in the United States. Today there are nearly five
million—and the game is really just starting to boom. It already
has a burgeoning pro circuit with substantial tournament prize
money up for grabs.

All over the country, racquetball clubs are being estab- 3
lished at an incredible rate. In addition, athletic clubs, YMCAs,
Jewish Centers, and colleges are building courts of their own.
Men and women in business, doctors and steelworkers,
youngsters and senior citizens—all sorts of people are taking
up racquetball.

What explains the sport's great popularity? 4

There are several reasons. The main one is that racquetball 5
is fun to play *right from the start.*

The game is played with an eighteen-inch-long racquet 6
that is easy to handle, and with a black rubber ball that is about
the size of a tennis ball, only much livelier. These features
permit beginners as well as experts to hit the ball many times
during rallies

Because the ball stays in play longer, you stay in motion 7
longer and so get a better workout than you would in playing
most other racquet sports. Only highly skilled tennis players or
squash players really can extend themselves fully in an hour
of playing those sports, for example. But after an hour or so
on the racquetball court, even the novice can feel pleasantly
exhausted.

In addition to being such a fun game, racquetball is an 8
excellent sport to play in order to remain physically fit. You can
practice on a court by yourself and still get a full workout.

In singles, you'll greatly enjoy playing against another 9
person at your own level. Even if you are both novices, you'll
still get a tremendous workout.

In doubles, where you have two teams of two persons 10
each, you will find that you can play for a longer period of time
because you don't have to cover as much of the court. Doubles
is becoming increasingly popular in racquetball because it gives
entire families and small groups of friends a chance to have fun
together.

Another reason racquetball is growing so rapidly is that 11
it is convenient to play. With all the new courts going up, people can schedule their matches or practice sessions for almost
any time of day. Many clubs are open from 6:00 A.M. to mid-
night, seven days a week. And you never have to worry about
being rained out in racquetball—courts are always fully enclosed, since the ceiling of the court is an integral part of the
game. 12

Finally, racquetball is inexpensive to play. Equipment and
clothing need not cost much, and there is a wide range of

membership fees available at racquetball clubs. A single person can join a club for as low as $25, with the cost of court-time running an additional $2.50–$5.00 per hour, depending on the time he or she wants to play. If you belong to a YMCA or a Jewish Center, it may be even less expensive to play—although court time at these places may be somewhat harder to come by.

COMPREHENSION

1. This article is mainly about
   a. how to play racquetball
   b. the reason racquetball is popular
   c. the equipment needed to play racquetball
   d. the convenience of playing racquetball
2. The writer indicates that
   a. beginners can play as well as experienced players
   b. only highly skilled tennis and squash players can play for a full hour
   c. even beginners get a fair amount of exercise on the court
   d. little skill is required
3. Racquetball is better exercise than tennis because
   a. the racquet is easy to handle
   b. the court is larger
   c. you can play by yourself
   d. the ball stays in play longer, so you stay in motion longer
4. One advantage of playing doubles is that
   a. you can play for a longer time because four people split the cost
   b. you can play longer because you don't have to cover as much of the court
   c. you can have more fun with small groups of people
   d. you can play against people who are at your own level
5. Racquetball is growing in popularity primarily because
   a. it's fun right from the beginning
   b. novices can feel pleasantly exhausted after a game
   c. you can play in teams of two persons each
   d. you don't have to worry about being rained out

VOCABULARY

Directions: *The meaning of the following terms from selection 3 cannot be clearly determined from the context. Using the dictionary entries, select the appropriate definition of the term as it is used in the reading selection.*

1. burgeoning (par. 2)
   a. sprouting
   b. putting forth
   c. growing
   d. thriving

bur·geon (bûr'jən) *v.* -geoned, -geoning, -geons. Also **bour·geon.** —*intr.* **1.** To put forth new buds, leaves, or greenery; begin to sprout, grow, or blossom. **2.** To develop rapidly; flourish. See Usage note below. —*tr.* To put forth (buds, for example); to sprout. —*n.* Also **bour·geon.** A bud, sprout, or newly developing growth. [Middle English *burgenen,* from *burjon,* a bud, from Old French, from Vulgar Latin *burriō* (stem *burriōn-*) (unattested), from Late Latin *burra,* shaggy garment (probably from the down on some buds). See **burl.**]
   Usage: The verb *burgeon* and its participle *burgeoning,* used as an adjective, are properly restricted to actual or figurative budding and sprouting, that is, to what is newly emerging: *the burgeoning talent of the boy Mozart.* They are not mere substitutes for the more general *expand, grow,* and *thrive,* as 51 per cent of the Usage Panel noted in rejecting the following example: *the burgeoning population of Queens.*

2. novice (par. 7)
   a. beginner
   b. postulant
   c. one who has
      taken vows
   d. religious person

nov·ice (nŏv'ĭs) *n.* **1.** A person new to any field or activity; beginner. **2.** A person who has entered a religious order, but who is on probation before taking final vows. Compare **postulant.** [Middle English *novyce,* from Old French *novice,* from Medieval Latin *novícius,* from Latin *novícius,* extension of *novus,* new. See **newo-** in Appendix.*]

DISCUSSION

1. Do you think racquetball is just a fad? What do you think will be the next sport to experience sudden popularity?
2. Do you think sports have any value in our lives? Why? What is their value?
3. How do you envision the life of a professional in a sport? Are there advantages? Disadvantages?

Difficulty level: B

4. To Lie or Not to Lie— The Doctor's Dilemma

Sissela Bok

Should doctors ever lie to benefit their patients—to speed recovery or to conceal the approach of death? In medicine as in law, government, and other lines of work, the requirements of honesty often seem dwarfed by greater needs: the need to shelter from brutal news or to uphold a promise of secrecy; to expose corruption or to promote the public interest. [1]

What should doctors say, for example, to a 46-year-old man coming in for a routine physical checkup just before going on vacation with his family who, though he feels in perfect health, is found to have a form of cancer that will cause him to die within six months? Is it best to tell him the truth? If he asks, should the doctors deny that he is ill, or minimize the gravity of the prognosis? Should they at least conceal the truth until after the family vacation? [2]

Doctors confront such choices often and urgently. At times, they see important reasons to lie for the patient's own sake; in their eyes, such lies differ sharply from self-serving ones. [3]

Studies show that most doctors sincerely believe that the seriously ill do not want to know the truth about their condition, and that informing them risks destroying their hope, so that they may recover more slowly, or deteriorate faster, perhaps even commit suicide. As one physician wrote: "Ours is a profession which traditionally has been guided by a precept that transcends the virtue of uttering the truth for truth's sake, and that is 'as far as possible do no harm.' " [4]

Armed with such a precept, a number of doctors may slip 5
into deceptive practices that they assume will "do no harm"
and may well help their patients. They may prescribe innumerable placebos, sound more encouraging than the facts warrant, and distort grave news, especially to the incurably ill and
the dying.

But the illusory nature of the benefits such deception is 6
meant to bestow is now coming to be documented. Studies
show that, contrary to the belief of many physicians, an overwhelming majority of patients do want to be told the truth,
even about grave illness, and feel betrayed when they learn
that they have been misled. We are also learning that truthful
information, humanely conveyed, helps patients cope with illness: helps them tolerate pain better, need less medication, and
even recover faster after surgery.

Not only do lies not provide the "help" hoped for by 7
advocates of benevolent deception; they invade the autonomy
of patients and render them unable to make informed choices
concerning their own health, including the choice of whether
to *be* a patient in the first place. We are becoming increasingly
aware of all that can befall patients in the course of their illness
when information is denied or distorted.

Dying patients especially—who are easiest to mislead and 8
most often kept in the dark—can then not make decisions
about the end of life: about whether or not to enter a hospital,
or to have surgery; about where and with whom to spend their
remaining time; about how to bring their affairs to a close and
take leave.

Lies also do harm to those who tell them: harm to their 9
integrity and, in the long run, to their credibility. Lies hurt their
colleagues as well. The suspicion of deceit undercuts the work
of the many doctors who are scrupulously honest with their
patients; it contributes to the spiral of litigation and of "defensive medicine," and thus it injures, in turn, the entire medical
profession.

Sharp conflicts are now arising. Patients are learning to 10
press for answers. Patients' bills of rights require that they be
informed about their condition and about alternatives for treatment. Many doctors go to great lengths to provide such information. Yet even in hospitals with the most eloquent bill of
rights, believers in benevolent deception continue their age-old
practices. Colleagues may disapprove but refrain from
remonstrating. Nurses may bitterly resent having to take part,
day after day, in deceiving patients, but feel powerless to take
a stand.

There is urgent need to debate this issue openly. Not only 11
in medicine, but in other professions as well, practitioners may
find themselves repeatedly in straits where serious consequences seem avoidable only through deception. Yet the public
has every reason to be wary of professional deception, for such
practices are peculiarly likely to become ingrained, to spread,
and to erode trust. Neither in medicine, nor in law, government, or the social sciences can there be comfort in the old saw,
"What you don't know can't hurt you."

COMPREHENSION

1. This selection is about
   a. why doctors don't always tell the truth
   b. the question of whether patients should be told the truth about their illnesses
   c. the benefits of not knowing the implications of an illness
   d. the circumstances in which a person should not be told the truth

2. A patient's bill of rights requires that patients be informed of
   a. all medical expenses
   b. their condition
   c. the doctor's credentials
   d. the anticipated schedule of recovery

3. Studies on the benefits of a doctor's deception about the seriousness of an illness show that
   a. people who are seriously ill do not want to know the truth
   b. the truth about the seriousness of an illnes destroys a patient's hope
   c. most patients want to know the truth about their illness
   d. many patients commit suicide when they are told the truth

4. Patients most easily misled are those who are
   a. entering the hospital
   b. about to have surgery
   c. dying
   d. children

5. The most unfortunate consequence of deception in the professions is that
   a. the practice will spread and erode trust
   b. colleagues disapprove
   c. nurses often tell patients the truth
   d. patients are unsure of their rights

VOCABULARY

Directions: *The meaning of the following terms from selection 4 cannot be clearly determined from the context. Using the dictionary entries, select the appropriate definition of the term as it is used in the reading selection.*

1. dwarfed (par. 1)
   a. small person
   b. ugly
   c. made smaller
   d. stunted

2. prognosis (par. 2)
   a. outcome
   b. recovery
   c. course
   d. prediction

dwarf (dwôrf) *n., pl.* **dwarfs** or **dwarves** (dwôrvz). **1. a.** A very small person, especially one afflicted with dwarfism. **b.** An atypically small animal or plant. **2.** A diminutive, often ugly, manlike creature of fairy tales and legend. **3.** A **dwarf star** (*see*). —*v.* **dwarfed, dwarfing, dwarfs.** —*tr.* **1.** To check the natural growth or development of; to stunt: "*the oaks were dwarfed from lack of moisture*" (Steinbeck). **2.** To cause to appear small by comparison: "*Together these two big men dwarfed the tiny Broadway office*" (Saul Bellow). —*intr.* To become stunted or grow smaller. —*adj.* **1.** Diminutive; undersized; stunted. **2.** *Biology.* Much smaller than the usual or typical kind: *dwarf gourami; dwarf zinnias.* [Middle English *dwerf, dwergh,* Old English *dweorg, dweorh,* from Germanic *dwerg-* (unattested).]

prog·no·sis (prŏg-nō′sĭs) *n., pl.* **-ses** (-sēz′). **1. a.** A prediction of the probable course and outcome of a disease. **b.** The likelihood of recovery from a disease. **2.** Any forecast or prediction. [Late Latin, from Greek *prognōsis,* from *progignōskein,* to foreknow, predict : *pro-,* before + *gignōskein,* to know (see **gnō-** in Appendix*).]

3. precept (par. 4)
   a. conduct
   b. principle
   c. law
   d. writ

pre·cept (prē'sĕpt') *n.* **1.** A rule or principle imposing a particular standard of action or conduct. **2.** *Law.* A writ. [Middle English, from Latin *praeceptum*, from *praecipere* (past participle *praeceptus*), to take beforehand, warn, teach : *prae*, before + *capere*, to take (see **kap-** in Appendix*).]

4. placebos (par. 5)
   a. inactive substances
   b. vesper services
   c. remedial values
   d. parts of a prayer

pla·ce·bo (plä-chā'bō *for sense 1;* plə-sē'bō *for senses 2 and 3*) *n., pl.* **-bos** or **-boes.** **1.** *Roman Catholic Church.* The service or office of vespers for the dead. **2. a.** *Medicine.* A substance containing no medication and given merely to humor a patient. **b.** An inactive substance used as a control in an experiment. **3.** Anything lacking intrinsic remedial value, done or given to humor another. [Medieval Latin, from the first word of the first antiphon of the service, *Placēbo* (*Dominō in rēgiōne vivōrum*), "I shall please (the Lord in the land of the living)," from *placēre*, to please. See **plāk-¹** in Appendix.*]

5. illusory (par. 6)
   a. tendency
   b. short term
   c. nature
   d. deceptive

il·lu·so·ry (ĭ-lōō'sə-rē, -zə-rē) *adj.* Tending to deceive; of the nature of an illusion; illusive.

6. benevolent (par. 7)
   a. kind
   b. easy
   c. well
   d. to wish

be·nev·o·lent (bə-nĕv'ə-lənt) *adj.* **1.** Characterized by benevolence; kindly. **2.** Of or concerned with charity: *a benevolent fund.* —See Synonyms at **kind.** [Middle English, from Latin *benevolēns*, "wishing well" : *bene*, well (see **deu-²** in Appendix*) + *volēns*, present participle of *velle*, to wish (see **wel-²** in Appendix*).] —**be·nev'o·lent·ly** *adv.*

7. autonomy (par. 7)
   a. governing
   b. group
   c. right of self-control
   d. community

au·ton·o·my (ô-tŏn'ə-mē) *n., pl.* **-mies.** **1.** The condition or quality of being self-governing. **2.** Self-government or the right of self-government; self-determination; independence. **3.** A self-governing state, community, or group. [Greek *autonomia*, from *autonomos*, AUTONOMOUS.] —**au·ton'o·mist** *n.*

8. remonstrating (par. 10)
   a. taking action
   b. objecting
   c. predicting an omen
   d. arguing

re·mon·strate (rĭ-mŏn'strāt') *v.* **-strated, -strating, -strates.** —*tr.* To say or plead in protest, objection, or reproof. —*intr.* To make objections; argue against some action. —See Synonyms at **object.** [Medieval Latin *remōnstrāre*, to demonstrate : Latin *re-*, completely + *monstrāre*, to show, from *monstrum*, an omen, a portent, from *monēre*, to warn (see **men-¹** in Appendix*).] —**re'mon·stra'tion** (rē'mŏn-strā'shən, rĕm'ən-) *n.* —**re·mon'stra·tive** (rĭ-mŏn'strə-tĭv) *adj.* —**re·mon'stra'tor** (rĭ-mŏn'strā'tər) *n.*

9. straits (par. 11)
   a. difficult position
   b. close quarters
   c. rigid feelings
   d. narrow area

strait (strāt) *n. Abbr.* **St., str. 1.** *Often plural.* A narrow passage of water joining two larger bodies of water. **2.** *Often plural.* A position of difficulty, perplexity, distress, or need: *He was in desperate straits for money.* —*adj. Archaic.* **1.** Narrow or constricted. **2.** Affording little space or room; restricted, confined, or close. **3.** Strict, rigid, or righteous. [Middle English *streit*, from Old French *estreit*, tight, narrow, from Latin *strictus*, from the past participle of *stringere*, to draw tight. See **streig-** in Appendix.*]

10. ingrained (par. 11)
    a. dyed
    b. made of fiber
    c. changed
    d. fixed in mind

in·grain (ĭn-grān') *tr.v.* **-grained, -graining, -grains. 1.** To impress indelibly on the mind or nature; to fix; infuse. **2.** *Archaic.* To dye or stain into the fiber of. —*adj.* **1.** Deeply rooted; instilled. **2.** Dyed in the yarn before weaving or knitting. **3.** Made of fiber or yarn dyed before weaving. Said especially of rugs. —*n.* **1.** Yarn or fiber dyed before manufacture. **2.** Any article made of ingrained yarns, as carpets. [IN- (in) + GRAIN (dye).]

DISCUSSION

1. If you were dying would you want to know the truth? Why?
2. In which profession is it most important to be honest—medicine, law, or government? Why?
3. If a member of your family were dying, would you want him or her to know the truth? Would you take the responsibility of providing the information?

Difficulty level: C

5. Mate Selection

Ian Robertson

A courtship system is essentially a marriage market, although different systems vary according to how much choice they permit the individual. The United States probably allows more individual freedom of choice than any other society. A parent who attempts to interfere in the choice of a son or daughter is considered meddlesome and is more likely to alienate than persuade the young lover. In our predominantly urban and anonymous society, young people—often equipped with automobiles—have an exceptional degree of privacy in their courting.

The practice of dating enables young people to find out about one another, to improve their own interpersonal skills in the market, to engage in sexual experimentation if they so wish, and finally to select a marriage partner. The metaphor of the "market" may seem a little unromantic, but in fact the participants do attempt to "sell" their assets—physical appearance, personal charms, talents and interests, and career prospects.

Who marries whom? In general, the American mate selection process is *homogamous:* individuals marry others much like themselves. Among the characteristics that seem to attract people to one another are the following:

Similar age. Married partners are usually of roughly the same age. Husbands are on average older than their wives, though rarely by more than five years, and even this difference in age is gradually declining. The 1970 census showed that the median age difference between partners was only two to four years.

Social class. Most people marry within their own social class. The reasons are obvious: we tend to live in class-segregated neighborhoods, to meet mostly people of the same class, and to share class-specific tastes and interests. Interclass marriages are relatively more common, however, among college students.

Proximity. People tend to marry people who live in the same area, even in the same neighborhood. In part this is because they are more likely to meet, in part because their common environment provides them with similar experiences and interests.

Religion. Most marriages are between people sharing the same religious faith: 93 percent of Jews, 91 percent of Catholics, and 78 percent of Protestants marry partners of the same religion. Interreligious marriages within Protestant denominations, however, are fairly common. Religious bodies generally oppose interfaith marriages, on the grounds that they may lead to personal conflicts, disagreements over the faith in which children should be raised, and an undermining of belief in a particular doctrine. Many intending spouses change their religion to that of their partner before marriage.

Education. Husbands and wives generally have a similar educational level. Since the number of years of schooling correlates strongly with social class, it is difficult to disentangle the influence of educational level from class status, but some degree of intellectual parity seems to be demanded by marital partners. The college campus is, of course, a marriage market in its own right, and college-educated people are especially likely to marry people of similar educational achievement. 8

Racial background. Interracial marriages are extremely rare. Several states had laws prohibiting interracial marriages until the sixties, and even today such marriages attract considerable social disapproval. Interracial marriages between blacks and whites are particularly rare; in the majority of these cases, the husband is black and the wife white. 9

Ethnic background. Members of the white ethnic groups are more likely to marry within their own group than outside it, but with the halt in new immigration and the steady assimilation of the ethnic groups into mainstream American society, this tendency is declining markedly. 10

Physical characteristics. People tend to marry partners who are physically similar to themselves in height, weight, and even in hair color, state of health, and basal metabolism. 11

Cupid's arrow, then, does not strike at random. We know very little about the personality characteristics that attract partners to one another. If a general psychological pattern exists, no researchers have yet been able to determine it with any certainty. But the social characteristics of marriage partners are much easier to establish, and all research findings point in the same direction: we tend to choose as mates people who have social characteristics similar to our own. 12

COMPREHENSION

1. This article is written to explain
   a. how people are attracted to each other
   b. the personality characteristics that influence the selection of a mate
   c. the social characteristics that influence the selection of a mate
   d. how to find a mate

2. In America the age of married partners
   a. differs significantly
   b. varies with social class
   c. varies with educational level
   d. is roughly the same

3. Interclass marriages
   a. never occur in America
   b. are affected by religious faith
   c. are more common among college students
   d. are unaffected by level of education

4. Religious institutions often oppose interfaith marriages for all of the following reasons *except*
   a. they may lead to personal conflict
   b. decisions have to be made about which faith the children should be raised in

c. one partner must change his or her religion

d. beliefs in special doctrines might be questioned or changed

5. Interracial marriages

   a. are still prohibited by law

   b. attract social disapproval

   c. occur among various ethnic groups

   d. only occur between black men and white women

VOCABULARY

Directions: *The meaning of the following terms from selection 5 cannot be clearly determined from the context. Using the dictionary entries, select the appropriate definition of the term as it is used in the reading selection.*

1. meddlesome (par. 1)

   a. curious

   b. interfering

   c. interested

   d. anxious

2. alienate (par. 1)

   a. to convey

   b. to turn away

   c. to change

   d. to transfer

3. metaphor (par. 2)

   a. simile

   b. literal

   c. denote

   d. comparison

4. homogamous (par. 3)

   a. alike in many ways

   b. simultaneous

   c. sisters

   d. of the same sex

5. proximity (par. 6)

   a. nearness in time

   b. nearness in order

   c. nearness in relation

   d. nearness in place

6. doctrine (par. 7)

   a. religious principle

   b. government policy

   c. method of teaching

   d. lessons

7. correlates (par. 8)

   a. implies

   b. places

   c. mutually connected

   d. established in order

8. parity (par. 8)

   a. equality

   b. regulation

   c. symmetry

   d. fixed rate

med·dle \'med-ᵊl\ *vi* **med·dled; med·dling** \'med-liŋ, -ᵊl-iŋ\ [ME *medlen,* fr. OF *mesler, medler,* fr. (assumed) VL *misculare,* fr. L *miscēre* to mix — more at MIX] : to interest oneself in what is not one's concern : interfere without right or propriety — **med·dler** \'med-lər, -ᵊl-ər\ *n*
syn MEDDLE, INTERFERE, INTERMEDDLE, TAMPER *shared meaning element* : to concern oneself with officiously, impertinently, or indiscreetly
med·dle·some \'med-ᵊl-səm\ *adj* : given to meddling *syn* see IMPERTINENT — **med·dle·some·ness** *n*

al·ien·ate (āl'yən-āt', ā'lē-ən-) *tr.v.* -ated, -ating, -ates. 1. To cause (someone previously friendly or affectionate) to become unfriendly or indifferent; estrange: *alienate a friend.* 2. To remove or dissociate (oneself, for example): *"man cannot alienate himself from his own consciousness"* (Wylie Sypher). 3. To cause to be transferred; turn away: *"he succeeded . . . in alienating the affections of my only ward"* (Oscar Wilde). 4. *Law.* To transfer (property) to the ownership of another. —See Synonyms at **estrange.** [Latin *aliēnāre,* from *aliēnus,* ALIEN.] —**al'ien·a'tor** (-ā'tər) *n.*

met·a·phor \'met-ə-ˌfȯ(ə)r *also* -fər\ *n* [MF or L; MF, *metaphore,* fr. L *metaphora,* fr. Gk, fr. *metapherein* to transfer, fr. *meta-* + *pherein* to bear — more at BEAR] 1 : a figure of speech in which a word or phrase literally denoting one kind of object or idea is used in place of another to suggest a likeness or analogy between them (as in *the ship plows the sea*) <using ~, we say that computers have senses and a memory —William Jovanovich>; *broadly* : figurative language — compare SIMILE 2 : an object, activity, or idea treated as a metaphor — **met·a·phor·ic** \ˌmet-ə-'fȯr-ik, -'fär-\ *or* **met·a·phor·i·cal** \-i-kəl\ *adj* — **met·a·phor·i·cal·ly** \-i-k(ə-)lē\ *adv*

ho·mog·a·my \hō-'mäg-ə-mē\ *n* [G *homogamie,* fr. *hom-* + *-gamie* -gamy] 1 a : a state of having flowers alike throughout b : the maturing of stamens and pistils at the same period 2 : reproduction within an isolated group perpetuating qualities by which it is differentiated from the larger group of which it is a part; *broadly* : the mating of like with like — **ho·mog·a·mous** \-məs\ *or* **ho·mo·gam·ic** \ˌhō-mə-'gam-ik, ˌhäm-ə-\ *adj*

prox·im·i·ty (prŏk-sĭm'ə-tē) *n.* The state, quality, or fact of being near or next; closeness. [Old French *proximite,* from Latin *proximitās,* from *proximus,* nearest. See proximate.]

doc·trine \'däk-trən\ *n* [ME, fr. MF & L; MF, fr. L *doctrina,* fr. *doctor*] 1 *archaic* : TEACHING, INSTRUCTION 2 a : something that is taught b : a principle or position or the body of principles in a branch of knowledge or system of belief : DOGMA c : a principle of law established through past decisions d : a statement of fundamental government policy esp. in international relations
syn DOCTRINE, DOGMA, TENET *shared meaning element* : a principle accepted as valid and authoritative

²**cor·re·late** \-ˌlāt\ *vb* -lat·ed; -lat·ing *vi* : to bear reciprocal or mutual relations ~ *vt* 1 a : to establish a mutual or reciprocal relation of b : to show a causal relationship between 2 : to relate so that to each member of one set or series a corresponding member of another is assigned 3 : to present or set forth so as to show relationship <he ~s the findings of the scientists, the psychologists, and the mystics —Eugene Exman> — **cor·re·lat·able** \-ˌlāt-ə-bəl\ *adj*

¹**par·i·ty** \'par-ət-ē\ *n, pl* **-ties** [L *paritas,* fr. *par* equal] 1 : the quality or state of being equal or equivalent 2 a : equivalence of a commodity price expressed in one currency to its price expressed in another b : equality of purchasing power established by law between different kinds of money at a given ratio 3 : an equivalence between farmers' current purchasing power and their purchasing power at a selected base period maintained by government support of agricultural commodity prices

9. assimilation (par. 10)
    a. merging
    b. conversion
    c. absorption
    d. photosynthesis

as·sim·i·la·tion \ə-ˌsim-ə-'lā-shən\ *n* **1 a** : an act, process, or instance of assimilating **b** : the state of being assimilated **2** : the incorporation or conversion of nutrients into protoplasm that in animals follows digestion and absorption and in higher plants involves both photosynthesis and root absorption **3** : adaptation of a sound to an adjacent sound <in the word *cupboard* the \p\ sound of the word *cup* has undergone complete ~> *syn* see RECOGNITION

10. basal metabolism (par. 11)
    a. high level of physical activity
    b. use of energy during rest
    c. basic living standard
    d. energy conversion

bas·al \'bā-səl, -zəl\ *adj* **1 a** : relating to, situated at, or forming the base **b** : arising from the base of a stem <~ leaves> **2 a** : of or relating to the foundation, base, or essence : FUNDAMENTAL **b** : of, relating to, or being essential for maintaining the fundamental vital activities of an organism : MINIMAL **c** : used for teaching beginners <~ readers> — **ba·sal·ly** \-ē\ *adv*
basal metabolic rate *n* : the rate at which heat is given off by an organism at complete rest
basal metabolism *n* : the turnover of energy in a fasting and resting organism using energy solely to maintain vital cellular activity, respiration, and circulation as measured by the basal metabolic rate

DISCUSSION

1. What is the value of dating? List some valuable things you have learned.
2. Which social characteristics mentioned in the article are (or were) particularly important to you in selecting a mate?
3. America is often said to be a classless society. Does the mate selection process described in the article support that idea?
4. The author describes the college campus as a "marriage market." Do you agree or disagree with this statement? Support your position by giving examples of behavior on your own campus.

Difficulty level: C

6. Violence in Sports

Robert C. Yeager

What is sports violence? The distinction between unacceptable viciousness and a game's normal rough-and-tumble is impossible to make, or so the argument runs. This position may appeal to our penchant for legalism, but the truth is most of us know quite well when an act of needless savagery has been committed, and sports are little different from countless other activities of life. The distinction is as apparent as that between a deliberately aimed roundhouse and the arm flailing of an athlete losing his balance. When a player balls his hand into a fist, when he drives his helmet into an unsuspecting opponent—in short, when he crosses the boundary between playing hard and playing to hurt—he can only intend an act of violence. 1

Admittedly, violent acts in sports are difficult to police. But here, too, we find reflected the conditions of everyday life. Ambiguities in the law, confusion at the scene, and the reluctance of witnesses cloud almost any routine assault and battery case. Such uncertainties, however, have not prevented society from arresting people who strike their fellow citizens on the street. 2

Perhaps our troubles stem not from the games we play but rather from how we play them. The 1979 meeting between hockey stars from the Soviet Union and the National Hockey League provided a direct test of two approaches to sport—the emphasis on skill, grace, and finesse by the Russians and the stress on brutality and violence by the NHL. In a startling upset, the Russians embarrassed their rough-playing opponents and debunked a long-standing myth: that success in certain sports requires excessive violence.   3

Violence apologists cite two additional arguments. First, they say, sports always have been violent; today things are no different. But arguments in America's Old West were settled on Main Street with six-guns, and early cave-dwellers chose their women with a club. Civilizing influences ended those practices; yet we are told sports violence should be tolerated. The second contention is that athletes accept risk as part of the game, and, in the case of professionals, are paid handsomely to do so. But can anyone seriously argue that being an athlete should require the acceptance of unnecessary physical abuse? And, exaggerated as it may seem, the pay of professional athletes presumably reflects their abilities, not an indemnification against combat injuries.   4

"Clearly we are in deep trouble," says perplexed former sportscaster and football player Al DeRogatis. "But how and why has it gotten so bad?"   5

COMPREHENSION

1. The writer's main thought is that
   a. violence in sports is illegal
   b. finesse is more important than aggression
   c. athletes should not be injured in sports
   d. violence in sports is not necessary
2. This article makes a distinction between
   a. legal and social definitions of violence
   b. viciousness and aggression
   c. assault and battery
   d. American and Russian hockey
3. A sports violence "apologist" probably thinks that
   a. violence in sports is a rare occurrence
   b. violence in sports is not necessary
   c. athletes are paid enough for their injuries
   d. professional athletes enjoy violence
4. In the last paragraph the author indicates that
   a. nothing can be done about violence in sports
   b. football players are concerned about violence in sports
   c. violence in sports is worse now than it ever was
   d. sportscasters are confused about what should be permitted in sports
5. The author feels that
   a. the personalities of athletes produce violent confrontations
   b. athletes should not have to accept unnecessary physical abuse
   c. athletes' salaries are already too high
   d. athletes need higher salaries to compensate for their injuries

VOCABULARY

Directions: *The meaning of the following terms from selection 6 cannot be clearly determined from the context. Using the dictionary entries, select the appropriate definition of the term as it is used in the reading selection.*

1. penchant (par. 1)
   a. hatred
   b. hanging
   continuation
   c. inclination
   d. definition

2. ambiguities (par. 2)
   a. multiple
   interpretations
   b. faulty clauses
   c. difficult conditions
   d. unusual
   circumstances

3. debunked (par. 3)
   a. shamed
   b. exaggerated
   c. ridiculed
   d. exposed falseness

4. cite (par. 4)
   a. to quote as
   authority
   b. to offer support
   c. rouse to action
   d. to set in motion

5. indemnification
   (par. 4)
   a. compensation
   b. insurance
   c. protection
   d. security

6. perplexed (par. 5)
   a. involved
   b. complicated
   c. puzzled
   d. intricate

pen·chant (pĕn'chənt) *n.* A strong inclination; a definite and continued liking. [French, from the present participle of *pencher*, to incline, from Vulgar Latin *pendicāre* (unattested), from Latin *pendēre*, to hang. See **spen-** in Appendix.*]

am·bi·gu·i·ty (ăm'bĭ-gyōō'ə-tē) *n., pl.* **-ties. 1.** The state of being ambiguous. **2.** Something ambiguous.
am·big·u·ous (ăm-bĭg'yōō-əs) *adj.* **1.** Susceptible of multiple interpretation. **2.** Doubtful or uncertain. [Latin *ambiguus*, uncertain, "going about," from *ambigere*, to wander about : *ambi-*, around + *agere*, to drive, lead (see **ag-** in Appendix*).] —**am·big'u·ous·ly** *adv.* —**am·big'u·ous·ness** *n.*
Synonyms: ambiguous, equivocal, obscure, recondite, abstruse, vague, cryptic, enigmatic. These adjectives mean lacking clarity of meaning. *Ambiguous* indicates the presence of two or more possible meanings, usually because of faulty expression. An *equivocal* statement is deliberately unclear or misleading, suggesting a hedging to avoid exposure of one's position. *Obscure* suggests meaning hidden in difficult form, sometimes not worth digging out. *Recondite* and *abstruse*, less pejorative, connote the erudite obscurity of the scholar: *a recondite allusion missed by most readers; abstruse works of philosophy. Vague* primarily indicates a lack of definite form. *Cryptic* suggests a puzzling terseness intended to discourage understanding, and *enigmatic*, great significance hidden in mysterious and challenging form.

de·bunk (dĭ-bŭngk') *tr.v.* **-bunked, -bunking, -bunks.** *Informal.* To expose or ridicule the falseness, sham, or exaggerated claims of. [DE- + BUNK (nonsense).] —**de·bunk'er** *n.*

cite (sīt) *tr.v.* **cited, citing, cites. 1.** To quote as an authority or example. **2.** To mention or bring forward as support, illustration, or proof. **3.** To commend (a unit or individual in the armed forces) in orders, for meritorious action. **4.** To call to attention or enumerate; to mention. **5.** To summon before a court of law. **6.** To call to action; rouse. [Middle English *citen*, to summon, from Old French *citer*, from Latin *citāre*, frequentative of *ciēre*, to set in motion, summon. See **kei-³** in Appendix.*]

in·dem·ni·fi·ca·tion (ĭn-dĕm'nə-fĭ-kā'shən) *n.* **1.** The act of indemnifying or the condition of being indemnified. **2.** Something that indemnifies.
in·dem·ni·fy (ĭn-dĕm'nə-fī') *tr.v.* **-fied, -fying, -fies. 1.** To protect against possible damage, legal suit, or bodily injury; insure. **2.** To make compensation to for incurred damage or hurt. [Latin *indemnis*, uninjured (see **indemnity**) + -FY.] —**in·dem'ni·fi'er** *n.*

per·plexed (pər-plĕkst') *adj.* **1.** Puzzled; bewildered; confused. **2.** Complicated; involved. —**per·plex'ed·ly** (pər-plĕk'sĭd-lē) *adv.* **per·plex·i·ty** (pər-plĕk'sə-tē) *n., pl.* **-ties. 1.** The state or condi-

DISCUSSION

1. What part do you think a coach plays in determining whether or not violence is an accepted part of a sport? Give some specific examples.
2. Do you think violence in sports is acceptable? Why?
3. Do spectators have a role in promoting violence in sports? Do you think people enjoy seeing human beings get hurt? Why?

Unit Two
Sentence Patterns

This unit is designed to help you express your ideas in a clear, understandable manner. A very basic but important unit of expression is the sentence. Sentences are the starting point for expressing anything more than immediate reactions and feelings. Even when you do not speak in complete sentences, your meaning is often understood as a sentence. Suppose you burn your finger on a stove; your immediate reaction may be to say "Ouch." However, a friend nearby will know that you hurt yourself. Similarly, when a two- or three-year-old child points to a plate of cookies and says "Cookie!" the parents know that he or she means "I want a cookie." You can see, then, that the sentence, whether expressed completely or not, is the basic vehicle for communicating ideas.

At this point you may be wondering, "If a listener can interpret a word or two as a complete thought, why must I, as a writer, express my ideas in a careful, precise way?" The answer is that when you hear someone say "Ouch" as he or she burns a finger, you have viewed the situation and can relate it to the verbal expression. However, if you just see the word "Ouch" printed on a page, you would have no idea of what had occurred, to whom, or why. In writing, then, you must provide your reader with more information than you do in speech. You must, in effect, describe to your reader what happened and to whom it happened. To do this you must write in complete sentences.

In Chapter 3 we will explain the basic sentence patterns and discuss how to read and write them more effectively. In Chapter 4 you will see how you can combine ideas into clearer, even more effective sentences. In Chapter 5 you will see how your sentences can combine ideas to show your reader how those ideas are related.

3. Basic Sentences

We all know that letters are arranged in a specific sequence to form words. In fact the same letters, depending on their arrangement, can form two different words. The letters w-a-s arranged one way form the word "was"; arranged another way they form the word "saw." Here are a few other examples: rat–tar; smile–miles; on–no; lead–deal. It is obvious that letter arrangement determines how a word is read and understood. Similarly, the way you arrange words in a sentence determines how the sentence is read and understood. In the following two examples, notice that by simply rearranging the word order, one can express two very different meanings:

EXAMPLE 1: The instructor liked the student.
The student liked the instructor.

EXAMPLE 2: The dog bit the snake.
The snake bit the dog.

In addition to how you arrange letters in writing a word, you must also be sure to include all the letters; otherwise the word may not be understood. For example, do these groups of letters mean anything to you?

mo	cande
ot	foth
ry	onl
wl	rea

They probably do not because one letter is missing in each. With the missing letter replaced, however, these groupings make sense.

mop	candle
got	forth
cry	only
owl	read

Similarly in a sentence, if you leave out a word or part of the sentence, the sentence may not make sense, or it may be misread. For instance, each of the following sentences is missing a word important to the meaning of the sentence. As you read each you will see that its meaning is not complete.

My _____ walked across the street.
(sister? wife? father? dog?)

My psychology instructor _____ yesterday.
(assigned a test? cancelled class?)

The purpose of this chapter, then, is to emphasize writing sentences that follow recognized arrangements (patterns) and that are complete in meaning. As a first step you must be able to identify the most basic sentence pattern, the simple sentence, and the parts that it contains. Next, you need to be able to write effective sentences that express clear, complete thoughts, as well as to identify common sentence errors that cause confusion for the reader.

IDENTIFYING SIMPLE SENTENCE PATTERNS

"A sentence is a group of words that expresses a complete thought." You probably have heard this definition at one time or another, but you may not have considered how it affects your writing and your ability to understand what you read. If you are to read and completely understand a sentence, you should be able to identify certain parts that carry the basic message of that sentence. Similarly, as a writer, you must be sure to include all necessary parts to convey a complete thought. To do either, you must be able to distinguish a complete from an incomplete thought.

Recognizing Complete Thoughts

You will notice that some information in the following statement is missing and that you are left with a question in mind after reading it.

INCOMPLETE THOUGHT: Walked to the car after the movie
(Who walked to the car?)

This statement is not a complete thought because it does not tell you *who* walked to the car. To express a complete thought, this statement could be expanded as follows:

COMPLETE THOUGHT: <u>George</u> walked to the car after the movie.

Here are a few more incomplete thoughts with examples of how information can be added to make them complete. The information added to the incomplete thought is underlined.

INCOMPLETE THOUGHT: Is difficult to understand
(Who or what is difficult?)

COMPLETE THOUGHT: <u>The textbook</u> is difficult to understand.

When information was included about *what* was difficult to understand, the thought was made complete.

INCOMPLETE THOUGHT: The instructor in the blue sweater
(What does the instructor do?)

COMPLETE THOUGHT: The instructor in the blue sweater <u>gives difficult exams</u>.

This thought was completed by including information about what the instructor does.

INCOMPLETE THOUGHT: After paying the bill
(Who did what?)

COMPLETE THOUGHT: The couple left the restaurant after paying the bill.

The completed thought tells you who (the couple) did what (left the restaurant).

In each of these examples you may have noticed that the complete thought had at least two parts. One part usually told *who* or *what* did something. The other part told *what was done* or *what happened*. Both of these parts must be present in order for a thought to be expressed in a complete sentence.

EXERCISE 3–1

Directions: *None of the following statements expresses a complete thought. Each is missing some important information, and reading it leaves a question in your mind. In the blank following each statement, write the question that is left unanswered.*

EXAMPLE: Went bowling three times a week *Who went bowling?*

1. A very violent movie _____

2. Well known as Rodeo King _____

3. Going to a movie on a rainy afternoon _____

4. The angry and upset student _____

5. A book called *Twins* _____

6. After hearing both sides of the argument _____

7. Whenever someone in the class asks an important question _____

_____

8. After spotting several UFOs _____

9. Writing his term paper late at night _____

10. A chocolate soda with vanilla ice cream _____

11. Assertively responding to the charges _____

12. A process used in plastic surgery for grafting skin _____

_____

13. A knot formed by a collection of nerve cells _____

_____

14. Studying similarities and differences of various cultures _____

_____

15. After identifying the source of the pollution _____

_____

EXCERCISE 3–2

Directions: *Read each statement and identify those which express a complete thought. In the blank at the right mark a C for complete thought and I for an incomplete thought.*

EXAMPLE: Driving slowly and carefully   *I*

1. He lost his book during lunch. _____

2. He got off the bus at the wrong stop. _____

3. Going home on the subway. _____

4. After buying the popcorn. _____

5. When he got a flat tire. _____

6. Because food prices have risen drastically. _____

7. Lasting friendships are often formed in college. _____

8. To cope with increasing energy costs. _____

9. Watching the candidates debate the issue. _____

10. The committee was formed to evaluate current grading practices on campus. _____

11. Often due to fine particles of dust or smoke suspended in the air. _____

12. Played in an enclosed court that measures 20 feet wide and 34 feet long. _____

13. The grouse, a species of game bird, is found in the colder climates. _____

14. Comparing the life cycles of the house fly and the honeybee. _____

15. Unlike the other vital necessities of civilized man. _____

Identifying Sentence Core Parts

In the previous section you learned that a sentence or complete thought must have two parts. The *subject* tells who or what the thought is about. The *predicate* tells you what, in general, was done or happened. Together the subject and predicate contain all the words in the sentence.

However, not all the information contained in the subject and predicate is absolutely essential to the basic message of the sentence. The most important part of the subject is called the *simple subject*. It consists of the word or words that name the main person, place, object, or idea that is discussed in the sentence. The basic information in the predicate is provided by the *verb*. The verb is the word or group of words that expresses action, or tells you that something exists, or helps to complete a statement. These two important parts of the sentence are known as its *core parts*. If you can pick out the core parts in a sentence, you can find the basic idea of most sentences because the core parts express the essential meaning of the sentence. All the other words in the subject and predicate contribute more information about the primary message of the sentence. For example, in the sentence:

The X-rated movie about two teenagers was playing at the drive-in.

The core parts are "movie" (the simple subject) and "was playing" (the verb). These words tell you the basic idea of what the sentence is about and what is happening. The other words in the sentence tell you more about the movie—that it was X-rated, that it concerns two teenagers, and that it was being shown at a drive-in theatre.

In the following arrangements of words, only the core parts of a sentence are given. Notice that you can understand what is happening even when you only have two core parts to read.

1. Car overturned
2. Orchestra played
3. Child cried
4. Instructor grades
5. Sam argued

Here are the same core parts included in complete sentences. Notice that you learn more about the subject and that you find out how, when, or where the action occurred.

1. The orange car overturned while rounding a corner.
2. The school orchestra played several difficult marches.
3. The young child cried when he dropped his ice cream cone.
4. The psychology instructor grades all written exams on a pass/fail basis.
5. Sam, a new member of the football team, argued with the coach about training rules.

What Verbs Tell the Reader

The primary function of verbs is to express action or to indicate state of being. Here are a few examples:

EXAMPLE 1: The reporter <u>interviewed</u> the crash victims.

77

In this sentence the verb "interviewed" expresses action, or indicates what the reporter did.

> EXAMPLE 2: The waitress is angry.

The verb "is," in this example, indicates that a certain state or condition (anger) exists for the waitress.

> EXAMPLE 3: The student was studying for the exam last night.

In this example the verb is "was studying." the word "was" is part of the verb because it helps to explain what the student did and when he did it. Basically, then, verbs indicate action or state of being.

As you have seen from these examples, the *verb* is the word or words that expresses action or indicates state of being, but the verb is part of the *predicate* of the sentence, or the part of the sentence that, as a whole, says something more about the subject. For example, in the sentence

> My brother will leave for Mexico tomorrow.

the verb is "will leave," but "will leave for Mexico tomorrow" is the predicate.

Compound Core Parts

Some sentences may have more than one subject or more than one verb. That is, a sentence may be about more than one thing, or more than one action may be described. When this happens there is a *compound subject* or *compound verb*.

Each of the following sentences has a compound subject:

> Sam and Joe were good friends last year.

> Boston and New York are interesting cities to visit.

> Corned beef, swiss cheese, and sauerkraut are used to make a Reuben sandwich.

The first sentence above mentions some information about two people. The second sentence is about two places, and the third sentence mentions three ingredients, which make up a compound subject.

Each of the following sentences has a compound verb:

> You should call your parents or write them a letter.

> My sister always worries and complains.

> Neil is afraid of stray dogs and never walks alone at night.

The first example mentions two things you should do; the next one, likewise, relates two actions the sister is always involved in; and the last one shows Neil's condition and what action he never does. All three sentences contain at least two actions or statements of being for one subject.

A sentence may have both a compound subject and a compound verb:

The nurses and doctors rushed to the accident site and helped the victims.

Many men and women fought and died in World War II.

In each sentence two groups of people carried out the same two actions. In the first sentence nurses and doctors rushed and helped; in the second sentence men and women both fought and died.

EXERCISE 3–3

Directions: *Read each of the following sentences. Underline the subject and circle the verb.*

EXAMPLE: The radio station (gives) the weather report every half hour.

1. I read the assignment three times.
2. The lawn mower broke down.
3. The child chewed and swallowed two aspirins.
4. Sue answered two of the three essay questions.
5. The snack bar closes at ten P.M.
6. Letters of complaint frequently bring results.
7. Both inflation and the high unemployment have caused many families to readjust their lifestyles.
8. Women's clothing fashions have changed drastically since the 1960s.
9. Interior decorators often use house plants to fill empty spaces.
10. Radio and television stations often dramatize news events.
11. Drowning is caused by the lungs filling with water instead of air.
12. The English Channel is a narrow sea extending from the Scilly Isles to the Straits of Dover.
13. Aicurus, a Greek philosopher, owned a school in Athens where he taught women as well as men.
14. Equinox occurs when the sun's center crosses the celestial equator.
15. Folk dances are often the primitive expression of rituals or joy through group dances.

Expanded Sentences

As you now know, all sentences contain two basic parts—the simple subject and verb, which carry the most basic meaning of the sentence. However, sentences usually contain more than just a subject and verb.

They also include other words that provide further information and detail about the subject and the verb. These words or groups of words have various grammatical labels. It is not necessary to be able to identify and label all the various grammatical parts of the sentence, but it is important to realize how these parts can be used to expand and enhance sentence meaning. These various parts will simply be called *sentence expanders*. The function of sentence expanders is to explain the thought expressed by the core parts. Expanders usually explain the core parts of the sentence by answering such questions about the subject or the action of the sentence as *what, where, who, which, when, how,* or *why.* In the following sentence

George drove his car <u>across the bridge</u>.
where

you find out *where* George drove his car—across the bridge.
Or in the sentence

who
Sheila Warren, <u>the first mayor of the town</u>, was reelected <u>last month</u>.
when

you find out *who* Sheila Warren was and *when* she was reelected—last month.
And in this sentence

The couple danced <u>slowly and gracefully</u>.
how

you learn *how* the couple danced—slowly and gracefully. You can see in these examples that expanders provide additional information about the sentence's core parts.

How Expanders Affect Meaning

You have just seen how expanders supply additional information about the core parts, and how they can be used to "add in" information about the subject and verb, making the message more complete. However, you should also recognize how expanders can affect sentence meaning by qualifying, restricting, or limiting the meaning of a message. For example:

Those senators <u>hoping for a pay raise</u> voted against the budget cut.

In this sentence the group of words "hoping for a pay raise" indicates that not all senators, but only those hoping for a pay raise, voted against the budget cut. This expander is very important to the overall meaning of the sentence because it further describes the subject of the sentence.

Expanders can make a message more specific by providing additional detail.

On their way to the party, the couple stopped to buy gas.

The core parts (couple, stopped) in this sentence give only very general information. The expanders (underlined) describe the specifics of when and why the couple stopped.

Writers often use expanders to provide background information:

EXAMPLE: While waiting for their friends to arrive, Pete and Gloria decided to straighten up their kitchen.

The underlined expander explains the conditions under which the main action of the sentence occurred. You learn that Pete and Gloria straightened up their kitchen while they were waiting for their friends to arrive.

Expanders can also make the basic meaning of the sentence more clear, vivid, or accurate:

EXAMPLE: The angry woman, screaming and cursing, slammed the door.

In this sentence the underlined expanders help you to understand and visualize the situation being described.

EXERCISE 3–4

Directions: *Read each of the following sentences and circle the core parts. Then decide what the underlined part of each sentence tells you about the core parts. Write* who, what, which, when, where, how, *or* why *in the space provided to the right of each sentence.*

EXAMPLE: The plumber charged the housewife twenty-five dollars.

who

In this example, the underlined words tell who the plumber charged.

1. Gloria Nickerson lives in Rochester. _____

2. The senator voted for the tax increase. _____

3. The footprints in the snow led the policemen to the criminal's door. _____

4. The New Orleans Mardi Gras is fun and exciting. _____

5. Sal got the job because he had the most experience. _____

6. <u>After swimming all afternoon</u>, we ached all over. _____

7. I read <u>with enthusiasm</u> the editorial on unemployment and inflation. _____

8. The cruise ship that sails every Sunday from Miami allows <u>plenty of time for relaxation</u> before reaching its final destination. _____

9. Fast-food restaurants, <u>located throughout the country</u>, are gradually increasing the variety of the food they serve. _____

10. Tofu, or bean curd, <u>a custardlike substance</u>, is made from curdled soybean milk. _____

11. Over the past decade, federal support for social services has increased <u>due to several new poverty-reduction programs</u>. _____

12. High interest rates from time-deposit savings accounts are often available <u>only after a stated period of time</u>. _____

13. Solar ponds, or shallow pools of salt water, are one of the newest developments <u>in the field of solar energy</u>. _____

14. <u>Studying deaths resulting from a tornado</u>, researchers found that the victims tried to outrace the storm. _____

15. Corporate law firms recruit law students who have high scores <u>on their bar exams</u>. _____

WRITING BASIC SENTENCES

In composing a sentence, writers do not choose core parts deliberately and then build a sentence around those parts. Instead, because they are thinking of ideas, writers often write down words as they come to mind. You are probably wondering at this point why, then, it is necessary to learn about subjects, verbs, and modifiers. The answer is that a knowledge of them makes revision of unclear sentences easier. Often your ideas, as you express them in writing, will already be in a clear, understandable pattern. At other times, however, you will need to revise a sentence so that it expresses your idea more clearly; but to revise a sentence you first have to recognize what is wrong with it.

Expressing Complete Thoughts

If you think about any system (for example, a stereo sound system, a lighting system, a registration system), you will realize that all systems have parts, and those parts work together to produce certain results. All languages are systems of communication, and the sentence is one of many parts that function within the system. Sentences also have parts, and the core parts of the sentences, the simple subject and verb, work together to express complete thoughts. Make sure then, that every sentence you write contains both a subject and a verb and expresses a complete idea.

Using Verbs to Indicate Time

A verb can be one word or a group of words that shows action or expresses a state of being. The added words that make up the verb are called auxiliary or helping verbs because they help a verb make a statement by confining the action to a specific time period. In the following examples, the main verb is underlined twice and the helping verb is underlined once.

EXAMPLES: The boat was blowing its horn.

I have heard that song before.

I will have completed my paper before next week.

Some forms of verbs are spelled in several different ways, or they sometimes have different endings depending on the time period they indicate. Verbs express action that takes place at a certain time. To express the time when the action took place, the spelling or ending of the verb changes, or a helping verb may be added. The different times that these changes in the forms of verbs show are known as verb *tenses*. There are three most commonly used tenses: present, past, and future. Here a few basic examples of these tenses:

	Present	*Past*	*Future*	
I	(see,	saw,	will see)	the mountains.
I	(work,	worked,	will work)	at home.
I	(qualify,	qualified,	will qualify)	for the job.

Further changes are made in the form of verbs in order to provide more information about the action and when it is occurring. For example, if an action is occurring immediately in the present, -ing and a form of the verb "to be" may be added to the present form, as in the following example:

I am walking home.

Sometimes the present tense is used to show facts that do not change.

Human beings are mortal.

Habitual action is expressed in present tense.

She <u>goes</u> to work every day.

Historical events can also be discussed in the present tense.

The United States <u>decides</u> to drop the atom bomb on Hiroshima.

Sometimes a future action can be expressed in the present tense.

We <u>leave</u> for Florida on the first available flight.

The past tense also has varied uses; for example, verbs can describe an action that occurred in the past and is still affecting the present:

I <u>have studied</u> for my test, but I don't understand the material.

An action that was completed in the past but is not necessarily affecting what is happening in the present is expressed in another form of the past tense:

I <u>was studying</u> with my friend last night.

A past action that has occurred before another action has taken place is expressed in a past tense:

I had <u>given</u> a contribution <u>before the campaign began</u>.

An action completed in a definite time in the past is expressed in the simple past, which is the form that is most familiar to the majority of people:

Last week he <u>asked</u> for a final decision.

The future is expressed in several different ways, too. You've seen the example of the simple future:

I <u>will see</u> the movie.

But, if an action that will occur in the future will extend or be continued over a period of time, you use the following form of the verb:

I <u>shall be traveling</u> for three months.

or

I <u>will be living</u> in Paris for one year.

However, if a future action will be completed before another action that is also in the future it will be expressed as in the following example:

I <u>will have completed</u> my assignment before the due date.

You will probably not use all these verb tenses frequently, but when you are revising sentence structure consider the specific time period you want your reader to think about in relation to the event or idea you are expressing.

EXERCISE 3–5

Directions: *Each of the following statements is a part of a sentence. Complete each sentence; circle the core part that you added; then rewrite each sentence by changing the verb so that the action occurs at a different time.*

EXAMPLE: The girl in the bookstore *forgot her wallet.*

The girl in the bookstore will forget her wallet if she is distracted.

1. The student in my class _____

    _____ .

    _____

2. _____ went to New York City last summer.

    _____

3. My desk _____ .

    _____

4. The instructor from Cornwell University _____

    _____ .

    _____

5. My parents _____ .

    _____

6. Adolescents in our society _____ .

    _____

7. _____ have always provided security and stability.

    _____

8. _____ is torn between acting ~~like~~ ^{as} a child and ~~as~~ ^{like} an adult.

    _____

9. The purpose of the chemistry lab demonstration _____

    _____ .

    _____

10. Children often _____.

    _____

11. Forming clear occupational goals _____

    _____ .

    _____

12. _____ is boring and time-consuming.

    _____

13. From their earliest years, some individuals _____

    _____ .

    _____

14. _____ have caused damage and destruction.

    _____

15. _____ is dangerous to your health and well-being.

    _____

Combining Core Parts

One way that you can improve your writing is to combine sentences that express similar actions or have related subjects to make a shorter or more concise statement. For instance, suppose you had written the following sentences describing what happened in your psychology class today:

My psychology instructor discussed Chapter 2 in class.

My psychology instructor assigned Chapter 3 for homework.

To express these ideas more concisely, you could combine these sentences into one sentence, as follows:

COMBINED SENTENCE: My psychology instructor discussed Chapter 2 in class and assigned Chapter 3 for homework.

Similarly, you can combine two sentences with two different subjects into a single sentence as follows:

Sharon went to the library.

Agnes also went to the library.

SINGLE SENTENCE: Sharon and Agnes went to the library.

It is also possible to combine more than one subject and more than one verb in a sentence so that the sentence contains both a compound subject and a compound predicate.

<u>Mike</u> <u>traveled</u> to Lake George and <u>sailed</u> his boat in the race.

<u>Chuck</u> traveled to Lake George and sailed his boat in the race.

SINGLE SENTENCE: <u>Mike</u> and <u>Chuck</u> <u>traveled</u> to Lake George and <u>sailed</u> their boats in the races.

EXERCISE 3–6

Directions: *Combine the following pairs or groups of single sentences into one simple sentence that has compound core parts.*

EXAMPLE: Jennifer went to the science fair at school.

Dale went to the science fair at school.

Jennifer and Dale went to the science fair at school.

1. John finished his homework early.
   John went to dinner with his friends.

2. Nancy had to study for exams.
   Diane had to study for exams.
   Sandy had to study for exams.

3. I plan to take sociology in the fall.
   I plan to complete my social science electives in the fall.

4. Ed and Tom chopped down the dead trees.
   Ed and Tom cut the wood in the forest.

5. Pat, Kathy, and Mary drove to Florida.

   Pat, Kathy, and Mary flew back to Virginia.

   _____

6. We drove through the isolated desert town.

   We stopped to look at some buildings that were still standing at the edge of town.

   _____

   _____

7. The reporter tried to interview the political candidate.

   The reporter tried to photograph the political candidate.

   _____

   _____

8. Joan and Bill drove to the train station.

   Joan and bill took the train into the city.

   _____

   _____

9. The tornado ripped out everything in its path.

   The tornado left a trail of destruction.

   The tornado left hundreds homeless.

   _____

   _____

10. Phil, John, and Mark drove home over the weekend.

    Phil, John, and Mark couldn't get back in time for their biology exam.

    _____

    _____

11. The curator of the museum presided over the opening of the new exhibition.

    The curator gave a lecture.

    _____

    _____

12. Money serves as a medium of exchange.
    Money is used to measure and compare value.

    _____

    _____

13. The rocket lifted from the launching pad.
    The rocket soared upward until it was out sight.

    _____

    _____

14. Karen studied for her exam and missed the basketball game.
    Karen completed her term paper.

    _____

    _____

15. Inflation reduces buying power.
    Inflation forces people to change the way they live.

    _____

    _____

Expanding Sentences

Another way to write more effective sentences is to use sentence expanders to combine ideas and clarify meaning. Let us assume that your instructor has asked you to write a description of the person sitting next to you in class and to describe what he or she is doing. You might write the following sentences:

The girl has dark hair.

The girl's hair is long.

The girl has blue eyes.

The girl is writing in a notebook.

Or you could write this sentence:

The girl with blue eyes and long, dark hair is writing in a notebook.

Notice that this sentence combines all the information given in four short simple sentences into one longer sentence. Although this sentence is easier to read and less repetitious than the four shorter sentences, all the information of the four sentences is packed into it.
    Now read this sentence:

The girl is writing a letter to her parents who live in California.

3. Basic Sentences

In this example, too, additional information is included about the core parts of the sentence (girl, is writing). The writer has included the facts that the girl is writing the letter to her parents and that they live in California. These additional pieces of information change or modify the basic message by offering more information about it. As a writer then, you can use expanders to include further information about the core parts of your sentence. Notice, in the following example, how many additional facts can be included about the core parts (underlined) of the sentence.

> *EXAMPLE:* The physical education <u>instructor</u> <u>wrote</u> an article on physical fitness that appeared in the student newspaper.

Additional Facts Supplied About the Core Parts

1. The instructor taught physical education.
2. The instructor wrote an article.
3. The article was about physical fitness.
4. The article appeared in the student newspaper.

EXERCISE 3–7

Directions: *Expand and rewrite each of the following sentences to include at least two additional pieces of information. That is, include at least two additional pieces of information that expand one or both of the core parts.*

> *EXAMPLE:* Sam read the newspaper.
>
> *My brother Sam read the newspaper before dinner.*

1. Dean graduates in June.

   _____

   _____

2. Diane cannot decide on a college.

   _____

   _____

3. The book is on the best seller list.

   _____

   _____

4. Jim will serve as treasurer this year.

   _____

   _____

5. My homework assignment is due Tuesday.

_____

_____

6. The car gets good mileage.

_____

_____

7. George attended a meeting.

_____

_____

8. A large family lives in that house.

_____

_____

9. The concert was successful.

_____

_____

10. The student almost failed a test.

_____

_____

11. The dorm rooms are small.

_____

_____

12. The lecture was about freedom.

_____

_____

13. The issue sparked riots.

_____

_____

14. Prices are unrealistic.

_____

_____

15. Weather affects the economy.

_____

_____

AVOIDING COMMON PROBLEMS ENCOUNTERED IN WRITING

After you have expressed your ideas in writing, it is important to revise what you have written; specifically, you should reread the ideas you have expressed and evaluate how clearly you have expressed them. At this point, one thing you should look for is common sentence errors. To analyze sentence errors you will need to apply your knowledge of the basic structure of the sentence and to be alert to several of the most common and most serious types of sentence errors. These common problems will be discussed in the following section.

Sentence Fragments

A sentence fragment is a statement that does not express a complete thought. A fragment may lack a subject or a verb, or it may be a statement that is incomplete in some other way. Here are a few examples of the various types of fragments. Notice that after reading each fragment you are left with a question in your mind, indicating that the thought is incomplete. The core part in each fragment is underlined.

Fragments without a subject:

Going home on the subway (Who went home?)

Which certainly tastes good on a winter evening (What tastes good?)

Determined to win the contest (Who was determined to win?)

In these examples none of the statements has a subject. Action occurs, but you do not know whom or what the statement is about.

Fragments without a verb:

Nobody from the college except me

Many situations like this over the last twenty years

The question about reproduction on my biology exam

None of these statements describes any action. The subject (underlined) is stated, but you do not know what action occurred.

Fragments that lack a verb expressing action about the subject:

Even <u>George</u>, who doesn't like dancing

Some good <u>movies</u> for people who like comedies

My <u>sister</u> from a town where everyone goes to church

In these examples the subject is stated (underlined), but there is no action expressed about the subject. There is a verb in each statement, but it expresses action about another word in the sentence. In the last example the words in the phrase "goes to church" tells what everyone in the town did, but it does not tell what action the subject (sister) performed.

Fragments that do not express a complete thought:

After <u>I left</u> the party at 11 P.M. (What happened after you left?)

If <u>she is</u> late for her appointment (Then what will happen?)

Each of these statements has a subject and a verb (underlined), but its thought is not complete because it depends on another idea. Also, sentence fragments can be produced when a verb is used incorrectly in a statement. The following statement is incomplete:

Sam and George arguing about what movie to see.

As it is written there is no action that Sam and George perform. The phrase "arguing about what movie to see" only provides descriptive information about them. However, if the verb is changed from "arguing" to "were arguing," then the statement becomes a sentence.

To avoid writing sentence fragments check each sentence to be sure that it has both a subject and a verb. Then check to be sure that the verb expresses action about the subject. Finally, read each sentence to check that it expresses a complete thought that does not depend on another idea.

The Run-on Sentence

A run-on sentence, in a sense, is the opposite of a sentence fragment. Whereas a sentence fragment contains too little information to express a complete thought, a run-on sentence contains too much information. It is a sentence that does not end when it should. It contains more than one thought and more than one set of core parts. Run-on sentences are considered errors because they do not express ideas clearly or because they express too many thoughts at one time and tend to confuse the reader. When too much information is presented, the ideas and their relationships to each other are no longer clear.

Frequently, a run-on sentence occurs when you try to include too much information in one sentence. This problem can usually be corrected by developing a second sentence to present some of the information. For example,

RUN-ON: We left Toronto just before dusk, a strong wind was blowing, dark clouds indicated a storm coming from the north.

It could be broken down into two sentences like this:

REVISED: We left Toronto before dusk.

A strong wind was blowing, and dark clouds indicated a storm was coming from the north.

In many situations, however, a run-on sentence is really an error in punctuation. Two or more ideas can be combined into a single sentence, but punctuation must be used to separate these ideas. In the next two chapters you will learn how to combine two or more ideas and how to punctuate them correctly to avoid writing a run-on sentence.

Subject-Verb Agreement

A serious sentence error is made when the subject and verb in a sentence do not agree or match. That is, a subject that refers to one person, place, or thing must be consistent with the verb that refers to that person, place, or thing. Both subjects and verbs have singular and plural forms. Singular means one—or *a single*—whereas plural means more than one, or many. When a subject is singular, it must be matched with a verb that is also singular. Similarly, a plural subject must be matched with a plural form of the verb.

A subject is singular if it refers to a single person, place, thing, or idea. Most subjects are easy to identify as either singular or plural. Movie, book, restaurant, car, and instructor are all singular. Movies, books, restaurants, cars, and instructors are all plural. Although there are many exceptions, a general rule is that subjects that end in -s or -es are plural.

The spelling or ending of a verb is also changed when it changes from singular to plural. Here are a few examples of verbs in the singular and plural form in the present tense. A subject has been included with each to make the change clearer.

SINGULAR: Sandra <u>watches</u> the television.

Sam <u>does not</u> watch television.

PLURAL: The people <u>watch</u> television.

Sam and Pete <u>do not</u> watch television.

Notice that all of the above examples were in the present tense. In the past tense, the same verb form is often used for the singular and the plural, as in the following examples:

SINGULAR: The runner stumbled.

The dancer fell.

PLURAL: The runners stumbled.

The dancers fell.

When a pronoun is used to replace the subject then the pronoun and the verb must agree. The guidelines to follow in these cases are discussed in the next section. As you write sentences be sure to make the subject and verb agree. A singular subject requires a singular verb, and a plural subject requires a plural verb. A few other special cases of subject-verb agreement are discussed below:

1. *Common plural words*, such as several, few, both, and many, are always plural. Always use a plural verb with these words.
2. *A compound subject* joined by "and" takes a plural verb.

   EXAMPLE: Hal <u>and</u> Anne <u>are</u> going to Florida.

   However, if two singular subjects are joined by "or" or "nor," then a singular verb is used.

   EXAMPLE: Either Fred <u>or</u> Mary <u>is</u> coming to the cocktail party.

3. *Subjects that refer to a group* are "collective." That is, the noun is in a singular form, but its meaning could be plural when it refers to a number of separate individuals or singular when it refers to a group. The following words are used with either singular or plural verbs: administration, army, audience, band, class, committee, crowd, faculty, family, government, orchestra, public, team.

   GROUP: The faculty is always present at graduation.

   INDIVIDUALS: The faculty are attending the ceremony.

   There are also some words that refer to numbers and take a singular or plural verb depending on what is being discussed. The context provides the information for these decisions. Such words as majority, minority, or mass can be thought of as separate items or as a unit. When meant as separate items they are plural, but they are singular when they refer to a unit. Consider the following examples:

   SEPARATE ITEMS: The majority of students are applying for student loans.

   UNIT: The majority is composed of hardworking, middle-class men and women.

   The mass of the crowd is near the building.

Pronoun Agreement

A pronoun is a word that is used in place of a noun. The noun the pronoun replaces is called its *antecedent*. Pronouns can be used to avoid the repetition of the same word throughout a piece of writing. Here is a group of sentences written without the use of pronouns.

   Mary is the most ambitious student in the class. Mary plans to major in biology. Mary will probably apply to medical school.

These statements can be revised so that after Mary's name has been mentioned for the first time, the pronoun "she" replaces it, as in these sentences:

   Mary is the most ambitious student in the class. <u>She</u> plans to major in biology. <u>She</u> will probably apply to medical school.

The use of pronouns will make your writing less repetitious. However, as you use pronouns, you should be conscious of pronoun agreement. Just as subjects and verbs must agree, so must a pronoun agree with the word it replaces.

In the following sentences, notice that the choice of pronoun depends on the word it is replacing. A singular noun is replaced with a singular pronoun and a plural noun is replaced with a plural pronoun.

Mike said that he forgot about the exam.

The students said that they forgot about the exam.

Personal Pronoun–Indefinite Pronoun Agreement

Pronouns that refer to a specific being or object are called personal pronouns. In this sentence, the pronoun "she" is a personal pronoun because it refers to a specific person—Meg:

Because she lost her wallet, Meg had to cancel her credit cards.

A second type of pronoun does *not* refer to a specific person, place, or thing. These pronouns are called indefinite pronouns because it is *not* definite (or clear) to whom or what they refer. Here are a few examples:

Someone lost a pen.

One never knows what can happen.

Nobody attended the ceremony.

When a personal pronoun and an indefinite pronoun are used together, they must agree. An indefinite pronoun may be singular or plural. If the pronoun is singular, then it must be used with singular personal pronouns.

Each of the girls lost her scarf.

One of the workers forgot his lunch.

Even if a phrase comes between the pronoun and the noun it replaces (the antecedent) there is no change in agreement. In the following sentence, notice that the phrase "of the artists" is placed between the pronoun and indefinite antecedent "one," but that a singular verb is still necessary.

One of the artists destroyed his own sketch.

The reason for this rule is that although the artist is one of a group of artists, only *one* artist destroyed his sketch.

Two Singular Antecedents Joined by "And." When two antecedents joined by "and" are referred to by one pronoun, the pronoun should be plural, as in the following examples:

Jim and Frank did their best.

Phil and his brother helped their uncle repair his car.

If you think of the two singular nouns, or antecedents, *together,* they are more than one and then require a plural pronoun.

Two or More Singular Antecedents Joined by "Or" or "Nor". When a singular antecedent is connected to another by the words "or" or "nor," a singular pronoun is used. Here are a few examples:

Neither <u>Ross</u> nor <u>Pat</u> did <u>his</u> best.

Either <u>Steve</u> or <u>Matt</u> can bring <u>his</u> dog.

To remember this rule, remember that only one or neither of the two antecedents can perform the action, and since only one or neither can complete the action, a singular pronoun is necessary.

Pronoun-Verb Agreement

Some indefinite pronouns (such as some, any, most, all, or none) also take either the plural or the singular verb form depending on the context. Here are some examples:

<u>Some</u> of the cereal <u>is</u> spoiled.

<u>Some</u> <u>are</u> coming later.

<u>None</u> of us <u>is</u> better than the other.

<u>None</u> of us <u>are</u> happy with the decision.

<u>Most</u> of us <u>are</u> employed.

<u>Most</u> of the group <u>is</u> here.

When a pronoun is the subject of a sentence, you must be sure that the verb of the sentence agrees with the pronoun. Suppose an indefinite pronoun is the subject of a sentence. Then the verb must agree with that pronoun. Here are a few examples:

<u>Everybody</u> in the class <u>takes</u> the same bus.

<u>Someone</u> <u>drives</u> a station wagon.

If a phrase comes between an indefinite pronoun subject and the verb of the sentence, the agreement is *not* changed.

<u>None</u> of his friends <u>believe</u> him.

In the above example, "friends" is plural, but the subject of the sentence is "none," and it refers to a group that is understood to be more than one.

EXERCISE 3-8

Directions: *Read each statement carefully, paying particular attention to completeness of sentences, to subject-verb agreement, and to pronoun agreement. Revise each sentence so it is correct.*

1. While you were looking the other way it happens. Without even noticing the car ran the red light at Third Street.

2. Whenever a student needed advice, they could feel free to talk to Mr. Dempsey.

3. Entertained thousands with a musical comedy every Memorial Day.

4. The actress wore an old, baggy jogging suit, no one recognized her.

5. Each member of the faculty had at least one committee assignment which they were to report on each month.

6. Kindergarten is usually a child's first experience at school, and they are very excited about learning.

7. After finishing the semester. They stayed in their ocean-front cottage.

8. Drunken drivers should be severely penalized in fact they should lose their driver's licenses for at least one year.

9. Most of the records was destroyed by the fire.

10. Each of the sisters hold a New Year's party.

11. My brother is proud of his sports car. Which he restored after buying it from a junkyard.

12. The price of concert tickets have doubled over the past year.

13. Many blue-collar workers receive at least one cash bonus per year, however, the bonus does little to help them keep pace with inflation.

14. There is two ways in which a inexperienced swimmer can drown.

15. Waiting for my math class to begin. I reviewed last night's assignment and found two errors.

EXERCISE 3–9

Directions: *Choose a reading selection from the end of this unit. Preread and read the selection. Write the title and subject of the reading in these spaces:*

TITLE: _____

SUBJECT: _____

Using the subject of the selection as a starting point, follow each of these steps:

1. *Prewriting.*
   a. Narrow the subject into three possible topics:

   _____

   _____

   _____

   b. Select one topic and use a five-minute free-writing exercise or write several questions that occur to you about the topic to generate ideas.
2. *Composing.* Select the most important ideas you see in your prewriting exercise. Develop these ideas into a paper consisting of an introduction, body, and conclusion. Include the details your reader will need in order to have a clear understanding of your purpose and message.
3. *Checking the Content and Organization.* Read over the rough draft you have written, considering the sequence or order of your ideas. Decide whether you need to change the order of your ideas, and rewrite the outline so it shows how your ideas will progress.
4. *Revising.* Read through your rough draft and circle sentences that you can expand by making verb changes, adding compound core parts, or adding modifiers. On a separate sheet rewrite the circled sentences; try several variations until you are pleased with a version. Rewrite the brief discussion, making any necessary changes and including the revised sentences. Then reread your paper again and check to see if you have (1) written any sentence fragments, (2) included any run-on sentences, (3) used correct subject-verb agreement, and (4) used correct pronoun agreement. Read through the paper to see if there are any other sentences you would like to change, then write a clean copy of the paper.
5. *Proofreading.* Read your final copy, looking for spelling and particularly punctuation errors; in rewriting sentences you can easily overlook a comma or period that is incorrectly placed. Place a check on the proofreading checklist next to each item that you correct. List a description of each error you corrected in the column on the right.

PROOFREADING CHECKLIST

Essay Title _____

Date _____

TYPE	✔	ERROR	FREQUENCY	DESCRIPTION
GRAMMAR		Run-on Sentence Sentence Fragment Subject/Verb Agreement Verb Tense Pronoun Agreement		
MECHANICS		Capitalization Italics Abbreviation		
PUNCTUATION		, (Comma) ; (Semicolon) ' (Apostrophe) " (Quotation Marks) . (Period) ! (Exclamation Point) ? (Question Mark) : (Colon) — (Dash) ( ) (Parentheses) - (Hyphen)		

		ERROR	CORRECTION	
SPELLING ERRORS				

SUMMARY

In this chapter we discussed the simplest pattern in which words can be arranged to express a complete idea. Recognition of this basic pattern, called the simple sentence, can help you to better understand what you read. Simple sentences are made up of core parts that identify the subject and express the action, and expanders that provide additional information about the core parts. A knowledge of this basic sentence pattern and its component parts will enable you to write more effective sentences, to revise unclear sentences, and to avoid common errors in writing sentences. The common errors discussed in this chapter are sentence fragments, run-on sentences, lack of subject-verb agreement, and lack of pronoun agreement.

4. Sentences That Combine Ideas

In the previous chapter you learned to write effective sentences that express one complete thought. However, if you take a moment to listen to an instructor lecturing or a group of friends talking, you will find that people do not use only simple sentences. Similarly, if you choose a page out of your textbook or out of a magazine, you will find numerous sentences that express more than one complete thought. The simple sentence, then, is often inadequate to express complex related ideas. Read the following paragraph:

> I have to go to the grocery store. I am going to a party tonight. It is being given by a friend. I used to work with him several years ago. He asked everyone to bring some type of party food. I can't decide what to buy. I could buy some cheese. I could take some chips and dip.

Although this paragraph was constructed with complete sentences that logically follow each other, you probably found it dull and monotonous to read. If you look back to the individual sentences, you can see that some of them could be combined. For instance, the last two sentences could be combined as

> I could buy some cheese, or I could take chips and dip.

Not only is this sentence a little more interesting, but the relationship of the two ideas is clearer. In the original paragraph you probably guessed that cheese or chips and dip were alternative choices the writer was considering, but the word "or" in the revised sentence tells you specifically that the writer will decide to take one of the two. The purpose of this chapter is to show you how to combine closely related, equally important ideas using a sentence pattern called the *compound sentence*. First, we will explain the structure of compound sentences and offer suggestions for reading this sentence pattern. Then we will show how you can combine related ideas by using the compound sentence pattern and appropriate punctuation.

USING THE COMPOUND SENTENCE TO COMBINE IDEAS

The simple sentence is an independent clause consisting of a subject and predicate. A compound sentence, however, has two or more independent clauses that contain closely related ideas. Independent clauses in a compound sentence are connected in one of two ways. First, they may be connected by a comma and a conjunction. That is, a comma follows the first independent clause, and it is followed by a word such as and, but, or, nor, for, so, yet. This type of compound sentence would look like the following model, which uses "and" to join the independent clauses.

| independent clause | , and | independent clause | .

Second, the two independent clauses may be joined by a semicolon:

| independent clause | ; | independent clause | .

For example, consider the following two simple sentences:

| The city received eleven inches of snow. |

| All city streets were impassable. |

These sentences can be combined by use of a comma and a conjunction, forming a compound sentence consisting of the two independent clauses.

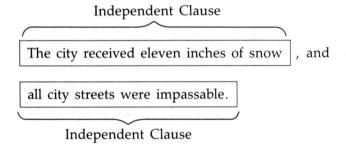

The same two sentences can also be made into a compound sentence by using a semicolon:

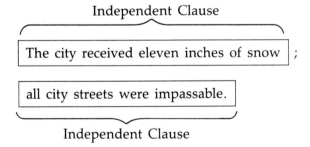

The comma and conjunction, as well as the semicolon, serve as connectors for the two related thoughts, and they also show that these thoughts are more or less equivalent as well as related.

How Compound Sentences Relate Ideas

When a writer combines two or more ideas in a compound sentence, he or she is giving you some additional information about the relationship between the ideas. First, you know that there is a strong connection between the ideas. Only very closely related ideas can be combined into one sentence. Second, the writer is telling you that the two ideas are of equal importance. As a reader, then, you know that you must pay equal attention to both ideas. You cannot afford to miss one of the ideas, and you have to consider both as equally important. For example, in this sentence

The local hockey team won the game, but the fans were disappointed with the final score.

the writer is communicating two ideas and, to the writer, the fact that the fans were disappointed is just as important as the fact that the local team won.

Notice that in each of the following sentences, the two ideas are related and equally important.

He was ready to run the marathon; he felt confident and eager to begin.

The store offered special discounts, but only a few people took advantage of the savings.

The student was late for class, and he missed the quiz.

Understanding Compound Sentences

When reading a compound sentence, look for two or more sets of core parts. A compound sentence is made up of two or more complete thoughts or independent clauses, each of which contains a subject and verb, so there will always be at least two subjects and two verbs in a compound sentence. For example, consider the compound sentence:

<u>Jane Bell</u> <u>wants</u> to become an accountant, so <u>she</u> <u>has registered</u> for all business courses.

In the first half of this sentence, the subject is "Jane Bell," the action is indicated in the verb "wants," and in this part of the sentence you find out what she wants. In the second half of the sentence, the subject is "she" (Jane Bell), the action is indicated in the verb "has registered," and the remainder of the sentence tells you that she has registered for business courses.

If you have trouble understanding a difficult compound sentence, split it into two parts. Read the first independent clause, then locate the core parts and modifiers. Stop. Tell yourself in your own words what the clause means. Then read the second half. Put its meaning into your own words. Then add the two together and put both in your own words. Be sure you understand how they relate to each other. Try this procedure with the following sentence:

The purpose of advertising is to influence the behavior, attitudes, and beliefs of others, and television commercials aimed at children clearly demonstrate this purpose.

In this sentence you see that the first part of the sentence states the purpose of advertising—to influence the behavior, attitudes, and beliefs of others. The second half tells you that television commercials that are intended for children are good examples of this purpose. The two parts of the sentence are related in that the second independent clause gives a particular instance that illustrates the first statement.

EXERCISE 4–1

Directions: *Read each of the following sentences and mark an X in the space to the right of each* compound *sentence. Then, for each compound sentence, underline the two sets of core parts.*

> *EXAMPLE:* <u>Nancy finished</u> her homework, and <u>she went</u>
>
> to the cafeteria to meet her friends.   _X_

1. My friends had an argument about what to do Saturday night.   _____

2. Sam, a dean's list student, works as a tutor.   _____

3. Some <u>students were</u> very interested in history; <u>others were</u> quite bored with it.   _X_

4. <u>Miami Beach and Fort Lauderdale are</u> fun, but <u>I prefer</u> smaller resort areas.   _X_

5. My favorite <u>dessert is</u> cheesecake, and <u>I make</u> a different kind each week.   _X_

6. Some <u>writers tend</u> to use a very complicated style, and <u>they do</u> not <u>realize</u> that some readers find their style difficult to read.   _X_

7. <u>Selecting</u> a college <u>is</u> a difficult choice; <u>it is</u> often influenced by financial and social factors.   _X_

8. Many <u>customers complained</u> about the poor quality of the food, but the <u>restaurant continued</u> to make a profit.   _X_

9. Many shoppers clip coupons to help cut down food costs and to help reduce the profits of large food stores.   _____

10. Some <u>students think</u> they can learn the material in a textbook by reading it once; <u>you would</u> need to have a photographic memory to do this.

11. Good <u>photography</u> is not easy; <u>it requires</u> knowledge, skill, and an understanding of composition.

12. Everyone must make a number of important decisions including occupational, educational, and ethical choices.

13. <u>Marriage consists</u> of shared experiences and ambitions, and <u>both are</u> influenced by the values of each partner.

14. The <u>purpose</u> of the text <u>is</u> to teach basic principles of psychology as applied to children and adolescents.

15. <u>Computers</u> have become part of our daily lives, but their <u>role</u> in today's classrooms <u>has</u> not yet been realized, understood, or fully explored.

WRITING SENTENCES THAT COMBINE IDEAS

Your writing will improve if you use a variety of sentence patterns that enable you to combine ideas and to show the relationship between or among them. Although the simple sentence does express ideas clearly and accurately, it is not always the most effective sentence pattern to use. For example, suppose you wanted to explain that you cannot decide between two activities for Saturday evening. You could express each alternative in a separate sentence, as in the following examples, but then your reader would not be told directly that you have a choice to make.

On Saturday night I could go to Sal's party.

On Saturday night I could help my sister paint her kitchen.

However, if you combine the two sentences and connect them with the word "or," it is clearer to your reader that a choice is involved, as demonstrated in the following sentence.

On Saturday night I could go to Sal's party, or I could help my sister paint her kitchen.

When to Use Compound Sentences

Compound sentences allow you to combine two closely related ideas into one sentence. However, there must be a strong and clear relationship between the ideas in order for you to combine them effectively. In fact, the relationship between the ideas is an important aspect in deciding whether to use two separate sentences or to combine the two ideas into a compound sentence. A compound sentence is a signal to your reader(s) that a relationship exists; therefore you should combine ideas only when you want your reader to relate them.

For example, the following sentence is not effective because it attempts to combine two ideas that have very little to do with each other. Notice that the second part of the sentence has no logical connection with the first.

> The main character of the movie was a teenage drug addict, and the theatre was crowded and noisy.

The fact that the theatre was crowded and noisy has little to do with the content of the movie, so there is no reason to combine the ideas in a compound sentence. However, in the following sentence the two ideas are closely related, and this compound sentence effectively shows the connection between the ideas.

> You should stand back from the curb, or you will get splattered with mud.

A second important aspect to consider in deciding whether to combine ideas is the relative importance of the ideas. If the two ideas are equally important, it is appropriate to use the compound sentence to combine them. However, if one idea is more important than the other, then they should not be combined into a compound sentence. For example, the following sentence inappropriately combines two ideas into a compound sentence. Notice that the second thought is much less important than the first and as a result the sentence seems unbalanced.

> I failed my history test, and I got the question on the dates of World War I wrong.

Failing an exam is more important than getting any one particular question wrong, so the sentence appears unbalanced.

Ways to Connect Independent Clauses

As you have seen, there are two ways that you can connect the independent clauses to form a compound sentence. The clauses may be joined with a conjunction and a comma, or they may be connected by a semicolon.

Using Conjunctions to Connect Two Clauses

When ideas are combined in compound sentences, the way they are related determines which conjunction should be used. Conjunctions must relate the ideas in a way that makes sense and clarifies the connection. Look at the following sentence.

> John completed his experiment, but it did not work out well.

The conjunction used here implies that the events in the second clause do not support the expectations implied in the first clause. The conjunction "but" implies contrast.

In the following sentence the word "but" does *not* accurately connect the two ideas.

John completed his experiment, but it worked out well.

Instead, the conjunction "and" should be used because the second idea is the expected outcome of the event that occurred in the first clause. The most common conjunctions used to join independent clauses are listed below.

Conjunctions that can connect clauses

and	or
so	nor
for	but
yet	

Another set of conjunctions can also be used to connect independent clauses in a compound sentence. These conjunctions occur in pairs. They are called *correlative conjunctions* because together they relate two clauses to each other.

Correlative conjunctions that relate clauses

both . . . and	either . . . or
neither . . . nor	not only . . . but also

Look at the examples that show how correlative conjunctions connect clauses.

Either we can go together, or we can drive our own cars.

Mary not only speaks English, but she also speaks French and Italian.

Notice that if you leave out the conjunctions you will have two independent clauses:

We can go together.

We can drive our own cars.

Mary speaks English.

She also speaks French and Italian.

Using Semicolons to Connect Independent Clauses

The semicolon can be used to connect independent clauses in a compound sentence. Used alone, the semicolon shows that the clauses are closely related, but it does not specify in any way how they are related. However, an adverb can be used along with a semicolon to show the relationship between the two independent clauses.

The choice of adverb strongly affects the meaning of the sentence, so always make sure the adverb you use demonstrates the relationship you have in mind. Adverbs that are used in compound sentences are called *conjunctive adverbs* because they connect. These connectors are preceded by a semicolon, and they are followed by a comma when they join two independent clauses. The following examples show how clauses can be made into compound sentences when joined by a semicolon and a conjunctive adverb. The conjunctive adverb is underlined.

He had not planned to stay overnight; <u>however</u>, he quickly changed his mind when the weather changed so abruptly.

Sophie hated to do homework; <u>similarly</u>, she hated tests.

Some common adverbs that can connect independent clauses

accordingly	likewise	therefore
besides	moreover	then
furthermore	indeed	similarly
however	namely	still
hence		

Types of Ideas to Combine

There are five relationships that you can express within a compound sentence. The proper choice of conjunction can help you to make these relationships clear. However, in each of these relationships, keep in mind that the two ideas must be of equal importance.

Parts of a Whole

A discussion of equally important parts of a process, event, or description may be combined in a compound sentence. In this case the conjunction *and* is used to join the two ideas. Here are several examples:

TWO PARTS OF A PROCESS:	Jane cooked the dinner, and Sally cleaned up the dishes.
TWO PARTS OF A DESCRIPTION:	His shirt was dirty, and his shoes were worn.
TWO PARTS OF AN EVENT:	Amy failed to see the signal, and she went through a red light.

Contrasting Ideas

Opposite or contrasting ideas can be combined using a compound sentence if the ideas are equally important. When contrasting ideas are combined, they are connected with the words "but" or "yet." Here are a few examples:

The lecture was very long, <u>but</u> no one seemed bored.

Many students were absent, <u>yet</u> classes met as usual.

Explanations or Reasons

Clauses may be combined when one idea in a clause explains or gives a reason for the other. In this case, the sentences are joined by the conjunction "for." Here are a few examples:

Gerry had very little time to study, <u>for</u> he works thirty hours a week at Penny's.

Ellen received the award, <u>for</u> she sold more than anyone else.

Choices or Alternatives

If two ideas, when joined, express a choice or alternative, they can be connected by the conjunctions "or" or "nor" or by the correlative conjunctions "either . . . or" and "neither . . . nor." Look at the examples:

You should apologize, <u>or</u> she will never speak to you again.

We cannot force men to think, <u>nor</u> can we force them to be reasonable.

Results or Consequences

When one idea is the result or consequence of the other, the two ideas can be connected using the conjunction "so," as in the following example:

Sam did not want to frighten his parents, <u>so</u> he did not tell them about the robbery.

When you write compound sentences remember that combining independent clauses into one sentence pattern does not happen without some reason. The ideas in the clauses have to be related to each other in some way, and the way in which you connect them has to contribute to your reader's understanding of the relationship.

EXERCISE 4–2

Directions: *Combine the sentences below by connecting them with conjunctions or semicolons.*

EXAMPLE: I got up early.

I ate a huge breakfast.

I got up early, and I ate a huge breakfast.

or

I got up early, so I ate a huge breakfast.

1. Sue went to bed early.
   She got up late.

   _____

   _____

2. Sue had planned to call her mother.
   Her mother's plane left very early in the morning.

   _____

   _____

3. She was disappointed and lonely.
   She called her brother.

   _____

   _____

4. The biology midterm was easy.
   The final was difficult.

   _____

   _____

5. I underlined the important ideas in the chapter.
   I wrote a summary.

   _____

   _____

6. She had never been to the West Coast.
   She was excited about the trip to California.

   _____

   _____

7. The walls were brown and dreary.
   The room lacked character without the furniture.

   _____

   _____

8. The steel mills belched thick smoke into the air.

    The environmentalists were aware that government officials were investigating the matter.

    _____

    _____

    _____

9. The cross country runners practiced every day.

    Rain never stopped them.

    _____

    _____

10. Television offers entertainment.

    Television also features some educational programs.

    _____

    _____

11. The statue was corroded.

    It had been in the cave for many years.

    _____

    _____

12. The ivy-covered walls have been a landmark for nearly two centuries.

    Many students have passed through the halls and wandered across the campus.

    _____

    _____

    _____

13. The eccentric millionaire was a recluse.

    His home was not concealed by the high fences.

    _____

    _____

14. During the afternoon, the restored Victorian mansion was finally opened to the public.

    Guided tours were scheduled every hour in the morning for school groups.

    _____

    _____

    _____

15. Knights were supposed to be chivalrous and honorable.

    They would be ostracized from the Round Table for bad deeds.

    _____

    _____

    _____

EXERCISE 4–3

Directions: *Combine the following pairs of sentences by joining them with a conjunctive adverb.*

   EXAMPLE: Summer is a pleasant season.

   Summer is a leisurely time.

   Summer is not only a pleasant season,
   but it is also a leisurely time.

1. Accounting is my major.

   I have to have a good math background.

   _____

   _____

2. We'll go home for Christmas.

   We'll go to Florida for two weeks in January.

   _____

   _____

3. I ran out of money.

   I had to write home to ask for a loan.

   _____

   _____

4. I will take three liberal arts courses next semester.
   My friend will also take three.

   _____

   _____

5. Jim laughed a lot.
   His nickname was "Giggles."

   _____

   _____

6. Film has developed as an art form over the last twenty-five
   years.
   It has also developed as an industry.

   _____

   _____

7. Anthropology is a social science.
   It is a required course in the social science curriculum.

   _____

   _____

8. I plan to major in business administration.
   I expect to get a good job after I graduate.

   _____

   _____

9. Dancing is often a central part of an ethnic festival.
   It is sometimes an aspect of religious ritual.

   _____

   _____

10. Most people pack too many clothes for a trip overseas.
    They have difficulty carrying their luggage through airports and
    train stations.

    _____

    _____

11. Environmentalists have suggested extraordinary measures for the preservation of our natural resources.

    The cost of implementation is prohibitive.

    _____

    _____

12. Petroleum resources in America have dwindled considerably since the initial discovery of oil.

    Research in the production of alternative or synthetic fuels is important.

    _____

    _____

    _____

13. The state of the economy in the seventies has created a financial climate similar to that of the thirties.

    Students are selecting business and career-oriented programs in college.

    _____

    _____

    _____

14. The computer industry has developed into a major international business.

    It has changed the way business is conducted.

    _____

    _____

15. Executives in business and industry have complained that college graduates are technically overtrained.

    They are encouraging colleges to add more humanistically oriented courses to their technical programs.

    _____

    _____

    _____

EXERCISE 4–4

Directions: *Choose a reading selection from the end of this unit. Preread and read the selection. Write the title and subject of the reading here:*

TITLE: _____

SUBJECT: _____

Using the subject of the selection as a starting point, follow each of the steps listed below.

1. *Prewriting.*
   a. Narrow the subject into three possible topics:

   _____

   _____

   _____

   b. Select one topic and use a five-minute free-writing exercise or write several questions that occur to you about the topic to generate ideas.

2. *Composing.* Select the most important ideas you see in your prewriting exercise. Develop them into a paper consisting of an introduction, body, and conclusion. Include the details your reader will need in order to have a clear understanding of your purpose and message.

3. *Checking the Content and Organization.* Read over the rough draft you have written, considering the sequence or order of your ideas. Decide whether you need to change the order, and rewrite the outline so it shows how your ideas will progress.

4. *Revising.* Read through your rough draft and underline sentences that you can combine in compound sentences. On a separate sheet rewrite the sentences expressing appropriate relationships. (Refer to pages 109–110, on Types of Ideas to Combine, if you need to review the relationship of ideas demonstrated in compound sentences.) Rewrite the paper, including the revised sentences you have combined, then read through it. See if there are any other changes you want to make. Also, check for the following errors: (1) sentence fragments, (2) run-on sentences, (3) subject-verb agreement, and (4) pronoun agreement.

5. *Proofreading.* Read your final copy looking for spelling and particularly punctuation errors; in rewriting sentences you can easily overlook a comma or period that is inappropriately used. Place a check on the proofreading checklist next to each item that you correct. List a description of each error you corrected in the column on the right.

PROOFREADING CHECKLIST

Essay Title _____

Date _____

TYPE	✔	ERROR	FREQUENCY	DESCRIPTION
GRAMMAR		Run-on Sentence Sentence Fragment Subject/Verb Agreement Verb Tense Pronoun Agreement		
MECHANICS		Capitalization Italics Abbreviation		
PUNCTUATION		, (Comma) ; (Semicolon) ' (Apostrophe) " (Quotation Marks) . (Period) ! (Exclamation Point) ? (Question Mark) : (Colon) — (Dash) ( ) (Parentheses) - (Hyphen)		

		ERROR	CORRECTION	
SPELLING ERRORS				

SUMMARY

In this chapter we presented techniques for reading and writing compound sentences. You learned that a compound sentence is made up of two independent clauses that express closely related ideas. When reading compound sentences, it is important to identify two or more sets of core parts. The compound sentence structure indicates that each complete idea expressed within the sentence is of equal importance. In writing, compound sentences can be used to combine two or more ideas of equal importance. Conjunctions or semicolons may be used to connect closely related ideas. A conjunction often provides information about the relationship between or among the ideas. Correlative conjunctions and conjunctive adverbs can also connect two independent clauses in a compound sentence.

5. Sentences That Show Relationships

You have already seen some alternatives to the basic simple sentence that can make your writing more effective. You have learned how to combine ideas into a single sentence using compound subjects and compound predicates. You know how to use expanders to include additional information about the sentence core parts. Also, you can combine two closely related, equally important ideas into a compound sentence.

Now you need to learn one last sentence pattern that will enable you to combine ideas that are closely related but not of equal importance. This pattern is called the *complex sentence;* it contains two ideas, one of which is more important than the other. In this chapter we will explain the structure of the complex sentence and the compound-complex sentence and then discuss how to read complicated sentences. Then, you will learn when and how to combine complex sentences and compound sentences to express your ideas more effectively.

THE STRUCTURE OF COMPLEX SENTENCES

The structure of a complex sentence can be understood easily by looking at an example. In the following complex sentence the more important idea is that Mary decided not to become a teacher, and that information is included in an independent clause within the sentence.

> EXAMPLE: Since Mary was terrified of large groups, she decided against becoming a teacher.

The first part (underlined) of this sentence is of less importance, and its purpose is to explain more about Mary's decision. That portion of the sentence is referred to as a *dependent clause*. It depends on the other complete idea contained in the independent clause to make its meaning clear. Notice that the dependent clause in the example has a subject (she) and a verb (was terrified), but it is not a sentence by itself because it relates to and depends on the other idea in the sentence. In fact, the word "since" tells you that one idea depends on another. Dependent clauses are incomplete statements, and they cannot stand alone as sentences.

Each of the following is a dependent clause. Each has a subject and predicate, but you can see that you do not have all the information you need to understand the idea. You are still left with a question in mind about the meaning.

> DEPENDENT CLAUSES: Because I missed the bus (What happened?)
>
> After I left the party (What happened?)

Who walks beside her (Who walks beside her?)

Unless I earn $500 (What will happen?)

Which has six lanes (What has six lanes?)

If I fail the course (Then what will happen?)

What he decides (What about what he decides?)

Because a dependent clause is missing information (or it depends on other information) and is not a complete thought, it can never be a sentence by itself; it must be combined with an independent clause that can stand alone as a complete sentence.

When we add an independent clause to each of the dependent clauses shown above, the result is a complex sentence.

COMPLEX SENTENCES: Because I missed the bus, I was late for work.

After the party, I felt sick.

Mary loves the dog who walks beside her.

Unless I earn $500, I will not be able to pay my tuition.

The highway which has six lanes is heavily traveled.

If I fail the course, I will not graduate.

Regardless of what he decides, Sam will always be respected by his friends.

Depending on the sentence order, the dependent clause may be separated from the independent clause by a comma. Complex sentences can be arranged in several ways, as diagramed here.

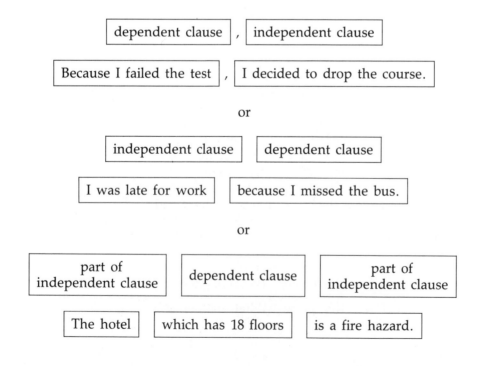

120

Understanding Complex Sentences

To read complex sentences effectively you should pay attention to both the independent and dependent clauses. Each will have a set of core parts, but the independent clause will make sense by itself, whereas the dependent clause will not. To understand the sentence completely, you must understand the relationship between these two parts. The independent clause will supply the information that is missing in the dependent clause. The ideas expressed in the dependent clause will *depend on* the ideas contained in the independent clause.

When a writer combines two ideas into a complex sentence, one idea is always more important than the other. The main, or most important, idea is expressed in the independent clause. Less important, or subordinate, information is given in the dependent clause. Thus, when reading complex sentences you should pay more attention to information contained in the independent clause than in the dependent clause. Information contained in the independent clause should be carried in your mind as you continue reading the remainder of the paragraph. For instance, in the following sentence:

Although it was raining, Sam decided to go jogging.

It is more important for you to know and remember that Sam decided to go jogging than it is to remember that it was raining.

So you see, the structure of the sentence can help you to distinguish important facts and ideas from less important ones. Your knowledge of sentence structure can pay off for you in textbook reading by helping you to identify the important part of each sentence. If you have trouble understanding a long or difficult complex sentence, read just the independent clause by itself. Locate its core parts and identify any modifiers. Put the meaning of the independent clause in your own words. Then read the dependent clause and try to see how it relates to or depends on the independent clause. For example, in the sentence:

Although hypnosis has been practiced for centuries and used to treat various mental and physical illnesses, only recently has hypnosis been widely accepted by the medical profession.

The core parts of the independent clause are "hypnosis" and "has been accepted." The modifiers tell you *when* and *by whom* hypnosis has been accepted. The dependent clause gives you background information. It tells you that hypnosis has been used for a long time to treat both mental and physical problems.

In reading complex sentences, you should realize that dependent clauses give you further information about the more important parts of the sentence. Dependent clauses give additional information about the basic meaning expressed in the sentence. Dependent clauses often explain relationships of *time, place, purpose, cause, condition,* or *manner.*

EXAMPLE: Unless she can get a discount, Jan won't be able to buy the coat.

In this example, the dependent clause explains the *conditions* under which Jan can buy the coat. Or, in the following example, the dependent clause indicates the place *where* the main action of the sentence occurred.

> *EXAMPLE:* <u>Where Highways 401 and 23 meet</u>, Sam found his stolen car.

When reading complex sentences, then, be sure to notice *how* the dependent clause relates to the more important independent clause. Also notice *how* the dependent clause changes or qualifies the sentence meaning.

EXERCISE 5-1

Directions: *For each of the following complex sentences, underline the more important part of each sentence. (Be sure that you underline the independent clause, not the dependent clause.)*

> *EXAMPLE:* When George called on Wednesday, <u>I was working on my term paper</u>.

1. If it is too noisy in a room, I cannot concentrate.
2. Betty bought a new jacket, which she wears every day.
3. Because I missed so many classes, I failed the test.
4. Although the food was well prepared, the service in the restaurant was very slow.
5. As I was driving home, I went through a red light.
6. Although many commercials seem ridiculous, they are effective in selling products.
7. Even if you are motivated to study, you may have difficulty concentrating on your work.
8. Because the child enjoys television, she always sits directly in front of the set.
9. Although the statistics were very convincing, the committee rejected the proposal.
10. If you give a plant too much water, it will wilt and die.
11. As far as we can tell from available evidence, humankind has been on this earth for several million years.[1]
12. The anthropological linguist is concerned primarily with languages that have no written form, although written languages are not ignored by any means.[2]
13. Although the pattern may vary dramatically from group to group, the basic components of social organization are always the same.[3]
14. Although a feather and a stone will fall equally fast in a vacuum, they fall quite differently in the presence of air.[4]
15. As the members of a group interact over a period of time, their interpersonal exchanges follow increasingly predictable patterns.[5]

READING MORE COMPLICATED SENTENCES

Throughout this unit you have gained skill in reading the basic sentence patterns: simple, compound, and complex. However, many sentences that you will encounter in your textbooks may seem more difficult than many of the sentences used as examples throughout these chapters. Authors of textbooks do follow these basic patterns, but they also use a combination of these patterns. Professional writers also use numerous modifiers, and as a result their sentences appear long and complicated. Because writers often use words that you are unfamiliar with, you may not understand the sentence. These problems will be discussed briefly now.

Sentence Structure

The way sentence parts are put together, as well as the number and types of these parts included in a sentence, can make a sentence difficult to read. The simple sentence is usually the easiest structure to read. Compound and complex sentences can be more difficult to follow. Possibly even more difficult to read are sentences that use a combination of structures. Although it is not necessary for you to learn each possible combination, here are a few structures.

COMPOUND-COMPLEX: Since I spoke with him yesterday, I knew Sam was unhappy, but I did not guess that he would cancel his trip.

COMPOUND-COMPOUND: I chose a good movie, and I was satisfied with my choice, but the main character was poorly developed, and the sound effects were weak.

You might question why writers use complicated structures if such structures are difficult to read. It is probably because complicated sentence structures make it possible to express in a concise manner several ideas, actions, and events that are dependent on one another. These relationships often are difficult to express fully in simple sentences. Relationships and connections often are more easily understood when ideas are combined into more complicated sentences. The compound and complex sentences are the most common forms of sentences that allow a writer to show relationships of ideas. You recall that the use of the compound sentence suggests that the two ideas expressed in the independent clauses are of equal importance. You should also recall that the complex sentence permits a writer to show how one idea depends on another.

How to Read Sentences with Complicated Structure

In reading sentences that are complicated or that have numerous expanders and dependent clauses, use the following procedure. Start by reading the whole sentence through once. Then, if you don't understand it, follow these steps:

1.   Look for the independent clause or clauses that the rest of the sentence is built around. Read it, and ignore everything else. Identify the core parts. Try to phrase the meaning in your own words.

2. Include any expanders. Notice how they change or add to the meaning of the core parts.
3. Read any dependent clauses that depend on the main part of the sentence. Decide what additional information each dependent clause gives you.
4. Read any other sentence parts such as introductory phrases and parenthetical information (look for commas to help you locate these). Notice how these parts further explain the basic sentence meaning.
5. Read the sentence through again completely and put the meaning in your own words.

This is a procedure in which you "strip away" all but the core parts of the sentence. Then, piece by piece, you "add in" other sentence parts, noticing what each contributes to overall sentence meaning. Let's use this procedure on a sample complicated sentence.

> EXAMPLE: Frustration, the result of blocking needs or motives, occurs frequently in daily life and, unless a person learns to cope with it, it can cause severe mental problems.

(1) Identify the independent clause(s) and then locate the core parts. In this sentence there are two: "Frustration . . . occurs" and "it [frustration] can cause." (2) Notice any expanders. The phrase "in daily life" tells you where frustration occurs frequently. (3) Identify any dependent clauses. In this sentence it is "unless a person learns to cope with it." This clause sets a condition or describes the situation under which frustration can cause mental problems. (4) Include any parenthetical information. The phrase "the result of blocking needs or motives" explains the term "frustration." (5) Put the meaning in your own words. You might say, "Frustration is the result of blocking needs or motives. It happens frequently in everyday life. Unless a person learns how to handle frustration, it can cause mental problems."

Sentence Length

The length of a sentence also can make it difficult to read. In reading a very long sentence you will have trouble keeping it all in mind until you finish reading it. Some sentences also have many long clauses and modifiers and are difficult to read. Finally, long sentences can be difficult to read because the subject and verb often are separated by modifiers, and this makes it difficult to identify and understand the core parts of the sentence.

How to Read Long Sentences

To read long sentences, follow the same steps you would for reading sentences with complicated structure.

Vocabulary

Any sentence, regardless of its structure or length, is difficult to read if you do not know the meaning of the words used. The following sentence uses simple sentence structure and is very short, yet it is difficult to understand because of the vocabulary used.

> *EXAMPLE:* The prosimians include the lemur, the loris, and the tarsier.

Most texts and material you will be reading in college will not be as difficult as this example. It is more likely that there will be one or, at the most, two words in a sentence that you will not know. Our example contains highly technical terminology and requires specific knowledge of the terms.

How to Handle Difficult Vocabulary

When you read a sentence that contains a word you do not know, your first impulse may be to skip over the word and continue reading. This impulse is partially correct because you may be able to get the meaning later in the passage. You definitely should continue reading and finish the sentence. Sometimes, by the time you have finished reading the sentence, or even the next few sentences, you will have found a clue to what the word means. A word (or words) that gives you a clue about the meaning of an unknown word is called a *context clue*. Often, the context a word is found in gives you enough information so that you can figure out what the word means.

If you cannot figure out the meaning of a word from the way it is used in the sentence, use the following steps:

1. Try to pronounce the word. Sometimes hearing the word will help you recognize it, or you might remember hearing it or a closely related term before.
2. Look for the parts of the word that might be familiar and that might give you a clue to the word's meaning. For example, you could see the word "culture" in the term "acculturation" or the word "line" in the term "linearly."
3. If neither of these approaches helps, you will need to look up the word in a dictionary. After looking the word up, be sure to jot the meaning in the margin so you won't have to look it up again later when reviewing or studying. Writing the meaning down will also help "fix" the word in your memory. Later, transfer each new word and its meaning to an index card. Write the new word on the front and its meaning on the back. Then carry these cards with you so you can, in spare moments, go through them, testing yourself to see if you can recall each word and its meaning.

PUNCTUATION AS AN AID TO UNDERSTANDING SENTENCES

Most students know that punctuation is important in writing, but few students realize that punctuation is also an aid to reading. Punctuation helps you to understand what you read because it separates ideas. It can also give you signals about what is to follow next in a sentence.

Basically there are seven punctuation marks that are commonly used in writing. Of course, the period, question mark, and exclamation point mark the end of a sentence. The other four types of punctuation—the comma, semicolon, colon, and dash—are used within the sentence to separate ideas or to signal what is to follow. They will be discussed in the following sections and their functions are summarized on page 128.

The Comma

Commas are always used to separate parts of sentences. They can help you to understand a sentence because they can help you to see the relationship of ideas. Commas may also give you clues about the relative importance and location of the core parts within the sentence. There are several specific uses of the comma in simple sentences.

Parenthetical Use of the Comma

One way a comma is used in a single sentence is to separate qualifying or added information from the core parts of the sentence. This use of the comma is called *parenthetical*. That portion of a sentence set off by commas is information that is nonessential or less important than the basic sentence meaning.

> EXAMPLE: My philosophy instructor, Mr. Warren, gives too many reading assignments.

Because the instructor's name is not essential to the basic meaning of the sentence, it is separated by commas from the remainder of the sentence. The description is separated because it provides additional or qualifying information; it is not the core information the sentence was written to express.

Serial Use of the Comma

Another use of the comma in simple sentences is to separate the items in a group, list, or series from one another. For example, in the sentence

> Paul stopped at the store to buy beer, pretzels, and soda pop for the party.

the items beer, pretzels, and soda pop are separated from one another by commas.

Or, in the sentence

> Sue, Joan, Sam, and George decided to go to the beach.

the comma is used to separate the names in the compound subject of the sentence.

The serial use of the comma indicates that the items separated from one another have equal importance in the sentence. It also suggests that all the items have the same relationship to each other and to other sentence parts. In our first example beer, pretzels, and soda pop are all things Paul bought for the party, and they are all equally important.

Introductory Use of the Comma

A third use of the comma is to separate an introductory phrase from the main part of the sentence. For example, in the sentence

In summary, there are three rules to keep in mind in learning to ski.

the opening phrase "In summary" is set apart by a comma from the remainder of the sentence. The introductory use of the comma helps you to distinguish and separate nonessential information from the main part of the sentence. In many cases the comma will help you to locate the core parts of the sentence; you know that the core parts of the sentence will appear after the comma.

Use in Complicated Sentences

As you have already learned, the comma is used to separate clauses within a sentence. When used along with a conjunction, the comma separates two independent clauses. It may also be used to separate a dependent clause from an independent clause. The use of the comma in complicated sentences helps you to locate the sentence core parts. It may also signal to you that you should look for more than one set of core parts.

The Semicolon

The most common use of the semicolon is to connect two simple sentences that make up the compound sentence. When you see a semicolon you should realize that you are reading a compound sentence. You should then look for two sets of core parts—one set before the semicolon and one set after it.

The semicolon is often used in a compound sentence when the second simple sentence explains the first:

EXAMPLE: The students became somewhat confused during the lecture; no one could understand the foreign phrases used.

Notice that the second part of the sentence explains or tells more about the students' confusion.

The semicolon has one other, very particular, use. It can be used to separate items in a series when one or more of the items themselves contain commas or any other punctuation.

EXAMPLE: The class discussion on ethics was led by Sam Smith, a philosophy major; George Havin, a biology major; and Helen Holmes, a literature major.

In this example semicolons are used to separate the names and majors from each other, indicating that each name and major is a set.

PUNCTUATION AS A READING AID

Punctuation mark	Main function	Aid to the reader
Period	marks end of sentence	tells you complete thought has been expressed
Question mark	marks end of sentence	tells you information has been requested
Exclamation point	marks end of sentence	tells you the writer expressed the idea with emotion or emphasis
Comma	separates information within a sentence	
parenthetical	separates qualifying or additional information from rest of sentence	tells you information set off is nonessential to basic sentence meaning
serial	separates items in list	tells you all items are of equal importance; all items have single relationship to one another
introductory	separates nonessential opening comments from main sentence	helps you locate the core parts by setting aside introductory information
with conjunction in a compound sentence	separates the two independent clauses that form a compound sentence	tells you to expect two sets of core parts
Semicolon		
in a compound sentence	separates the two or more independent clauses that form a compound sentence	tells you to expect two or more sets of core parts
in items in a series	separates items from one another	tells you items are equally important and have a single relationship to one another
Colon	separates main clause from statement or list	tells you a list or further information will follow
Dash	separates additional information from main clause	tells you there has been a change of thought

The Colon

The colon is most commonly used to introduce a list, statement, or quotation. Here, the colon indicates that a list will follow:

My desk was cluttered with all kinds of papers: memos, reports, bills, and phone messages.

Usually the list, statement, or quotation further explains an idea previously stated in the sentence. When you are reading a sentence and you find a colon, you have an idea about what to expect in the remainder of the sentence.

The Dash

The dash signals a sharp break or change in the thought pattern of a sentence. Usually it separates parenthetical information or details included in order to clarify an idea in the rest of the sentence. Often a writer may use the dash to emphasize the material that is separated from the rest of the sentence.

EXERCISE 5–2

Directions: *Read each of the following sentences using the procedure given in this chapter for reading complicated sentences. Underline the independent clause(s) and cirlce the core parts. Then underline the dependent clause with a single line.*

> EXAMPLE: Because they feel superior to children, both in terms of knowledge and authority, adults ignore children.

1. If you really want to understand what you are reading, paraphrase, or put ideas into your own words.
2. On entering the room, I found a group of young seamen, studying by dim light a chart of the channel.
3. Women, who outnumber men, seldom reach the upper levels of power, responsibility, or authority in politics, business, or professional careers.
4. Many people buy clothing from mail-order stores, such as Sears or Penny's, because it is easy and convenient or because clothing is cheaper than in local department stores.
5. After a time of dating or casual relationships with various people, most people choose a partner and make a commitment to marriage.
6. We are frequently told by parents, teachers, and Fourth of July orators that we live in the greatest democracy in the world, where everyone is equal before the law, and free to pursue his or her own happiness in freedom and dignity.[6]

7. Of all people, Americans today tend to be quite distrustful of their government, perhaps as a result of the events of the last decade, which have made us aware that our leaders are humans too.[7]

8. Even if we could convince every single American that the strategy of deterrence through the development of increasingly powerful weapons is suicidal or that the communist hordes are not on our doorstep, the manufacturing of lethal weapons would not stop.[8]

9. Although intelligence and personality tests are not customarily considered as vehicles for observation, they are, in fact, very short samples of behavior and are extremely important in terms of their ability to disclose useful information.[9]

10. The relationship of the arts to leisure in American nineteenth century society was therefore quite simple; those who had leisure traveled to the places where art was to be found, those who had money sometimes bought it and brought it back, and they, or some of those who visited the museums to which it eventually found its way, learned to enjoy it.[10]

11. Piaget's research has touched on many areas, but all of his investigations have had as a central aim the discovery of the nature of intelligence—its function, structure, and content—as well as the means by which it changes with age and experience.[11]

12. Although the statement "the emotional stability of the child is dependent upon the emotional stability of the parent" lacks confirmation through research, it is quite evident that an unstable home environment, for whatever cause, may have harmful implications for the child's psychological adjustment.[12]

WRITING SENTENCES THAT SHOW RELATIONSHIPS

To effectively communicate your ideas in writing, you should try to show readers how your ideas are related and help them to follow your train of thought easily. You can do this by using the complex sentence to provide clues about the relationship of your ideas.

Suppose you had written the following sentences in a first draft of a paragraph.

Alex liked his job at the theatre.

He had to spend most of his time collecting tickets.

Two ideas are expressed and each idea is clear and understandable. However, the connection between the two ideas is not clear. At this point, it is left for the reader to reason or figure out what, if any, relationship exists between the two ideas. You can make the relationship clear by combining the two sentences as follows:

> Although he had to spend most of his time collecting tickets, Alex liked his job at the theatre.

Now your reader would understand that Alex liked his job *in spite of* the fact that he spent most of his time collecting tickets. If you wanted to indicate that Alex's favorite part of his job was collecting tickets, you might combine the two sentences as follows:

> Alex liked his job at the theatre because he had to spend most of his time collecting tickets.

Notice that each of these complex sentences contains a word (although, because) that describes how the two ideas are related. Also notice that one sentence remains unchanged in each example, while the other is changed by the addition of a word. That is, one sentence has been changed into a dependent clause; it has a subject and verb, but because a word was added the statement is no longer complete. Instead it has become dependent on the other clause in the combined sentence.

When to Use Complex Sentences

When you combine ideas into the complex sentence pattern, the two ideas *cannot* be equally important. One idea must be less important and depend on the other more important idea. The more important idea is expressed in the independent clause, and the idea of lesser importance is expressed in the dependent clause. For example, in the following sentence the more important idea is that Marcia rushed to call her sister:

> As soon as Marcia heard about the plane crash, she rushed to the phone to call her sister.

The dependent clause "as soon as Marcia heard about the plane crash" provides additional information about why she called her sister and suggests that the one situation (hearing about the plane crash) caused the other action (calling her sister).

There are a number of situations in which you can use complex sentences to express relationships between ideas. They can be used to show relationships of time, purpose, condition, cause or effect, or place. Each of these situations will be briefly discussed.

Expressing Time Relationships

When events happen in a certain order or when there is a time sequence involved, a complex sentence can be used to express this relationship. Here are a few examples of two ideas that have been combined into a complex sentence to show a relationship in time.

> While I was driving home, I heard an interesting song on the radio. (One event happened at the same time another was going on.)

After I left the library, I met an old friend in the parking lot.
(One event happened later than another.)

When Mr. Pritchard finished his lecture, he gave the class a quiz.
(One event immediately followed another.)

Expressing Purpose or Reason

The complex structure can be used to show for what purpose an action is taken or the reason why an event, action, or situation exists, as in the following sentences:

Willie and Pete left early so they could avoid the rush hour traffic.
(Their purpose in leaving early was to avoid the traffic.)

Because Joe got an "A" in his psychology course, he decided to take another psychology course next semester.
(Joe's high grade was the reason why he decided to take another psychology course.)

Expressing Conditional Relationships

When one idea, event, or action depends on another, the complex sentence can be used to express this relationship.

If Sue passes the final exam, she will pass the course.
(This sentence describes the condition under which Sue will pass the course.)

Greg will meet us this evening unless he doesn't finish his term paper.
(This sentence tells the condition under which Greg will not meet us.)

Expressing Cause-Effect Relationships

When one event causes another or when something happens as a result of something else, you can use the complex sentence form to show the connection between the two events.

Since she disliked the instructor, Sara dropped her philosophy course.
(Her dislike for the instructor caused Sara to drop the course.)

Including Descriptive or Qualifying Information

Complex sentences can also be used to include descriptions in sentences. In this case a dependent clause further explains or describes a noun (person, place, thing, or idea) or pronoun. The following examples illustrate this function.

The company wanted an operator who could speak French.

In this sentence the underlined dependent clause ("who" is the subject, "could speak" is the verb) describes the type of operator the company wanted.

> The college <u>where my brother teaches</u> has a four-week winter vacation.

The clause "where my brother teaches" provides further information about the subject of the sentence—"college."

> Mr. Everett, the man whom I work for, was in an auto accident.

The clause "the man whom I work for" further describes Mr. Everett. As a rule, a dependent clause that provides descriptive or qualifying information begins with words such as who, whose, whom, which, that, where, when, why, after.

EXERCISE 5–3

Directions: *Combine each set of sentences into one complex sentence.*

> EXAMPLE: Ed Smith is the president of the freshman class.
>
> Ed Smith is transferring to another school.
>
> *Ed Smith, who is president of the freshman class, is transferring to another school.*

1. The math teacher is patient.
   The math teacher makes his class interesting.

   _____

   _____

2. He arrived.
   It was late.

   _____

   _____

3. He is the runner.
   He won the first race.

   _____

   _____

4. He agreed with my suggestions.
   He didn't want to admit it.

   _____

5. John has been upset.
   John moved out of the dorm.

   _____

   _____

6. One of the most creative art forms today is film.
   Film is a growing industry.

   _____

   _____

7. Sue won't move into the dorm.
   Sue thinks she won't be able to study in the dorm.

   _____

   _____

8. The environmental group are likely to picket the chemical plant.
   They are opposed to manufacturing the pesticide.

   _____

   _____

9. We must decide on a destination.
   We can make our airline reservation early.

   _____

   _____

10. Some students find history difficult.
    Some students don't have good memories.

    _____

    _____

11. The hill was dangerously steep.

    John skied the hill with great care.

    _____

    _____

12. The Renaissance began around the end of the fourteenth century.

    The Renaissance lasted about two hundred years.

    _____

    _____

13. The computerized data showed negative results.

    The data had been collected by political volunteers.

    The volunteers were not trained in interviewing techniques.

    _____

    _____

    _____

14. The scientists will prove their hypothesis is true.

    The results of the tests are positive.

    _____

    _____

    _____

15. The anthropologist collected his information in the jungles of South America.

    The anthropologist published his research in a prominent journal.

    _____

    _____

    _____

THE COMPOUND-COMPLEX SENTENCE PATTERN

Many thoughts, actions, situations, and events are complicated. That is, certain ideas depend on other ideas for their clear expression, so they seldom occur by themselves, unrelated to anything else. For example, if you think about going to a particular movie, you begin to think about related ideas. You wonder what it will be about, whether you will like it, or if there will be a line at the ticket window. Think of a particular action or event. Suppose you spilled your coffee. There had to be a reason why you spilled it; something probably happened as a result of it, and you probably did something after it spilled.

Because thoughts and actions do not occur in isolation, when you write about them it is often necessary to show the relationships to make clear the connections between or among these ideas. Both the compound sentence and the complex sentence can be used to combine ideas, to show their relative importance, and to indicate the relationships. However, since many ideas that you express are even more complicated, containing several relationships, you might need to use a sentence pattern that enables you to combine ideas and to describe several different types of relationships at the same time. Here are three simple sentences that describe a situation.

> Barb had spilled her coffee.
>
> Sam wiped off the table.
>
> Mark lifted up her books.

As these sentences are now written, the reader is not shown in any way that the three actions are related. To begin to show that they are related, you could combine the actions into two sentences instead of three by using one compound sentence and one simple sentence.

> Barb had spilled her coffee, and Sam wiped off the table.
>
> Mark lifted up her books.

However, these two sentences do not yet clearly express the relationship of the three actions. Barb's action is now connected with Sam's action, but you still do not know if Mark's action is directly related to the situation. To connect Mark's action to the situation, you could combine the sentences as follows:

> After Barb had spilled her coffee, Sam wiped off the table.
>
> After Barb had spilled her coffee, Mark lifted up her books.

These two sentences are an improvement over the first two. At least you now begin to see that two actions each happened as a result of another. However, the three actions are still not directly connected together. The following sentence finally ties the three ideas together and shows how they are related.

> After Barb had spilled her coffee, Mark lifted up her books, and Sam wiped off the table.

This sentence is a compound-complex sentence. It consists of one dependent clause and two independent clauses. You might think of a compound-complex sentence as a compound sentence combined with a dependent clause, or as a complex sentence to which an additional independent clause has been added.

When to Use Compound-Complex Sentences

The compound-complex sentence pattern is useful when you want to combine several ideas that are related to one another. However, the ideas should not be of equal importance. The material in the independent clauses should be the most important information; the material in the dependent clause should be of lesser importance. Also, the two independent clauses must contain information that is closely related. The information in the dependent clause must "depend on" or relate to the ideas presented in the independent clauses.

Punctuation in Compound-Complex Sentences

There are two alternatives in the punctuation of compound-complex sentences. Look at these two examples.

EXAMPLE 1: When spending increases faster than production, prices rise ☐ and we have inflation.

EXAMPLE 2: When spending increases faster than production, prices rise ☐ and we have inflation.

Notice the difference in punctuation. In the first example the two independent clauses are joined by a comma and a conjunction. In the second the two independent clauses are joined by a semicolon and a conjunction. A semicolon indicates a separation that is stronger than a comma; the choice of whether to use a comma or a semicolon depends on how distinctly you want to separate the independent clauses.

EXERCISE 5–4

Directions: *Combine each set of sentences into a compound-complex sentence.*

EXAMPLE: Memory is an important aspect of successful study skills.

Students should use as many study aids as possible.

Underlining important ideas in textbooks is one of the most effective study aids.

Underlining important ideas in textbooks helps the memory.

Since a good memory is an important aspect of successful study skills, students should use as many study aids as possible, and underlining important ideas in textbooks is one of the most effective study aids that helps the memory.

1. I saw a group of students studying their notes.

   The students were having an informal study session in philosophy.

   The study session should improve their understanding of philosophy.

   _____

   _____

   _____

2. The cottage was large.

   We found we were crowded.

   We looked forward to having our own rooms again.

   _____

   _____

   _____

3. The coach helped the basketball player get up.

   The basketball player was injured.

   The basketball player wanted to finish the game.

   The coach made him sit on the bench for the rest of the game.

   _____

   _____

   _____

4. Paraphrasing is putting ideas in your own words.

   Paraphrasing can be used as a test.

   The test will show that you understand what you are reading.

   _____

   _____

   _____

5. Some people think a degree in English is impractical.

   Communication is an important aspect of the legal profession.

   Many successful lawyers have a bachelor's degree in English.

   _____

   _____

   _____

6. Running is a skill.

   It can be improved just like any other skill.

   You have to coordinate the sequence, direction, and timing.

   _____

   _____

   _____

7. Many novice runners have a tendency to overstride.

   Overstriding results in the lead foot hitting the ground ahead of the center of gravity.

   _____

   _____

   _____

8. No magic formula exists for determining optimal stride length.

   Studies are under way.

   Considerable mileage must be logged before stride characteristics are apparent.

   _____

   _____

   _____

9. Runners frequently complain of a tightening in shoulder muscles.

   The tightness wastes energy and should be avoided.

   Trying to achieve an overall sense of relaxation is important.

   _____

   _____

   _____

10. Efficiency may be a more important factor than previously realized.

    Runners often improve with age.

    Running thousands of miles over the years will make a runner more efficient.

    _____

    _____

    _____

11. Toys stimulate the imagination.

Toys are satisfying.

Toys take the place of real things.

Real things are not always obtainable.

_____

_____

_____

12. Toys are like science fiction.

Toys often show the shape of things to come.

Toy airplanes were made in the nineteenth century before we had real airplanes.

_____

_____

_____

13. Toys can do things that real-life machines cannot do.

Toys can even violate engineering principles.

Toys do not have to be efficient.

_____

_____

_____

14. Man's aspiration to fly led to interesting and imaginative toys.

Some small balloons supported rowboat compartments.

The rowboat compartments had little men in them.

_____

_____

_____

15. New physical principles are always being discovered.

Sometimes physical principles are first expressed in toys.

The first use of the wheel may have been in a toy.

_____

_____

_____

The Compound-Complex Sentence Pattern

EXERCISE 5–5

Directions: *Each group of ten sentences in this exercise can be combined to make several long sentences. Using any of the sentence patterns you have learned, combine several sentences from each group to form a longer, more complicated sentence. Read through the sample exercise before you begin.*

Simple Sentences:
a. The Newfoundland dog resembles a St. Bernard.
b. Newfoundlands are usually black.
c. Some Newfoundlands are brown.
d. Some Newfoundlands are gray.
e. The males can reach a weight of 200 pounds.
f. The females are slightly smaller than the males.
g. Newfoundlands are noted for their gentle temperament.
h. Newfoundlands are good with children.
i. Newfoundlands are good swimmers.
j. Newfoundlands love people.

Combined Sentences:

1. The Newfoundland dog resembles a St. Bernard, but Newfoundlands are usually black.

2. Some Newfoundlands are brown or gray.

3. Although the males can reach a weight of 200 pounds and the females are slightly smaller, the Newfoundlands are noted for their gentle temperament.

4. Newfoundlands are good swimmers, and they love people and are good with children.

1. Simple Sentences:
   a. Glass has come a long way in its 3,500 years.
   b. There is no other material that man has used for so many purposes.
   c. Glass was used in ancient religious ceremonies.
   d. Glass is used in ordinary day-to-day living.
   e. Glass is used in spaceships and telecommunications fibers.
   f. Glass begins as a mixture of soda, silica, and lime.
   g. The mixture is heated in a furnace.
   h. The mixture changes into a glowing orange mass.
   i. Glass was probably discovered by accident.
   j. It would be difficult to get along without glass in our modern society.

141

Combined Sentences:

1. _____

_____

2. _____

_____

3. _____

_____

2. *Simple Sentences:*
   a. Cross country skiing began thousands of years ago in Scandanavia.
   b. Cross country skiing later developed as a tactical maneuver in winter warfare.
   c. Cross country skiing became a sport in Norway in the nineteenth century.
   d. Norway has a famous cross country race.
   e. The race is called the Birkebeiner.
   f. The race actually celebrates a dramatic historical escape.
   g. Seven centuries ago the heir to the throne was smuggled to safety.
   h. Soldiers on skis carried the infant across the mountains.
   i. They took the child to Lillehammer.
   j. Now the cross country race alternately starts or finishes at Lillehammer.

Combined Sentences:

1. _____

_____

2. _____

_____

3. _____

_____

3. *Simple Sentences:*
   a. Sailors used to get scurvy after spending long periods at sea.
   b. Scurvy is a disease caused by a lack of Vitamin C.
   c. It is well known that nineteenth-century British sailors were nicknamed "limeys."
   d. They were nicknamed limeys because of the quantity of fruit they consumed to ward off scurvy.
   e. Few people realize that the practice was a law.
   f. The Merchant Shipping Act of 1894 required that all crew members be given one ounce of lime or lemon juice.

g. The lime or lemon juice had to be given to crew members after a ship had been at sea for ten days.

h. The lime or lemon juice was often mixed with a potent West Indian rum.

i. The rum acted as a preservative.

j. Half a century later scientists discovered that lemons were two or three times richer in Vitamin C than limes.

Combined Sentences:

1. _____

_____

2. _____

_____

3. _____

_____

_____

EXERCISE 5–6

Directions: *Choose a reading selection from the end of this unit. Preread and read the selection. Write the title and subject of the reading here:*

TITLE: _____

SUBJECT: _____

Using the subject of the selection as a starting point, follow each of these steps:

1. *Prewriting.*
   a. Narrow the subject into three possible topics:

   _____

   _____

   _____

   b. Select one topic and use a five-minute free-writing exercise or write several questions that occur to you about the topic to generate ideas.

2. *Composing.* Select the most important ideas you see in your prewriting exercise. Develop these ideas into a paper consisting of an introduction, body, and conclusion. Include the details your reader will need in order to have a clear understanding of your purpose and message.

3. *Checking the Content and Organization.* Read over the rough draft you have written, considering the sequence of your ideas.

Decide whether you need to change the order and rewrite the outline so it shows how your ideas will progress.

4. *Revising.* Read through the rough draft you have written. Make a brief list of the sentences you have written that express the following: time relationships, purpose or cause, conditional relationships, cause-effect relationships, and descriptive or qualifying information. Look at each sentence separately, then read it as it appears in the context of the entire paper. Consider the sentences preceding and following each sentence on your list. Check to see if you can effectively combine the sentences on your list with other sentences by making one sentence a dependent clause. Rewrite as many sentences as you feel are necessary. Next, check for the following errors: (1) sentence fragments, (2) run-on sentences, (3) subject-verb agreement, and (4) pronoun agreement. Then make a clean copy of the final piece of writing.

5. *Proofreading.* Reread the paper, checking carefully for punctuation and spelling errors. Pay particular attention to the comma and make sure you have not left any dependent clauses standing as sentences. Place a check on the proofreading checklist next to each item that you correct. List a description of each error you corrected in the column on the right.

SUMMARY

A complex sentence combines two complete ideas in one sentence. However, in the complex sentence one idea becomes dependent on the other; thus, the clause containing the dependent idea is called a dependent clause and the other clause, which can stand alone as a complete sentence, is called an independent clause. Compound-complex sentences combine the forms of complex sentences and compound sentences. Compound-complex sentences have two or more independent clauses and one or more dependent clauses. They use the same types of internal modifiers as the complex and compound sentences. Independent clauses in a compound-complex sentence are joined together by a comma and a conjunction or just a semicolon. Both complex sentences and compound-complex sentences are used to combine ideas while providing clues about the relationships existing among the ideas.

PROOFREADING CHECKLIST

Essay Title _____

Date _____

TYPE	✔	ERROR	FREQUENCY	DESCRIPTION
GRAMMAR		Run-on Sentence Sentence Fragment Subject/Verb Agreement Verb Tense Pronoun Agreement		
MECHANICS		Capitalization Italics Abbreviation		
PUNCTUATION		, (Comma) ; (Semicolon) ' (Apostrophe) " (Quotation Marks) . (Period) ! (Exclamation Point) ? (Question Mark) : (Colon) — (Dash) ( ) (Parentheses) - (Hyphen)		

		ERROR	CORRECTION	
SPELLING ERRORS				

Unit Two Reading Selections

Difficulty level: A

7. Kids' Country

Shana Alexander

Children are a relatively modern invention. Until a few hundred years ago they did not exist. In medieval and Renaissance painting you see pint-size men and women, wearing grown-up clothes and grown-up expressions, performing grown-up tasks. Children did not exist because the family as we know it had not evolved. In the old days most people lived on the land, and life was a communal affair.

Children today not only exist; they have taken over. God's Country has to an astonishing degree become Kids' Country— in no place more than in America, and at no time more than now. Once more 'tis the season, holiday time has begun, the frantic family skedaddle from pumpkin to holly when Kids' Country runs in its jumpingest high gear.

But it is always Kids' Country here. Our civilization is child-centered, child-obsessed. A kid's body is our physical ideal. Weightwatchers grunt and pant. Sages jog from sea to shining sea. Plastic surgeons scissor and tuck up. New hair sprouts, transplanted, on wisdom's brow. One way or another we are determined to "keep in shape," and invariably this means keeping a kid's shape—which we then outfit in baby-doll ruffles, sneakers, and blue jeans.

The food we live on is kids' food: pizza, hot dogs, fried chicken, ice cream, hamburgers. This bizarre diet is the reason we have such trouble maintaining our kids' bodies.

The stuff we now drink has thrown the beverage industry into turmoil. Our consumption of soft drinks has risen 80 percent in a decade. Americans not only are switching *en masse* from hot coffee to iced tea, and bitter drinks to sweet. The popularity of alcoholic soda pop—the so-called "fun" wines like Thunderbird and apple wine—has jumped 168 percent in five years!

Children hate spinach, vitamins, and *haute cuisine*. They like their food kooked, not cooked: you pop, thaw, dissolve, or explode it into eatability. To buy it you push around a wire perambulator, and at the end of the supermarket line you get prizes of colored stamps.

In Kids' Country, every day must be prize day. Miss America, Miss Teen-Age America, Miss Junior Miss America and probably Miss Little Miss America trample each other down star-spangled runways. Volume mail-order giveaways will shortly silt up our postal system entirely. All day long TV shows like "Concentration," "Dating Game," "Hollywood Squares," and "Jackpot" hand out more toys: wrist watches, washing machines, trips to Hawaii.

The rest of the world may be in fee to the Old Boy Network, carried on to the point of senility, but here there are no elder statesmen left. Seniority in an American politician no longer denotes wisdom, only power or tenure. The old age of the present Congress is a major hindrance. No one considers the Héberts and Eastlands as Athenian men.

Our contemporary heroes are a series of golden boys. A direct line links Charles Lindbergh to Billy Graham to the astronauts to John F. Kennedy—and to his kid brothers.

The philosopher-kings of Kids' Country are professors like Erich Segal and Charles Reich, who saw in Woodstock and the flower children a new golden age of innocence he called Consciousness III. The totem animal in Kids' Country just now is a talking, philosophizing seagull who soars on vast updrafts of hot air, and the beloved bogeyman is a wicked movie *mafioso* with a heart of gold.

The ideal of American parenthood is to be a kid with your kid. Take him to Disneyland; take him fishing, take him out to the ball game. Our national pastimes are kids' games, and we are all hooked. When the Redskins are blacked out in Washington, the President holes up in New York so as not to miss the big game. Bobby Fischer, the quintessential smart boy of every school, turns the whole country on to chess. "The Boys of Summer" becomes a best seller. In nostalgia's golden haze, we forget the poet's full line, "I see the boys of summer in their ruin."

In Kids' Country we do not permit middle age. Thirty is promoted over fifty, but thirty knows that soon his time to be overtaken will come. Middle-aged man must appear to run, even if it is only running in place. Often the big kid outruns his heart. In our over-sixty population there are ten widows for every man.

Like a child's room, Kids' Country is a mess. New York City seems about to disappear under its load of litter, graffiti, and dog droppings. How is it that China can eliminate the house fly, and we can't even clean up Central Park?

In Kids' Country, not so ironically, Mommy and Daddy are household gods, and so we have two immense national holidays, elsewhere virtually unknown, called "Mother's Day" and "Father's Day."

We are the first society in which parents expect to learn from their children. Such a topsy-turvy situation has come about at least in part because, unlike the rest of the world, ours is an immigrant society, and for immigrants the *only* hope is in the kids. In the Old Country, hope was in the father, and how much family wealth he could accumulate and pass along to his children. In the growth pattern of America and its ever-expanding frontier, the young man was ever advised to Go West; the father was ever inheriting from his son: the topsy-turviness was built in from the beginning. In short, a melting pot needs a spoon. Kids' Country may be the inevitable result.

Kids' Country is not all bad. America is the greatest country in the world to grow up in *because* it's Kids' Country. We not only wear kids' clothes and eat kids' food; we dream kids' dreams, and make them come true. It was, after all, a boys' game to go to the moon. 16

Certainly as a people we thrive. By the time they are sixteen, most American kids today are bigger, stronger—and smarter—than Mommy and Daddy ever were. And if they are not precisely "happier," they may well be more "grown up." But being a civilization with no genuine rites of passage, what we are experiencing now seems in many ways the exact opposite of medieval and Renaissance life. If in the old days children did not exist, it seems equally true today that adults, as a class, have begun to disappear, condemning all of us to remain boys and girls forever, jogging and doing push-ups against eternity. 17

COMPREHENSION

1. The central theme of this essay is that
   a. modern American children are basically the same as children of the Renaissance
   b. American civilization is "child-centered, child-obsessed"
   c. American kids are spoiled brats and poor students
   d. Medieval and Renaissance children were better than modern American kids
2. The author says that in medieval and Renaissance times "kids" did not exist because
   a. children were dressed like adults
   b. children were seen but never heard
   c. the family as we know it did not exist
   d. children were not permitted to appear in public until they were eighteen
3. Alexander argues the modern American father and mother are
   a. too severe with their children
   b. too free with their children
   c. "household gods"
   d. not interested in family life
4. According to the author, American civilization is the first in which
   a. both parents work
   b. parents play kids' games
   c. parents expect to learn from their children
   d. children are truly happy
5. Alexander feels that modern adults attempt to
   a. control and dominate children
   b. imitate the diet and dress of children
   c. ignore their children
   d. treat them as adults

VOCABULARY

Directions: *The meaning of the following terms from selection 7 cannot be clearly determined from the context. Using the dictionary entries, select the appropriate definition of the term as it is used in the reading selection.*

1. perambulator (par. 6)
   a. instrument for measuring distance
   b. odometer
   c. carriage for a child
   d. one who perambulates

   per·am·bu·la·tor \pə-'ram-byə-ˌlāt-ər, *for 2 also* 'pram-\ *n* **1** : one that perambulates **2** *chiefly Brit* : a baby carriage — per·am·bu·la·to·ry \-lə-ˌtōr-ē, -ˌtȯr-\ *adj*

2. totem (par. 10)
   a. clan
   b. primitive group
   c. symbol
   d. object

   to·tem (tō'təm) *n.* **1.** An animal, plant, or natural object that serves as a symbol of a clan or family and is claimed by the members as an ancestor. **2.** A representation of this being or object. [Ojibwa *nintōtēm*, "my family mark."] —to·tem'ic (tō-tĕm'ĭk) *adj.*

3. quintessential (par. 11)
   a. ether
   b. typical example
   c. power
   d. fire, air, water, earth

   quin·tes·sence \kwin-'tes-ᵊn(t)s\ *n* [ME, fr. MF *quinte essence,* fr. ML *quinta essentia,* lit., fifth essence] **1** : the fifth and highest essence in ancient and medieval philosophy that permeates all nature and is the substance composing the heavenly bodies **2** : the essence of a thing in its purest and most concentrated form **3** : the most typical example or representative — quint·es·sen·tial \ˌkwint-ə-'sen-chəl\ *adj*

DISCUSSION

1. In paragraph 11, the author says that "The ideal of American parenthood is to be a kid with your kid." Explain what she means.
2. Do you agree, or disagree, with the author's attitude(s) about "kids" in our society? Why?
3. What are some of the differences Alexander sees between modern "kids" and the Renaissance child?

Difficulty level: A

8. Angels on a Pin

Alexander Calandra

Some time ago, I received a call from a colleague who asked if I would be the referee on the grading of an examination question. He was about to give a student a zero for his answer to a physics question, while the student claimed he should receive a perfect score and would if the system were not set up against the student. The instructor and the student agreed to submit this to an impartial arbiter, and I was selected. 1

I went to my colleague's office and read the examination question: "Show how it is possible to determine the height of a tall building with the aid of a barometer." 2

The student had answered: "Take the barometer to the top of the building, attach a long rope to it, lower the barometer to the street, and then bring it up, measuring the length of the rope. The length of the rope is the height of the building." 3

I pointed out that the student really had a strong case for full credit, since he had answered the question completely and correctly. On the other hand, if full credit were given, it could well contribute to a high grade for the student in his physics course. A high grade is supposed to certify competence in physics, but the answer did not confirm this. I suggested that the student have another try at answering the question. I was not surprised that my colleague agreed, but I was surprised that the student did.

I gave the student six minutes to answer the question, with the warning that his answer should show some knowledge of physics. At the end of five minutes, he had not written anything. I asked if he wished to give up, but he said no. He had many answers to this problem; he was just thinking of the best one. I excused myself for interrupting him, and asked him to please go on. In the next minute, he dashed off his answer, which read:

"Take the barometer to the top of the building and lean over the edge of the roof. Drop the barometer, timing its fall with a stopwatch. Then, using the formula $S = \frac{1}{2} at^2$, calculate the height of the building."

At this point, I asked my colleague if *he* would give up. He conceded, and I gave the student almost full credit.

In leaving my colleague's office, I recalled that the student had said he had other answers to the problem, so I asked him what they were. "Oh, yes," said the student. "There are many ways of getting the height of a tall building with the aid of a barometer. For example, you could take the barometer out on a sunny day and measure the height of the barometer, the length of its shadow, and the length of the shadow of the building, and by the use of a simple proportion, determine the height of the building."

"Fine," I said. "And the others?"

"Yes," said the student. "There is a very basic measurement method that you will like. In this method, you take the barometer and begin to walk up the stairs. As you climb the stairs, you mark off the length of the barometer along the wall. You then count the number of marks, and this will give you the height of the building in barometer units. A very direct method.

"Of course, if you want a more sophisticated method, you can tie the barometer to the end of a string, swing it as a pendulum, and determine the value of 'g' at the street level and at the top of the building. From the difference between the two values of 'g,' the height of the building can, in principle, be calculated."

Finally he concluded, there are many other ways of solving the problem. "Probably the best," he said, "is to take the barometer to the basement and knock on the superintendent's door. When the superintendent answers, you speak to him as follows: 'Mr. Superintendent, here I have a fine barometer. If you will tell me the height of this building, I will give you this barometer.'"

At this point, I asked the student if he really did not know the conventional answer to this question. He admitted that he did, but said that he was fed up with high school and college instructors trying to teach him how to think, to use the "scientific method," and to explore the deep inner logic of the subject in a pedantic way, as is often done in the new mathematics, rather than teaching him the structure of the subject. With this in mind, he decided to revive scholasticism as an academic lark to challenge the Sputnik-panicked classrooms of America.

COMPREHENSION

1. The major point of this essay is that
   a. students *should not* question an instructor's evaluation
   b. a student should question an instructor's grade if he has good reasons
   c. students should be encouraged to think creatively
   d. physics is a boring subject
2. The student objected to his examination grade because
   a. he did not think his instructor knew what he was talking about
   b. the question was unfair
   c. the question was ambiguous
   d. he was tired of instructors trying to teach him how to think
3. After his first discussion of the problem with the instructor Calandra felt that
   a. the student was wrong
   b. the student deserved another chance
   c. the question was unfair
   d. the instructor was biased
4. After the student had retaken the test, the instructor
   a. insisted that the student should fail
   b. argued with Calandra about his evaluation
   c. agreed to pass the student with almost full credit
   d. refused to talk to the student
5. When asked if he did not know the conventional answer to the question the student said
   a. that he did
   b. that he did not
   c. that he did not understand the question
   d. that he felt the question was irrelevant

VOCABULARY

Directions: *The meaning of the following terms from selection 8 cannot be clearly determined from the context. Using the dictionary entries, select the appropriate definition of the term as it is used in the reading selection.*

1. pedantic (par. 3)
   a. formal
   b. show-off
   c. experienced
   d. paying too much attention to booklearning

ped·ant (pĕd'nt) *n.* **1.** A person who pays too much attention to book learning and formal rules without having an understanding or experience of practical affairs. **2.** A person who shows off his learning or scholarship. [Old French, from Italian *pedante*.] —**pe·dan'tic** (pə-dăn'tĭk) or **pe·dan'ti·cal** *adj.* —**pe·dan'ti·cal·ly** *adv.*

2. scholasticism (par. 3)
   a. metaphysics
   b. Christian
      philosophy
   c. Aristotelianism
   d. use of traditional
      methods

scho·las·ti·cism \skə-'las-tə-ˌsiz-əm\ *n* **1** *cap* **a :** a philosophical movement dominant in western Christian civilization from the 9th until the 17th century and combining religious dogma with the mystical and intuitional tradition of patristic philosophy esp. of St. Augustine and later with Aristotelianism **b :** NEO-SCHOLASTICISM **2 a :** close adherence to the traditional teachings or methods of a school or sect **b :** pedantic adherence to scholastic methods

DISCUSSION

1. The title of this essay was drawn from a popular debate among scholastic philosophers in the Middle Ages about how many angels could stand on a pin. Although it was considered seriously at that time, it is now regarded as an example of the trivial use to which logic can be put. How does the title affect the meaning of the essay?
2. What point does the author make about education? Is it valid in your opinion?
3. Why do you think Calandra ended the story as he did?

Difficulty level: B

9. Thermography—A Fabulous New Way of "Seeing"

James Lincoln Collier

At five feet, it can warn of a tumor no bigger than a pinprick deep in the breast. It can look at the wall of a house and spot where faulty insulation is letting heat out. It can scan the wall of a fiery industrial furnace and indicate dangerous weak spots. It can examine a human leg and show a malfunctioning blood vessel that is causing varicose veins. Incredibly, it can even take a photograph of a past event. 1

This remarkable technique is called thermography, and it has given human beings a new way of seeing. Thermography depends upon the fact that all objects give off infrared energy. The strength of these infrared emissions depends on the temperature of the body from which they come. Although scientists have long been able to measure the strength of infrared emissions, the problem was to turn these measurements into some sort of "picture." 2

Attempts were not notably successful until 1956, when Dr. Ray Lawson, of Montreal, made the first thermograms of the human body. Progress in the science has been rapid ever since, as industrial companies in Europe and the United States —led by the Swedish concern AGA—have come up with new developments. 3

Today's thermograph looks, for the most part, like a small television camera. You point it at the subject, make a few fairly simple adjustments—and on an accompanying screen appears 4 a black-and-white heat picture of the subject. Normally the warm areas are light, the cold areas dark, and the picture looks something like an ordinary photograph negative. However, in some systems, black and white are reversed, and in still others the picture comes out in brilliant colors, with the various tones representing given temperatures.

Using one of these systems, experimenters made a picture of the past. Focusing on an empty chair after someone had been sitting in it for a few minutes, they were able to see the heat pattern left by the body, still emanating from the chair's fabric. The picture was so clear that they could detect that the sitter's legs had been crossed.

Thermography's most valuable use has been in the field of medicine. Already it has helped to save lives, and added to doctors' skills in treating disease. It has proved especially helpful in detecting breast tumors. (The extra heat frequently generated by a growth shows up in contrast with the surrounding skin temperatures.)

The standard examinations for breast cancer are mammography (X ray of the breast) and clinical examination. But, says Dr. Harold Isard, of Albert Einstein Medical Center in Philadelphia, who has used thermography to examine some 20,000 women for breast cancer, "The two methods do not catch everything. Thermography can indicate the possibility of some small cancers that have been missed. And it's safe and cheap. We can do a thermogram in a couple of minutes, and although the machines cost around $30,000 each, the price of operating them is a matter of pennies."

The American Cancer Society, working with the federal government, has begun pilot programs to screen for breast cancer 270,000 women in the over-35 age range during the next six years, via 27 centers around the country. The women will be checked by mammography, thermography and clinical examination. Says Dr. Isard, "With the addition of thermography to the other two methods, we can get about 92 percent accuracy in detecting breast cancer."

COMPREHENSION

1. This article is about
   a. a new way of detecting cancer
   b. the history of thermography
   c. the value of thermography
   d. how to interpret a thermogram
2. Thermography depends on
   a. television cameras
   b. infrared energy
   c. photograph negatives
   d. temperatures
3. The most valuable use of thermography has been in the field of
   a. medicine
   b. industry
   c. science
   d. energy conservation
4. The advantage in using thermography to detect cancer is that it
   a. is helpful in detecting breast cancer

b. can indicate very small cancers

c. adds to doctors' skill in treating disease

d. saves lives

5. Producing a thermogram is

a. costly because of the high voltage the machine requires

b. a time-consuming process

c. inexpensive after the machine is purchased

d. an unsafe procedure

VOCABULARY

Directions: *The meaning of the following terms from selection 9 cannot be clearly determined from the context. Using the dictionary entries, select the appropriate definition of the term as it is used in the reading selection.*

1. infrared (par. 2)

a. short waves

b. red rays

c. radio waves

d. heat rays

in·fra·red (in′frə-red′), *adj.* designating or of those invisible rays just beyond the red of the visible spectrum: their waves are longer than those of the spectrum colors but shorter than radio waves, and have a penetrating heating effect.

2. emissions (par. 2)

a. money

b. discharge

c. fluid

d. shares

e·mis·sion (i mish′ən), *n.* **1.** the act or an instance of emitting. **2.** something that is emitted; discharge; emanation. **3.** the act or an instance of issuing, as paper money. **4.** *Electronics.* a measure of the number of electrons emitted by the heated filament or cathode of a vacuum tube. **5.** an ejection or discharge of semen or other fluid from the body. **6.** the fluid ejected or discharged. [< L ēmissiōn- (s. of ēmissiō) = ēmiss(us) (ptp. of ēmittere to EMIT) + -iōn- -ION] —**e·mis·sive** (i mis′iv), *adj.*

3. emanating (par. 5)

a. coming forth

b. belonging to

c. flowing out of

d. starting

em·a·nate (ĕm′ə-nāt′) *v.* -**nated, -nating, -nates.** —*intr.* To come forth or proceed, as from a source or origin; issue; originate: "*there was no light of any kind emanating from lamp or candle*" (Poe). —*tr.* To send forth; emit. [Latin ēmānāre, flow out : ex-, out + mānāre, to flow (see mā-³ in Appendix*).] —**em′a·na′tive** *adj.*

DISCUSSION

1. Can you think of other possible uses of thermography? What advantage would its use provide in those contexts?

2. The article states that "experimenters made a picture of the past." Do you find that statement misleading? Why or why not?

3. Are you aware of any programs in your community, medical or otherwise, that use thermography? Do you think the field of thermography might present opportunities for a good career? Why?

Difficulty level: B

10. The New (and Still Hidden) Persuaders

Vance Packard

People keep asking me what the hidden persuaders are up to nowadays. So, for a few months, I revisited the persuasion specialists. The demographers and motivational researchers, I found, are still very much with us, but admen today are also listening to other kinds of behavior specialists. It's a less wacky world than 20 years ago perhaps, but more weird.

Admen seek trustworthy predictions on how we the con- 2
sumers are going to react to their efforts. Years ago they learned
that we may lie politely when discussing ads or products, so,
increasingly, the advertising world has turned to our bodies for
clues to our real feelings.

Take our eyes. There is one computerized machine that 3
tracks their movement as they examine a printed ad. This spots
the elements in the ad that have the most "stopping power."
For overall reactions to an ad or commercial, some admen have
been trying the pupillometer, a machine that measures the
pupil under stimulation.

The pupil expands when there is arousal of interest, 4
although this can lead to mistaken conclusions. A marketer of
frozen french fries was pleased by reports of significant dilation
during its TV ad. But further analysis indicated that it was the
sizzling steak in the ad, not the french fries, that was causing
the dilation. What's more, the pupillometer cannot tell whether
a viewer likes or dislikes an ad. (We are also aroused by ads
that annoy us.) This caused some of its users to become
disgruntled, but others stick with it as at least helpful. Arousal
is *something*. Without it the admen are inevitably wasting
money.

There are also machines that offer voice-pitch analysis. 5
First, our normal voices are taped and then our voices while
commenting on an ad or product. A computer reports whether
we are offering lip service, a polite lie or a firm opinion.

In the testing of two commercials with children in them, 6
other kids' comments seemed about equally approving. The
mechanical detective, however, reported that one of the commercials simply interested the kids, whereas the other packed
an emotional wallop that they found hard to articulate.

Viewing rooms are used to try out commercials and pro- 7
grams on off-the-street people. Viewers push buttons to
indicate how interested or bored they are.

One technique for gauging ad impact is to measure brain 8
waves with electrodes. If a person is really interested in
something, his brain emits fast beta waves. If he is in a passive,
relaxed state, his brain emits the much slower alpha waves. An
airline has used brain-wave testing to choose its commercial
spokesman. Networks have used the test to check out actors
and specific scenes in pilot films that need a sponsor.

Admen also seek to sharpen their word power to move 9
us to action. Some have turned to psycholinguistics—the deep-
down meaning of words—and to a specialty called psychographic segmentation.

A few years ago Colgate-Palmolive was eager to launch a 10
new soap. Now, for most people, the promise of cleanliness
ranks low as a compelling reason for buying soap. It's assumed.
So soap makers promise not only cleanliness but one of two gut
appeals—physical attractiveness (a tuning up of complexion)
or a deodorant (a pleasant smell).

Colgate-Palmolive turned to psychographic segmentation 11
to find a position within the "deodorant" end of the soap field.
The segmenters found a psychological type they called
Independents—the ambitious, forceful, self-assured types with

a positive outlook on life, mainly men, who like to take cold showers.

Their big need, over and above cleanliness, was a sense of refreshment. What kind of imagery could offer refreshment? Colgate researchers thought of spring and of greenery and that led them to think of Ireland, which has a nationally advertised image epitomizing cool, misty, outdoor greenery. 12

So the Colgate people hired a rugged, self-assured male with a bit of a brogue as spokesman and concocted a soap with green and white striations. The bar was packaged in a manly green-against-black wrapper (the black had come out of psychological research), and they hailed it as Irish Spring— now a big success in the soap field. 13

Advertising people have long fretted about not being able to say much in a 15- or 30-second commercial. So they experimented with faster talking. Typically, when you run a recorded message at speeds significantly faster than normal you get Donald Duck quackery. But psychologists working with electronic specialists came up with a computerized time-compression device that creates a normal-sounding voice even when the recording is speeded up by 40 percent. Research has also indicated that listeners actually preferred messages at faster-than-normal speed and remembered them better. 14

Meanwhile, at one of the world's largest advertising agencies, J. Walter Thompson, technicians forecast that by 1990 many TV messages will be coming at us in three-second bursts, combining words, symbols and other imagery. The messages will be almost subliminal. 15

The subliminal approach is to get messages to us beneath our level of awareness. It can be a voice too low for us to hear consciously. It can be a message flashed on a screen too rapidly for us to notice, or a filmed message shown continuously but dimly. It can even be a word such as SEX embedded in the pictures of printed ads. 16

Subliminal seduction has been banned by most broadcasters, but nothing prevents its use in stores, movies and salesrooms. Several dozen department stores use it to reduce shoplifting. Such messages as "I am honest, I will not steal" are mixed with background music and continually repeated. One East Coast retail chain reported a one-third drop in theft in a nine-month period. 17

The sale of imagery and symbols continues to fascinate admen. In one experiment, 200 women were questioned, ostensibly about color schemes in furniture design. For their co-operation the women were given a supply of cold cream. They were to take home and try out two samples. When they came back for their next advice-giving session, they would be given an ample supply of the cold cream of their choice. 18

Both sample jars were labeled "high-quality cold cream." The cap of one jar had a design with two triangles on it. The cap of the other jar had two circles. The cold cream inside the jars was identical, yet 80 percent of the women asked for the one with the circle design on the cap. They liked the consistency of that cream better. They found it easier to apply and definitely of finer quality. All because, it seems, women prefer circles to triangles. 19

The use of sexuality in the media has become standard. 20
Interestingly, a research report stated that women now are
more aroused by nudity in ads than men. This may account for
one twist recently employed by admen. In 1980, a highly successful campaign for men's Jockey-brand underwear was aimed
at women, based on the finding that women often buy clothing
for their mates.

For this campaign the star was the handsome pitcher of 21
the Baltimore Orioles, Jim Palmer. In the ads he was nude
except for the snug-fitting Jockey briefs. Sales soared—as did
Palmer's female fan mail.

Today, as when I first reported on persuasion techniques 22
in advertising, our hidden needs are still very much on admen's
minds. One need that has grown greatly in two decades—
perhaps because of all the moving and the breaking up of
families—is warm human contact.

The American Telephone and Telegraph Company used 23
this need to generate more long-distance calls. Historically,
such calls were associated with accidents, death in the family
and other stressful situations. AT&T wanted long-distance calling to become casual spur-of-the-moment fun. Hence the
jingle, "Reach out, reach out and touch someone," played
against various scenes filled with good friendship.

Then there was a manufacturer of hay balers who sought 24
more farmers to buy his machine. Psychologist Ernest Dichter,
an old master at persuasion, came up with a technique based
on the theory that instant reward is better in creating a sense
of achievement than long-delayed reward—in this case a check
for the hay two months later.

Dichter recommended attaching a rear-view mirror and a 25
bell to the baler. Every time a bundle of hay was assembled as
the machine moved across a hayfield, the farmer could see it
in the mirror. And when the bale dropped onto the field the
bell rang. Thus the reward was not only instant but visual and
audible. Farmers loved it. And so did the manufacturer, who
started ringing up the hay-baler sales.

COMPREHENSION

1. This article is mainly about
   a. how the advertising industry judges the impact of an ad
   b. how to write ads
   c. how machines contribute to advertising technology
   d. subliminal seduction
2. A pupillometer is a machine that
   a. measures arousal
   b. shows whether a viewer likes or dislikes an advertisement
   c. tracks eye movement
   d. measures the pupil under stimulation
3. The impact of an ad can be judged by
   a. observing the audience in a viewing room
   b. measuring brain waves
   c. measuring the degree of viewers' ego involvement
   d. analyzing a viewer's linguistic patterns

4. The subliminal approach
   a. consists of three-second bursts of words and symbols
   b. always uses sex
   c. has been banned in all forms of advertisement
   d. gets ideas to us in such a way that we are not aware we are receiving the message
5. According to the article, in the future we can expect commercials to
   a. contain more blatant sexual images
   b. become shorter
   c. contain more subliminal messages
   d. use more color and light appeal

VOCABULARY

Directions: *The meaning of the following terms from selection 10 cannot be clearly determined from the context. Using the dictionary entries, select the appropriate definition of the term as it is used in the reading selection.*

1. demographers (par. 1)
   a. people who research birth
   b. people who research marriages
   c. people who research vital statistics
   d. people who research death

de·mog·ra·phy (di mog′rə fē), *n.* the science of vital and social statistics, as of the births, deaths, marriages, etc., of populations. —**de·mog′ra·pher,** *n.* —**de·mo·graph·ic** (dē′-mə graf′ik, dem′ə-), *adj.* —**de′mo·graph′i·cal·ly,** *adv.*

2. gauging (par. 8)
   a. extending
   b. determining
   c. marking
   d. conforming

gauge (gāj), *v.,* **gauged, gaug·ing,** *n.* —*v.t.* **1.** to appraise, estimate, or judge. **2.** to determine the exact dimensions, capacity, quantity, or force of; measure. **3.** to make conformable to a standard. **4.** to mark or measure off; delineate. **5.** to chip or rub (bricks or stones) to a uniform size or shape. —*n.* **6.** a standard of measure or measurement; dimension, size, or quantity. **7.** any device for measuring or testing something, esp. for measuring a dimension, quantity, or mechanical accuracy. **8.** a means of estimating or judging; criterion. **9.** extent; scope; capacity. **10.** *Ordn.* a unit of measure of the internal diameter of a shotgun barrel, determined by the number of spherical lead bullets of a diameter equal to that of the bore that are required to make one pound. **11.** *Railroads.* the distance between the inner edges of the heads of the rails in a track, usually 4 feet 8½ inches (**standard gauge**), but sometimes more (**broad gauge**) and sometimes less (**narrow gauge**). **12.** the distance between a pair of wheels on an axle. **13.** the thickness or diameter of various, usually thin, objects, as sheet metal or wire. **14.** the fineness of a knitted fabric as expressed in loops per every 1½ inch: *15-denier, 60-gauge stockings.* **15.** *Naut.* the position of one vessel as being to the windward or to the leeward of another on an approximately parallel course. Also, *esp. in technical use,* **gage.** [ME < ONF (F *jauge*) < Gmc] —**gauge′a·ble,** *adj.* —**gauge′a·bly,** *adv.*

3. segmentation (par. 11)
   a. cell division
   b. subdivision of an organism
   c. division into parts
   d. equivalent parts

seg·men·ta·tion (seg′mən tā′shən), *n.* **1.** division into segments. **2.** *Biol.* **a.** the subdivision of an organism or of an organ into more or less equivalent parts **b.** cell division.

4. seduction (par. 17)
   a. sexual
   b. act
   c. means
   d. enticement

se·duc·tion (si duk′shən), *n.* **1.** the act or an instance of seducing, esp. sexually. **2.** the condition of being seduced. **3.** a means of seducing; enticement. Also, **se·duce·ment** (si-dōōs′mənt, -dyōōs′-). [< L *sēductiōn-* (s. of *sēductiō*) a leading aside = *sēduct(us)* (ptp. of *sēdūcere* to SEDUCE) + *-iōn--ION*]

5. ostensibly (par. 18)
   a. apparently
   b. clearly
   c. conspicuously
   d. obviously

os·ten·si·ble (o sten′sə bəl), *adj.* **1.** given out or outwardly appearing as such; professed; pretended. **2.** apparent; conspicuous: *the ostensible truth of his theories.* [< F < L *ostens(us)* displayed (see OSTENTATION) + F *-ible -IBLE*] —**os·ten′si·bil′i·ty,** *n.* —**os·ten′si·bly,** *adv.*

DISCUSSION

1. What makes your favorite commercial successful?
2. Consider the possible outcome of subliminal persuasion. Do you think its effects are harmful or not?

3.   Think of a product that you could improve to make it more appealing to people. Would the improvement be in the product or the packaging?

Difficulty level: C

11. What You See Is the Real You

Willard Gaylin

It was, I believe, the distinguished Nebraska financier Father Edward J. Flanagan[1] who professed to having "never met a bad boy." Having, myself, met a remarkable number of bad boys, it might seem that either our experiences were drastically different or we were using the word "bad" differently. I suspect neither is true but rather that the Father was appraising the "inner man," while I, in fact, do not acknowledge the existence of inner people.

Since we psychoanalysts have unwittingly contributed to this confusion, let one, at least, attempt a small rectifying effort. Psychoanalytic data—which should be viewed as supplementary information—is, unfortunately, often viewed as alternative (and superior) explanation. This has led to the prevalent tendency to think of the "inner" man as the real man and the outer man as an illusion or pretender.

While psychoanalysis supplies us with an incredibly useful tool for explaining the motives and purposes underlying human behavior, most of this has little bearing on the moral nature of that behavior.

Like roentgenology, psychoanalysis is a fascinating, but relatively new, means of illuminating the person. But few of us are prepared to substitute an X-ray of Grandfather's head for the portrait that hangs in the parlor. The inside of the man represents another view, not a truer one. A man may not always be what he appears to be, but what he appears to be is always a significant part of what he is. A man is the sum total of *all* his behavior. To probe for unconscious determinants of behavior and then define *him* in their terms exclusively, ignoring his overt behavior altogether, is a greater distortion than ignoring the unconscious completely.

Kurt Vonnegut[2] has said, "You are what you pretend to be," which is simply another way of saying, you are what we (all of us) perceive you to be, not what you think you are.

Consider for a moment the case of the 90-year-old man on his deathbed[3] (surely the Talmud must deal with this?) joyous and relieved over the success of his deception. For 90 years he has shielded his evil nature from public observation. For 90 years he has affected courtesy, kindness, and generosity—

[1](1886–1948), founder of Boys' Town orphanage near Omaha, Nebraska.
[2]American novelist, author of *Cat's Cradle* (1963); *God Bless You, Mr. Rosewater* (1964); *Slaughterhouse-Five* (1969); and *Breakfast of Champions* (1973).
[3]Book of orthodox Jewish civil and religious law.

suppressing all the malice he knew was within him while he calculatedly and artificially substituted grace and charity. All his life he had been fooling the world into believing he was a good man. This "evil" man will, I predict, be welcomed into the Kingdom of Heaven.

Similarly, I will not be told that the young man who earns   7
his pocket money by mugging old ladies is "really" a good boy. Even my generous and expansive definition of goodness will not accommodate that particular form of self-advancement.

It does not count that beneath the rough exterior he has a   8
heart—or, for that matter, an entire innards—of purest gold, locked away from human perception. You are for the most part what you seem to be, not what you would wish to be, nor, indeed, what you believe yourself to be.

Spare me, therefore, your good intentions, your inner   9
sensitivities, your unarticulated and unexpressed love. And spare me also those tedious psychohistories which—by exposing the goodness inside the bad man, and the evil in the good—invariably establish a vulgar and perverse egalitarianism, as if the arrangement of what is outside and what is inside makes no moral difference.

Saint Francis may, in his unconscious, indeed have been   10
compensating for, and denying, destructive, unconscious Oedipal impulses identical to those which Attila projected and acted on. But the similarity of the unconscious constellations in the two men matters precious little, if it does not distinguish between them.

I do not care to learn that Hitler's heart was in the right   11
place. A knowledge of the unconscious life of the man may be an adjunct to understanding his behavior. It is *not* a substitute for his behavior in describing him.

The inner man is a fantasy. If it helps you to identify with   12
one, by all means, do so; preserve it, cherish it, embrace it, but do not present it to others for evaluation or consideration, for excuse or exculpation, or, for that matter, for punishment or disapproval.

Like any fantasy, it serves your purposes alone. It has no   13
standing in the real world which we share with each other. Those character traits, those attitudes, that behavior—that strange and alien stuff sticking out all over you—*that's the real you!*

COMPREHENSION

1. The main idea in this article is that
   a. a person's unconscious determines his personality
   b. a person is not really what he appears to be
   c. a person can pretend to be someone else
   d. a person's behavior reflects what he is
2. Father Flanagan claimed
   a. he never met a good boy
   b. he never met a bad boy
   c. that inner man did not exist
   d. that only outward action is important

3. Psychoanalytic data should be viewed as
   a. alternative explanation
   b. supplementary information
   c. superior explanation
   d. an illusion
4. The 90-year-old man on his deathbed
   a. was an evil man all his life
   b. behaved as a courteous, kind, and generous man only when he was with other courteous people
   c. deceived himself
   d. thought he was evil but behaved as a good man
5. The author's point of view is that
   a. character traits, attitudes, and behavior reflect the real person
   b. there is good in evil
   c. psychoanalysis is a waste of time
   d. Saint Francis and Attila were the same kind of person

VOCABULARY

Directions: *The meaning of the following terms from selection 11 cannot be clearly determined from the context. Using the dictionary entries, select the appropriate definition of the term as it is used in the reading selection.*

1. financier (par. 1)
   a. business transaction
   b. financial corporation
   c. a person skilled in financial operations
   d. a person engaged in public service

   fin·an·cier (fin′ən sēr′, fī′nən-; *Brit.* fi nan′sē ər), *n.* **1.** a person who is skilled in or engaged in financial operations, whether public, corporate, or individual. —*v.t.* **2.** to finance. —*v.i.* **3.** to act as a financier. [< F]

2. rectifying (par. 2)
   a. calculating
   b. putting right
   c. changing
   d. purifying

   rec·ti·fy (rek′tə fī′), *v.t.*, **-fied, -fy·ing. 1.** to make, put, or set right; remedy; correct. **2.** to put right by adjustment or calculation. **3.** *Chem.* to purify (esp. a spirit or liquor) by repeated distillation. **4.** *Elect.* to change (an alternating current) into a direct current. **5.** to determine the length of (a curve). **6.** *Astron., Geog.* to adjust (a globe) for the solution of any proposed problem.

3. supplementary (par. 2)
   a. additional
   b. unknown
   c. deficient
   d. correct

   sup·ple·ment (*n.* sup′lə mənt; *v.* sup′lə ment′), *n.* **1.** something added to complete a thing, supply a deficiency, or reinforce or extend a whole. **2.** a part added to a book, document, etc., to supply additional or later information, correct errors, or the like. **3.** an additional part of a newspaper or other periodical. **4.** *Math.* the quantity by which an angle or an arc falls short of 180° or a semicircle. —*v.t.* **5.** to complete, add to, or extend by a supplement; form a supplement or addition to. **6.** to supply (a deficiency). [ME < L *supplēment(um)* that by which anything is made full = *sup-* SUP- + *plē-* (s. of *plēre* to fill) + *-mentum* -MENT] —**sup′ple·men·ta′tion,** *n.* —**sup′ple·ment′er,** *n.* —**Syn. 1.** reinforcement, extension, addition. **2.** addendum, postscript. **5.** See **complement.**
   sup·ple·men·tal (sup′lə men′t³l), *adj.* supplementary (def. 1). —**sup′ple·men′tal·ly,** *adv.*
   sup·ple·men·ta·ry (sup′lə men′tə rē), *adj., n., pl.* **-ries.** —*adj.* **1.** of the nature of or forming a supplement; additional. —*n.* **2.** a person or thing that is supplementary.

4. roentgenology (par. 4)
   a. medical branch
   b. diagnosis and therapy by X-rays
   c. study of X-rays
   d. reading of X-rays

   roent·gen·ol·o·gy (rent′gə nol′ə jē, -jə-, runt′-), *n.* the branch of medicine dealing with diagnosis and therapy through x-rays. —**roent·gen·o·log·ic** (rent′gə nᵊloj′ik, -jə-, runt′-), **roent′gen·o·log′i·cal,** *adj.* —**roent′gen·ol′o·gist,** *n.*

5. overt (par. 4)
   a. concealed
   b. open to view
   c. private
   d. hostility

   o·vert (ō vûrt′, ō′vûrt), *adj.* open to view or knowledge; not concealed or secret: *overt hostility.* [ME < OF, ptp. of *ouvrir* to open < VL *ōperīre,* var. of L *aperīre*] —**o·vert′ly,** *adv.*

6. vulgar (par. 9)
   a. lewd
   b. ordinary
   c. obscene
   d. current

   vul·gar (vul′gər), *adj.* **1.** characterized by ignorance of or lack of good breeding or taste; unrefined; crude. **2.** indecent; obscene; lewd. **3.** of, pertaining to, or constituting the ordinary people in a society: *the vulgar masses.* **4.** current; popular; common: *a vulgar success.* **5.** spoken by, or being in the language spoken by, the people generally; vernacular: *a vulgar translation of the Greek text of the New Testament.* —*n.* **6.** *Archaic.* the common people. **7.** *Obs.* the vernacular. [late ME < L *vulgār(is)* = *vulg(us)* the general public + *-āris* -AR¹] —**vul′gar·ly,** *adv.* —**vul′gar·ness,** *n.* —**Syn. 1.** inelegant, low. See **common. 5.** colloquial.

7. perverse (par. 9)
   a. a cranky mood
   b. persistent
   c. wicked
   d. contrary

per·verse (pər vûrs´), *adj.* **1.** willfully determined not to do what is expected or desired; contrary. **2.** characterized by or proceeding from such a determination: *a perverse mood.* **3.** petulant; cranky. **4.** persistent or obstinate in what is wrong. **5.** turned away from what is right, good, or proper; wicked. [ME *perverse* < L *pervers(us)* askew, orig. ptp. of *pervertere*. See PERVERT] —per·verse´ly, *adv.*, —per·verse´ness, *n.* —**Syn. 1.** contumacious, disobedient. **4.** stubborn, headstrong. See **willful. 5.** evil, bad, sinful. —**Ant. 1.** agreeable. **4.** tractable.

8. egalitarianism (par. 9)
   a. belief in equality
      of all men
   b. belief in asserting
      one's rights
   c. person who believes
      in self-assertion
   d. person who believes
      in equality

e·gal·i·tar·i·an (i gal´i târ´ē ən), *adj.* **1.** asserting, resulting from, or characterized by belief in the equality of all men. —*n.* **2.** a person who adheres to egalitarian beliefs. [alter. of EQUALITARIAN with F *égal* r. EQUAL] —**e·gal´i·tar´i·an·ism,** *n.*
é·ga·li·té (ā gA lē tā´), *n. French.* equality.

9. exculpation (par. 12)
   a. freeing from blame
   b. blaming
   c. fraud
   d. freeing from fraud

ex·cul·pate (ek´skul pāt´, ik skul´pāt), *v.t.*, **-pat·ed, -pat·ing.** to clear from a charge of guilt or fault; free from blame; vindicate. [< L *exculpāt(us)* freed from blame = *ex-* EX-¹ + *culpātus* blamed (ptp. of *culpāre;* see CULPABLE)] —**ex·cul·pa·ble** (ik skul´pə bəl), *adj.* —**ex´cul·pa´tion,** *n.*

DISCUSSION

1. Gaylin says that the inner man is a fantasy. What is your point of view?

2. The author quotes Kurt Vonnegut as saying, ". . . you are what we (all of us) perceive you to be, not what you think you are." If this is true, how does it affect your attitudes about yourself?

3. What is the confusion that Gaylin says psychoanalysts have contributed to? What is the danger of this confusion?

Difficulty level: C

12. The Unique Human Time Sense

Samuel A. Goudsmit and R. Claiborne

1   Man's puzzlement and preoccupation with time both derive ultimately from his unique relationship to it. All animals exist in time and are changed by it; only man can manipulate it.

2   Like Proust, the French author whose experiences became his literary capital, man can recapture the past. He can also summon up things to come, displaying imagination and foresight along with memory. It can be argued, indeed, that memory and foresightedness are the essence of intelligence; that man's ability to manipulate time, to employ both past and future as guides to present action, is what makes him human.

3   To be sure, many animals can react to time after a fashion. A rat can learn to press a lever that will, after a delay of some 25 seconds, reward it with a bit of food. But if the delay stretches beyond 30 seconds, the animal is stumped. It can no

LIFE-SCIENCE LIBRARY/Time, by Samuel A. Goudsmit, Robert Claiborne, and the Editors of Life. Time-Life Books Inc. Publisher. ©1966 Time, Inc.

longer associate reward so "far" in the future with present lever-pressing.

Monkeys, more intelligent than rats, are better able to deal with time. If one of them is allowed to see food being hidden under one of two cups, it can pick out the right cup even after 90 seconds have passed. But after that time interval, the monkey's hunt for the food is no better than chance predicts.

With the apes, man's nearest cousins, "time sense" takes a big step forward. Even under laboratory conditions, quite different from those they encounter in the wild, apes sometimes show remarkable ability to manipulate the present to obtain a future goal. A chimpanzee, for example, can learn to stack four boxes, one atop the other, as a platform from which it can reach a hanging banana. Chimpanzees, indeed, carry their ability to cope with the future to the threshold of human capacity: they can make tools. And it is by the making of tools—physical tools as crude as a stone chopper, mental tools as subtle as a mathematical equation—that man characteristically prepares for future contingencies.

Chimpanzees in the wild have been seen to strip a twig of its leaves to make a probe for extracting termites from their hole. Significantly, however, the ape does not make this tool *before* setting out on a termite hunt, but only when it actually sees the insects or their nest. Here, as with the banana and the crates, the ape can deal only with a future that is immediate and visible—and thus halfway into the present.

When the small-brained ape-man *Australopithecus* began to make tools, some two million years ago, his first crude stone choppers, like the chimpanzee's stripped twig, may have been improvised to meet an immediate and visible future. Before long, however, he evolved to the point where he began carrying his improvisations about with him. A piece of shaped quartz, unearthed several miles from the nearest quartz deposit, shows that its maker possessed at least enough foresight to hold on to a rock that he had taken the trouble to batter into a useful shape.

With bigger brains came greater foresight. More than 400,000 years ago, submen in China used fire. And the regular use of fire, as the anthropologist F. Clark Howell says, implies men "provident enough to keep supplies of fuel on hand and skillful enough to keep fires going."

Certainly by this time, and probably much earlier, man had developed his most remarkable tool, and one which revolutionized his relationship to time: language. Words are not simply means of communication; many beasts and birds communicate. Words are the best tools for "moving" things in time. To name a thing or an action is to call it to mind, to summon it up, from past or future. (Even today, to "speak of the Devil" is to invite his presence!) With the aid of words, man could mull over past time and plan for future time with new precision. (Try deciding what you are going to have for dinner without naming things.) He could instruct his sons at leisure on how to meet the charge of some future mammoth or wild ox, instead of having to reserve his gestured or grunted warnings for the moment of peril.

COMPREHENSION

1. This article is about
   a. how apes understand time relationships
   b. man's preoccupation with past and future events
   c. how man's time sense separates him from animals
   d. time sense in animals

2. The author states that
   a. monkeys and apes are almost as intelligent as man
   b. memory and foresight contribute to intelligence
   c. man developed from apes
   d. man's brain is larger than it used to be

3. The tool that changed man's relationship to time was
   a. fire
   b. hunting equipment
   c. language
   d. stone choppers

4. It is significant that chimpanzees make tools, but it is more important that
   a. the tools are crude
   b. they stack items to make platforms
   c. they can make up simple equations
   d. they never make tools before they need them

5. From the clause "Like Proust, the French author whose experiences became his literary capital, man can recapture the past," you can tell that Proust
   a. wrote about past experiences
   b. described man's development of time sense
   c. discovered things about the future by reliving the past
   d. wrote primarily to improve his future life

VOCABULARY

Directions: *The meaning of the following terms from selection 12 cannot be clearly determined from the context. Using the dictionary entries, select the appropriate definition of the term as it is used in the reading selection.*

1. contingencies (par. 5)
   a. events that may occur
   b. incidental thought
   c. dependent conditions
   d. uncertainties

   con·tin·gen·cy (kən-tĭn′jən-sē) *n., pl.* **-cies. 1. a.** An event that may occur but that is not likely or intended; a possibility. **b.** A possibility that must be prepared against; future emergency. **2.** The condition of being dependent upon chance; uncertainty; fortuitousness. **3.** Something incidental to something else.

2. improvised (par. 7)
   a. executed
   b. recited without preparation
   c. invented from available materials
   d. provided

   im·pro·vise (ĭm′prə-vīz′) *v.* **-vised, -vising, -vises.** —*tr.* **1.** To invent, compose, or recite without preparation. **2.** To make or provide from available materials. —*intr.* To invent, compose, recite, or execute something offhand. [French *improviser*, from Italian *improvvisare*, from *improvviso*, unforeseen, impromptu, from Latin *imprōvīsus*, : *in-*, not + *prōvīsus*, past participle of *prōvidēre*, to foresee, PROVIDE.] —**im′pro·vis′er** *n.*

3. provident (par. 8)
   a. frugal
   b. able to look ahead
   c. economical
   d. eventful

prov·i·dent (prŏv′ə-dənt, -dĕnt′) *adj.* **1.** Providing for future needs or events. **2.** Frugal; economical. [Middle English, from Latin *prōvidēns,* present participle of *prōvidēre,* to foresee, PROVIDE.] —**prov′i·dent·ly** *adv.*

4. gestured (par. 9)
   a. use of body movement
      to express meaning
   b. offering a sign
      of friendship
   c. emphasizing speech
   d. giving directive
      language

ges·ture (jĕs′chər) *n.* **1.** A motion of the limbs or body made to express or help express thought or to emphasize speech. **2.** The act of moving the limbs or body as an expression of thought or emphasis. **3.** Any act or expression made as a sign, often formal, of intention or attitude; especially, a sign of friendship or good intentions. —*v.* **gestured. -turing, -tures.** —*intr.* To make gestures. —*tr.* To show, express, or direct by gestures. [Medieval Latin *gestūra,* bearing, carriage, from Latin *gestus,* past participle of *gerere,* to carry, act. See **gerere** in Appendix.*] —**ges′tur·er** *n.*

DISCUSSION

1. In discussing the time sense of apes the authors state that an "ape can deal with a future that is immediate and visible and halfway into the present." Where does the past end and when does the present begin? When does the present end and the future begin?
2. When you recall an incident in the past does the recall depend on language? Can you recall an incident without using language?
3. Not all languages handle time in the same way. Many languages have a wide variety of tenses to show how time is organized, whereas others may have only a few tenses. If you had no way of expressing the past through verb tense, how might your thinking differ from the way it is now?

Unit Three
Paragraph Structure

You probably *cannot* recall hearing a conversation such as the following:

> *HE:*   "I think I'll call in sick for work tonight."
> *SHE:* "I saw a car accident on the way home."
> *HE:*   "My history instructor does not review assigned chapters."
> *SHE:* "There's a big sale on camping equipment at K-Mart this week."

This is a very unlikely conversation because each person is discussing separate, unrelated ideas; neither person is communicating with the other.

Similarly, you probably cannot recall reading sentences such as the following, grouped together to form a paragraph.

> The price of new cars is unbelievable. Only two-income families can afford to buy a new car. Children are neglected when both parents work full-time. Often grandparents take over care of the children.

These sentences are not a paragraph because they do not all relate to one topic.

You can see then that ideas, whether spoken or written, are usually arranged together in meaningful, related groupings called paragraphs. In most of your reading you will find related sentences grouped together in paragraphs; and in your writing you will need to relate ideas and to group them into paragraph form.

However, paragraphs are more than just related ideas grouped together. They have a specific structure, and they are organized in a particular way. Most paragraphs contain three essential elements: a topic, a main idea, and details, and in reading, recognizing these three elements will help you to better understand most paragraphs. In writing, organizing your ideas so that each paragraph clearly presents these three elements will strengthen the presentation of your ideas. This unit provides you with techniques for identifying these paragraph elements in reading and procedures for organizing these elements in your writing.

6. Focusing the Topic

The topic of a paragraph is one of three essential elements that make up a paragraph. Basically the topic is the one person, place, or idea that is discussed throughout the paragraph. When reading you should be able to identify the topic of each paragraph. When writing you must focus the topic to make it clear and understandable to your reader. That is, the topic must be narrowed and developed throughout the paragraph. The first part of this chapter will present techniques for identifying the topic of a paragraph. In the second part of this chapter you will learn the steps to follow in focusing a topic in writing, and you will learn how to avoid common problems in focusing a topic.

IDENTIFYING THE TOPIC

The *topic* of a paragraph is a specific idea that is discussed throughout the whole paragraph. Every sentence in the paragraph relates to this topic. In the following paragraph, for example, all the sentences tell you more about newspaper advertising.

> Newspaper advertising has a number of advantages. First, it reaches large numbers of people within one area. Second, it can be accomplished rapidly. An ad can be placed and run within a two- to three-day period. Finally, newspaper advertising is less expensive than other forms.

Notice that each sentence refers to newspaper advertising and gives you more information about it.

Here is another example. As you read this paragraph, notice what each of the sentences is about.

> Another natural reaction to unmet needs is anger. You may become angry when you are afraid of something or somebody, when someone or something frustrates you, when you feel insecure in your ability to deal with a situation. You may get angry when you feel rejected. You may feel anger when you face indecision, either in yourself or in another person, because you would prefer a clear-cut situation. Tension, conflict, disappointment, or lack of respect from other people can all trigger anger.[1]

You should have noticed that each sentence in the paragraph discusses anger. Each sentence presents a cause of anger and contributes to the discussion of the paragraph's general topic—anger.

Every paragraph has a topic and is limited to that one general topic. The following group of sentences is not a paragraph because the sentences do not refer to one idea. Instead, each sentence could be viewed as a statement about a specific topic that could be developed into a paragraph if other sentences were added.

Alcohol is the most commonly used drug on the college campus. Some students receive financial aid, whereas others must hold part-time jobs. Most colleges have a bookstore on campus.

Among these sentences several items are mentioned: alcohol use, financial aid, and college bookstores. Each sentence has something to do with college, but it is unclear what all the sentences have to do with each other. There is nothing that connects or relates the ideas to one another. There is no topic.

General versus Specific

To help you identify topics in paragraphs, you will find it useful to distinguish "general" terms and ideas from "specific" terms and ideas. A general idea or term is one that is broad or applies to every member of a group or class. A specific idea or term is more detailed or particular. For example, the word "car" is a general term, whereas Chevrolet, Ford, and Buick are more specific terms. "Buick Skylark" is an even more specific term. Here are a few more examples to consider:

GENERAL: Clothing
SPECIFIC: hats
mittens
shirts
dresses

GENERAL: Soup
SPECIFIC: onion
split pea
chicken noodle

GENERAL: Bread
SPECIFIC: rye
whole wheat
pumpernickel

GENERAL: People
SPECIFIC: man
woman
child

GENERAL: States
SPECIFIC: Oregon
California
Nevada

You will notice that the items listed under the heading "specific" are types or kinds or examples of the general terms. The terms hats, mittens, shirts, and dresses are specific because these items are all types of clothing. The term "clothing" is general because it is a label for this list of articles.

Each specific item on the list can be made even more specific. In the fourth example, for instance, the word "man" could be made more specific by using the following terms: bachelor, widower, father, or grandfather. The term "child" could be narrowed to girl, boy, toddler, etc.

Here are a few more examples of general terms or ideas and their more specific parts. Notice that these examples are concerned with parts, ideas, concepts, or procedures rather than objects.

GENERAL: Parts of plants
SPECIFIC: stem
leaves
flowers

GENERAL: Memory techniques
SPECIFIC: focus your attention
select what is important
organize the information

GENERAL: How stars differ
SPECIFIC: in color
in temperature
in distance from earth

Each of these specific examples can also be made more specific. In the first example, the term "flower" could be further divided into petals, stamen, nectar.

EXERCISE 6-1

Directions: *For each grouping of general and specific topics, fill in the missing word(s) in the blank provided.*

EXAMPLE: General: Writing instruments
Specific: pen
pencil

Crayon

magic marker

1. General: Cakes
Specific: chocolate
coconut

_____

_____

2. General: _____

Specific: apples
grapefruit
lemons
pears

3. *General:* Alcoholic beverages

    Specific: _____

    _____

    _____

    _____

4. *General:* Parts of an automobile

    Specific: _____

    _____

    _____

5. *General:* _____

    Specific: racquetball
    baseball
    golf

6. *General:* _____

    Specific: love
    fear
    hate

7. *General:* Musical groups

    Specific: _____

    _____

    _____

8. *General:* Differences among people

    Specific: _____

    _____

    _____

9. *General:* _____

    Specific: poetry
    sculpture
    ballet
    drama

10. *General:* Conformity

    Specific: _____

    _____

    _____

11. *General:* Reasons for divorce

    Specific: _____

    _____

    _____

12. *General:* How to choose a movie

    Specific: _____

    _____

    _____

EXERCISE 6–2

Directions: *In each group of words, underline the most general term.*

EXAMPLE: milk, beverage, Coke, beer, coffee

1. red, blue, green, color, purple
2. chair, sofa, coffee table, furniture, love seat
3. steak, pork chops, hamburger, meat
4. washer, household appliance, dryer, dishwasher
5. Honda, Toyota, car, Cutlass, Buick
6. inches, feet, distance, meters
7. sister, brother, relative, mother, father
8. TV, radio, newspaper, magazine, media
9. food, housing, transportation, living expenses, utilities
10. reading, watching TV, playing tennis, leisure time activities
11. geology, natural sciences, chemistry, physics
12. novels, poems, drama, literature, essays
13. basic needs, food, shelter, love, security
14. personality traits, aggressive, timid, authoritarian

General versus Specific Ideas within Paragraphs

Much of what we experience daily is organized according to a general-specific scheme. In a very ordinary context, an aisle in the grocery store might be labeled "snacks," and in that aisle you would expect to find potato chips, pretzels, and popcorn. In a more formal context, libraries are also organized in a general-specific scheme. One section of the library contains psychology books and in that area you would expect to find books on child psychology, adolescent psychology, social psychology, and experimental psychology.

Most paragraphs contain one general idea and a number of related specific ideas. The topic of the paragraph is the general idea, and the parts of the paragraph that tell you more about the topic are the specifics. Later these specifics will be referred to as details. The topic of a paragraph must be general, or broad enough, so that all the specifics in the paragraph can be related to it. In the following paragraph notice that the underlined words are general enough to cover all the other ideas expressed in the paragraph. Therefore, it is the topic of the paragraph and tells what the whole paragraph is about.

Many different <u>systems</u> are used for <u>filing</u> records. The three most common <u>systems</u> are alphabetical, numerical, and topical. An alphabetical filing <u>system</u> arranges information by names of persons or companies. Numerical arrangement records by an established numbering system, and topical filing records according to topics.

The ideas expressed in this paragraph can be diagrammed as follows:

GENERAL: Filing systems
SPECIFIC: alphabetical
numerical
topical

In general, the topic of a paragraph may be compared to a label or a title. The topic consists of a word or two that tells you what the paragraph is about. Just as the label on a can of soup tells you what kind of soup is inside, the topic of the paragraph tells you what is covered in the paragraph.

How to Find the Topic

The easiest way to find the topic of a paragraph is to ask yourself one of these questions:

What is the one object or concept this whole paragraph is about?

or

What is the one object or concept the author is discussing throughout this paragraph?

What you provide as an answer should be the topic of the paragraph. For example:

Deductible expenses are those the government allows taxpayers to deduct from their taxable income. A list of

deductible expenses is included in the tax instruction
booklet. Some examples of deductible expenses are
charitable contributions, medical expenses, and interest
payments. Taxpayers should keep a record of all deductible
expenses each year.

In that paragraph, the answer to the question "What is the one concept
the author is discussing throughout this paragraph?" is "deductible
expenses."

After you think you have found the topic of a paragraph, check to
see if you are correct by considering each sentence to be sure that it is
a specific comment about the topic you discovered. In the above
paragraph, for example, you can see that each idea in the paragraph
explains or tells more about deductible expenses. The following exercises
will give you an opportunity to practice identifying paragraph topics.

EXERCISE 6-3

Directions: *Read each paragraph. Then write the topic of the paragraph in
the space provided.*

1. A unique festival is now held each June in Santee, California. It
   features a long, colorful Saturday morning parade that starts
   from a shopping center and ends at the town's sewage treatment
   plant. For the remainder of the weekend, as many as ten thousand people celebrate the recent construction of five beautiful
   man-made lakes laid out in a line for the better part of a mile.
   At this "Festival of the Lakes," people fish, picnic, boat and
   swim, with little concern that nearly every drop of the water is
   supplied by Santee's municipal sewage system.[2]

   TOPIC: _____

2. It is always a queer shock, part a sudden upwelling of grief,
   part unaccountable amazement. It is simply astounding to see an
   animal dead on a highway. The outrage is more than just the
   location; it is the impropriety of such visible death, anywhere.
   You do not expect to see dead animals in the open. It is the
   nature of animals to die alone, off somewhere, hidden. It is
   wrong to see them lying out on the highway; it is wrong to see
   them anywhere.[3]

   TOPIC: _____

3. Prejudice against blacks was invisible to most white Americans
   for many years. When blacks finally started to "mention" it, with
   sit-ins, boycotts, and freedom rides, Americans were incredu-
   lous. "Who, us?" they asked in injured tones. "*We're* prejudiced?"
   It was the start of a long, painful reeducation for white America.
   It will take years for whites—including those who think of
   themselves as liberals—to discover and eliminate the racist attitudes they all actually have.[4]

   TOPIC: _____

4. The Picturephone is a new kind of telephone equipment—it lets you see the person you are talking to and he sees you. The Picturephone is rather expensive, but it may prove to be a valuable aid to business firms. Conferences and sales demonstrations can be conducted over the Picturephone. This, of course, will save a great deal of time and expense. The Picturephone is being introduced gradually—first in Pittsburgh, then in Chicago, Washington, Detroit, Cleveland, Newark, New York, and Philadelphia. In the beginning it will be available in business areas only, and calls can be made to other firms in the area.[5]

   TOPIC: _____

5. Greek mythology is largely made up of stories about gods and goddesses, but it must not be read as a kind of Greek Bible, an account of the Greek religion. According to the most modern idea, a real myth has nothing to do with religion. It is an explanation of something in nature; how, for instance, any and everything in the universe came into existence: men, animals, this or that tree or flower, the sun, the moon, the stars, storms, eruptions, earthquakes, all that is and all that happens. Thunder and lightning are caused when Zeus hurls his thunderbolt. A volcano erupts because a terrible creature is imprisoned in the mountain and every now and then struggles to get free. The Dipper, the constellation called also the Great Bear, does not set below the horizon because a goddess once was angry at it and decreed that it should never sink into the sea.[6]

   TOPIC: _____

6. Science fiction is an undefined term in the sense that there is no generally agreed-upon definition of it. To be sure, there are probably hundreds of individual definitions but that is as bad as none at all. Worse, perhaps, since one's own definition gets in the way of an understanding of the next man's viewpoint. Under the circumstances, I think it best to make a personal definition. I should stress that my own definition is not necessarily better than the next man's or more valid or more inclusive or more precise. It simply expresses my way of thinking.[7]

   TOPIC: _____

7. In addition to having developed language, man has also developed means of making, on clay tablets, bits of wood or stone, skins of animals, and paper, more or less permanent marks and scratches which *stand for* language. These marks enable him to communicate with people who are beyond the reach of his voice, both in space and in time. There is a long course of evolution from the marked trees that indicated Indian trails to the metropolitan daily newspaper, but they have this in common: They pass on what one individual has known to other individuals, for their convenience or, in the broadest sense, instruction. Many of the lopstick trails in the Canadian woods, marked by Indians long since dead, can be followed to this day. Archimedes is dead, but we still have his reports on what he

observed in his experiments in physics. Keats is dead, but he can still tell us how he felt on first reading Chapman's Homer. From our newspapers and radios we learn with great rapidity facts about the world we live in. From books and magazines we learn how hundreds of people whom we shall never be able to see have felt and thought. All this information is helpful to us at one time or another in throwing light on our own problems.[8]

TOPIC: _____

8. Most animals possess some kind of "signaling" communication system. Among the spiders there is a complex system for court-ship. The male spider, before he approaches his lady love, goes through elaborate gestures to inform her that he is indeed a spider and not a crumb or a fly to be eaten. These gestures are invariant. One never finds a "creative" spider changing or adding to the particular courtship ritual of his species.[9]

TOPIC: _____

9. Embedding refers generally to the practice of hiding emotionally loaded words or pictures in the backgrounds of ads. Embedded words and picture illusions are part of most advertising throughout North America today. These subliminal stimuli, though invisible to conscious perception, are perceived instantly at the unconscious level by virtually everyone who perceives them even for an instant![10]

TOPIC: _____

10. There are almost as many definitions of meditation as there are people meditating. It has been described as a 4th state of con-sciousness (neither waking, sleeping, nor dreaming); as a way to recharge one's inner batteries; as a state of passive awareness, of "no mind." Some teachers regard meditation as the complement to prayer: "Prayer is when you talk to God; meditation is when you listen to God." Meditation teaches the conscious mind to be still. The mind must learn to be still and listen, whether it listens to God, to the subconscious, or to an outside influence. Which of these one listens to depends on one's point of view and on which of the many forms of meditation one is attempting.[11]

TOPIC: _____

11. I believe, quite simply, that writing is our chief means, as indi-viduals, of discovering knowledge, and eventually of discovering values and what is valid. Reading, of course, takes us well into that territory, as do lectures and TV and films and talk and all the rest of our experience, raw and otherwise. But only by *realizing*—making real—our new ideas by writing them out do we really discover them fully and as our own. We discover what we know by writing it out, bringing up from our tumbling mists of thought and intuition, our perpetual daydreams, those con-cepts we hardly knew we had. On blank paper we shape thoughts from what we thought were our blank minds. We discover that we know something after all. Only on paper can

we hold those thoughts still, straighten them out, test them out. Like our inner dialogues, speech helps, of course, so we warm up our ideas with discussion. But only writing makes the full discovery of thought.[12]

TOPIC: _____

12. In the general run of human activity currently there seems to be a pervasive idea, adhered to by many but perhaps not really accepted, that given time and effort anyone can master anything of an intellectual nature. Thus, the concept of elitism in education has become almost obsolete. It has come to be associated with a high position in society, being better born, rich, and so on. The idea that one individual may be better endowed than another for a particular function or pursuit has remained respectable only in some less essential, although not less interesting, areas such as sports and entertainment.[13]

TOPIC: _____

EXERCISE 6–4

Directions: *Select one of the readings at the end of this unit. Read the selection, following these steps:*

1. *Prereading.* Preread the selection to become familiar with its overall content and organization.
2. *Establishing a Purpose for Reading.* Based on your prereading of the selection, write several questions you want to answer as you read. Write them in the space provided.

   _____

   _____

   _____

3. *Reading.* Read the selection, looking for the answer to your questions. Then reread the selection and, as you read, write the topic of each paragraph in the margin.
4. *Reviewing.* Go back through the selection, reading the parts that will help you to remember the important ideas presented in the selection.
5. *Reacting.* Think about and react to what you read. You will have an opportunity to express your ideas about this subject in the writing exercise at the end of this chapter.

FOCUSING YOUR TOPIC IN THE STAGES OF WRITING

To write effective paragraphs, you need to focus and develop each paragraph around a single topic or general idea. As you will see, focusing your topic is a procedure that continues throughout all the stages of writing, from prewriting to proofreading.

Prewriting: Narrow Your Topic

Suppose you decided to write a paragraph on part-time jobs. At the prewriting stage you would need to narrow your topic. There are many types of part-time jobs, and there are many things to consider when looking for part-time jobs. You could not possibly discuss all things about all part-time jobs in a single paragraph. Therefore, it would be necessary to narrow "part-time jobs" to a more manageable topic.

You could narrow your topic by breaking the topic into specifics; or, you could do a free-writing exercise, and from that exercise, select an idea, characteristic, or concern about part-time jobs that could be discussed in a single paragraph. A third approach would be to write questions about the topic of part-time jobs, then select one question that you could handle effectively in one paragraph.

Suppose you decided to use the questioning approach to narrow the topic. You might write questions like this:

TOPIC: Part-Time Jobs
QUESTIONS:
1. What are the best part-time jobs?
2. How many hours should I work?
3. Will references from part-time jobs help me get a job after college?
4. Does having a part-time job interfere with education?
5. How much money can I make before I have to pay a lot of taxes?
6. Is it better to get a work-study job?
7. What is the best way to find a part-time job?
8. Should I work all year or just summers?
9. How much loyalty should I have to a part-time employer?
10. Should I be honest and say that I only intend to work for the summer, or should I just not say anything about my plans for the fall?

Let's say that, after rereading the questions, you chose question 10.

Composing: Develop Your Topic

After you have narrowed the topic, the next step is to compose, or to begin developing ideas and statements that relate to your topic. On the topic of "Being Honest With Employers" a student wrote the following sentences.

How honest will an employer be with me? If I say I won't work after school starts, I probably won't get a job. I would hate to lie though. Especially if my parents knew the person. It must be easier in a big city than in a small town. Even so I guess it's not right. That's like saying it's okay to rip off someone you don't

179

know. If it's unskilled work and there's no training, maybe it doesn't matter. The problem is I have to get a job or I can't go to school. I didn't even get to vote and I'm being affected by budget cuts. I have to look out for myself. If there's no more work, the boss wouldn't worry about laying me off. I could always change my mind. So many people want jobs it wouldn't be hard to replace me. My buddy quit one part-time job for a better one, and the guy said he could work all year but then he laid him off after two months. Now he's out of a job. How fair is that? What are students supposed to do anyway?

You can see that the student was struggling with an issue involving his personal feelings. The sentences reveal his indecision. The student realized that his topic was not manageable because he did not really know how he felt about the issue. The student had several options; for example, he could have gone back to his questions and selected a different question to consider; he could have made a decision about what the right course of action is, or he could have looked for a point of departure to further expand. In this instance the student selected the last option and wrote more about how he felt.

There are a number of things to think about before you accept a part-time job. You have to think about your own needs, but you also have to think about the needs of the employer. If the job is just labor and there's no training involved, replacing a part-time worker isn't difficult. Also, if you are going away to school, you know you can't work in the fall. If you're not going away to school, then you might want to continue working through the year. Finally, if you are honest, you will probably be better off.

Notice that in the last sentence the student has made a decision. Sometimes writing involves investigation and decision making. It took the writer some time and effort to come to terms with his ideas about the topic, but once he knew what he wanted to write about, he no longer had to struggle with the topic. It took some time, but the student finally composed the following piece of writing on a revised topic: Look for a Part-Time Job that Will Suit Your Needs.

When you look for a part-time job, you have to know your own needs, and you have to know how much time you can give to the job. When you look for a part-time job, it is best to spend some time looking for jobs that fit your needs and the employer's needs. If you are going away to school, don't waste your time looking for jobs that require training. If you take the time to figure out what you can do and who needs what you have to offer, you can avoid problems for both yourself and your employer.

This paragraph differs considerably from the first attempt, and it still needs work. However, from this point the writing is at the stage of polishing rather than developing. Always reread what you have written in the composing stage and try to find a sentence that states the overall idea you want to express about your topic. This is the topic sentence. The topic sentence expresses the general most important idea that is discussed throughout the paragraph. If there is no single sentence that expresses the most important idea, then try to write one at this time.

Checking the Content and Organization

After composing your ideas on the topic you should reread your statements, eliminating those ideas which do not directly relate to the topic. Also, at this time you should add any additional statements you can think of that directly support your topic. In the following example, the same paragraph appears as it was finally written in the composing step. Notice that the order of the sentences has been changed, and additional sentences have been included.

If you take the time to investigate your own skills and find out which businesses need what you have to offer, you can avoid problems for both yourself and your potential employer. When you look for a part-time job, you have to know your own needs and you have to know how much time you intend to give to the job. If you're going away to school, don't waste time applying for jobs that require training. Jobs are difficult to find, but if you establish yourself as a dependable worker and obtain good references, finding your next job will not be so difficult.

Revising

Always reread and rewrite your paragraphs to improve their effectiveness. Notice how the following paragraph has been revised. Sentences have been added; sentences have been rewritten. The sentences appear in a different order, and different words and phrases have replaced previous wording.

As part of the revision process, be sure to read the paragraph to check that each sentence is related to the topic. Each sentence must directly explain or support the topic. Eliminate any ideas that do not directly relate to the topic. Notice that the writer shortened some statements to make his sentences more concise, after he had already made revisions. Revision should take place constantly in writing.

If you take the time to investegate your own skills and find out which businesses needs what you have to offer you can avoid problems for yourself and your potential employee. When you look for a part-time job you should know how much time you can give to the job. It your going away to school, don't waste an employer's time and money by applying for jobs that require training. Jobs are difficult to find, but if you establish yourself as a dependible worker, and obtain good character references, ~~your next job will be easier to find~~. employers will be more likely to hire you.

Proofreading

Reread the entire paragraph to check for errors in spelling, punctuation, and sentence structure. The writer circled errors that he caught during proofreading. He was unsure about punctuation errors and the use of so or as, but after reading the sentence aloud and checking with a friend, he made his corrections. Compare the final corrected copy and the copy that was proofread.

If you take the time to investegate your own skills and find out which businesses needs what you have to offer, you can avoid problems for yourself and your potential employee When you look for a part-time job,^(comma) you should know how much time you can give to the job. If ^(you're)~~your~~ going away to school, don't waste ^(an employer's) time and money by applying for jobs that require training. Jobs are difficult to find, but if you establish yourself as a depend^(a)ible worker, and obtain good ^(character)references, ~~your next job will be easier to find.~~ employers will be more likely to hire you.

Final Copy

If you take the time to investigate your own skills and find out which businesses need what you have to offer, you can avoid problems for yourself and your potential employer. When you look for a part-time job, you should know how much time you can give to the job. If you're going away to school, don't waste an employer's time and money by applying for jobs that require training. Jobs are difficult to find, but if you establish yourself as a dependable worker and obtain good character references, employers will be more likely to hire you.

COMMON PROBLEMS IN FOCUSING A TOPIC

As you narrow and focus a topic, there are some common problems that you might experience.

Straying from the Topic

Often, in writing a paragraph, one idea leads to another, and that idea leads to another, and so forth. Eventually you may end up with an idea that is related to one of your previous ideas but does not directly relate to the topic. The following paragraph illustrates the problem of straying from the topic. The writer's purpose in this paragraph is to explain how to get ready for a job interview.

There are several ways you can prepare for a job interview. First, you should learn about the company or business with whom you are interviewing. Find out as much as you can about how they operate, what they sell, how many branches they have, etc. Next, try to anticipate the kind of questions an interviewer might ask you and think about your answers. For example, you should know why you want to work for the company, what you can offer the company, and why you feel you deserve the job. When you answer, try to be positive about yourself. If you don't believe in yourself, no one else will either. Once my

sister applied for a job as a ticket agent. She had never
worked as a ticket agent before, but when she went for her
interview she told them she was sure she could handle the
job. She got the job.

In this paragraph you can notice that the one idea led to another and
the writer ended up describing something his or her sister did when he
or she really intended to list ways to prepare for a job interview. The last
two sentences, then, stray from the topic and should be taken out. The
last three sentences of the paragraph are not directly related to the
topic—preparation for a job interview. When the paragraph is revised,
these sentences which describe the sister's experience should be
eliminated. This sample paragraph is a good example of how a writer can
stray from the topic and include irrelevant information that does not
directly pertain to the topic.

A quick way to see if you have included irrelevant information is to
read each sentence separately, starting with the last sentence in the
paragraph. For each sentence decide whether the sentence directly explains, develops, or supports your topic.

Lack of Detail

A second major problem that often occurs in writing is the lack of
specific information that supports or continues an idea throughout a
paragraph. The result is a paragraph that does not clearly explain or focus
the topic in any particular direction. The following paragraph does not
have a focus because it lacks specifics. The writer of this paragraph
intended to discuss what he likes about college; however, he never really
explains his reasons for thinking that college is fun.

College is fun for a lot of reasons. You can really have
a good time in college. Your classes are a lot of work, but
you can have fun, too. It is not the same as in high school,
but you really can enjoy yourself in college.

To identify this type of problem, try outlining what you have written, using only a few words for each sentence. The resulting outline will
help you to realize if you haven't provided enough information or detail
to explain your idea. If you outlined the above paragraph, it might look
like this:

I.   Reasons why college is fun
      A. You can have a good time
      B. Classes are a lot of work
      C. Classes are not like high school
      D. You can enjoy yourself

By studying this outline you can see that more information is
needed. The writer does not say how you can have a good time, or how
college is different from high school, or why classes are a lot of work.
The writer's statement that classes are not like high school is not
developed either. You may wonder how the classes are different.

You might evaluate your outline of a paragraph by asking this question: Do the details in the outline answer the questions who? what?

when? where? how? or why? about the topic. If none of these questions are answered, you probably lack sufficient detail in your paragraph. At this point you might need to go back to the prewriting stage to generate additional ideas that could be used to develop the topic.

EXERCISE 6–5

Directions: *This exercise is intended to give you some practice in focusing the topic of a paragraph. Work through each of the steps listed below. Choose a reading selection from the end of this unit. Preread and read the selection. Write the title and subject of the reading here:*

TITLE: _____

SUBJECT: _____

1. *Prewriting.*
   a. Narrow the subject into three possible topics:

   _____

   _____

   _____

   b. Select one topic and use a five-minute free-writing exercise or write several questions that occur to you about the topic to generate ideas.

2. *Composing.* Select the most important ideas you see in your prewriting exercise. Develop these ideas into a paper consisting of an introduction, body, and conclusion. Include the details your reader will need in order to have a clear understanding of your purpose and message.

3. *Checking the Content and Organization.* Briefly outline the order of your ideas as they are written in each paragraph. Check to see that all ideas are related to the topic and that your paragraph includes specific information that develops and explains your topic. Answer the following questions:
   a. Which sentence in each paragraph best expresses the topic?
   b. Circle each detail that supports the topic.
   c. Do the details in each paragraph answer the questions who? what? where? how? or why? about the topic?
   d. Is the topic of each paragraph immediately apparent? Write the topic in the margin next to each paragraph. Do you need a stronger statement of the topic?

4. *Revising.* Reread your rough draft and cross out any sentences that do not support your topic. At this time, add any statements that are needed to explain your topic. Then continue with the revision process by checking the organization, the wording of sentences, terminology and presentation of ideas. Use the five questions on pages 26–27 to guide your revision.

5. *Proofreading.* Read your final copy looking closely for spelling and punctuation errors. Place a check on the proofreading checklist next to each item that you correct. Describe the errors you corrected in the column on the right.

PROOFREADING CHECKLIST

Essay Title _____

Date _____

TYPE	✔	ERROR	FREQUENCY	DESCRIPTION
GRAMMAR		Run-on Sentence Sentence Fragment Subject/Verb Agreement Verb Tense Pronoun Agreement		
MECHANICS		Capitalization Italics Abbreviation		
PUNCTUATION		, (Comma) ; (Semicolon) ' (Apostrophe) " (Quotation Marks) . (Period) ! (Exclamation Point) ? (Question Mark) : (Colon) — (Dash) ( ) (Parentheses) - (Hyphen)		

		ERROR	CORRECTION	
SPELLING ERRORS				

SUMMARY

In this chapter we discussed the *topic*—the first of three essential elements within a paragraph. When reading a paragraph think of the topic as the most general or the broadest idea within the paragraph. To identify the topic of a paragraph, a reader should ask, "What is the one object or concept the whole paragraph is about?" In composing a paragraph, a writer must clearly focus and develop the topic. All sentences in the paragraph must directly relate to and support this topic.

7. Developing the Main Idea

In the previous chapter you learned that the topic is one of the essential elements of a paragraph. In this chapter we will discuss the second important element of a paragraph—the main idea. First you will learn how to identify the main idea as you read, and you will see that, in many paragraphs, a single sentence expresses the main idea. Then you will learn how to express the main idea, and you will also learn where to place the sentence that expresses the main idea.

IDENTIFYING THE MAIN IDEA

The *main idea* of a paragraph makes the most important statement about the topic of the paragraph. Usually the topic sentence states this main idea. As you have seen, the topic of a paragraph is also its focus. The main idea, however, is what the author wants you to know about the topic or what he or she is telling you about the topic. For example, a topic of a paragraph might be "cross country skiing," but the main idea could be that "cross country skiing is safer than downhill skiing"; the main idea is the point the author wants to make about cross country skiing.

Here are some other simple examples of topics and main ideas. Reading through them will help you to understand the relationship between topic and main idea.

> *TOPIC:*   Plants
> *MAIN IDEA:* Plants require sufficient light and water to remain healthy.
>
> *TOPIC:*   Advertising
> *MAIN IDEA:* Advertising often misleads the buyer.
>
> *TOPIC:*   Violence
> *MAIN IDEA:* The increase in violence is frightening.

Basically, the topic of a paragraph can be stated as a noun—a person, place, thing, or concept—whereas the main idea is often stated as a sentence because it represents a complete thought.

Locating the Topic Sentence

The topic sentence directly states the main idea. To find this sentence ask yourself the following question:

What does the author want me to know about the topic?

As you read, look for a sentence that answers this question. In many cases, the subject in this sentence is the topic of the paragraph.

> *EXAMPLE:* Hypnosis can be used to eliminate bad habits and to control pain. Through hypnosis, a person can learn to control cigarette smoking, overeating, and various nervous habits. Some medical doctors use hypnosis instead of anesthetics for women during childbirth. Other doctors have found hypnosis to be effective in eliminating severe headaches.

The topic of this paragraph is hypnosis. Notice in this example that the question "What does the author want me to know about hypnosis?" leads you directly to the sentence that states the main idea. The first sentence answers this question and tells you what you should know about hypnosis. None of the other sentences in the paragraph contain enough information to answer your question.

To be sure that you have found the topic sentence of a paragraph, read over the remaining sentences and check that each sentence explains or tells you more about the main idea. If one or more sentences does not support your choice, then your choice is probably incorrect.

Placement of the Topic Sentence

The topic sentence may be placed anywhere in the paragraph. However, there are several positions in which topic sentences most frequently appear. As you will see when you begin to improve the organization of your own paragraphs, the position of the topic sentence is not left to chance. Rather, a writer plans carefully where in the paragraph the main idea will be stated. A writer's choice of the position of the topic sentence is determined by the method of development of ideas he or she wishes to employ. Here are the most common positions for the topic sentence:

Topic Sentence First

Usually the main idea is expressed first in the paragraph. In fact, in the style of writing used in many textbooks, the main idea is stated first about 80 percent of the time. The main idea is then explained in the remainder of the paragraph. Such paragraphs may be diagrammed as follows:

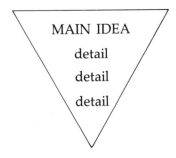

EXAMPLE: <u>A conscientious student, in order to study effectively, carefully organizes each study session before beginning to work</u>. First, the student deliberately selects a place to study where he or she can concentrate and work with a minimal number of distractions or interruptions. Then, before beginning to study, he or she collects all necessary materials, including pens, paper, texts, notebooks, and reference books. Next, the student outlines what needs to be studied and the order in which subjects will be studied. Finally, a time limit or goal is established for each activity.

Topic Sentence Last

The second most common position for the topic sentence is last in the paragraph. In a paragraph using this arrangement, the writer leads up to his idea throughout the paragraph and states it at the very end. Such a paragraph can be diagrammed as follows:

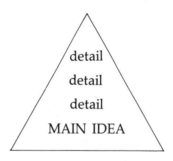

EXAMPLE: Before beginning to study, the conscientious student deliberately selects a place to study where he or she can concentrate and work with a minimal number of distractions or interruptions; and he or she collects all necessary materials, including pens, paper, texts, notebooks, and reference books. Then, the student outlines what needs to be studied and the order in which subjects will be studied. Finally, he or she establishes a time limit or goal for each activity. <u>As you can see, a conscientious student, in order to study effectively, carefully organizes each study session before beginning to study.</u>

Topic Sentence in the Middle

Occasionally, the main idea appears in the middle of a paragraph. In that case, the writer leads up to or introduces the main idea, states it, and then further explains or supports the idea. The details given before the main idea may introduce the idea, set the scene, connect the paragraph with a previous paragraph, or provide background information.

EXAMPLE: Before beginning to study, the conscientious student deliberately selects a place to study where he or she can concentrate and work with a minimal number of distractions or interruptions. Then, the student collects all necessary materials, including pens, paper, texts, notebooks, and reference books. As you are beginning to see, the conscientious student carefully organizes each study session before beginning. Also, the student outlines what needs to be studied and the order in which subjects will be studied. Finally, a time limit or goal is established for each activity.

Topic Sentence First and Last

Sometimes a writer will state his or her main idea, explain it, and then restate it at the end of the paragraph. Although the exact wording may differ, the first and last sentences convey essentially the same meaning. Writers often use this arrangement to emphasize an important idea or to restate an idea in a different way to help you understand it.

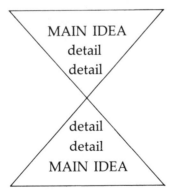

EXAMPLE: A conscientious student, in order to study effectively, carefully organizes each study session before beginning. First, the student deliberately selects a place to study where he or she can concentrate and work with a minimal number of distractions or interruptions. Then, before beginning to study, he or she collects all necessary materials, including pens, paper, texts, notebooks, and reference books. Next, the student outlines what needs to be studied and the order in which subjects will be studied. Finally, a time limit or goal is established for each activity. <u>Organization and planning are essential to effective study</u>.

You can see from these diagrams and examples that the topic sentence has four common positions within the paragraph. Although you will occasionally find some paragraphs that do not follow any of these methods of development, the majority will employ one of them.

EXERCISE 7–1

Directions: *Read each of the following paragraphs and underline the sentence that states the main idea.*

1. Friendship rests on accurate communication. We relate to each other by communicating how we feel and what we know. Communicating is not limited to talking; it involves both sending and receiving, and talking is but one form of sending. Facial expression, body posture, hands and legs, all send messages; often these nonverbal channels of communication are at least as important to understanding as the verbal channels.[1]

2. The schoolmaster was watching the two men climb toward him. One was on horseback, the other on foot. They had not yet tackled the abrupt rise leading to the schoolhouse built on the hillside. They were toiling onward, making slow progress in the snow, among the stones, on the vast expanse of the high, deserted plateau. From time to time the horse stumbled. Without hearing anything yet, he could see the breath issuing from the horse's nostrils. One of the men, at least, knew the region. They were following the trail although it had disappeared days ago under a layer of dirty white snow. The schoolmaster calculated that it would take them half an hour to get onto the hill. It was cold; he went back into the school to get a sweater.[2]

3. I am an invisible man. No, I am not a spook like those who haunted Edgar Allan Poe; nor am I one of your Hollywood-movie ectoplasms. I am a man of substance, of flesh and bone, fiber and liquids—and I might even be said to possess a mind. I am invisible, understand, simply because people refuse to see me. Like the bodiless heads you see sometimes in circus sideshows, it is as though I have been surrounded by mirrors of hard, distorting glass. When they approach me they see only my surroundings, themselves, or figments of their imagination— indeed, everything and anything except me.[3]

4. It was a dark autumn night. The old banker was walking up and down his study and remembering how, fifteen years before, he had given a party one autumn evening. There had been many clever men there, and there had been interesting conversations. Among other things they had talked of capital punishment. The majority of the guests, among whom were many journalists and intellectual men, disapproved of the death pen-

alty. They considered that form of punishment out of date, immoral, and unsuitable for Christian states. In the opinion of some of them the death penalty ought to be replaced everywhere by imprisonment for life.[4]

5. All languages change with time. It is fortunate for us that though languages change, they do so rather slowly compared to the human life span. It would be inconvenient to have to relearn our native language every twenty years. In the field of astronomy we find a similar situation. Because of the movement of individual stars, the stellar configurations we call constellations are continuously changing their shape. Fifty thousand years from now we would find it difficult to recognize Orion or the Big Dipper. But from year to year the changes are not noticeable. Linguistic change is also slow, in human if not astronomical terms. If a person were to turn on a radio and miraculously receive a broadcast in his "native language" from the year 3000, he would probably think he had tuned in some foreign language station. Yet from year to year, even from birth to grave, we hardly notice any change in our language at all.[5]

6. It was two years ago, on a beach near East Hampton, on Long Island, that I first heard the phrase with which so many of today's young adults consign those over 30 to the scrap heap of humanity. It was used by a long-limbed, graceful girl of perhaps 25 to a friend of mine, a youthful-looking, divorced man in his mid-40s. Their conversation had been roaming freely from black humor to foreign movies, discothèques and the risks and rewards of smoking marijuana. But despite mutual good will, they seemed unable to agree about any of these things, and finally she said, laughing, "Carl, you just don't understand. It's that same old problem—it's the generational gap." Carl guffawed and tried to look amused, but I saw dismay in his eyes; he had just been classified as obsolescent and hopelessly out of touch with "what's happening."[6]

7. Getting at the truth of "flying saucers" has been extraordinarily difficult because the subject automatically engenders such instantaneous reactions and passionate beliefs. Nearly all of my scientific colleagues, I regret to say, have scoffed at the reports of UFOs as so much balderdash, although this was a most unscientific reaction since virtually none of them had ever studied the evidence. Until recently my friends in the physical sciences wouldn't even discuss UFOs with me. The subject, in fact, rarely came up. My friends were obviously mystified as to how I, a scientist, could have gotten mixed up with "flying saucers" in the first place. It was a little as though I had been an opera singer who had suddenly taken it into his head to perform in a cabaret. It was all too embarrassing to bring up in polite conversation.[7]

8. Burger King Corporation offers both a service and a product to its customers. Its service is the convenience it offers the consumer—the location of its restaurants and its fast food service—in catering to his or her lifestyle. Its product, in essence, is *the total Burger King experience,* which starts from the time you drive into the restaurant's parking lot and ends when you drive out. It includes the speed of service, the food you order, the price you pay, the friendliness and courtesy you are shown, the intangible

feeling of satisfaction—in short, an experience. Burger King, then, is marketing a positive experience, as promised by its advertising and promotional efforts and delivered by its product.[8]

9. Art deals with the whole spectrum of human experience and the artist interprets and expresses these experiences in a distinctive manner. While the various arts vary in their characteristic subject matters because of the differences of media, they are alike in their basic objective. They are all preoccupied with interpreting human experience. The stimuli for such experiences are often varied due to sociocultural influences, but whatever, whenever, and wherever they occur, the artist seeks to re-create and interpret them for his fellow men.[9]

10. In trying to determine the boundaries of music periods, we observe that they rarely show decisive signs of their beginnings and endings. Certain monumental events or creations tend to accentuate the origins or high points, but generally the new style grows out of the old in a wavelike motion. That is, the main style gradually attains its peak and then slowly recedes, only to be replaced by a new wave representing a new creative ideal. Furthermore, the progression and recession of these style waves seem to be governed by the *Zeitgeist* (prevailing spirit) of the times.[10]

11. The current distinction between analytic and speculative philosophy can be traced to Socrates. He was analytic in that he distinguished clearly the meanings of terms and formulated carefully his definitions and assumptions; he was speculative in that he reflected upon the highest ends of moral conduct and attempted to relate the parts of experience within a larger coherent framework of meaning. A study of Socrates' life, methods, and beliefs (such as he admitted to) can therefore present to the beginning student the basic problems that must be grappled with as he or she strives toward a rationally and morally justifiable commitment.[11]

12. Regardless of the different experiences the respective partners bring to their wedding, the legal procedure for getting married remains the same. A couple must obtain a marriage license, signify their willingness to get married in a ceremony performed by someone legally permitted to do so, and have two witnesses of legal age verify the event. Following the ceremony, the couple, official, and witnesses must sign the marriage license. It is then sent, usually by the religious official or justice of the peace, to the state capital where it is recorded and filed.[12]

When the Main Idea Is Unstated

Occasionally you will find a paragraph in which the main idea is not directly stated in any one sentence. Instead, it is up to you, the reader, to infer (figure out) the main idea. Often it will be apparent but not directly stated, as in the following paragraph.

When buying a used car, be sure to check the mileage. Also check the condition of the body of the car. Inspect the tires and check to see that all accessories function properly.

Although there is no one sentence that directly states it, you know that the main idea of the paragraph is "There are several things you should check when buying a used car."

In the following paragraph the main idea is not directly stated.

> Belle Carpenter had a dark skin, grey eyes, and thick lips. She was tall and strong. When black thoughts visited her she grew angry and wished she were a man and could fight someone with her fists. She worked in the millinery shop kept by Mrs. Kate McHugh and during the day sat trimming hats by a window at the rear of the store. She was the daughter of Henry Carpenter, bookkeeper in the First National Bank of Winesburg, and lived with him in a gloomy old house far out at the end of Buckeye Street.[13]

The main idea of the paragraph is the description of Belle Carpenter. There is no sentence in the paragraph stating that this paragraph describes Belle Carpenter. The reader has to infer that the main idea here is the description.

Finding an Unstated Main Idea

If you ask yourself the question, "What does the author want me to know about the topic?" but you cannot find a single sentence that clearly answers your question, then you will know that it is up to you to figure out the main idea. You should then reread the paragraph with this question in mind:

What do all these facts or details say together?

For example, in the following paragraph, each sentence seems to offer a reason why cigarette smoking is harmful to your health.

> Cigarette smoking is related to lung cancer. A large number of deaths occur each year which are caused by lung cancer. Smoking can shorten your life span and make you more susceptible to other diseases. Smoking also causes excessive coughing and shortness of breath.

Each sentence gives a fact about cigarette smoking. Taken together, these facts suggest that smoking is harmful, which is the main idea in this paragraph. You can see that in determining the main idea of a paragraph when it is not directly stated, you must use your sense of logic and decide what each sentence has in common about the topic of the paragraph. Then you can create your own topic sentence in your mind.

EXERCISE 7–2

Directions: *None of the following paragraphs contains a sentence that directly states the main idea of the paragraph. Read each paragraph and then, in the space provided, write what you consider to be the main idea of the paragraph.*

1. I want a wife who will take care of my physical needs. I want a wife who will keep my house clean. A wife who will pick up after me. I want a wife who will keep my clothes clean, ironed,

mended, replaced when need be, and who will see to it that my personal things are kept in their proper place so that I can find what I need the minute I need it. I want a wife who cooks the meals, a wife who is a good cook. I want a wife who will plan the menus, do the necessary grocery shopping, prepare the meals, serve them pleasantly, and then do the cleaning up while I do my studying. I want a wife who will care for me when I am sick and sympathize with my pain and loss of time from school. I want a wife to go along when our family takes a vacation so that someone can continue to care for me and my children when I need a rest and change of scene.[14]

MAIN IDEA: _____

2. When shopping, remember that larger, rougher, dark-skinned Florida avocados are usually better-behaved houseplants than the smaller California variety. Any kind of avocado will sprout and give forth leaves, however, if you allow it to germinate and plant it in decent soil. Sometimes roots start to sprout even before you get the pit out of the fruit. If so, wash the pit in warm water and proceed. If not, either peel it or just leave it in a warm place for a day or so until the skin dries up and falls off.[15]

MAIN IDEA: _____

3. Crowded with strollers on summer evenings, the broad promenade that fronts the gaudy palaces in the World of Fun and Frivolity is deserted, and dirty drifted snow lies in the sheltered niches. Across the boulevard where a milk truck scurries to more lucrative fields lies the sea and miles of empty beach on which thousands come to bask and bathe in summer. The empty lifeguard towers look out to sea; their boats are gone; no human being in sight. The wind and the waves alone are moving and the only sound is the sea.[16]

MAIN IDEA: _____

4. According to Judeo-Christian beliefs, God gave Adam the power to name all things. Similar beliefs are found throughout the world. According to the Egyptians, the creator of speech was the god Thoth. According to the Babylonians, the language giver was the god Nabû. According to the Hindus, we owe our unique language ability to a female god; Brahma was the creator of the universe, but language was given to man by his wife, Sarasvati.[17]

MAIN IDEA: _____

5. Aging paints every action gray, lies heavy on every movement, imprisons every thought. It governs each decision with a ruthless and single-minded perversity. To age is to learn the feeling of no longer growing, of struggling to do old tasks, to remember familiar actions. The cells of the brain are destroyed with thousands of unfelt tiny strokes, little pockets of clotted blood wiping out memories and abilities without warning. The body

seems slowly to give up, randomly stopping, sometimes starting again as if to torture and tease with the memory of lost strength. Hands become clumsy, frail transparencies, held together with knotted blue veins.[18]

MAIN IDEA: _____

6. Although you may be at a proper distance from a piece of sculpture, you may not be in a right relationship or perspective to enjoy it. Or, if you are straining your neck to see a movie, you may not experience an aesthetic response to the film. When visiting the seashore while suffering an allergy, you may not appreciate the beauty of the experience. Or if you try to study a poem while you have a raging headache, you may not appreciate the literary or aesthetic value of the poem.

MAIN IDEA: _____

7. Twenty research papers are submitted in one freshman composition section; nine are plagiarized. A sharp-eyed history professor, disheartened by yearly bumper crops of plagiarists, gives up on the term paper: "I even have graduate students do annotated bibliographies now." Another professor in the social sciences retains papers, but with cynical fatalism: "Plagiarism? Sure, there's lots of it, but I'm busy and try not to look too closely." An allegedly original English paper is submitted bearing a fresh top-sheet over the unaltered text of a roommate's year-old paper, unaltered even to the roommate's name and the original instructor's comments and grade.[19]

MAIN IDEA: _____

8. One theory of drama states that drama appeals to an audience because it offers an entertaining or engaging story. The play holds the spectators' attention and takes their minds away from the daily problems that surround them. Another theory insists that the appeal of drama relates to man's desire to witness and become emotionally involved with the dramatization of the characters' trials and victories. The dramatic experience has also been interpreted as spiritual. That is, tragedy can evoke a catharsis, or a feeling of cleansing or purging of base, mean, or immoral feelings.

MAIN IDEA: _____

9. Later in the afternoon the sun went down with a riotous swirl of gold and varying blues and scarlets, and left the dry, rustling night of Western summer. Dexter watched from the veranda of the Golf Club, watched the even overlap of the waters in the little wind, silver molasses under the harvest moon. Then the moon held a finger to her lips and the lake became a clear pool, pale and quiet. Dexter put on his bathing suit and swam out to the farthest raft, where he stretched dripping on the wet canvas of the springboard.[20]

MAIN IDEA: _____

EXERCISE 7–3

Directions: *Select one of the reading selections included at the end of this unit. Read the selection, following these steps:*

1. *Prereading.* Preread the selection to become familiar with its overall content and organization.
2. *Establishing a Purpose for Reading.* Using your prereading of the selection, make up several questions you want to answer as you read. Write them in the space provided.

_____

_____

_____

3. *Reading.* Read the selection, looking for the answers to your questions. Then reread the selection and, as you read, underline the sentence that expresses the main idea of each paragraph. If the main idea is unstated, write your own statement of the main idea.
4. *Reviewing.* Go back through the selection, reading the parts that will help you to remember the important ideas presented in the selection.
5. *Reacting.* Think about and react to what you read. You will have an opportunity to express your ideas about this subject in the writing exercise at the end of this chapter.

DEVELOPING THE MAIN IDEA

You have seen how locating the main idea in a topic sentence can make reading paragraphs easier. Now you are ready to learn to write a main idea in a sentence that will make the paragraphs you write clearer and easier to read.

You might not consciously sit down and think, "Now I will write the sentence that will express the main idea in this paragraph." However, you should have a purpose in mind while you are writing your ideas in sentences. When writing the first draft of a paragraph, you do not have to decide exactly how to arrange your ideas, but each paragraph you write should contain a sentence that makes the most important or most general statement about the topic of the paragraph.

Many instructors and writers refer to this sentence as a topic sentence. However, as a reader you know that not all paragraphs have topic sentences. There are some paragraphs in which you cannot find a particular sentence that expresses the main idea; instead, the reader comes to realize what the main idea is by considering all the ideas in the paragraph. Although it is certainly not necessary to have a topic sentence in every paragraph, your writing will be clearer and easier to read if you write paragraphs that have topic sentences, at least until you become more experienced with the various methods of paragraph development.

How to State the Topic Sentence

The purpose of the topic sentence is to help your reader understand what the paragraph is about. It should announce your main idea and focus your reader's attention on it, and it should provide some clues about your attitude or feelings about the topic. To write an effective topic sentence, keep the following guidelines in mind.

1. State your idea in a direct, straightforward manner. A fairly short, simple sentence is often effective, and the main idea should be the subject of the sentence. For example, "Forest fires are an annual threat in California." Notice that forest fires is the subject, and an attitude about forest fires is expressed by the word "threat." You know, then, that the writer has a negative attitude about forest fires and will probably explain that they are destructive. Also, because of the word "annual," you could expect the writer to discuss conditions that make forest fires possible every year. Then, the addition of "in California" limits the discussion further because only forest fires in California will be discussed.

2. Try not to include explanatory information in the topic sentence; usually it detracts from the main idea and draws the reader's attention away.

    > *EXAMPLE:* Forest fires are an annual threat in California because of the dry winds, often called the Santa Annas, that blow across the desert into fertile areas that need rain.

    This sentence contains too much information to be an effective topic sentence. The reader could expect several discussions—for example, a discussion of the Santa Anna winds, the effects of drought, or even cycles in the weather. The sentence could easily distract a reader. Let the paragraph, rather than the topic sentence, provide the details.

3. Be sure that it is broad enough to include all the details you want to include in the paragraph. An effective topic sentence is written so that the rest of the paragraph explains, or supports the main idea.

4. Be specific enough that your reader knows what the paragraph will discuss. Look at the following examples.

    > *TOO LITTLE DETAIL:* Forest fires are an annual threat.

    > *TOO MUCH DETAIL:* Forest fires are an annual threat in California because of the dry winds, often called the Santa Annas, that blow across the desert into fertile areas that need rain.

    > *ADEQUATE DETAIL:* Forest fires are an annual threat in many parts of California.

Notice that the addition of "many parts" makes this statement more specific than the sentence you saw earlier. "Many" is a qualifying word; it places some restrictions on the statement. Qualifying words, such as few, several, sometimes, usually, often, and some are often used to make it clear to the reader that the discussion is true in a limited context. In other words, the statement does not apply in every situation.

Stating Main Ideas in Paragraphs

You can state a main idea anywhere in the paragraph. However, there are four most common positions for the main idea. It may be placed first, last, in the middle, or first and last. These positions can be diagrammed as follows:

1. *Main Idea First*

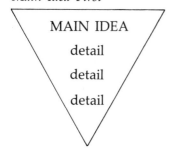

2. *Main Idea Last*

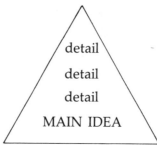

3. *Main Idea in the Middle*

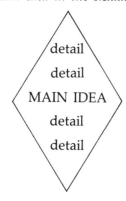

4. *Main Idea First and Last*

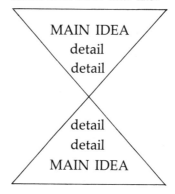

Where to Place the Main Idea

Although, strictly speaking, it is possible to place the topic anywhere in the paragraph, usually the context in which the paragraph occurs should be considered in deciding where to place it. If, for example, a paragraph will stand alone, as it might if it is an answer on an essay exam, the last pattern of organization, the main idea stated first and then restated at the end, might be best. This structure would enable your reader to view the paragraph as having a beginning, middle, and end, and the main idea would be emphasized. However, if the paragraph is part of a large piece of writing, then you will need to consider the structure and context of what came before a particular paragraph and what will follow it. For instance, if a previous paragraph ended with an example, you may not want to start the next paragraph with another example or detail. In this situation, then, you might consider placing the topic sentence first, so that it signals the beginning of a new thought and separates the examples and details from one another.

Your purpose for writing and the audience you are writing for are also important in determining the placement of the topic sentence. Various paragraph arrangements produce different effects that depend, in part, on the placement of the main idea. Some effects created by each of the common placements are described here:

1. *Main Idea First.* When the main idea is stated in the first sentence, it announces what the paragraph will be about. This pattern provides the reader with the most guidance and structure. The reader knows what idea is being explained and is able to follow the thought pattern easily. If you want to produce very direct, clear explanations this arrangement is effective.

2. *Main Idea Last.* When the main idea is stated at the end of the paragraph, it requires the reader to use different skills than when it is stated first. The reader is not told what the paragraph is about until he or she has nearly finished reading it. The reader must follow the train of thought with less guidance and direction.

    You might place the main idea last when you want to lead the reader step by step through a thought process or line of reasoning. Or, you might state the main idea last when you want to build up to a conclusion or general statement. Finally, when you want to summarize ideas already stated, you might place the topic sentence last.

3. *Main Idea in the Middle.* In some paragraphs you may wish to begin by setting a scene, providing some background information, or connecting the main idea with ideas expressed in previous paragraphs. In these instances, then, the topic sentence would appear in the middle of the paragraph, and details and explanation would follow.

4. *The Main Idea First and Last.* Stating the main idea twice, once in the beginning and again at the end of a paragraph, is an effective way of emphasizing an important idea. You can also use this pattern when you want to restate your idea in a different way to ensure that your reader will understand. Restating the idea at the end also results in "fixing" the idea in the reader's mind, encouraging retention.

EXERCISE 7–4

Directions: *This exercise is intended to give you some experience in stating main ideas. Choose a reading selection from the end of this unit. Preread, then read the selection. Write the title and subject of the reading here:*

TITLE: _____

SUBJECT: _____

1. *Prewriting.*
    a. Narrow the subject into three possible topics:

    _____

    _____

    _____

b. Select one topic and use a five-minute free-writing exercise or write several questions that occur to you about the topic to generate ideas.

2. *Composing.* Select the most important ideas you see in your prewriting exercise. Develop these ideas into a paper consisting of an introduction, body, and conclusion. Include the details your reader will need in order to have a clear understanding of your purpose and message.

3. *Checking the Content and Organization.* Outline each paragraph, showing the relationship between the main idea and the details in the paragraphs. Write the following symbols next to each paragraph to show where the main idea is stated:

(Refer to page 200 if you have forgotten what the drawings represent.) Now, look carefully at your outline and your rough draft. Do you need to change the placement of the main idea in any of the paragraphs?

4. *Revising.* Use the questions on pages 26–27 to help you revise your paper. Rewrite any of the paragraphs where the main idea needed better placement. Look closely at the sentences containing main ideas. Answer the following questions.
   a. Is the sentence structure correct?
   b. Could you expand or combine any sentences to make them more effective?
   c. How appropriate is the terminology?
   d. Are the words specific or general?
   e. Can you combine any of the sentences that contain details? Make all the necessary changes, then write your final copy, making further changes as you write, if necessary.

5. *Proofreading.* Read your final copy looking closely for spelling and punctuation errors. Place a check on the proofreading checklist next to each item that you correct. Describe the errors you corrected in the column on the right.

SUMMARY

In this chapter we discussed the main idea, the most general statement of what the entire paragraph is about. The main idea expresses what the writer wants the reader to know about the topic. It is usually expressed in one sentence, called the topic sentence. The topic sentence can be placed in various positions within a paragraph. Its placement produces differing effects.

PROOFREADING CHECKLIST

Essay Title _____

Date _____

TYPE	✔	ERROR	FREQUENCY	DESCRIPTION
GRAMMAR		Run-on Sentence Sentence Fragment Subject/Verb Agreement Verb Tense Pronoun Agreement		
MECHANICS		Capitalization Italics Abbreviation		
PUNCTUATION		, (Comma) ; (Semicolon) ' (Apostrophe) " (Quotation Marks) . (Period) ! (Exclamation Point) ? (Question Mark) : (Colon) — (Dash) ( ) (Parentheses) - (Hyphen)		
SPELLING ERRORS		ERROR	CORRECTION	

8. Using Supporting Details

In previous chapters in this unit you have learned how the topic and main idea express the broad, general thought that an entire paragraph is about. This chapter will discuss the third element of the paragraph—the details that explain, prove, or support the main idea. First you will learn how to identify supporting details and how to distinguish between more and less important details. Then you will see how to use supporting details to develop and explain your main ideas. You will also discover how outlining can be used to help you organize your ideas and include sufficient details to support your main idea.

IDENTIFYING SUPPORTING DETAILS

Sometimes, when reading certain paragraphs, you can become confused by all the facts and details that they contain; a large number of details can prevent you from "seeing" the most important ideas contained in a paragraph. Similarly, in reading textbooks, you may become so concerned with remembering every piece of information in every paragraph that you lose sight of the larger ideas contained in a chapter.

To be able to recall everything you read is nearly impossible, and few college instructors expect you to do so on the first reading. Instead, you should identify and try to remember only the most important details. Specifically, you should concentrate on those ideas which directly explain or prove the main idea. These ideas or details are called *supporting details.*

Supporting details include all the facts and ideas in a paragraph that explain the main idea; each tells you more about the main idea. There are many types of details: facts, examples, explanations, definitions, proof, evidence, and descriptions can all be used to support the main idea. You will learn more about these types of details and their relationships to main ideas in Chapter 9.

In order to identify supporting details, you must first know the topic and locate the main idea; then you can identify supporting details by asking yourself a simple question:

How does the author prove or explain the main idea?

or

What does the author say to prove or explain the main idea?

Your answer will lead you directly to the important supporting details in the paragraph. For example, in the following paragraph, the topic is physical dependence. The main idea is expressed in the first sentence. To find the supporting details you would ask, "How does the author explain physical dependence?"

Physical dependence is what was formerly called addiction. It is characterized by tolerance and withdrawal. Tolerance means that more and more of the drug must be taken to achieve the same effect, as use continues. Withdrawal means that if use is discontinued, the person experiences various unpleasant symptoms. When I quit smoking cigarettes, for example, I went through about five days of irritability, depression, and restlessness. Withdrawal from heroin and other narcotics is much more painful, involving violent cramps, vomiting, diarrhea, and other symptoms that continue for at least two or three days. With some drugs, especially barbiturates, cold-turkey (sudden and total) quitting can result in death, so severe is the withdrawal.[1]

And, in this paragraph, the answer to your question is:

Physical dependence is characterized by tolerance and withdrawal.

You can see other pieces of information that are also important such as:

1. Tolerance means that over a length of time more and more of the same drug is needed to achieve the same effect.
2. Withdrawal means that if someone stops taking a drug, that person will experience unpleasant symptoms.

Both of these facts contribute to the overall meaning of the paragraph by clarifying and further explaining the main idea.

However, this paragraph also contains other facts that do not directly explain the main idea. Rather, they further explain one or more of the supporting details. These are often called *secondary details*. For example, the fact that the writer quit smoking cigarettes for five days and experienced irritability only indirectly supports the main idea, but it is useful because it further explains what withdrawal means.

To further clarify the concept of supporting details and secondary details, read the following paragraph. The main idea is stated in the first sentence, in italics. The supporting details are marked with a double line; the secondary details that explain one of the supporting details are marked with a single line.

Conformity may be defined as the attempt to maintain a standard set by a group. When a child wears sneakers without laces to school because his friends all wear sneakers without laces, the child is conforming. It should be emphasized that conformity is voluntary. That is, it is something one chooses to do. Speaking English, for example, is not conformity because few of us have any choice. But using the same type of notebook as everyone else in the class is conformity.

<u>Degree of conformity varies from group to group</u>. <u>Children
in a swim club may have a higher degree of conformity
than employees in a particular department store</u>.

In this paragraph the topic is conformity. The writer's main idea is
that conformity means attempting to maintain a standard set by a group.
The rest of the paragraph explains and provides examples of conformity.
The writer presents two important, additional facts about conformity:
that it is voluntary and that it varies in degree from group to group. The
other sentences in the paragraph are of secondary importance. They provide examples of the more important supporting details in the paragraph,
or they restate the important supporting details.

As you read paragraphs, be sure to pay more attention to supporting
details than to secondary details. You should try to remember *how* the
author explains the main idea. However, in all but unusual circumstances, it is not necessary to remember all the additional facts or
secondary details the author includes to explain the supporting details.

Relating Supporting Details to the Topic

A useful way to fully understand the function of supporting details
in a paragraph is to refer to the concept of general versus specific that
was presented in Chapter 5. You will recall that topics are broad, general
items and that specifics are smaller, individual pieces of a larger category.
One of the same examples used earlier is repeated here:

GENERAL: States
SPECIFIC: Oregon
California
Nevada

In a paragraph, the main idea works as a general statement, whereas the
supporting details can be seen as specific statements. Now, read the
following paragraph:

Retirement usually means an abrupt change in lifestyle.
For some it is an unhappy switch from activity to boredom.
The daily routine of a job is destroyed, and the retired person is left with excess leisure time. For others retirement
means the loss of freedom and independence. Retirees feel
restricted physically, socially, and financially.

In this paragraph the topic is retirement, and the main idea is "retirement
means an abrupt change in lifestyle." The rest of the paragraph tells you
more about the changes that occur. You could divide the ideas presented
in this paragraph into general and specific as follows:

GENERAL: Changes in lifestyle
SPECIFIC: change from activity to boredom
loss of independence

You can see, then, that the supporting details in a paragraph function as
specifics, or parts, that prove or explain the main idea of the paragraph.

Outlining the Supporting Details

Outlining, or listing the ideas presented in the paragraph in brief form, is an effective way to be sure that you have understood the ideas expressed in the paragraph and that you see the relationships among them. Outlining is also an effective way to help you remember what you read, and it can be a good starting point for preparing summary sheets to use when you review for an exam. A formal outline normally uses Roman numerals, capital letters, and numbers in an arrangement like this:

I.
   A.
      1.
      2.
   B.
      1.
      2.

However, when outlining for the purposes of understanding the organization of a paragraph, it is not necessary to follow this formal structure. Instead you should try to make a working outline—one that simply shows the relationships among ideas in the paragraph.

To outline a paragraph express each idea in as few words as possible. Try to use your own words rather than the writer's exact words and phrases. Use a separate line for each idea and use a system of indentation that will show the relative importance of the major ideas included in the outline. The main idea should be farthest toward the left margin, supporting details should be indented a few spaces, and secondary details, if included, should be indented even further. Unless you are required to remember every detail in a reading assignment, you may omit secondary details. An outline might look like this:

MAIN IDEA
   Supporting Detail
      Secondary Detail
   Supporting Detail
   Supporting Detail

For example, the paragraph on conformity above might be outlined as follows:

MAIN IDEA: Conformity—doing what others in a group do.

SUPPORTING DETAIL: Conformity is done by choice.

SUPPORTING DETAIL: Amount of conformity is different for different groups.

Outlining helps you to understand and remember what you read in several ways. First, knowing that you will have to outline the ideas forces you to direct your concentration toward your reading. Second, the outline is a summary or list of important information contained in the paragraph. Third, the outline is a useful study aid because often it saves you the time and effort involved in rereading each paragraph.

EXERCISE 8–1

Directions: *The following numbered sentences are main ideas. Each is followed by a number of details. Check off those details which directly support or explain the main idea.*

1. Employment agencies can help you learn how to find a job.

   _____ Some employment agencies offer tips on how to handle a job interview.

   _____ Most employment agencies charge a fee for their services.

   _____ Many agencies have counselors that help you to prepare a resume.

   _____ Other agencies may show you how to dress when applying for a job.

2. Not all electric typewriters are efficient and easy to use.

   _____ Some typewriters have a crowded keyboard.

   _____ For one brand of typewriter it takes ten minutes to change the ribbon.

   _____ Some typewriters are sold without a carrying case.

   _____ Some typewriters do not have features for correcting errors.

3. Television has become an important educational tool.

   _____ Many schools have TVs permanently installed in the classrooms.

   _____ Many programs have been developed which provide new and updated information on current subjects.

   _____ Commercials sometimes interrupt the learning process.

   _____ Teachers need to learn how to use television more effectively.

4. Every college student should own a dictionary.

   _____ A dictionary is useful for checking the spelling of words.

   _____ Dictionaries can tell you how to pronounce words.

   _____ Hardbound dictionaries contain more words than paperback versions.

   _____ Some dictionaries index slang words; others do not.

5. Magazine advertising can be more effective than newspaper advertising.

_____ Magazines have a wider distribution and circulation than newspapers.

_____ Magazines can use colored print and other graphic aids.

_____ Newspapers are read by thousands of people each day.

_____ Magazine advertising is more expensive than any other form.

6. The instructor acted nervous and ill at ease.

_____ As he spoke, the instructor paced back and forth across the room.

_____ As he picked up his notes, his hands shook slightly.

_____ He seemed to be staring at the women seated in the back row.

_____ Frequently, he grasped for a word or mixed up two words.

7. The quality and content of a book are not the only factors that determine whether a book becomes a best seller.

_____ The amount of publicity a book receives influences its sales.

_____ A book written by a well-known author has a better chance of becoming a best seller than a book by an unknown writer.

_____ The amount of time and effort spent by the author in verifying the factual content of a book influences sales.

_____ The timing of the advance publicity and the actual release date of the book affects sales.

8. Stamp collecting has become a form of financial investment.

_____ During 1979, U.S. stamp values had achieved a growth rate of 23 percent.

_____ Competition for higher quality stamps will drive prices even higher.

_____ Some companies offer to help you build a rare stamp investment portfolio.

_____ Each stamp purchased from a dealer is accompanied by a certificate of authenticity.

9. From infancy to adulthood women demonstrate superiority in verbal and linguistic functions.

   _____ Men achieve highly on tests that measure arithmetic reasoning.

   _____ Women learn foreign languages much more rapidly and accurately than men.

   _____ Girls begin to talk earlier than boys and learn to speak in sentences earlier than boys.

   _____ Women have fewer reading difficulties and disabilities than boys.

10. Reading speed should vary according to the reader's purpose and the difficulty of the material.

    _____ Complicated scientific material should be read more slowly than a newspaper article.

    _____ The average speed for most college students and adults is 250 words per minute.

    _____ Textbook chapters in which high comprehension and retention are required should be read faster than a murder mystery.

    _____ An essay that contains long, difficult sentences should be read at the same speed as a letter from a friend.

11. Jobs for college graduates are plentiful in technical fields and business areas but prospects are bleak for the liberal arts areas.

    _____ Job openings in the fields of accounting and computers are up as much as 16 percent over last year.

    _____ There is too little career counseling provided too late to students making career decisions.

    _____ Competition for jobs in journalism and sociology is aggressive and frantic.

    _____ For every ten job applicants in the liberal arts field, there is one job opening.

12. Vandalism in public schools is becoming a financial problem of growing proportions.

    _____ A school in Detroit reported $10,000 damage per year to a particular school facility.

    _____ Vandalism is caused by students' lack of respect for public property.

_____ The Board of Education in a midwestern town reported a 50 percent increase in maintenance and repair costs due to vandalism over the past two years.

_____ Parents should assume responsibility for the behavior and actions of their children.

EXERCISE 8–2

Directions: *Select one of the reading selections included at the end of this unit. Read the selection, following these steps:*

1. *Prereading.* Preread the selection to become familiar with its overall content and organization.
2. *Establishing a Purpose for Reading.* Using your prereading of the selection, write several questions you want to answer as you read.

_____

_____

_____

3. *Reading.* Read the selection, looking for the answer to your questions. Then reread the selection, making a brief outline of the important supporting details that explain the main idea.
4. *Reviewing.* Go back through the selection, reading the parts that will help you to remember the important ideas presented in the selection. Also, review the outline you prepared in step 3.
5. *Reacting.* Think about and react to what you read. You will have an opportunity to express your ideas about this subject in the writing exercise at the end of this chapter.

DEVELOPING PARAGRAPHS

In writing, your primary purpose is to communicate information and ideas as clearly as possible. You have to provide enough information and explanation to enable your reader to understand what you are saying, and one of the best ways to make your meaning clear is to be sure that each paragraph has enough detail to explain to your reader exactly what you have in mind.

Suppose that a new restaurant had just opened near campus and in your writing class you were asked to write a paragraph that describes the restaurant. Someone in your class wrote this description:

A new restaurant called "Fat Man's Got It All" just opened on Church Street near campus. The food is just great at Fat Man's. Everything that my friend and I ordered was well prepared. The service was good, too. I would recommend Fat Man's to anyone interested in good food.

Does the information included in this paragraph interest you in trying this restaurant? What does the writer really tell you about the restaurant? Actually, all the writer really said was that he or she liked both the food and the service. For the most part, this paragraph was not effective because it included only vague, general statements rather than particular facts and details. Now suppose another student who had visited the restaurant wrote the following paragraph:

> "Fat Man's Got It All" is a new restaurant that just opened two blocks from campus. The atmosphere is informal and casual. There are large tables in the center that can seat 12 to 14 people, and smaller tables are situated near the walls. The menu lists 37 types of sandwiches and 24 ice cream desserts. We tried the Fat Man's Special—a cheeseburger on grilled rye, topped with bacon. It was well prepared and more than we could eat. I would recommend "Fat Man's Got It All" to anyone interested in a casual restaurant that serves a wide variety of sandwiches and desserts.

This paragraph is much more effective than the first. Rather than making vague, general statements, this writer included specific details and examples. After reading this paragraph you have an idea of what the restaurant is like and what is served. The primary difference between the two paragraphs is the type of supporting statements that were used and the manner in which they were used to develop and explain the main idea. As you can see from the two examples, your choice of supporting details in a paragraph largely determines its effectiveness.

Selecting Details that Support the Topic

The information included in a topic sentence will not usually express thoroughly the main idea of a paragraph, so additional facts or ideas need to be presented in other sentences in order to "round out" the main ideas. Supporting details are all the facts and ideas in a paragraph that directly explain or support the main idea.

When you write a paragraph, then, one of your major goals is to thoroughly develop your main idea, so that your reader will have a clear grasp of it. To help yourself select appropriate details you might ask this question:

> What do I need to say so that my reader will understand the situation as I want him to?

Thinking of this question as you write a paragraph will help you select details that clarify and support your main point about the topic.

A common error in developing a paragraph is to stray from the topic. Usually, this happens when you include details that do not directly support the topic. The following diagram of a paragraph shows how details should relate to the topic.

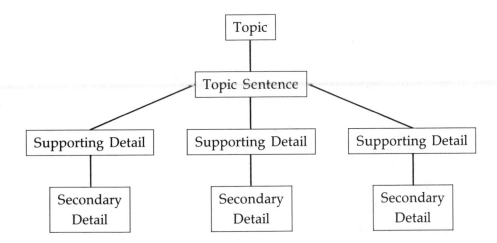

In this diagram the ideas move from general to specific. The topic is the most general concept in the paragraph, and the topic sentence expresses the main idea, which explains one general idea about that topic. The supporting details are specifics that explain, support, or tell more about the main idea. The secondary details are the most specific because they further explain a supporting detail.

Of course, an actual paragraph could include more supporting details and secondary details than are shown here. Also, there may be more than one secondary detail for each supporting detail, or some supporting details may not need any secondary details for further explanation. As you select details, then, be sure that each directly explains the main idea or provides further information about one of the supporting details.

As you gain more experience in writing, you will discover that models such as this one serve as examples of organization. You may not always write paragraphs that have, for example, a topic sentence. However, as you are developing your skills try to follow the suggested patterns of organization that have proven to be effective and use them as a point of departure.

Methods of Paragraph Development

One of the most effective aspects of a well-written paragraph is in the development of supporting details that explain, prove, describe, or in some way support your main idea. There are a number of ways to develop a paragraph, but some of the most effective methods are listed here.

1. *Facts.* One way that you can develop or tell more about a main idea is to provide factual detail. That is, you can support a statement by giving facts such as numbers, dates, events, places, names, and so forth. For example, suppose you are writing a paragraph about violence and television programs, and your main idea states that too much violence is shown on television programs. You might further explain this idea by giving some evidence of television violence. Using one day or one evening on a particular channel, you could indicate how many crimes, deaths, or personal injuries were shown.

2. *Examples.* A main idea can be explained by using details that are examples. That is, you can explain a particular happening, situation, or condition that illustrates and clarifies your main idea. To develop the topic of violence on television, you could give a detailed description of several particularly violent incidents.

3. *Definition.* If the purpose of your paragraph is to explain what a new term, concept, or idea means, then you might develop the main idea by definition. You would include sentences containing details that define or clarify the meaning of your topic. Suppose that you were asked to define the term "violence" on a short-answer portion of a psychology exam. Your answer would be a paragraph explaining the meaning and use of that term.

4. *Reasons.* A paragraph may be developed by giving reasons to support the main idea. Suppose the main idea of a paragraph you are writing is that violence on television should be carefully regulated. Then you could develop the paragraph by giving reasons for your position.

5. *Process.* If the purpose of the paragraph is to explain how to do something, you can develop the paragraph by listing and explaining each step. For instance, suppose you were asked to explain how to change a flat tire. The clearest and simplest way to do this would be to explain each step in the order in which it should be done.

The five methods we described are among the most basic ways to develop ideas in a paragraph. They can also be used in various combinations. You should realize, however, that these are not the only methods you can use. You will learn about other factors to consider in developing and organizing paragraphs in Chapter 9.

Using Outlining to Organize Your Ideas

You must be certain each detail relates directly to the topic and you must also be sure to include a sufficient amount of detail and to organize the details into a logical sequence.

Outlining is a useful tool for both including sufficient detail and organizing the details into a sequence. An outline of your paragraph will help you determine if you have included enough detail and whether your ideas are arranged in an appropriate order. From the length and complexity of the outline, you get an idea of whether you have explained your idea sufficiently. Here are three examples of outlines, one that has too little detail, one that has too much detail, and one that has sufficient detail.

TOO LITTLE DETAIL: I. Studying for Exams
    A. Read assignments
    B. Study material

TOO MUCH DETAIL: I. Studying for Exams
    A. Read assignment
    B. Underline main ideas
    C. Make study notes
    D. Review text and notes
    E. Get a good night's sleep
    F. Take appropriate materials with you
    G. Arrive at the exam room on time
    H. Read the whole test through first

SUFFICIENT DETAIL: I. Studying for Exams
    A. Read assignment
    B. Underline main ideas
    C. Make study notes
    D. Review text and notes

If you produce outlines like the first example, your supporting details are probably too broad and general. You should try to subdivide your ideas and explain each one. For instance, in this example it is not clear that when you read textbook assignments, you not only read, but you also underline and take notes.

If your outlines are similar to the second example, you are probably including too many details, or you may be straying from the topic of studying. For instance, details such as getting a good night's rest, arriving at the exam room on time, and reading the whole test through first do not directly relate to the topic. These details do not discuss how to study for exams; they are more appropriately called test-taking skills rather than study skills. To correct this problem of too many details, you might try to combine details or eliminate details that are repetitious or not directly related to the topic.

The third example shows a reasonable amount of detail and includes only those details which are directly related to the topic of studying for exams. Secondary details might be included to round out a paragraph, but the outline should present the most important details.

By studying the arrangement of ideas in an outline you can often recognize ideas that are out of order, ideas that do not directly relate to the topic, and ideas that may require further explanation or additional secondary detail. In the following outline can you recognize the detail that does not belong? Can you see a better way to arrange the details?

I.   Opening a Checking Account
    A. Get full information about the bank's service charges and penalties.
    B. Choose a bank that is convenient to your residence.
    C. When opening the account be prepared to fill out forms.
    D. Some young people automatically choose the bank where their parents conduct their business.
    E. You may be given temporary checks to use until your personal checks are printed.

In this outline, statement D does not belong in a paragraph that describes the procedure for opening a checking account. Also, statement B should appear first, since a logical way to arrange these ideas would be to make them follow the order one would follow to open an account.

EXERCISE 8–3

Directions: *This exercise is intended to give you some experience in developing and organizing supporting details. Choose a reading selection from the end of this unit. Preread and read the selection. Write the title and subject of the reading here:*

TITLE: _____

SUBJECT: _____

Using the subject of the selection as a starting point, follow each of the following steps:

1. *Prewriting.*
   a. Narrow the subject into three possible topics:

   _____

   _____

   _____

   b. Select one topic and use a five-minute free-writing exercise or write several questions that occur to you about the topic to generate ideas.

2. *Composing.* Select the most important ideas you see in your prewriting exercise. Develop these ideas into a paper consisting of an introduction, body, and conclusion. Include the details your reader will need in order to have a clear understanding of your purpose and message.

3. *Checking the Content and Organization.* Write an outline of the details you have presented in each paragraph. Check to be sure that you have included sufficient detail and that your ideas are logically sequenced. Decide what additional details are necessary and eliminate any that do not directly support the main idea in each paragraph. Consider also how the details can be rearranged to make the paragraph more effective. Write a new outline, if necessary, to guide you in revision.

4. *Revising.* Reread your paper and cross out any sentences that do not support the topic of each paragraph. Add any additional statements needed to support the topic of the paragraph. Look carefully at sentence structure and vocabulary. Circle any sentences or words that might confuse your reader. Then answer the following questions.
   a. List any facts you used to develop each paragraph. Do you have enough facts to support your main ideas?

   _____

   _____

   _____

   _____

   _____

   b. List any examples you included to develop each paragraph. Are the examples clear? Are they appropriate for your audience?

   _____

   _____

_____

_____

_____

    c. List any definitions you supplied for your reader. Are the definitions accurate?

_____

_____

_____

_____

_____

    d. List any reasons you provided to develop each paragraph. Do your reasons make sense? Will your reader know why you included them?

_____

_____

_____

_____

_____

5.   *Proofreading.* Read your final copy, looking closely for spelling and punctuation errors. Place a check on the proofreading checklist next to each item that you correct. Describe the errors you corrected in the column on the right.

SUMMARY

Supporting details are those facts and ideas which explain the main idea of the paragraph, giving the reader more information. Secondary details are facts and ideas that further explain one or more of the supporting details but do not directly explain the main idea. Supporting details may present facts, examples, definitions, or reasons. In reading, outlining is a useful technique for understanding the relationship among ideas. In writing, outlining is useful for checking the organization of your ideas and determining whether you have included sufficient detail to explain your ideas.

		PROOFREADING CHECKLIST		
Essay Title _____				
Date _____				

TYPE	✔	ERROR	FREQUENCY	DESCRIPTION
GRAMMAR		Run-on Sentence Sentence Fragment Subject/Verb Agreement Verb Tense Pronoun Agreement		
MECHANICS		Capitalization Italics Abbreviation		
PUNCTUATION		, (Comma) ; (Semicolon) ' (Apostrophe) " (Quotation Marks) . (Period) ! (Exclamation Point) ? (Question Mark) : (Colon) — (Dash) ( ) (Parentheses) - (Hyphen)		

TYPE	✔	ERROR	CORRECTION	
SPELLING ERRORS				

9. Paragraph Organization

This chapter is concerned with the arrangement or organization of ideas within a paragraph. First you will learn some of the most common patterns of organization. You will also learn how signal words, or words that indicate a change in thought, can help you to follow an author's thought pattern. Then you will learn how to arrange your ideas using various organizational patterns and how to use signal words to indicate a change in your thought pattern.

UNDERSTANDING PARAGRAPH ORGANIZATION

You are already aware of the three main parts of a paragraph—*topic, main idea,* and *details*—and how they are related to each other. You have learned how to identify them, and you have practiced isolating them while reading paragraphs. Now it will be helpful to develop some techniques for storing and remembering the ideas and details that you read. Following the author's train of thought as you read is just such a technique. The first part of this chapter will show you how to recognize the arrangement and organization of details in a paragraph. Recognizing the organizational pattern of a paragraph can help you to follow the progression of ideas and to remember what you have read.

Paragraph organization refers to the arrangement of ideas and details within a paragraph. You learned in Chapter 7, "The Main Idea," that main ideas can be situated in a variety of places in the sentence and that the position of the main idea within a sentence affects the relationship of ideas. For example, the most important ideas are expressed in independent clauses whereas less important ideas can be placed in dependent clauses as part of a complex or compound-complex sentence. Likewise, details in a paragraph can be formed into a variety of patterns or arrangements to suit the writer's purpose. Efficient readers are aware of the most common patterns and how they can be put to work for them.

How Paragraph Organization Aids Retention

Recognition of a paragraph's organizational pattern improves your understanding of the material you are reading, and recognition of the paragraph structure makes reading easier. Once you have the pattern of thought and structure of a paragraph in mind, you will be able to predict what type of ideas will come next in the paragraph. Also, recognition of the pattern will enable you to identify supporting details and distinguish them more easily from secondary details. Finally, recognition of patterns enables you more clearly to understand the relationship between the main ideas and the details.

Recognition of patterns also helps you retain, or remember, what you read. Many students complain that they are unable to remember what they read. They seem to understand while they are reading, but when they have finished a page they do not remember anything they have read. Recognizing paragraph organization (understanding how the details are tied together) is one way to overcome this problem.

By identifying paragraph organization you are actually identifying a pattern, and items that are arranged in a pattern are easier to remember than those that are not. To illustrate, test yourself and see which string of letters and which string of numbers are easier to remember or take less time to memorize.

LETTERS: AB AB CD CD EF EF
            A G Y K L F E N O X

NUMBERS: 1, 8, 5, 9, 4, 2, 7, 0
            2, 4, 6, 8, 8, 6, 4, 2, 0

Of course, the first string of letters and the second string of numbers were easier to remember. In each you could identify a pattern, and it was easier to remember the items in the pattern than to remember each item in a random series. Similarly, in paragraphs, if you can identify an organizational pattern you will be able to remember the information because you will not have to memorize each detail separately within the paragraph.

Types of Paragraph Organization

There are many types of paragraph organization. We will be concerned with the most common types for both textbook writing and literary essays: chronological order, statement-support, comparison-contrast, classification, cause-effect, definition, and description.

Chronological Order

One of the simplest patterns to identify is chronological order. In this pattern, the details are presented in the order in which they happened. That is, whatever happened first appears first in the paragraph; whatever happened next appears next in the paragraph; and so forth. This pattern may also be called *time order* or *sequence of events*. The following paragraph is written in chronological order. As you read it, notice how details follow one another in time.

> On April 23, 1564, William Shakespeare was born in Stratford-on-Avon in England. He attended a local grammar school in the town. At the age of eighteen he married Ann Hathaway. Several years later he traveled to London. By the time he was twenty-eight he had established his reputation by acting and writing plays. Other than these facts, little is known of Shakespeare's early life.

When you become aware that a paragraph is organized chronologically, you will be able to expect that whatever appears next in the paragraph occurs next within the time sequence. You will begin to notice how one idea is connected to or depends on another in time. You will be able to remember each separate fact, detail, or step because they fit together in an orderly fashion.

Paragraphs that describe a process, give directions, or detail a procedure are often arranged in chronological order. That is, the first step in the process or procedure is given first in the paragraph, the second step next, and so forth. The following paragraph describes a procedure for becoming familiar with a textbook. Notice the arrangement of details.

> Becoming familiar with a textbook before reading it involves several steps. First, read the front pages. Be sure to look at the foreword, introduction, and table of contents. Then turn to the end of the book. Notice whether the book has an index, appendix, and glossary. Finally, flip through a chapter in the middle of the book. Learn how difficult the book will be by noticing the size of print, the number of difficult words, the sentence patterns, and the length of the paragraphs.

You will find the chronological pattern frequently used in textbooks as well as in literature. History texts, for example, will often use this pattern for presenting details. Natural science texts employ chronological order to describe the steps in an experiment or process. Narrative essays tell a story or describe an event and frequently use this form of paragraph arrangement. Chronological order is also frequently used in novels and short stories to describe events and action.

Statement-Support

Another very common pattern used in both texts and essays is statement-support. In this form the main idea is stated and the rest of the paragraph explains or proves it. A writer may explain or prove his or her idea by giving examples, as here:

> Many people rationalize, or explain away, their difficulties in a fashion that protects their view of themselves. That is, they rationalize their mistakes and weaknesses by inventing excuses for them. For example, if a student failed an exam, he or she might say the exam was unfair or that the instructor did not teach what was on the test. Or, if your friend got a speeding ticket, he could rationalize that the police officer stopped the wrong car, that the speed was not posted, or that the speedometer was not working accurately.

Or, a writer may explain by listing additional facts, figures, or other forms of proof:

> Suicide is a serious problem affecting society. In 1978 over 25,000 Americans killed themselves. This is a rate of 11.7 suicides per 100,000 people. Statistics show this rate is fairly constant over the years. Suicide attempts are twice as common among women as among men, and the suicide rate is higher among whites than among minority groups.

Once you have determined that the statement support pattern is operating within a paragraph, you begin to develop a certain set of expectations. You would expect the details in the paragraph to prove, explain, or support the main idea. You would expect to find facts, statistics, examples, or descriptions of events that lend support to the main idea. Recognition of this pattern enables the reader to predict what will come next and to evaluate the usefulness of the support offered. The statement support pattern is commonly used in textbooks and in essays where concepts or ideas need to be explained. It is especially common in explanatory or expository writing when ideas are presented and then explained.

Comparison-Contrast

The comparison-contrast pattern is used when the similarities or differences of two or more actions, ideas, or events are being discussed. A paragraph may discuss only similarities or only differences. Sometimes, though, both similarities and differences are contained in the same paragraph. In the following paragraph only similarities are discussed; two types of tests are compared.

> Multiple-choice and matching tests have much in common. Both tests are tasks of recognition. That is, both require the test taker to recognize the correct answer from among given choices. Neither test requires the test taker to recall or produce information. Also, both tests are primarily used to test knowledge of factual or objective information. The tests do not usually involve organization, reasoning, evaluation of, or reaction to information.

In the following paragraph only differences are discussed—the differences between high school and college.

> Most beginning college students quickly realize that college is very different from high school. In college, students have a great deal of freedom. They can build their own time schedules, choose their own instructors, and decide whether to attend classes. In high school, however, freedom is more restricted. Most high schools operate within a controlled time frame; teachers and schedules are assigned, not selected by the student, and class attendance is required.

The next paragraph contains both comparison and contrast. Both the similarities and differences between red raspberries and black raspberries are presented.

> Both red raspberries and black raspberries grow wild in the United States. Both grow on canes approximately five feet tall and have compound leaves. Both berries ripen in July or early August. However, black berries are much more plentiful, and they are easier to find than red raspberries. Black raspberries grow easily in forests and wooded areas, whereas red raspberries require more light and space.

When you become aware that a comparison or contrast pattern is developing within a paragraph, you should begin to look for similarities or differences between the items discussed. Begin by identifying the two or more items involved. Usually the topic sentence of the paragraph states the basic relationship between the items or ideas. This sentence will state, in a general way, the similarities or differences between the two items or ideas. Decide whether the paragraph is written to discuss only similarities, only differences, or both.

Next, try to determine if the paragraph is written to clarify one item or idea by comparing or contrasting it to others or whether it is written to explain each of two or more ideas by contrasting them. For example, a paragraph may be written primarily to explain the concept of divorce, and that concept may be explained by contrasting it to a separation. In this case the concept of separations is used only as an explanatory device. On the other hand, a paragraph may be written to explain the two options that may lead to the termination of a marriage. In this case, both divorce and separation are equally important, and you should pay equal attention to both concepts.

You can expect to find the comparison-contrast pattern used frequently in the social sciences textbooks where governments, economies, social groups, behaviors, and cultures are studied. Many literary essays also use this pattern.

Classification

The classification pattern organizes information about a topic by dividing it into parts. These parts are selected on the basis of things they have in common. For example, a paragraph written about health foods may explain what health foods are by discussing various types. The foods may be grouped according to nutritional type (protein, carbohydrate) or according to type of food (soups, desserts, salads). In either case health foods are explained by dividing them up or grouping them according to common features or characteristics.

The following paragraph is organized by classification. As you read it, notice that the topic is vocabulary and that this topic is divided into four types of vocabulary levels.

> Most people do not realize that they have more than one vocabulary level. In fact, everyone has four different vocabularies—a reading vocabulary, a listening vocabulary, a writing vocabulary, and a speaking vocabulary. There are words that you understand when you hear them, but you may not use them in your daily speech. And there are words that you recognize when you read that you may not normally use in your own writing. Similarly, there are words and expressions that you use in your speech but not in writing.

When reading paragraphs that use classification, first identify the general topic or category being explained. Usually the topic sentence will name this general group or category. Next, determine how and on what basis the topic has been divided. Then, as you read, look for the distinguishing characteristics that make one subdivision different from another.

Remember that the writer's purpose is to show how various parts of the classification have a common base and also to show how they differ within that common base. This pattern is used whenever a topic can best be explained by subdividing it and explaining the individual parts. It is commonly used in textbooks, and it also appears in many types of brochures and catalogs.

Cause-Effect

When an event or action is caused by another event or action, the cause-effect pattern is used. The primary characteristic of cause-effect paragraphs is explanation by telling why or how something happened. The cause-effect pattern describes how two or more events are related or connected. A single event may produce a single effect or several effects (results) may be related to a single cause. A tornado, for example, may have multiple effects—cars overturned, homes destroyed, flooding. Or a paragraph can present several events together that resulted in a single effect. For example, diet, exercise, and self-control (causes) may result in weight loss (effect). Finally, multiple causes may be related to multiple effects. For example, a student missed the bus and got lost on campus (causes), so he missed his sociology class and did not get to the bookstore in time to buy the textbook for the course (effects).

In the following paragraph, several reasons are given for the expansion of government.

In the past century, government has expanded and become involved in many new fields and aspects of life. One reason for this change is that government has more to do because the population has increased by 600 percent over the past 100 years. More rules and regulations are needed to keep larger numbers of people living and working together peacefully. Another reason for government expansion is the growth of cities. The government has been forced to accept responsibility for the water supply, transportation, fire and police protection, and waste disposal in urban areas.

Basically, then, the cause-effect pattern describes the connection or relationship between two or more events or actions. Be sure to watch for the type of paragraph that works backward by describing the result first and finally identifying the cause. Regardless of how a cause-effect paragraph is organized, the writer's purpose is to show how one or more events lead directly to another event or set of events.

In reading paragraphs that describe cause-effect relationships, start by carefully reading or rereading the topic sentence. Usually it states the primary cause(s) and the primary effect(s). It usually also explains the basic cause-effect relationship that is detailed throughout the paragraph. Now determine the connection between the causes and effects: *Why* did one event cause another? *Why* did one action occur as a result of a previous action?

The cause-effect pattern is commonly used in the natural and life sciences where the focus of study is often physical occurrences, their causes, and their effects. You may also find the cause-effect pattern used in the reporting of current events in newspapers and magazines, and in description of historical events in history texts and reference material.

Definition

A writer who introduces or uses a term that he or she feels the reader won't understand often includes a definition and explanation of the term. The purpose in writing a definition paragraph is to clarify a term and eliminate confusion with similar terms. Often a writer provides clues that the paragraph is intended to define a term or concept, and the term being defined is often printed in italics or darkened (bold) print, underlined, or otherwise made to stand out. In the following paragraph, for example, the term "family therapy" is defined and explained.

> *Family therapy* is a method of helping troubled families work out their problems and conflicts. Therapy involves discussion sessions directed by a trained therapist. All members of the family are encouraged to come to the sessions. The goal of each session is to work out possible solutions to a particular problem.

The topic sentence of a paragraph that uses definition usually provides a general meaning of the term. The rest of the paragraph narrows the meaning of the term to the specific situation intended. A writer may use examples, illustrations, facts, or other devices to narrow and clarify the meaning of the term. The overall structure of the definition pattern, then, is to move from general to specific, from a literal definition to a situational meaning.

When reading a definition paragraph, pay close attention to the topic sentence. It will identify the term and suggest the overall context in which the term is commonly used. Next, notice how details that follow narrow or specify the author's intended meaning of the word. To be sure that you have understood the definition, try to express it in your own words without referring to the passage. If you can, you will know that you have understood the paragraph. If you cannot, reread the paragraph and try to restate each sentence in your own words. Then, when you have finished reading the paragraph, try again to state the definition of the term in your own words.

The definition pattern frequently occurs in textbooks where new terms are regularly introduced. It is also found in many other types of writing, including newspapers, magazines, and directions for assembling an item.

Description

A writer who wants to create a word picture of an event, person, object, idea, or theory, often uses the descriptive pattern. This type of paragraph often consists of a list of descriptive facts or characteristics. These particular pieces of the description may not seem to have an easily identifiable order, but writers do not arrange their descriptive details randomly. They usually arrange them in some order. Details can be arranged chronologically, placing events in a time sequence:

> The old man walked in the room, looked around, and chose a seat.

Or the details can be arranged spatially, describing how the object appears or is positioned in space (up, down, beside, in front of, etc.):

> The dog was warming itself in front of the fireplace, and to the left his master was dozing in his rocking chair.

Or the descriptive details may be arranged logically so that they lead the reader to a conclusion, create a feeling, or establish a visual picture in the mind. For example, a man's ugly facial features, poor posture, and dirty torn clothing could be described to show the reader that the man's physical appearance was unpleasant.

> The bent over old man with the distorted, scarred face apologized for his tattered shirt, muddy shoes, and threadbare jacket.

The descriptive paragraph may have a stated main idea, but more frequently the main idea is unstated. It is often left for the reader to determine what the writer is trying to convey about the topic of the paragraph.

In the following paragraph the author's topic is Oliver Bacon's flat, and the entire paragraph provides details that describe his flat. There is no sentence that directly states the author's main idea.

> Oliver Bacon lived at the top of a house overlooking the Green Park. He had a flat; chairs jutted out at the right angles—chairs covered in hide. Sofas filled the bays of the windows—sofas covered in tapestry. The windows, the three long windows, had the proper allowance of discreet net and figured satin. The mahogany sideboard bulged discreetly with the right brandies, whiskeys and liqueurs. And from the middle window he looked down upon the glossy roofs of fashionable cars packed in the narrow straits of Piccadilly. A more central position could not be imagined.[1]

The steps involved in reading a descriptive paragraph are quite different from the steps followed in reading other types of paragraphs. Many descriptive paragraphs lack a stated main idea, so it is left up to the reader to "piece together" the various parts of the description to form an overall picture. In this unusual situation read the paragraph more than once. On the first reading try to identify who or what is being described and form a general impression of that person or item. Then reread the entire paragraph to fill in the details, noticing how they contribute to the overall impression. Notice the writer's choice of words and try to create a visual picture of the topic that is described. Finally, try to determine how the writer feels about the topic and what purpose he or she had in writing the paragraph. At this last stage, factors such as word choice, tone, and the arrangement of ideas are important.

Descriptive paragraphs are used in textbooks, but they also occur in newspapers, magazines, advertisements, and other literature you come across on nearly a daily basis. Many authors of fiction owe a great deal of their success to their talent for accurately describing a person, event, or item so that the reader is able to visualize the scene.

Signal Words and Paragraph Organization

Writers often use special words and phrases to connect ideas, to lead into an idea, or to make the transition from one idea to another. These words or phrases have many names; they may be called transitional words or linking words. But the most descriptive name is *signal words*. Signal words alert or signal the reader about what is to follow. Just as the driver of a car uses a directional or hand signal before changing his or her course of direction, so does a writer signal the reader of changes that are about to occur and of what is to follow. For example, notice that within the following sentence the writer signals by using the word "but" to show that a different idea will follow.

> I planned on ordering a steak, but at the last minute I decided to order shrimp.

In the following two sentences, the signal words "as a result" indicate that the first situation caused the second.

> The driver of the car was busy laughing and joking with his passengers. As a result, he failed to stop at the intersection and struck another car.

In the next paragraph, notice how the words connect each event and signal the reader that the events are arranged chronologically.

> Salesmen often follow an established routine in making a sale. First, the salesman establishes his credibility by making you aware of his knowledge and familiarity with the product. Next, the salesman attempts to discover how the customer feels about the product. Then, the salesman tries to actively involve the customer in a discussion of the merits of the product. Finally, the customer is encouraged to make a positive statement about or commitment to the product.

You probably discovered that in addition to connecting ideas, signal words often give the reader a clue about a paragraph's pattern of organization. The following chart lists some frequently used signal words and indicates the organizational pattern they suggest.

Organizational pattern	Commonly used signal words
Chronological Order	first, second . . . , then, next, following, finally
Statement-Support	for example, to illustrate, in fact
Comparison	similarly, to compare, likewise, by comparison
Contrast	but, however, in contrast, on the other hand, instead, on the contrary
Classification	first, second . . . , one, another
Cause-Effect	because, thus, consequently, as a result
Definition	is, can be defined as, means, refers to
Description	above, beside, next to, below

EXERCISE 9–1

Directions: *Read each paragraph and identify the predominant organizational pattern. Write the name of the pattern in the space provided*

1. In simplest outline, how is a President chosen? First, a candidate campaigns within his party for nomination at a national convention. After the convention comes a period of competition with the nominee of the other major party and perhaps the nominees of minor parties. The showdown arrives on Election Day. The candidate must win more votes than any other nominee in enough states and the District of Columbia to give him a majority of the electoral votes. If he does all these things, he has won the right to the office of President of the United States.[2]

   PATTERN: _____

2. All life is a game of power. The object of the game is simple enough: to know what you want and get it. The moves of the game, by contrast, are infinite and complex, although they usually involve the manipulation of people and situations to your advantage. As for the rules, these are only discovered by playing the game to the end.[3]

   PATTERN: _____

3. It was market-day, and over all the roads round Goderville the peasants and their wives were coming towards the town. The men walked easily, lurching the whole body forward at every step. Their long legs were twisted and deformed by the slow, painful labors of the country—by bending over to plough, which is what also makes their left shoulders too high and their figures crooked; and by reaping corn, which obliges them for steadiness' sake to spread their knees too wide. Their starched blue blouses, shining as though varnished, ornamented at collar and cuffs with little patterns of white stitch-work, and blown up big around their bony bodies, seemed exactly like balloons about to soar, but putting forth a head, two arms, and two feet.[4]

   PATTERN: _____

4. If animals could talk, what wonderful stories they would tell. The eagle already knew the earth was round when men were still afraid of falling off its edge. The whale could have warned Columbus about a barrier between Europe and India and saved that explorer a lot of anxiety. Justice would be more properly served if animals could give testimony. There would be a reduction in crime, no doubt, and quite possibly an increase in the divorce rate. All of us would have to alter our behavior in some way or another, for our environment would be considerably changed.[5]

   PATTERN: _____

5. This process of selecting details favorable or unfavorable to the subject being described may be termed *slanting*. Slanting gives no explicit judgments, but it differs from reporting in that it deliberately makes certain judgments inescapable. Let us assume for a moment the truth of the statement "When Clyde was in New York last November he was seen having dinner with a show girl. . . ." The inferences that can be drawn from this statement are changed considerably when the following words are added: ". . . and her husband and their two children." Yet, if Clyde is a married man, his enemies could conceivably do him a great deal of harm by talking about his "dinner-date with a New York show girl." One-sided or biased slanting of this kind, not uncommon in private gossip and backbiting, and all too common in the "interpretative reporting" of newspapers and news magazines, can be described as a technique of lying without actually telling any lies.[6]

   PATTERN: _____

6. Many children of this generation have never witnessed the birth of a baby or experienced the death of a family member. Nowadays, children are born in the hospital, a sterile environment detached from the family. And when a family member becomes seriously ill or approaches death, he is transferred to a hospital where children are forbidden to visit terminally ill patients. Children are deprived of feelings and situations related to birth and death. As a result, children do not develop healthy, natural attitudes toward either experience.

   PATTERN: _____

7. So Grant and Lee were in complete contrast, representing two diametrically opposed elements in American life. Grant was the modern man emerging; beyond him, ready to come on the stage, was the great age of steel and machinery, of crowded cities and a restless, burgeoning vitality. Lee might have ridden down from the old age of chivalry, lance in hand, silken banner fluttering over his head. Each man was the perfect champion of his cause, drawing both his strengths and his weaknesses from the people he led.[7]

   PATTERN: _____

8. The tax structure ensures that, as incomes rise for individual taxpayers, they move into higher tax brackets. They pay higher taxes and thus are only able to spend a smaller portion of their higher incomes. On the other hand, as incomes fall, lower tax rates go into effect and help keep consumer spending stable.[8]

   PATTERN: _____

9. Studies of different cultures have shown that there are many people in the world who as a group are friendly and kind. Anthropologist Margaret Mead (1939) found that the Arapesh, a

primitive tribe living in the mountains of New Guinea, were a peaceful people who thought that all human beings were naturally cooperative, unaggressive, self-denying, and primarily concerned with growing food to feed growing children. Curiously enough, a neighboring tribe, the Mungudumor, were highly aggressive, warlike, and cruel. Early studies of American Indians also indicate the peaceful nature of some tribes, such as the Hopi, Zuni, and Pueblo; while others, such as the Apaches and Comanches, were aggressive and warlike.[9]

PATTERN: _____

10. Various kinds and degrees of determinism have been argued since ancient times. The great dramatic tragedies of Aeschylus and Sophocles, for example, are pervaded by the ancient Greek belief that men and women are, in the last analysis, the pawns of fate. There is an inevitability to their actions, an end from which they cannot escape. This fatalism is clearly illustrated in the well-known legend of Oedipus. In trying to avoid fulfilling the oracle's prophecy that he would kill his father and marry his mother, Oedipus turned headlong into fate's trap and unwittingly did as prophesied. A later example is the Calvinist doctrine of predestination, which holds that at birth every individual has already been elected to salvation or condemned to damnation.[10]

PATTERN: _____

11. All human societies overcome death by creating and maintaining institutions that are handed on from one generation to another. Sex is a still more awkward feature of our biological inheritance than death, and our nineteenth-century Western society handled sex with relative success. By postponing the age of sexual awakening, it prolonged the length of the period of education. It is this, together with the seventeenth-century Western achievement of learning to think for oneself instead of taking tradition on trust, that accounts for the West's preeminence in the world during the last few centuries.[11]

PATTERN: _____

12. In contrast to the ease of becoming involved in a heterosexual relationship on today's university campus, overwhelming obstacles faced young adults in the early eighteenth century. Not only were coeducational opportunities nonexistent, but an introduction of the boy to the girl's parents had to precede any conversation between the partners. If her parents decided that the boy was not suitable, no relationship would develop. And even if her parents approved of the suitor, the time the couple could be together was limited. Both the girl and the boy were involved in chores or studies, and the little leisure time that was available to them was usually spent with other family members.[12]

PATTERN: _____

EXERCISE 9-2

Directions: *Select one of the reading selections included at the end of this unit. Read the selection, following these steps:*

1. *Prereading.* Preread the selection to become familiar with its overall content and organization.
2. *Establishing a Purpose for Reading.* Using your prereading of the selection, write several questions you want to answer as you read.

   _____

   _____

   _____

3. *Reading.* Read the selection, looking for the answer to your questions. Then reread the selection, identifying the organizational pattern of each paragraph and writing it in the margin next to the paragraph.
4. *Reviewing.* Go back through the selection, reading the parts that will help you to remember the important ideas presented in the selection.
5. *Reacting.* Think about and react to what you read. You will have an opportunity to express your ideas about this subject in the writing exercise at the end of this chapter.

DEVELOPING PARAGRAPHS

Earlier in this chapter you learned how to *recognize* the structure and organization of a paragraph and then use that organization to follow and remember the writer's progression of ideas. Now, as the writer, you must provide the structure and organization of details in the paragraph in a manner that helps *your* reader to follow *your* progression of ideas.

Organizing Paragraphs

You have already looked at the types of paragraph organization from the reader's perspective. Now think of organization from the writer's point of view. Most people do not always think in an organized, systematic way. Often ideas occur to us in a random fashion, and details are not always clear. In order to make a group of ideas make sense to someone else, we try to impose some order on the arrangement of main ideas and details. Think of how you organize an area of your own home. For the sake of convenience you might group certain things together. This grouping process, or categorization, is different for each person and depends on how an individual looks at the world around him or her. Some people might be content to put all kinds of clothing in one drawer, whereas someone else might separate types of clothing and store each type in a different drawer. Some people may keep all their sports equipment in one closet, whereas someone else might store each type, or the equipment for each sport, in a different place. This organization depends on preference or choice.

In writing you must organize your ideas so they make sense to more than just you because you cannot depend on anyone else to view things in *exactly* the same way you do. Since alert readers are usually looking for certain patterns of organization, you can use them to aid your reader.

Methods of Paragraph Development

In developing a paragraph, a central task is to decide how you want your reader to respond to your ideas. Often, the way you want your reader to respond, as well as the content of your paragraph, determines how you organize the paragraph.

Chronological Order

The simplest pattern of organization to identify when reading is chronological order. However, to write a paragraph using chronology is not as simple. You must make sure that the sequence of events follows in the right order. You also have to decide how many details to include and make sure they contribute to the reader's understanding of the sequence of events. The sequence may not seem logical if an important detail is left out. You can ask yourself these questions when you are planning to describe a sequence of events or a time-ordered pattern.

1. At what point did the chain of events really begin? That is, did some important detail that preceded the events contribute to their cause?
2. Would my description of the sequence lead my reader to expect the conclusion?
3. Would my reader be bored by the time he or she finished reading and perhaps skip over some of the events?

To develop a paragraph using chronological order you might use the following steps:

1. Prewrite, making a list of the steps or events in order.
2. Construct a topic sentence that states what it is you are explaining or describing.
3. Write out the details in sentence form.
4. Write a summary or concluding sentence that restates the idea or adds a new direction of thought.
5. Revise and proofread your paragraph.

Look at the following sample, which shows how a student used these steps to develop a paragraph that related a sequence of chronological events.

> TOPIC: How to register a car with the New York State Department of Motor Vehicles

STEP 1: Prewriting (list the steps)

Get title form from previous owner or bank

Get registration form

Get car inspected

Get insurance

Go to the N.Y.S. Department of Motor Vehicles with forms and cash or check for fee

STEP 2: Construct a Topic Sentence

Registering a car with the New York State Department of Motor Vehicles requires several steps.

STEP 3: Write Out Details

a. Make sure you have the form that tells who holds the title to the car.

b. Obtain a registration form from the N.Y.S. Department of Motor Vehicles and answer the questions.

c. Get the required amount of liability insurance from an insurance company. The insurance company will give you a set of cards as proof that you have insurance for the car.

d. Take the car to a service station to be inspected. The service station must be licensed by the N.Y.S. to do inspections. The inspector will put a new sticker on the window and stamp the registration form you have filled out.

e. Take all the forms to the N.Y.S. Department of Motor Vehicles and pay the fee and sales tax.

The writer then wrote the following paragraph.

STEP 4: Write a Summary or Concluding Sentence

> Registering a car with the Department of Motor Vehicles requires several steps. First, you have to provide proof of ownership. Next, you have to arrange for car insurance and get insurance cards to put in the glove compartment of the car, and the car has to be inspected by a licensed service station. An inspection sticker is placed on the window and the inspector stamps your registration form. Finally, you take all the forms, along with a check or cash, and stand in long lines to show all the necessary items to clerks who process your forms and stamp your registration form.

The writer realized that this paragraph was too vague.

STEP 5: Make Necessary Revisions

> Registering a car with the N.Y.S. Department of Motor Vehicles requires several steps, which have to be done in the following order. First, you have to ~~have~~ obtain the form ~~which~~ that shows who has title to the car, either from the dealer or the previous owner or the bank. ~~Next~~ Second, you should have the car inspected by a ~~licensed N.Y.S.~~ service station licensed to do N.Y.S. inspections; the next step, is to get insurance. ~~But these two steps can be done~~

At this point the writer discovered why he was having difficulty. The procedures for registering new cars and used cars are slightly different, but he had been trying to generally describe both procedures. He realized that his topic had to be narrowed before he could go on. Look at the final paragraph about how to register a used car.

STEP 6: Second Revision

> ~~There are several steps to~~
> Registering a used car with the
> N.Y.S. Dept. of Motor Vehicles requires
> several steps. First, you have to have
> ~~the~~ a part of the ~~old~~ previous owner's
> registration, showing that you have
> purchased the car. You also need a
> receipt for the amount you paid for the
> car. ~~Next,~~ ^Second,^ you have to get cards from
> your insurance company that show you
> have the required amount of insurance.
> ~~The next step is to have the car inspected~~
> ~~by a service station licensed to do N.Y.S.~~
> ~~inspections. Finally, you take all the~~
> ~~The inspector will stamp the new~~
> ~~registration form~~
> ^As long as^
> ~~If~~ the inspection sticker has not expired,
> you do not have to have the car inspected.
> ~~If it has expired then take it the car~~
> ~~to a service station and have it~~
> Finally, take the old registration form,
> receipt, and insurance cards to the
> Dept. of Motor Vehicles. Fill out a new
> registration form and pay N.Y.S. sales
> tax, ~~so as~~ and ^the^ ~~a~~ registration ~~free~~ fee.
> After all the fees have been paid and
> you've turned in ~~the~~ ^an^ insurance card,
> you will be issued a new registration
> form.

Notice how much revising the writer did while he was writing. You can see that the paragraph posed some difficulties, and the writer had to make choices about what information to include and where to include it. This writing task proved to be difficult even though the writer followed each step.

There are several situations for which chronological order is the clearest and most effective way to express your ideas. Most commonly, it is used to describe a chain of events. It can also be used to describe a process or steps to follow in completing a task. You could describe how to change a tire or how to make a pizza by listing each step in the order in which it should be done. Also, you might discuss or trace the development of an idea or concept by using chronological order when providing a reader with background information. When including historical background, chronology can again be an effective way to structure your ideas.

EXERCISE 9–3

Directions: *The following exercise is written to give you an opportunity to practice developing a paragraph using chronological order.*

1. Make a list of *one* of the following:
   a. five things you had to do in order to register for your college courses
   b. the steps required in dropping and adding a course at your college
   c. the steps you would take to look for a part-time job
2. Make sure the sequence is correct. Then write a topic sentence that states what it is you are explaining.
3. Using your list, write out the details in sentence form.
4. Write a summary or concluding sentence.
5. Revise and proofread your paragraph.

Statement-Support

Statement-support is another pattern of organization that you will use frequently. In this form you must make a statement and explain it by adding supporting details. The statement will be your main idea in the paragraph.

A writer can also support a statement by supplying examples. An example is a typical instance or a sample. Examples provide the reader with something specific to visualize. They must be relevant to the statement, and the reader must be able to understand them. In developing a paragraph using the statement-support pattern, use the following steps as a guide.

1. Identify your topic and decide what position you will take on that topic.
2. Write several statements that support your position. Review these statements, eliminating any that are not directly related to your topic.
3. Write a topic sentence that expresses the main idea you plan to develop.
4. Arrange your supporting statements into a paragraph that supports the topic sentence.
5. Write a summary or concluding sentence.
6. Revise and proofread your paragraph.

Read through the following example, showing how a writer used the first three steps to write a paragraph about the advantages of studying history.

TOPIC:	The Advantages of Studying History
POSITION:	It's good to study history.
STEP 1:	Identify topic and decide on a position.
STEP 2:	Write several statements. History gives you a better view of life. You can learn to understand problems. You see what the world is like. You see where you fit.
STEP 3:	Write a topic sentence. Studying history gives you a new way of looking at life.

Now, look at the paragraph the writer produced after completing all of the steps.

> Studying history gives you a new way of looking at life. When you learn about the past, you begin to see that your lifetime is only part of a larger picture. Also, history can help you understand problems better. You begin to see why the world is as it is and what events caused it to be this way. Finally, history allows you to think of yourself in a different way. In looking at everything that has happened before us, we as individuals seem small and unimportant.

Notice that the very first sentence in this paragraph is a statement, and each sentence that follows supports the statement that "History provides a new way of looking at life." Each detail in the paragraph explains how the study of history can give a person a new way of looking at life.

EXERCISE 9–4

Directions: *This exercise is designed to give you some experience in developing a paragraph using the statement-support pattern.*

1. Decide your position on *one* of the following topics:
   a. whether the parents of girls under eighteen should be notified if their daughters are provided with birth control pills or devices
   b. whether women should be required to register for the draft
   c. whether books in libraries should be restricted for use among specific age groups
2. Write several statements that support your position.
3. Next, introduce the main idea in a statement of position that will be your topic sentence.
4. Organize your supporting statements into a paragraph that develops your main idea.
5. Write a summary or concluding sentence.
6. Revise and proofread your paragraph.

Comparison-Contrast

The comparison-contrast paragraph can be used whenever you discuss the similarities or differences between two ideas, events, or actions. This pattern enables you to show connections between two or more ideas, objects or events.

There are two situations in which you might use this comparison-contrast method of development. In the first situation, you have one item or concept in mind and your purpose is to explain or describe it to the reader. You might also use the comparison-contrast pattern if you decide that the item or concept can be best explained in relation to something that is familiar to the reader. For instance, if you were to describe how an uncommon or unusual food such as rabbit or bear tastes, you might compare or contrast it to chicken or beef.

The second situation in which you might use this pattern is when you wish to discuss the comparative qualities or characteristics of two or more items. You might compare two cars you are thinking of buying, two movies you've seen recently, or three people you have just met.

One of the first steps in using a comparison-contrast pattern is to decide whether you should compare, contrast, or both compare and contrast the two or more items you are discussing. One way to decide is to ask yourself these questions:

How are these items alike?

How are these items different?

Of course, if you find mostly likenesses, then you would compare the items; and if you find mostly differences, then you would contrast the items. However, more frequently, there will be some similarities and some differences, and it will not be easy to decide. To develop a comparison-contrast paragraph, use the following steps as a guide.

1. Determine whether there are more similarities or more differences. This diagram may clarify how to make this decision.

Degrees of Likeness

Figure 1   Figure 2

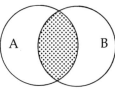 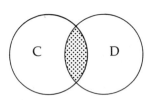

Four objects—A, B, C, and D—are each represented by a circle. The shaded area in each figure represents likenesses (things A and B or C and D have in common). In Figure 1 it makes sense to *compare* the objects, but in Figure 2 it would make better sense to *contrast* the two objects.

2. Mention that there are differences or briefly note any similarities, but devote most of the discussion to the stronger areas of likenesses or differences.

In the following sample paragraphs a student discussed types of snow skis—downhill, mountain, and cross country. Notice that in each paragraph the number of likenesses and differences controls the focus—comparison, contrast, or a combination of the two.

> John and Tom's downhill skis are similar even though they are different brands. Both pairs of skis are 190 centimeters long, and they are fairly stiff, so they are stable at high speeds. Also, the two pairs of skis are narrow and handle better in hard-packed snow than in light powdery snow.

In this first paragraph the student compared the skis owned by two friends since there are more likenesses than differences.

> Cross country skis and downhill skis are very different. Cross country skis are used to glide over fairly level terrain, whereas downhill skis are used to ski down steep slopes. Cross country skis are lightweight and very narrow, and the bottom is curved so the ski does not lie flat on the snow. Downhill skis are broader and heavier, and they have a flatter bottom. Unlike cross country skis, downhill skis have steel edges, and the bindings keep the entire boot clamped to the ski. On the other hand, the bindings on cross country skis do not keep the heel clamped down, since the long running strides characteristic of cross country skiing depend on free movement of the heel.

In the second paragraph the student contrasted the cross country and downhill skis since there are more differences than likenesses.

> Mountain skis and downhill skis are alike in several ways. Both mountain skis and downhill skis have steel edges, and they can be used to ski on steep terrain. However, the bindings on mountain skis permit the skier to unclamp the heel of the boot for skiing over level terrain whereas the bindings on downhill skis always keep the heel of the boot firmly clamped in place.

In this paragraph the student combined comparison and contrast because both types of skis are similar in some ways, but they are also very different in other ways.

When you use comparison-contrast as a means of organization, your topic sentence must contain certain information. Read the following topic sentences.

Novels and short stories have much in common.

A novel is very different from a short story.

Although there are similarities between them, a novel and short story have very different purposes.

Notice that each topic sentence identifies the two items to be discussed and then tells the reader what approach will be used.

The topic sentence in a comparison-contrast paragraph should accomplish two important tasks. First, it should identify the two or more ideas, events, or actions that will be discussed in the paragraph. Second, your topic sentence should indicate whether you will discuss similarities or differences or whether you will discuss both. Having stated this information, you can add details related to the comparison or contrast, or to a combination.

EXERCISE 9–5

Directions: *This exercise is designed to give you some practice in developing paragraphs using the comparison-contrast pattern.*

1. Make a list of similarities between *one* of the following pairs:
   a. two of your instructors
   b. two of your favorite entertainers
   c. two of your friends
2. Write a statement that expresses the most significant area of likeness in the comparison.
3. Now write a paragraph comparing the two people. Be sure to include a topic sentence that states the most significant area of likeness in the comparison.
4. Next, make a list of five differences between the two people.
5. Write a statement that expresses the most significant area of difference in the contrast between the two individuals.
6. Write a paragraph contrasting the two persons. Be sure to include a topic sentence that states the major area of difference.
7. Use your lists of likenesses and differences to formulate the main idea of a new paragraph that will compare and contrast the two individuals. Write down the items you will include in the paragraph.
8. Write a statement that shows the most important likenesses and the most important differences between the two people.
9. Write a paragraph that compares and contrasts the two persons. Use the statement you wrote in step 8 to begin your paragraph.
10. Revise and proofread each paragraph you have written.

Classification

A major job in writing is sorting out or grouping facts and ideas. Putting those ideas and facts into special categories helps the writer to convey ideas clearly to the reader. Classifying is the creation of groups of facts or ideas that share similar qualities. It is not a simple mechanical process of listing ideas; it must depend on some organizing principle. That is, the facts and ideas must be divided up in some consistent way based on common characteristics. The following examples illustrate the differences between lists and classification.

SAMPLE A: *Students*
     Catholics
     local residents
     sociology majors
     under 25 years old
     females

SAMPLE B: *Students*
>   sociology majors
>   math majors
>   art majors
>   drafting majors

Sample A is just a list of characteristics that might apply to some people in a school; there seems to be no single purpose for this list. One student could be all of these things. However, sample B is a classification because it separates students on the basis of their course of study.

To develop a paragraph using classification, use the following steps as a guide.

1. Decide how to divide your topic into groups that would help to explain or clarify your ideas.
2. Use your purpose as a means to divide your topic.
3. Write a topic sentence that clearly indicates the organizing principle you used.

In using classification try to decide how you could divide your topic into groups that would help to explain or clarify your ideas.

Classification is an effective way to discuss a large number of items or persons in an organized way. Suppose you wanted to describe the thirty-five students in your math class. Probably there is a wide variety of students. They differ in age, interests, goals, living arrangements, physical appearance, etc. So, unless you decided to describe each student individually it would be necessary to find some way of grouping them on the basis of something they all have in common. The way you divide them up depends on your purpose—or what you want to show about these students. If your purpose is to discuss their math ability then you could divide them into A, B, C, and D grade students. Or, if you want to discuss their religious background you could divide them into Protestants, Catholics, Moslems, Jews, etc.

Classification is also a useful method for developing a topic that is quite broad and has many parts. If you are writing a paragraph about why students attend your college, you could probably mention hundreds of reasons. To discuss this topic effectively in a paragraph, you would need to group similar reasons together. You might organize your paragraph like this:

I. Reasons Why Students Attend My College
    A. Financial Reasons
    B. Social Reasons
    C. Academic Reasons

Each category—A, B, and C—would include a group of related ideas, and the entire list of reasons would represent a classification of the reasons why students go to your college. The important element in classification is separation. In a classification the items in one group should be distinct from the items in another.

A student wrote the following paragraph about why students attend a certain college. Notice that each set of reasons is integrated into the paragraph by the topic sentence.

The three categories that describe the reason students attend my college are financial, social, or academic. The college I attend is a community college, which makes it somewhat less expensive because the students still live at home. Also, it is a state school, so the cost of tuition is more reasonable than it might be in a private college. Since the students commute to school and the student body is small, it is easy to get to know a lot of people. Most of the students are people who went to the same high school, so there is not a long period of social adjustments. Finally, many of the students who attend my college are either committed to a particular vocational program, or they have not yet made up their minds about a career. A community college gives them the opportunity to experiment for a couple of years before they decide.

You cannot help but notice that the items mentioned in this paragraph were separated and classified under specific labels. Classification depends on the separation and isolation of distinguishing features; then each set of features can be discussed.

EXERCISE 9–6

Directions: *This exercise is designed to give you some experience in developing a paragraph using the classification pattern.*

1.   Make a list of *one* of the following:
       a. leisure time activities you enjoy (for example, bowling, parties)
       b. types of films (for example, horror, space, comedies)
       c. types of people (overly friendly, businesslike, serious)
2.   Rearrange your list into categories or general types. (For example, you might divide leisure activities into sports, socializing, and special interests.)
3.   Write one general statement that describes how the items have been placed in specific groups.
4.   Write a paragraph that discusses your classification of the topic you selected. Include a topic sentence and supporting details.
5.   Revise and proofread your paragraph.

Cause-Effect

As a writer you will often find it necessary to explain the causes and effects of actions or events. You may want to describe *why* something happened, or you may want to tell what happened as a result of an action or event.

When developing a paragraph that involves causes and effects, there are a number of factors you need to consider:

1.   *Be sure that the cause-effect relationship you are discussing is valid.* That is, be sure that the event you are writing about was actually *caused* by the action or event you have identified. Suppose, for example, that a new ruling in your college permits beer to be served in the Student Center. The next week, more than half of the students in a particular history class are absent. If the instructor assumes that

the students were absent because they were in the Student Center drinking beer, he or she may not have correctly connected cause and effect. The students may have been absent because of a flu epidemic or because they were working on a term paper due the next day.

In determining the relationship between events, be sure you do not assume, as this instructor did, that two events that occur close together are causally related. To avoid this problem, connect events only when there is some evidence or reason for doing so.

2. *Distinguish between single and multiple causes and effects.* To help organize your ideas, decide whether:
   a. a single cause produced a single effect.
   b. a single cause produced multiple effects.
   c. multiple causes produced a single effect.
   d. multiple causes produced multiple effects.

   Once you have identified which of these four situations exists, then you can begin to arrange these cause(s) and effect(s) into an effective paragraph.

3. *Distinguish between immediate and long-range effects.* As you analyze the cause-effect relationship, identify which events were immediate, direct causes and immediate effects; then consider long-range and final causes or effects. Finally, decide whether you will discuss both immediate and long-range causes and effects or whether some can be eliminated.

   It is usually necessary to define the scope of your discussion in terms of your purpose. For instance, if you want to describe why an auto accident happened, you should focus on the immediate actions that caused the accident. The immediate cause may be that Joe went through a red light. Of course, if Joe was tuning in the radio and didn't see the light, that is also an immediate cause and should be included. However, the fact that Joe decided to drive rather than take the bus does not directly relate to your purpose—describing how the accident happened—and should not be included.

Organizing a Cause-Effect Paragraph. The topic sentence in a cause-effect paragraph should make a clear, general statement about the relationship of events discussed and suggest or state how they are connected. Here are a few sample topic sentences:

I passed my test in data processing because I used a new method for studying.

Due to many financial problems, my sister had to drop out of college.

Hal's behavior last night forced me to realize that he is a selfish person.

There are two basic ways to organize a cause-effect paragraph. One approach is to begin with the cause or causes and work toward the effect or effects. In this structure you lead your reader chronologically from one event to another, discussing events in the order in which they happened. This approach is most effective when there is a series of causes, a set of circumstances, or a chain of events that lead up to a particular effect or events. When you develop your idea in this way, you emphasize the causes and give your reader a clear, detailed picture of how or why something happened.

A second approach is to begin with the effect, or end result, and then explain how and why it happened. When using this method of development, in a sense you work backward. You begin with the event that occurred last in time and end with the initial cause. This approach emphasizes the result and works well when there are multiple effects.

Read the following sample paragraph written by a student and notice how the causes and effects are presented.

> Yesterday I was out sailing my Sunfish sailboat on a small lake. It was a nice day, and I was not expecting any heavy winds, so I was not being terribly cautious. My sail was tied down, and I was lying on the deck of the boat. All of a sudden there was a gust of wind. It took me by surprise, and I wasn't prepared. My boat tipped over, and I got soaking wet.

Notice that the writer outlines the causes that led up to several effects. The weather conditions and the sailor's expectations are mentioned, then the effects of these expectations—not being prepared for heavy wind—are made clear. The sail was tied down, so the wind easily tipped the boat over.

EXERCISE 9-7

Directions: *This exercise is intended to give you some practice in developing a paragraph using the cause-effect pattern. Follow these steps:*

1. Do a prewriting exercise on *one* of the following topics:
   a. why you did well or poorly on a recent test
   b. how your life would change if the United States went to war in Central America
   c. why you do or don't support nuclear research
2. Separate your ideas into two lists. In one column list causes; in the other list effects of each cause.
3. Write a statement that expresses the main idea behind the causes and effects listed in step 2.
4. Write a paragraph that discusses the various causes and effects you identified in step 2.
5. Revise and proofread your paragraph.

Definition

Definition is commonly called for in writing examinations, but it is also used in other types of writing, whenever you must explain the meaning of a term or word. There are two types of definitions that can be written for any word or term: denotative and connotative.

Denotative and Connotative Meaning. The denotative definition is the dictionary's description of the object. The connotative meaning is the meaning that can be associated with the object. The word "home," for example, is described by the dictionary as the place where a person or family lives. This is the denotative meaning of the word. The connotative meaning of the word is the impression the word "home" gives an individual. Most people will think of their own homes when they see the word, and thus the connotative definition of "home" could have various meanings depending on individual interpretation.

Look at the following example of a paragraph which defines utopia:

> Utopia is the name of an imaginary island described in a book written by Sir Thomas More in 1516. It was described as an ideal place to live because everyone acts according to reason. Today, when we think of utopia, we are referring to a situation, condition, place, or state of mind that is perfect. When someone says that an idea is "utopian," it means that it is almost perfect but impractical to apply in today's world.

This paragraph provides both the original denotative meaning of utopia and its connotative meaning. The denotative meaning of utopia is stated in the first two sentences: it is an imaginary island described in a book. The connotative meaning is given in the last two sentences, where there is an explanation of what the term has come to mean today. In this case the definition of utopia was made straightforward and obvious by direct statement of both denotative and connotative meanings.

You can see, then, that denotation and connotation are two basic approaches to writing definitions; several other methods will be described in the following sections.

Definition by Description. It is not always necessary to state the definition of a word. Sometimes it is more effective to explain a term or concept by describing it. For example, the following paragraph explains the meaning of the term "windsurfer," which is a relatively new concept in recreation for many people.

> The person who rides a windsurfer combines the skills of surfing and sailing. To windsurf well the rider must be able to handle a standard surfboard but also should know how to control a collapsible mast and sail. Windsurfing combines the best of surfing and sailing as the rider uses his sense of balance and the wind to drive him over the waves.

In this sample, a student defined a type of recreational object by describing how it looks and functions. Of course, a reader would have to be familiar with both surfing and sailing in order to relate to the appropriate mental image of combining surfing and sailing.

Definition by Example. Another effective way to define a term or concept is the use of examples. The following paragraph also defines a windsurfer, but it does so by giving specific examples.

> A windsurfer combines the design features of a surfboard and a small sailboat called a Sunfish, which is about 14 feet long, flat and broad, with a triangular shaped sail. The shape and weight of the board are similar to a surfboard's. A triangular sail is attached to a mast that pivots and is collapsible, so the weight of the rider is balanced by the force and direction of the wind. The rider both surfs and sails at the same time.

In this paragraph the student selected specific examples to show what a windsurfer is. Notice, too, that in providing specific design details the writer also used comparison to define the term.

Defining Abstract Terms. The most difficult definitions to write are those for abstract words such as truth, love, courage, democracy. This is so because these terms cannot be "pinned down" precisely with a denotative meaning. They are ideas rather than concrete objects, and they have a wide range of connotative meanings.

Since abstract terms carry different meanings for different people, it is often useful to focus your definition of them on areas of agreement. For example, the word "love" may have slightly different meanings to many people, but what these meanings have in common is "a strong emotional attachment," and this could form the basis for a definition. It may be useful, then, to extend this basic definition by describing or explaining the effects of the absence or presence of that quality on individuals.

Using the example of love again, you might go on to explain that people who share this quality, love, often behave in certain ways toward each other. Or you might show how those who no longer share the quality regard each other. Defining abstract terms can be quite involved, which is why writers have often devoted entire essays to defining such qualities.

EXERCISE 9–8

Directions: *This exercise will give you some practice in developing a paragraph using the definition pattern. Follow these steps:*

1. Write several statements that define *one* of the following:
    a. a "good friend"
    b. a mother or a father
    c. courage, love, beauty, *or* truth
2. Write a general statement that gives an overall impression of the way you define the item you chose in step 1.
3. Write a paragraph that defines your topic. Include a topic sentence and supporting details.
4. Revise and proofread your paragraph.

Description

The descriptive pattern of paragraph organization may be the most difficult of all for a writer to master. An effective descriptive paragraph conveys a clear mental picture of the idea, object, person, or event that you are trying to share with your readers. In order to make that picture a clear one, you might need to use some elements of the other organizational patterns to present descriptive details and to make effective word choices.

Suggestions for Writing Descriptive Paragraphs. Writing descriptive paragraphs is quite different from writing paragraphs in other organizational patterns. The purpose in writing a descriptive paragraph is to create a mental picture in the mind of your reader. The structure of a descriptive paragraph may also differ from that used in other paragraphs.

Often, descriptive paragraphs do not have a topic sentence that clearly states what is being described and what the writer wants you to know about that topic. Here are some suggestions to follow as you write a descriptive paragraph.

1. Develop a clear mental image of what you plan to describe. If you are going to describe a person, think of that person.
2. Decide what features about your topic you are going to discuss. If you are describing a person, decide whether you will describe his or her face, style of dressing, personality, lifestyle, and so forth.
3. Use a prewriting technique to select the details you will include.
4. As you compose the paragraph, try to organize your details in some manner. For instance, you might arrange them in a general-to-particular order, a spatial order, or a chronological order.
5. As you write try to use words that help the reader imagine or picture the topic you are describing. Read and compare the following sentences. Which one gives you a clearer picture of the applicant?
    a. The job applicant came to the interview dressed carelessly.
    b. The job applicant who came to the interview wore wrinkled jeans, sneakers, and a torn shirt.
    The second sentence actually *describes* the applicant's appearance, whereas the first only *tells* you in general how the person appeared.
6. As you reread your paragraph, compare the mental picture you created with your mental image of the thing described. Revise your paragraph so that it clearly communicates your mental image.

The difference between an effective, organized descriptive paragraph and one that is not is shown in the following paragraphs.

Not Effective
> My favorite room in the house is my bedroom. My room is a deep shade of blue that contrasts with the long, white drapes and the white bedspread on the comfortable bed. The bed and two dressers are made from dark pine wood. Ferns hang in front of the windows. The room is always quiet because it is the back of the house and overlooks the yard.

In the next paragraph notice that it is easier to form a mental image because the writer included specific references to location and more specific detail.

Effective
> My favorite room in the house is my bedroom, which is a deep shade of blue that contrasts with the long, white drapes on the two windows. A dark pine double bed, covered with a white down-filled comforter, extends from the middle of one wall to the center of the room. Across from the bed, on the opposite wall, is a dark pine dresser with a tall mirror and crystal lamps. Another tall pine chest of drawers stands against the wall opposite the door. Large, leafy green ferns hang in rustic clay pots in front of the multi-paned windows. Located in the back of the house, overlooking a green lawn, gardens, and a huge willow tree, my room is always serene and quiet.

EXERCISE 9-9

Directions: *This exercise is intended to give you some practice in using the descriptive pattern to develop a paragraph. Follow these steps:*

1. Choose *one* of the following topics.
    a. a special event you attended
    b. your favorite place
    c. the most moving or inspirational incident of your life
    Then, do a prewriting exercise to develop ideas.
2. Make a list of words that could help your reader construct a mental picture.
3. Write a statement that expresses the general impression you want to create about that event.
4. Write a paragraph that leads the reader to construct a mental picture of your topic. Include a topic sentence and supporting details. Use some of the descriptive words you listed in step 2 to create a more accurate, vivid picture.
5. Revise and proofread your paragraph.

Using Signal Words as an Aid to Paragraph Organization

As a reader you look for words and phrases that signal changes in thought or continuation of ideas. As a writer you will want to use these signal words to alert your reader to changes in thought. Signal words can also be used to emphasize ideas, show relationships, and connect ideas together.

There are several situations in which you should use signal words. First, use a signal word to indicate a change in thought. Remember that your reader is unfamiliar with your topic and how you have developed it. Unless you use signal words your reader may not know that you are moving to a different thought. Notice how the word *"but"* in the following sentence signals that a different thought is to follow.

I was planning to go to church, *but* I decided to go to the beach instead.

Signal words also can be used to emphasize important ideas. Again remember that *all* of your ideas are unfamiliar to your reader, and that it is necessary to lead him or her to identify what is important. Of course the topic sentence and the arrangement of details provide some clues about what is important, but signal words can be used to confirm and strengthen your existing structure.

Here is a paragraph written without the use of signal words. As you read it, notice that it is difficult to follow the ideas and that it appears choppy and unconnected.

The card catalog will help you to locate books easily and efficiently in the library. The card catalog drawers are arranged vertically and in alphabetical order. There are guides to indicate which letters of the alphabet are in each section. Guide cards are placed at intervals to indicate what part of the alphabet is contained between the guide cards.

Books on a topic can be found in three different places in
the card catalog. The card catalog contains subject, author,
and title cards.

Now, here is the same paragraph written with the use of signal words.

The card catalog will help you to locate books easily
and efficiently about topics you are investigating. *First,* the
card catalog drawers are arranged vertically and in alphabetical order with guides to indicate which letters of the
alphabet are in each section. *Next,* guide cards are placed at
intervals to indicate what parts of the alphabet are contained between the guide cards. *Finally,* books on a topic
can be found in three different places in the card catalog
because it contains subject, author, and title cards.

Notice that the italicized signal words indicate an arrangement of
ideas and tell the reader that there is a sequential procedure to consider
when using the card catalog. The words "first," "next," "finally," and
"because" draw the reader's attention to key concepts in the paragraph.
Signal words suggest various types of idea relationships and correspond quite closely to the organizational patterns presented in this
chapter. Review the list of signal words presented on page 227, and make
a conscious effort to include them in your writing.

EXERCISE 9–10

Directions: *Choose a reading selection from the end of this unit. Preread
and read the selection. Write the title and subject of the reading here:*

TITLE: _____

SUBJECT: _____

Using the subject of the selection as a starting point, follow these steps:

1. *Prewriting.*
    a. Narrow the subject into three possible topics:

    _____

    _____

    _____

    b. Select one topic and use a five-minute free-writing exercise or
       write several questions that occur to you about the topic to
       generate ideas.
2. *Composing.* Select the most important ideas you see in your
    prewriting exercise. Develop these ideas into a paper consisting
    of an introduction, body, and conclusion. Include the details
    your reader will need in order to have a clear understanding of
    your purpose and message.

3. *Checking the Content and Organization.* Write an outline of the details you have presented in each paragraph. Check to be sure that you have included sufficient detail and that your ideas are logically sequenced. Decide what additional details are necessary and eliminate any that do not directly support the main idea in each paragraph. Consider also how the details can be rearranged to make the paragraph more effective. Write a new outline, if necessary, to guide you in revision.

4. *Revising.* Use the five questions on pages 26–27 to help you revise your paper. Answer each question and write a list of changes you need to make. Next, look carefully at each paragraph and label the method of paragraph organization you used in each one. If you have combined methods of organization in one paragraph, consider carefully whether the combination is effective. Now check to see how many methods of organization you used and answer the following questions.

   a. Which paragraph is the most successful in relaying the main idea? Why?

   _____

   _____

   b. Which paragraph is the least successful in relaying the main idea? Is the failure caused by paragraph development or confusing sentence structure? Underline any confusing sentences.

   _____

   _____

   c. What signal words appear in the paragraphs? Are they effective? Do you need more signal words?

   _____

   _____

   d. Will the method of organization in each paragraph help the reader understand the subject you are writing about? List several reasons why this is so.

   _____

   _____

   Write a list of the changes you need to make, then begin rewriting sentences or paragraphs that need to be improved. After you have completed all the changes you needed to make, write a clean copy of the paper.

5. *Proofreading.* Read your final copy looking closely for spelling and punctuation errors. Place a check on the proofreading checklist next to each item that you correct. Describe the errors you corrected in the column on the right.

PROOFREADING CHECKLIST

Essay Title _____

Date _____

TYPE	✔	ERROR	FREQUENCY	DESCRIPTION
GRAMMAR		Run-on Sentence Sentence Fragment Subject/Verb Agreement Verb Tense Pronoun Agreement		
MECHANICS		Capitalization Italics Abbreviation		
PUNCTUATION		, (Comma) ; (Semicolon) ' (Apostrophe) " (Quotation Marks) . (Period) ! (Exclamation Point) ? (Question Mark) : (Colon) — (Dash) ( ) (Parentheses) - (Hyphen)		

		ERROR	CORRECTION	
SPELLING ERRORS				

Now go back to the first chapter and read through the right column of that proofreading checklist to see if you are still making the same errors. Cross off each error that you know you no longer make. Repeat this procedure for each chapter, including Chapter 9. Before you go on to Chapter 10, write all the types of errors you are still making in the right column of the proofreading checklist on page 251 of this unit. This new checklist will serve as an individualized guideline for you to consult each time you write a paper. With practice you should soon eliminate these errors from your writing, too.

SUMMARY

Paragraph organization refers to the arrangement of the ideas and details in a paragraph. In this chapter we presented various types of paragraph organization and showed you how to recognize the organizational pattern of a paragraph to help you remember what you read. You can use these patterns of organization to present your ideas when you write. The organizational patterns discussed in the chapter were chronological order, statement-support, comparison-contrast, classification, cause-effect, definition, and description.

Unit Three Reading Selections

Difficulty level: A

13. Dazzled in Disneyland

Aubrey Menen

. . . The next day I was taken to see the place for which all this ingenious work was going on. Disneyland is some miles out of Los Angeles in a flat stretch of country known as Anaheim. It rises from the plain like an island. It appears to be a haphazard jumble of constructions. There is a monorail, an imitation mountain, the tip of a giant space rocket and the turrets of a castle. All in all, it gives the impression of being nothing more than a large fairground. As I was shown through the turnstiles, I looked forward to tired feet, forced grins, bad food, and quarrelsome, overtired children.

Matters were not improved when a man or woman dressed as Mickey Mouse with a monstrous cardboard head insisted on shaking hands with me. Memories of the terrifying attentions of clowns when I was a child flooded back upon me. I was happy to see a tough schoolboy instantly square off into a fighting stance as the qrotesque figure walked toward him, a proper attitude to take toward monsters.

This was showmanship. A minute later all traces of that lowly craft were behind me, and I was in the middle of the private world of a genius.

All fairgrounds have a central avenue which is usually a blaring catchpenny road designed to make the visitor join in the fun or feel like a boor if he doesn't. Five minutes in such a place are usually enough to make me feel as gay as a Pilgrim Father. Here all was tranquil and detached. The visitors were not belabored into enjoyment; on the contrary, it seemed as though they were forgotten. They appeared to have wandered, by chance or some spell, into the past.

There was a square with green grass. There was a city hall, and a wide street lined with houses and shops. The architecture was that of a provincial American town in the late decades of the last century.

From time to time a surrey drove down the street, and then an automobile of the early years. There was the clatter of a bell, and a manual fire engine moved without very great haste to some invisible fire. Later there was the sound of music, and a brass band in red uniforms marched round the square playing old tunes.

At first glance, it all appeared to be an exact imitation. The architectural decorations were right, the windows perfect copies of the real thing. Yet it was unreal, or rather better than real. It seemed all to be of the right size. The shops were open, and people were going in and out of them. 7

A few days before, I had been driven round many similar streets in Hollywood, built up with enormous care to be settings for films. But they were dead places: it was impossible to delude oneself that anybody had really built them and lived in them. To see them was like peering close-to at a model. But Disney's town was alive, and this had nothing to do with the visitors, who formed no part of it. I was puzzled by this and set myself to find the reason. 8

Now, for some years I have gone about the streets of my own town—which is Rome—looking at the architecture, learning the principles of this most subtle of all the arts. I have trained my eye to look first at the proportions of the building, because it is by these that the architect makes his effect. He must, above all, get his proportions *right,* and for this there are rules which only a very fine creative artist can safely ignore. 9

I, therefore, studied the buildings in this strange main street with the same eye, and I immediately saw that the proportions were wrong. Everything on the first floor was as it should be. The doors were the right height for the people using them. But above them were windows that were too small; above them, again, were gables that were smaller still. The reduction in size as one's eye traveled upward was so beautifully done that it was almost imperceptible. 10

The great masters of the Baroque had studied this trick for a generation and only rarely dared to use it. Here it was done with the ease of a master; the effect was to give the street the reality of a dream—right, but wrong at the same time. 11

I asked who had thought of these subtle touches. I was told it was Disney. 12

I was next taken on what are known as "the rides." There are many in the park, but three will serve to show that Disney is himself again. 13

I went down Main Street to another square that was dominated by the medieval castle. Under the castle was a lake and a bandstand, and one or two other shelters. I did not examine them, because the effect was confused and garish. Disneyland is not laid out well. It consists of layers of ideas, like geological strata, and there are some fossils buried in it here and there. The piazza seems to be one of them, so I left it. I walked over to a gateway made of wood blocks, with the sign over it: FRONTIERLAND. I passed under the gateway, and in a moment order was restored. 14

I was in a frontier fort. There was a tall lookout tower, a sanded square and a trading post. One wall of the fort was missing; instead, there was a quay, and water beyond it. On the water, white and tall and beautiful, was a Mississippi paddle-wheel boat, it paddles turning slowly as it waited to cast off. The monarchs and grandees of Europe in the 18th Century spent fortunes designing parks with perspectives that gave onto Grecian temples or romantic ruins, to express their sense of history. None of their parks takes one back in time so suc- 15 cessfully and so quickly as this. Few grandees were rich enough to have ships in their pleasure gardens. Here there was not only one, there were two. Behind the paddle-wheeler was a three-masted bark moored in the middle of the lake.

I boarded the paddle-wheeler. The captain appeared on bridge, bells rang, and we moved off. In the middle of the lake was Tom Sawyer Island, green and full of little creeks and bays as it should be. On the island was another wooden fort. On the opposite bank, effigies of hostile Indians peered out of bushes or withdrew quickly as we passed. Rifle fire broke out from the fort, and a trumpet sounded. We rounded a promontory and saw that the Indians had set fire to a settler's hut. It burned furiously. More Indians came into view, friendly this time, and one lifted his hand in a salute as we passed. Then came a group of bears, moving their heads and tails. One stood up against a tree and, with the comic action peculiar to these animals, scratched his back. Somewhere on what seemed the horizon a train passed, and then a string of pack mules. All this was very real; and everything was life-sized.

I went on another ride in a most distant part of the grounds. Here the lake was very small. I boarded a painted barge, sitting down close to the water level. The barge waddled slowly round the shores of the lake, which was planted with miniature trees. From among these trees, scattered round the lake's margin, emerged a house, a castle, and a village. As we passed the house, an automobile horn sounded furiously. It was Toad Hall from *The Wind in the Willows*. Cinderella's castle came next, with a fantastic array of turrets and balconies that hung in the air. Then came the village, with its leaning houses and church steeples from which, as we passed, bells rang in a silvery carillon. This was where Pinocchio was born.

Now, where the bear and the Indians had been full-sized, all this was in miniature. The village was to the scale of the town of Lilliput, and I could have straddled over Toad Hall. The modeling was perfect, so that this village appeared like those little cities in the initial letters of medieval manuscripts over which artist-monks labored for months.

There are two kinds of legends: with one sort we can get inside them; with the other we are always spectators. I suppose there can be no American male who has not, at some time in his life, found himself alone in the countryside and explored Tom Sawyer island, or fought Indians, or crept on his belly up to a paleface fort. But nobody, I think, at any age plays Water Rat and Toad, or goes into Mole's house, or plays Prince Charming or Cinderella (unless driven to it by sentimental elders). These stories are too complete to have room for the outsider. We would know what to say to Pinocchio if we met him, or the Three Ugly Sisters. But we do not imagine ourselves being these people. A lesser man than Disney would not realize this. But here Tom Sawyer's island is big enough for children to play on; and Pinocchio's village is so small there is not even room in its streets to put one's foot. Once again Disney shows himself a master of the use of proportion.

The third ride shows another facet of the man. In another part of the park there is a third stretch of water through which move, in continuous procession, large gray submarines. They

16

17

18

19

20

cross the lake and disappear into a black cavern. At this point, to the people inside them, they appear to have plunged into the abyss of the ocean.

The submarines do not really submerge. They run on rails 21 through the lake and only the porthole windows along their sides are under water. But the dive is made convincing. The interior of the vessel rattles with the noise of the engines, sirens, and the loudspeaker commands from the captain. Bubbles appear outside the windows and rush upward until the required "depth" is reached. The submarine then glides slowly through a submarine landscape.

There is a forest of corals, glowing in their natural colors. 22 Shoals of iridescent fish swim among them or sport around huge octopuses that wave their arms. The light fades from the water for a while, and the monstrous fish of the great deep peer and yawn in at the portholes. A giant clam opens and shuts its enormous valves.

It is all very real. It threatens to be much too real, for it 23 seems that the whole elaborate box of mechanical tricks is only going to provide us with education in marine biology. But Disney has nothing of the schoolteacher in him, though he has a good deal of the schoolboy. Soon the submarine is passing a preposterously romantic wreck. It is plainly a pirate ship. Skeletons of pirates sit on its spars, and a treasure chest, half open as in the story books, spews out gold, huge jewels, and enormous pieces-of-eight. Then, as the submarine turns for home, there comes into view a master touch. An enormous white sea serpent undulates through the water toward the observation windows. It is a sort of dragon, but a friendly one with an eager, slightly wondering expression. It watched us pass like a small boy watching a passing train.

The submarine came to the surface, and I clambered out 24 into the sunshine. I had spent the morning riding through the dreams that lay somewhere at the bottom of my mind. We all have them: they lie there from our childhood, gathering dust. It is one of the functions of artists to blow away the dust and make them fresh again for a little while. It is a delicate operation that must be done with the sureness of a mature master who can still retain the vision of a child. "Tread softly," said a poet, "because you tread on my dreams."

A train runs around the borders of the park; it is a scaled- 25 down version of the early locomotives, with a high smokestack and a brass compression chamber. At one stage it passes through a long tunnel. On one side of the tunnel is a diorama of Rocky-Mountain scenery with animals. The beasts are stuffed, the sky is blue cloth. The hills are partly modeled and partly painted on the lower edge of the cloth. They faded into it with an attempt at perspective which would deceive nobody. The lighting is flat and unreal. In a word, it is the sort of diorama that was to be seen everywhere a generation ago. There is no sign of Disney in it.

In the heart of the park there is another stretch of moun- 26 tain scenery. This is also seen by means of miniature trains, but it has been designed by Disney. Just past the miniature station is a row of houses from a frontier town, scaled down to the height of a man. One wooden structure is labeled OPERA HOUSE. As the train moves off, a switch is automatically worked, and we hear a very bad soprano practicing a passage from an opera. It is a perfect touch of comedy. Then the track winds between big rocks, and at each turn it sets going a series of gadgets. A geyser erupts; a balancing stone threatens to slip off its pedestal onto the passengers' heads; a rattlesnake darts out of a rock and all but bites your hand—and so on. The dead diorama has been brought to life: it is real and more than real, because here and there Disney has illustrated his own opinion of wild nature—the cactus trees, for instance, have been turned by his art into vegetables that menace the passerby with frightening gestures, the suggestion of evil, leering faces. These, too, by means of mechanism, move in a slow and sinister fashion.

27   I crossed the park and entered an enclosure called *Tomorrowland*. There I found a triumph of gadgetry: a theater where a short play is performed with machinery as its only actors. This ride is called *A Voyage to the Moon*. A large rocket stands outside a round pavilion. Inside the pavilion there is a circular auditorium. The theater is designed to look like the interior of an enormous space craft. In the center of the area is a great circular screen. High in the roof is another. The theater darkens. The flight begins with a cascade of recorded hisses, roars and rattles. Suddenly one's chair begins to shudder. Below, on the screen, a white cloud of gas dissolves to show the launching pad disappearing below.

28   Slowly the rocket rises until one sees the curvature of the earth. On the screen above, the moon comes into view, comes closer until it is seen from a height of a hundred miles or so. The rocket reverses with a simulation of sounds that are inhuman and frightening. We return gratefully to the earth on the screen below. Our chairs shake violently. We land safely. The lights come on, and the ride is over.

29   Outside I realized that Disney had taken that elaborate but boring gadget, the planetarium, and turned it into a composition in space, sound, and time of high artistry. He had made machines tell a story. Once again there was something to point out the difference between an artist and a technician. Opposite the rocket was a film theater with a screen that ran round the whole building. A film was projected on the screen from several projectors. The effect, intended to be overwhelming, was merely irritating. You do not known where to look and end by staring at the places where the films should blend but don't. This inefficient side show is not by Mr. Disney.

30   But it will probably disappear along with the diorama and a lot of other things in the park. Every official I spoke to emphasized that Disneyland is not finished, and that it is Disney's intention it never will be. Every so often a creative mood seizes him, and he thinks up a new idea. Instantly his army of gadgeteers and artists are put to work to realize it. I saw this in progress. I had, that is, a glimpse round what is, in fact, Mr. Disney's studio—the strangest any artist ever had.

31   It was a vast hole in the ground. Bulldozers were at work—the artist's chisel as it were. They were digging out a

new lake, for Disney had devised a ride through the tropical jungle. Some distance away a monstrous structure of steel bars was being riveted together. This was to be a tree. Back in Los Angeles men were at work making its foliage and, following Disney's orders, they were making it leaf by leaf. When the tree was finished, it would house the huts of the Swiss Family Robinson. When the lake is finished, it will wind through a tropical landscape. The half-elephant I saw will be a full elephant and shower itself with water from a cataract along with half a dozen others. There will be a zoo full of moving animals. There will be head-hunters, and—unless he changes his mind—there will be a master touch of Disney: the boat with its sightseers will pass a hunter on an elephant. The hunter is aiming his rifle at a bush. Both he and the elephant are shaking with fright. As the boat passes the bush, the gun will go off. Behind the bush is a tiger. With an expression of thorough indignation, it is regarding its rear. The hunter has shot the tiger's skin, leaving him with a bare behind. . . .

I paid one more visit to Disneyland. I asked if I could see 32 it by night, because I wanted to see it with nobody there. Main Street was empty; only a few lights burned to guide watchmen. The skyrocket and the model of the Matterhorn were faint shapes against the sky. The woods with the Indians were full of shadows that seemed to move. The paddle-wheel boat floated on the dark waters of the lake like a ghost ship from the past. World upon world lay sleeping together, each born in the brain of the man who takes his art so seriously that he worries himself to tears.

My guide and I walked through the silent park, silent 33 ourselves. I thought of another masterpiece that I had once seen at nightfall. It was the great pleasure ground of Versailles, with its statues telling Greek legends, its miniature palaces and the imitation village with its dairy where Marie Antoinette played at making butter. It was a masterpiece of its age. It was built for the amusement of kings and their women. But this one was built for my pleasure and everybody else's. Versailles was copied all over Europe. This one, I think, will be copied all over the world.

COMPREHENSION

1. This essay is mainly about
    a. the rides at Disneyland
    b. dreams
    c. amusements
    d. Disney's creativity
2. The architectural features of Disneyland depend on
    a. a trick involving proportion
    b. subtle touches
    c. layering of ideas
    d. order

3. The author's attitude toward Disney can best be described as one of
   a. admiration
   b. surprise
   c. envy
   d. indifference

4. The reason that Pinocchio's Village is done in miniature is because
   a. there wasn't enough room to do it in a lifelike size
   b. Disney wanted to copy the cities in the initial letters of medieval manuscripts
   c. people cannot imagine being Pinocchio
   d. Pinocchio is not as important as Tom Sawyer

5. Disneyland will never be finished because
   a. there isn't enough money to complete it
   b. the workers are inefficient
   c. Mr. Disney constantly thinks up new ideas
   d. the Swiss Family Robinson project will take too long if the foliage has to be made leaf by leaf

VOCABULARY

Directions: *The meaning of the following terms from selection 13 cannot be clearly determined from the context. Using the dictionary entries, select the appropriate definition of the term as it is used in the reading selection.*

1. provincial (par. 5)
   a. rude
   b. countrified
   c. referring to the provinces of Canada
   d. limited

¹pro·vin·cial \prə-'vin-chəl\ *n* **1 :** the superior of a province of a Roman Catholic religious order **2 :** one living in or coming from a province **3 a :** a person of local or restricted interests or outlook **b :** a person lacking urban polish or refinement
²provincial *adj* **1 :** of, relating to, or coming from a province **2 a :** limited in outlook : NARROW **b :** lacking the polish of urban society : UNSOPHISTICATED **3 :** of or relating to a decorative style (as in furniture) marked by simplicity, informality, and relative plainness — **pro·vin·cial·ly** \-'vinch-(ə-)lē\ *adv*

2. Baroque (par. 11)
   a. curved, contorted architectural forms
   b. an irregular pearl
   c. a corrupt taste
   d. a style of writing

ba·roque (bə rōk′; *Fr.* bA RôK′), *n.* **1.** (*often cap.*) the baroque style or period. **2.** anything extravagantly ornamented, esp. something so ornate as to be in bad taste. **3.** an irregularly shaped pearl. —*adj.* **4.** (*often cap.*) of or pertaining to a style of art and architecture prevailing in Europe during the 17th and first half of the 18th centuries that was characterized by elaborate and grotesque forms and ornamentation. **5.** (*sometimes cap.*) of or pertaining to the musical period following the Renaissance, extending roughly from 1600 to 1750. **6.** irregular in shape: *baroque pearls.* [< F < Pg *barroco* rough pearl < ?]

Baroque cupboard
c1700

3. diorama (par. 25)
   a. scene viewed from a distance
   b. a painting
   c. three-dimensional figure
   d. translucent object

di·ora·ma \ˌdi-ə-'ram-ə, -'räm-\ *n* [F, fr. *dia-* + *-orama* (as in *panorama,* fr. E)] **1 :** a scenic representation in which a partly translucent painting is seen from a distance through an opening **2 a :** a scenic representation in which sculptured figures and lifelike details are displayed usu. in miniature so as to blend indistinguishably with a realistic painted background **b :** a life-size exhibit of a wildlife specimen or scene with realistic natural surroundings and a painted background — **di·oram·ic** \-'ram-ik\ *adj*

DISCUSSION

1. What is your favorite legend or fairy tale? How would you recreate the legend or fairy tale for other people so that it would be familiar to most people who know the legend or story?

2. What purpose do fantasy and make believe have in our culture?
3. Do you think it is possible for a person who has no awareness of American culture, literature, or tradition to enjoy Disneyland? Why?

Difficulty level: A

14. The Thin Grey Line

Marya Mannes

"Aw, they all do it," growled the cabdriver. He was 1
talking about cops who took payoffs for winking at double parking, but his cynicism could as well have been directed at any of a dozen other instances of corruption, big-time and small-time. Moreover, the disgust in his voice was overlaid by an unspoken "So what?": the implication that since this was the way things were, there was nothing anybody could do.

Like millions of his fellow Americans, the cabdriver was 2
probably a decent human being who had never stolen anything, broken any law or willfully injured another; somewhere, a knowledge of what was probably right had kept him from committing what was clearly wrong. But that knowledge had not kept a thin grey line that separates the two conditions from being daily greyer and thinner—to the point tht it was hardly noticeable.

On one side of this line are They: the bribers, the cheaters, 3
the chiselers, the swindlers, the extortioners. On the other side are We—both partners and victims. They and We are now so perilously close that the only mark distinguishing us is that They get caught and We don't.

The same citizen who voices his outrage at police corrup- 4
tion will slip the traffic cop on his block a handsome Christmas present in the belief that his car, nestled under a "No Parking" sign, will not be ticketed. The son of that nice woman next door has a habit of stealing cash from her purse because his allowance is smaller than his buddies'. Your son's friend admitted cheating at exams because "everybody does it."

Bit by bit, the resistance to an immunity against wrong 5
that a healthy social body builds up by law and ethics and the dictation of conscience have broken down. And instead of the fighting indignation of a people outraged by those who prey on them, we have the admission of impotence: "They all do it."

Now, failure to uphold the law is no less corrupt than 6
violation of the law. And the continuing shame of this country now is the growing number of Americans who fail to uphold and assist enforcement of the law, simply—and ignominiously—out of fear. Fear of "involvement," fear of "reprisal," fear of "trouble." A man is beaten by hoodlums in plain daylight and in view of bystanders. These people not only fail to help the victim, but, like the hoodlums, flee before the police can question them. A city official knows of a colleague's bribe but does not report it. A pedestrian watches a car hit a woman but leaves the scene, to avoid giving testimony. It happens

every day. And if the police get cynical at this irresponsibility, they are hardly to blame. Morale is a matter of giving support and having faith in one another; where both are lacking, "law" has become a worthless word.

How did we get this way? What started this blurring of what was once a thick black line between the lawful and the lawless? What makes a "regular guy," a decent fellow, accept a bribe? What makes a nice kid from a middle-class family take money for doing something he must know is not only illegal but wrong? 7

When you look into the background of an erring "kid" you will often find a comfortable home and a mother who will tell you, with tears in her eyes, that she "gave him everything." She probably did, to his everlasting damage. Fearing her son's disapproval, the indulgent mother denies him nothing except responsibility. Instead of growing up, he grows to believe that the world owes him everything. 8

The nice kid's father crosses the thin grey line himself in a dozen ways, day in and day out. He pads his expenses on his income-tax returns as a matter of course. As a landlord, he pays the local inspectors of the city housing authority to overlook violations in the houses he rents. When his son flunked his driving test, he gave him ten dollars to slip to the inspector on his second test. "They all do it," he said. 9

The nice kid is brought up with boys and girls who have no heroes except people not much older than themselves who have made the Big Time, usually in show business or in sports. Publicity and money are the halos of their stars, who range from pop singers who can't sing to ballplayers who can't read: from teen-age starlets who can't act to television performers who can't think. They may be excited by the exploits of spacemen, but the work's too tough and dangerous. 10

The nice kids have no heroes because they don't believe in heroes. Heroes are suckers and squares. To be a hero you have to stand out, to excel, to take risks, and above all, not only choose between right and wrong, but defend the right and fight the wrong. This means responsibility—and who needs it? 11

Today, no one has to take any responsibility. The psychiatrists, the sociologists, the novelists, the playwrights have gone a long way to help promote irresponsibility. Nobody really is to blame for what he does. It's Society. It's Environment. It's a Broken Home. It's an Underprivileged Area. But it's hardly ever You. 12

Now we find a truckload of excuses to absolve the individual from responsibility for his actions. A fellow commits a crime because he's basically insecure, because he hated his stepmother at nine, or because his sister needs an operation. A policeman loots a store because his salary is too low. A city official accepts a payoff because it's offered to him. Members of minority groups, racial or otherwise, commit crimes because they can't get a job, or are unacceptable to the people living around them. The words "right" and "wrong" are foreign to these people. 13

But honesty is the best policy. Says who? Anyone willing to get laughed at. But the laugh is no laughing matter. It con- 14 cerns the health and future of a nation. It involves the two-dollar illegal bettor as well as the corporation price-fixer, the college-examination cheater and the payroll-padding Congressman, the expense-account chiseler, the seller of pornography and his schoolboy reader, the bribed judge and the stealing delinquent. All these people may represent a minority. But when, as it appears now, the majority excuse themselves from responsibility by accepting corruption as natural to society ("They all do it"), this society is bordering on total confusion. If the line between right and wrong is finally erased, there is no defense against the power of evil.

Before this happens—and it is by no means far away—it might be well for the schools of the nation to substitute for the much-argued issue of prayer a daily lesson in ethics, law, and responsibility to society that would strengthen the conscience as exercise strengthens muscles. And it would be even better if parents were forced to attend it. For corruption is not something you read about in the papers and leave to courts. We are all involved. 15

COMPREHENSION

1. "The Thin Grey Line" is mostly about
   a. the corruption of government officials
   b. the responsibility we all share in the corruption of our society
   c. the corruption of the youth that is caused by show business heroes
   d. the difference between right and wrong
2. The cause of corruption in our culture can be attributed to
   a. income tax laws
   b. indulgent mothers
   c. irresponsibility
   d. show business
3. The most crucial reason why kids don't believe in heroes is because
   a. there are no heroes today
   b. heroes do not obtain wealth or fame
   c. heroes do not accept responsibility
   d. heroes must defend the right and fight the wrong
4. The main reason that corruption continues to spread is because
   a. everyone is corrupt in some way
   b. there is a growing number of people who are afraid to uphold and assist enforcement of the law
   c. the police are not doing their job
   d. there is nothing anybody can do to change it
5. To combat the growing corruption in our society, the author proposes that we
   a. erase the thin line between right and wrong
   b. conduct daily lessons in ethics, law, and responsibility in the school
   c. leave corruption to the courts
   d. accept corruption as natural to society

VOCABULARY

Directions: *The meaning of the following terms from selection 14 cannot be clearly determined from the context. Using the dictionary entries, select the appropriate definition of the term as it is used in the reading selection.*

1. impotence (par. 5)
    a. incapacity for sexual intercourse
    b. quality
    c. weakness
    d. lack of self-control

2. ignominiously (par. 6)
    a. markedly
    b. disgracefully
    c. deservingly
    d. fully

3. reprisal (par. 6)
    a. force
    b. seizure of property
    c. compensation
    d. retaliation

4. indulgent (par. 8)
    a. lenient
    b. prone
    c. compliant
    d. temporal

im·po·tence \'im-pət-ən(t)s\ *n* : the quality or state of being impotent
im·po·ten·cy \-ən-sē\ *n* : IMPOTENCE
im·po·tent \'im-pət-ənt\ *adj* [ME, fr. MF & L; MF, fr. L *impotent-, impotens*, fr. *in-* + *potent-, potens* potent] **1 a** : not potent : lacking in power, strength, or vigor : HELPLESS **b** : unable to copulate; *broadly* : STERILE — usu. used in males **2** *obs* : incapable of self-restraint : UNGOVERNABLE *syn* see STERILE *ant* virile, potent — **impotent** *n* — **im·po·tent·ly** *adv*

ig·no·min·i·ous \ˌig-nə-'min-ē-əs\ *adj* **1** : marked with or characterized by disgrace or shame : DISHONORABLE **2** : deserving of shame or infamy : DESPICABLE **3** : HUMILIATING, DEGRADING <suffered an ~ defeat> — **ig·no·min·i·ous·ly** *adv* — **ig·no·min·i·ous·ness** *n*
ig·no·mi·ny \'ig-nə-ˌmin-ē, -mə-nē; ig-'näm-ə-nē\ *n, pl* **-nies** [MF or L; MF *ignominie*, fr. L *ignominia*, fr. *ig-* (as in *ignorare* to be ignorant of, ignore) + *nomin-, nomen* name, repute — more at NAME] **1** : deep personal humiliation and disgrace **2** : disgraceful or dishonorable conduct, quality, or action *syn* see DISGRACE

re·pri·sal \ri-'prī-zəl\ *n* [ME *reprisail*, fr. MF *reprisaille*, fr. OIt *ripresaglia*, fr. *ripreso*, pp. of *riprendere* to take back, fr. *ri-* re- (fr. L *re-*) + *prendere* to take, fr. L *prehendere* — more at PREHENSILE] **1 a** : the act or practice in international law of resorting to force short of war in retaliation for damage or loss suffered **b** : an instance of such action **2** *obs* : PRIZE **3** : the regaining of something (as by recapture) **4** : something (as a sum of money) given or paid in restitution — usu. used in pl. **5** : a retaliatory act

¹in·dul·gence \in-'dəl-jən(t)s\ *n* **1** : remission of part or all of the temporal and esp. purgatorial punishment that according to Roman Catholicism is due for sins whose eternal punishment has been remitted and whose guilt has been pardoned (as through the sacrament of penance) **2** : the act of indulging : the state of being indulgent <treated her moody child with ~> **3 a** : an indulgent act **b** : an extension of time for payment or performance granted as a favor **4 a** : the act of indulging in something : the thing indulged in **b** : SELF-INDULGENCE
²indulgence *vt* **-genced; -genc·ing** : to attach an indulgence to <*indulgenced* prayers>
in·dul·gent \in-'dəl-jənt\ *adj* [L *indulgent-, indulgens*, prp. of *indulgēre*] : indulging or characterized by indulgence : LENIENT — **in·dul·gent·ly** *adv*

DISCUSSION

1. Is it possible to draw an absolute distinction between right and wrong? How does the meaning behind the thin grey line relate to the difference between right and wrong?
2. "The Thin Grey Line" was published in 1964. Do you see any changes in the society? What are those changes?
3. What are your feelings about the statement "failure to uphold the law is no less corrupt than violation of the law"? Is this statement true or false? Why?

Difficulty level: B

15. The Peter Principle

Laurence J. Peter and Raymond Hull

When I was a boy I was taught that the men upstairs knew what they were doing. I was told, "Peter, the more you know, the further you go." So I stayed in school until I graduated from college and then went forth into the world clutching firmly these ideas and my new teaching certificate. During the first year of teaching I was upset to find that a number of teachers, school principals, supervisors and superintendents appeared to be unaware of their professional responsibilities and incompetent in executing their duties. For example my principal's main concerns were that all window shades be at the same level, that classrooms should be quiet and that no one step on or near the rose beds. The superintendent's main concerns were that no minority group, no matter how fanatical, should ever be offended and that all official forms be submitted on time. The children's education appeared farthest from the administrator's mind.

At first I thought this was a special weakness of the school system in which I taught so I applied for certification in another province. I filled out the special forms, enclosed the required documents and complied willingly with all the red tape. Several weeks later, back came my application and all the documents!

No, there was nothing wrong with my credentials; the forms were correctly filled out; an official departmental stamp showed that they had been received in good order. But an accompanying letter said, "the new regulations require that such forms cannot be accepted by the Department of Education unless they have been registered at the Post Office to ensure safe delivery. Will you please remail the forms to the Department, making sure to register them this time?"

I began to suspect that the local school system did not have a monopoly on incompetence.

As I looked further afield, I saw that every organization contained a number of persons who could not do their jobs.

A UNIVERSAL PHENOMENON

Occupational incompetence is everywhere. Have you noticed it? Probably we all have noticed it.

We see indecisive politicians posing as resolute statesmen and the "authoritative source" who blames his misinformation on "situational imponderables." Limitless are the public servants who are indolent and insolent; military commanders whose behavioral timidity belies their dreadnought rhetoric, and governors whose innate servility prevents their actually governing. In our sophistication, we virtually shrug aside the immoral cleric, corrupt judge, incoherent attorney, author who cannot write and English teacher who cannot spell. At universities we see proclamations authored by administrators whose own office communications are hopelessly muddled; and droning lectures from inaudible or incomprehensible instructors.

Seeing incompetence at all levels of every hierarchy — political, legal, educational and industrial — I hypothesized that the cause was some inherent feature of the rules governing the placement of employees. Thus began my serious study of the ways in which employees move upward through a hierarchy, and of what happens to them after promotion.

Municipal Government File, Case No. 17

J. S. Minion* was a maintenance foreman in the public works department of Excelsior City. He was a favorite of the senior officials at City Hall. They all praised his unfailing affability.

* Some names have been changed, in order to protect the guilty.

"I like Minion," said the superintendent of works. "He has good judgment and is always pleasant and agreeable." 10

This behavior was appropriate for Minion's position: he was not supposed to make policy, so he had no need to disagree with his superiors. 11

The superintendent of works retired and Minion succeeded him. Minion continued to agree with everyone. He passed to his foreman every suggestion that came from above. The resulting conflicts in policy, and the continual changing of plans, soon demoralized the department. Complaints poured in from the Mayor and other officials, from taxpayers and from the maintenance-workers' union. 12

Minion still says "Yes" to everyone, and carries messages briskly back and forth between his superiors and his subordinates. Nominally a superintendent, he actually does the work of a messenger. The maintenance department regularly exceeds its budget, yet fails to fulfill its program of work. In short, Minion, a competent foreman, became an incompetent superintendent. 13

Service Industries File, Case No. 3

E. Tinker was exceptionally zealous and intelligent as an apprentice at G. Reece Auto Repair Inc., and soon rose to journeyman mechanic. In this job he showed outstanding ability in diagnosing obscure faults, and endless patience in correcting them. He was promoted to foreman of the repair shop. 14

But here his love of things mechanical and his perfectionism become liabilities. He will undertake any job that he thinks looks interesting, no matter how busy the shop may be. "We'll work it in somehow," he says. 15

He will not let a job go until he is fully satisfied with it. 16

He meddles constantly. He is seldom to be found at his desk. He is usually up to his elbows in a dismantled motor and while the man who should be doing the work stands watching, other workmen sit around waiting to be assigned new tasks. As a result the shop is always overcrowded with work, always in a muddle, and delivery times are often missed. 17

Tinker cannot understand that the average customer cares little about perfection—he wants his car back on time! He cannot understand that most of his men are less interested in motors than in their pay checks. So Tinker cannot get on with his customers or with his subordinates. He was a competent mechanic, but is now an incompetent foreman. 18

Military File, Case No. 8

Consider the case of the late renowned General A. Goodwin. His hearty, informal manner, his racy style of speech, his scorn for petty regulations and his undoubted personal bravery made him the idol of his men. He led them to many well-deserved victories. 19

When Goodwin was promoted to field marshal he had to deal, not with ordinary soldiers, but with politicians and allied generalissimos. 20

He would not conform to the necessary protocol. He could not turn his tongue to the conventional courtesies and flatteries. He quarreled with all the dignitaries and took to lying 21 for days at a time, drunk and sulking, in his trailer. The conduct of the war slipped out of his hands into those of his subordinates. He had been promoted to a position that he was incompetent to fill

AN IMPORTANT CLUE!

In time I saw that all such cases had a common feature. 22 The employee had been promoted from a position of competence to a position of incompetence. I saw that, sooner or later, this could happen to every employee in every hierarchy.

Hypothetical Case File, Case No. 1

Suppose you own a pill-rolling factory, Perfect Pill Incor- 23 porated. Your foreman-pill roller dies of a perforated ulcer. You need a replacement. You naturally look among your rank-and-file pill rollers.

Miss Oval, Mrs. Cylinder, Mr. Ellipse and Mr. Cube all 24 show various degrees of incompetence. They will naturally be ineligible for promotion. You will choose—other things being equal—your most competent pill roller, Mr. Sphere, and promote him to foreman.

Now suppose Mr. Sphere proves competent as foreman. 25 Later, when your general foreman, Legree, moves up to Works Manager, Sphere will be eligible to take his place.

If, on the other hand, sphere is an incompetent foreman, 26 he will get no more promotion. He has reached what I call his "level of incompetence." He will stay there till the end of this career.

Some employees, like Ellipse and Cube, reach a level of 27 incompetence in the lowest grade and are never promoted. Some, like Sphere (assuming he is not a satisfactory foreman), reach it after one promotion.

E. Tinker, the automobile repair-shop foreman, reached 28 his level of incompetence on the third stage of the hierarchy. General Goodwin reached his level of incompetence at the very top of the hierarchy.

So my analysis of hundreds of cases of occupational 29 incompetence led me on to formulate *The Peter Principle:*

In a Hierarchy Every Employee Tends to Rise to His Level of 30
Incompetence

A NEW SCIENCE!

Having formulated the Principle I discovered that I had 31 inadvertently founded a new science, hierarchiology, the study of hierarchies.

The term "hierarchy" was originally used to describe the 32 system of church government by priests graded into ranks. The contemporary meaning includes any organization whose members or employees are arranged in order of rank, grade or class.

Hierarchiology, although a relatively recent discipline, 33 appears to have great applicability to the fields of public and private administration.

THIS MEANS YOU!

My Principle is the key to an understanding of all hier- 34 archal systems, and therefore to an understanding of the whole structure of civilization. A few eccentrics try to avoid getting involved with hierarchies, but everyone in business, industry, trade-unionism, politics, government, the armed forces, religion and education is so involved. All of them are controlled by the Peter Principle.

Many of them, to be sure, may win a promotion or two, 35 moving from one level of competence to a higher level of competence. But competence in that new position qualifies them for still another promotion. For each individual, for *you*, for *me*, the final promotion is from a level of competence to a level of incompetence.

So, given enough time—and assuming the existence of 36 enough ranks in the hierarchy—each employee rises to, and remains at, his level of incompetence. Peter's Corollary states:

In time, every post tends to be occupied by an employee who is 37 *incompetent to carry out its duties.*

COMPREHENSION

1. This article tells you
   a. why Peter decided to find a new teaching position
   b. what happens to employees who are found to be incompetent
   c. the reasons why incompetent people are promoted
   d. why education is important in advancement
2. When Peter applied for certification in another province he found out that
   a. his application documents were with the Post Office
   b. his credentials were not in good order
   c. every organization contains a number of people who cannot do their jobs
   d. it was not worth his trouble because there was too much red tape
3. Occupational incompetence
   a. is confined to government
   b. is most evident in politics
   c. is present in all hierarchies
   d. is caused by lack of education
4. We accept occupational incompetence because
   a. we have become so used to it
   b. there is nothing we can do about it
   c. it is good for society
   d. people have rules to govern the placement of employees
5. Most people who are incompetent at a particular job
   a. improve and in time become competent
   b. have been promoted from a job in which they were competent
   c. are eventually demoted or fired
   d. voluntarily change jobs so that they can feel more competent

VOCABULARY

Directions: *The meaning of the following terms from selection 15 cannot be clearly determined from the context. Using the dictionary entries, select the appropriate definition of the term as it is used in the reading selection.*

1. monopoly (par. 4)
   a. pool
   b. syndicate
   c. exclusive control
   d. combination
2. indolent (par. 7)
   a. painless
   b. lazy
   c. giving pain
   d. disinclined
3. insolent (par. 7)
   a. presumptuous
   b. unusual
   c. audacious
   d. quaint
4. incoherent (par. 7)
   a. unconnected events
   b. disorderly thoughts
   c. inharmonious actions
   d. unable to express thoughts clearly

mo·nop·o·ly (mə-nŏp′ə-lē) *n., pl.* **-lies.** **1.** *Economics.* Exclusive control by one group of the means of producing or selling a commodity or service. Compare **oligopoly.** **2.** *Law.* A right granted by a government, giving exclusive control over a specified commercial activity to a single party. **3. a.** A company or group having exclusive control over a commercial activity. **b.** A commodity or service controlled exclusively by one company or group. **4.** Exclusive possession of or control over anything: *"the lexicographer had no monopoly of the problem of meaning"* (William V. Quine). [From Latin *monopōlium,* from Greek *monopōlion,* sole selling rights : MONO- + *pōlein,* to sell (see **pel-⁵** in Appendix*).] —**mo·nop′o·lism′** *n.* —**mo·nop′o·list** *n. & adj.* —**mo·nop′o·lis′tic** *adj.*

Synonyms: *monopoly, corner, pool, trust, cartel, syndicate, combination, combine. Monopoly* is a general term applicable to a condition or organization and the service or commodity involved; in none of these senses is illegality necessarily implied. *Corner* denotes only a condition. It is a short-term speculative monopoly created by individuals (not necessarily illegally) to control a market. *Pool* and *trust* denote intercorporate organizations (now illegal) designed to restrict competition within specific areas and industries over a long period. *Cartel* usually denotes an international pool or trust; in Europe the term often also applies to a pool or trust operating within a single country. *Syndicate* pertains to any group engaged in a short-term commercial venture involving large capital; monopoly is no longer usually implied. *Combination* denotes any sizable, relatively permanent intercorporate association; the term no longer indicates monopoly unless so qualified, as in *combination in restraint of trade. Combine* is used informally for a combination, and generally implies monopolistic practice for private gain.

in·do·lent (ĭn′də-lənt) *adj.* **1.** Disinclined to work; habitually lazy. **2.** *Pathology.* Causing little or no pain: *an indolent tumor.* [Late Latin *indolēns,* painless : Latin *in-,* not + *dolēns,* present participle of *dolēre,* to give pain, feel pain (see **del-³** in Appendix*).] —**in′do·lence** *n.*

in·so·lent (ĭn′sə-lənt) *adj.* **1.** Presumptuous and insulting in manner or speech; arrogant. **2.** Audaciously impudent; impertinent. [Middle English, from Latin *insolēns,* perhaps originally "unusual," "quaint" : *in-,* not + *solēns,* present participle of *solēre,* to use (see **obsolete**).] —**in′so·lent·ly** *adv.*

in·co·her·ent (ĭn′kō-hîr′ənt) *adj.* **1.** Not coherent; disordered; unconnected; inharmonious. **2.** Unable to think or express one's thoughts in a clear or orderly manner: *incoherent with grief.* —**in′co·her′ent·ly** *adv.* —**in′co·her′ent·ness** *n.*

DISCUSSION

1. Cite some cases of occupational incompetence that you have observed.
2. Where do you think occupational incompetence is the most harmful? the least harmful?
3. If the "men upstairs" do not know what they are doing what can be done about it?

Difficulty level: B

16. Euphemism

Neil Postman

A euphemism is commonly defined as an auspicious or exalted term (like "garbage man"). People who are partial to euphemisms stand accused of being "phony" or of trying to hide what it is they are really talking about. And there is no doubt that in some situations the accusation is entirely proper. For example, one of the more detestable euphemisms I have come across in recent years is the term "Operation Sunshine," which is the name the U.S. Government gave to some experiments it conducted with the hydrogen bomb in the South Pacific. It is obvious that the government, in choosing this name, was trying to expunge the hideous imagery that the bomb evokes and in so doing committed, as I see it, an immoral act. This sort of process—giving pretty names to essentially ugly realities—is what has given euphemizing such a bad name. And people like George Orwell have done valuable work for all of us in calling attention to how the process works. But there is another side to euphemizing that is worth mentioning, and a few words here in its defense will not be amiss.

To begin with, we must keep in mind that things do not have "real" names, although many people believe that they do. A garbage man is not "really" a "garbage man," any more than he is really a "sanitation engineer." And a pig is not called a "pig" because it is so dirty, nor a shrimp a "shrimp" because it is so small. There are things, and then there are the names of things, and it is considered a fundamental error in all branches of semantics to assume that a name and a thing are one and the same. It is true, of course, that a name is usually so firmly associated with the thing it denotes that it is extremely difficult to separate one from the other. That is why, for example, advertising is so effective. Perfumes are not given names like "Bronx Odor," and an automobile will never be called "The Lumbering Elephant." Shakespeare was only half right in saying that a rose by any other name would smell as sweet. What we call things affects how we will perceive them. It is not only harder to sell someone a "horse mackerel" sandwich than a "tuna fish" sandwich, but even though they are the "same" thing, we are likely to enjoy the taste of the tuna more than that of the horse mackerel. It would appear that human beings almost naturally come to *identify* names with things, which is one of our more fascinating illusions. But there is some substance to this illusion. For if you change the names of things, you change how people will regard them, and that is as good as changing the nature of the thing itself.

Now all sorts of scoundrels know this perfectly well and can make us love almost anything by getting us to transfer the charm of a name to whatever worthless thing they are promoting. But at the same time and in the same vein, euphemizing is a perfectly intelligent method of generating new and useful ways of perceiving things. The man who wants us to call him a "sanitation engineer" instead of a "garbage man" is hoping we will treat him with more respect than we presently do. He wants us to see that he is of some importance to our society. His euphemism is laughable only if we think that he is not deserving of such notice or respect. The teaher who refers us to use the term "culturally different children" instead of "slum children" is euphemizing, all right, but is doing it to encourage us to see aspects of a situation that might otherwise not be attended to.

The point I am making is that there is nothing in the process of euphemizing itself that is contemptible. Euphemizing is contemptible when a name makes us see something that is not true or diverts our attention from something that is. The hydrogen bomb kills. There is nothing else that it does. And when you experiment with it, you are trying to find out how widely and well it kills. Therefore, to call such an experiment "Operation Sunshine" is to suggest a purpose for the bomb that simply does not exist. But to call "slum children" "culturally different" is something else. It calls attention, for example, to legitimate reasons why such children might feel alienated from what goes on in school

I grant that sometimes such euphemizing does not have 5 the intended effect. It is possible for a teacher to use the term "culturally different" but still be controlled by the term "slum children" (which the teacher may believe is their "real" name). "Old people" may be called "senior citizens," and nothing might change. And "lunatic asylums" may still be filthy, primitive prisons though they are called "mental institutions." Nonetheless, euphemizing may be regarded as one of our more important intellectual resources for creating new perspectives on a subject. The *attempt* to rename "old people" "senior citizens" was obviously motivated by a desire to give them a political identity, which they not only warrant but which may yet have important consequences. In fact, the fate of euphemisms is very hard to predict. A new and seemingly silly name may replace an old one (let us say, "chairperson" for "chairman") and for years no one will think or act any differently because of it. And then, gradually, as people begin to assume that "chairperson" is the "real" and proper name (or "senior citizen" or "tuna fish" or "sanitation engineer"), their attitudes begin to shift, and they will approach things in a slightly different frame of mind. There is a danger, of course, in supposing that a new name can change attitudes quickly or always. There must be some authentic tendency or drift in the culture to lend support to the change, or the name will remain incongruous and may even appear ridiculous. To call a teacher a "facilitator" would be such an example. To eliminate the distinction between "boys" and "girls" by calling them "childpersons" would be another.

But to suppose that such changes never "amount to 6 anything" is to underestimate the power of names. I have been astounded not only by how rapidly the name "blacks" has replaced "Negroes" (a kind of euphemizing in reverse) but also by how significantly perceptions and attitudes have shifted as an accompaniment to the change.

The key idea here is that euphemisms are a means 7 through which a culture may alter its imagery and by so doing subtly change its style, its priorities, and its values. I reject categorically the idea that people who use "earthy" language are speaking more directly or with more authenticity than people who employ euphemisms. Saying that someone is "dead" is not to speak more plainly or honestly than saying he has "passed away." It is, rather, to suggest a different conception of what the event means. To ask where the "shithouse" is, is no more to the point than to ask where the "restroom" is. But in the difference between the two words, there is expressed a vast difference in one's attitude toward privacy and propriety. What I am saying is that the process of euphemizing has no moral content. The moral dimensions are supplied by what the words in question express, what they want us to value and to see. A nation that calls experiments with bombs "Operation Sunshine" is very frightening. On the other hand, a people who call "garbage men" "sanitation engineers" can't be all bad.

COMPREHENSION

1. The author suggests that euphemism
   a. is immoral
   b. is phony
   c. can have positive results
   d. should be used only in advertising
2. The author objected to the "Sunshine Operation" euphemism because it
   a. suggested that solar energy was connected with nuclear energy
   b. gives nuclear energy a bad reputation
   c. is a pretty name for an ugly reality
   d. gives euphemism a bad name
3. Euphemism may be regarded as one of our more important intellectual resources because it
   a. gives people a political identity
   b. can create new perspectives on a subject
   c. diverts our attention from the truth
   d. encourages positive thinking
4. Postman feels that the difference between the words "shithouse" and "restroom" is one of
   a. meaning
   b. morality
   c. honesty
   d. attitude toward privacy
5. According to Postman, euphemisms can create
   a. change in morality
   b. attitude change over time
   c. distortion in the development of language
   d. distrust

VOCABULARY

Directions: *The meaning of the following terms from selection 16 cannot be clearly determined from the context. Using the dictionary entries, select the appropriate definition of the term as it is used in the reading selection.*

1. auspicious (par. 1)
   a. one who is favored
   b. favorable
   c. fortunate
   d. prosperous

   aus·pi·cious \ȯ-'spish-əs\ *adj* **1** : affording a favorable auspice : PROPITIOUS <made an ~ beginning by getting an A> **2** : attended by good auspices : PROSPEROUS <an ~ year> *syn* see FAVORABLE *ant* inauspicious, ill-omened — **aus·pi·cious·ly** *adv* — **aus·pi·cious·ness** *n*

2. expunge (par. 1)
   a. to blot out
   b. to identify using dots
   c. to prick
   d. to mark

   ex·punge \ik-'spənj\ *vt* **ex·punged; ex·pung·ing** [L *expungere* to mark for deletion by dots, fr. *ex-* + *pungere* to prick — more at PUNGENT] **1** : to strike out, obliterate, or mark for deletion **2** : to efface completely : DESTROY *syn* see ERASE — **ex·pung·er** *n*

3. amiss (par. 1)
   a. improper
   b. appropriate
   c. beside the mark
   d. faulty

   ¹amiss \ə-'mis\ *adv* **1 a** : in a mistaken way : WRONGLY <if you think he is guilty, you judge ~> **b** : ASTRAY <something had gone ~> **2** : in a faulty way : IMPERFECTLY

271

4. semantics (par. 2)
   a. linguistic
      assumptions
   b. science of sounds
   c. science of symbolic
      relationships
   d. science of meanings

se·man·tics \si-'mant-iks\ *n pl but sing or pl in constr* **1** : the study of meanings: **a** : the historical and psychological study and the classification of changes in the signification of words or forms viewed as factors in linguistic development **b** (1) : SEMIOTIC (2) : a branch of semiotic dealing with the relations between signs and what they refer to and including theories of denotation, extension, naming, and truth **2** : GENERAL SEMANTICS **3 a** : the meaning or relationship of meanings of a sign or set of signs; *esp* : connotative meaning **b** : the exploitation of connotation and ambiguity (as in propaganda)

5. authentic (par. 5)
   a. veritable
   b. genuine
   c. trustworthy
   d. authoritative

au·then·tic \ə-'thent-ik, ȯ-\ *adj* [ME *autentik*, fr. MF *autentique*, fr. LL *authenticus*, fr. Gk *authentikos*, fr. *authentēs* perpetrator, master, fr. *aut-* + *-hentēs* (akin to Gk *anyein* to accomplish, Skt *sanoti* he gains)] **1** *obs* : AUTHORITATIVE **2** : worthy of acceptance or belief as conforming to fact or reality : TRUSTWORTHY **3 a** : not imaginery, false, or imitation <one of the few remaining ~ colonial buildings> **b** : conforming to an original so as to reproduce essential features <an ~ reproduction of a colonial farmhouse> **4 a** *of a church mode* : ranging upward from the keynote — compare PLAGAL 1 **b** *of a cadence* : progressing from the dominant chord to the tonic — compare PLAGAL 2 — **au·then·ti·cal·ly** \-i-k(ə-)lē\ *adv* — **au·then·tic·i·ty** \ȯ-ˌthen-'tis-ət-ē, -thən-\ *n*

6. categorically (par. 7)
   a. hypothetically
   b. logically
   c. absolutely
   d. explicitly

cat·e·gor·i·cal \ˌkat-ə-'gȯr-i-kəl, -'gär-\ *also* **cat·e·gor·ic** \-ik\ *adj* [LL *categoricus*, fr. Gk *katēgorikos*, fr. *katēgoria* affirmation, category] **1** : ABSOLUTE, UNQUALIFIED <a ~ denial> **2** : of, relating to, or constituting a category — **cat·e·gor·i·cal·ly** \-i-k(ə-)lē\ *adv*

7. propriety (par. 7)
   a. a peculiar condition
   b. true nature
   c. rules dictating
      behavior
   d. sense of what
      is proper

pro·pri·ety \p(r)ə-'prī-ət-ē\ *n, pl* **-eties** [ME *propriete*, fr. MF *proprieté* property, quality of a person or thing — more at PROPERTY] **1** *obs* : true nature **2** *obs* : a special characteristic : PECULIARITY **3** : the quality or state of being proper **4 a** : the standard of what is socially acceptable in conduct or speech : DECORUM **b** : fear of offending against conventional rules of behavior esp. as between the sexes **c** *pl* : the customs and manners of polite society

DISCUSSION

1. Do you consider any euphemisms to be immoral? Why?
2. What object or idea would you regard differently if it had a different name?
3. Do you think the tendency to identify names with things extends to people's names? For instance, do you associate special characteristics with specific names?

Difficulty level: C

17. Occupational Choice and Adjustment

James Coleman

As we have noted, people seek a great deal from their jobs in terms of good psychological conditions as well as good physical working conditions. Hence, the issue of occupational choice is a critical one, which most young people take very seriously. In this section we shall consider factors affecting job choiced as well as factors affecting the individual's satisfaction and success in his or her chosen work.

CHOOSING THE "RIGHT" OCCUPATION

Career choice, of course, is something relatively new. In earlier times—as well as in many other societies today—most people had their choices made for them or were at best severely limited in what they could choose. Of necessity, most males followed what their fathers had done or entered whatever apprenticeship training was available to them in their communities. Women remained in the home. Today most people have an almost unlimited choice of careers, within the range of their abilities and preparations.

The choices today offer new opportunities but also new problems. Besides the enormous variety of possibilities, there are many more white-collar positions than ever before, and pay is higher than ever before. Also, there are increased opportunities for women and minority workers. Nevertheless, in spite of these opportunities, there are still serious problems of discrimination as well as unsatisfying working conditions. Many occupations are oversupplied with workers; others that may be highly desirable require long years of education and preparation, as well as continuing study to keep abreast of advances in knowledge and technology. Hence, the person trying to decide about a career must be aware of both the opportunities and the obstacles associated with a particular occupational choice.

Characteristics of the Individual

Three questions appear to be of particular significance from the standpoint of personal characteristics.

1. What does the individual want to do? The answer to this question involves interests, motives, and values. Does the individual like to work with people? With ideas? With things? Does the person prefer a leisurely pace or thrive on pressures and deadlines? Other relevant questions concern what the individual would like to be doing ten or twenty years hence and what he or she would like their occupational experience to help them become.

2. What can the individual do—or learn to do? The answer to this question involves abilities and aptitudes. What is the person's general level of intelligence? What knowledge and skills does he or she possess? What is the individual's potential for acquiring further competence in particular areas? What outstanding special abilities, such as artistic, athletic, or mechanical skills, does the individual possess? Does the individual have any special physical or mental limitations that might rule out a particular occupational area?

3. Are the individual's goals likely to change drastically in the near future? Psychologists have devised a number of assessment instruments for obtaining information about interests, abilities, values, and other personal characteristics and then matching this information against the requirements of given occupations. Such assessment information may be useful, but it is information pertaining to *now.* It cannot be used to predict an individual's interests, abilities, or other personal characteristics five or ten years in the future. While we all change with time, some people are definitely unclear about what they really want to do and become. With learning and experience, they may show drastic changes in their life goals. Thus, it seems desirable to exercise caution in relating an individual's present characteristics to long-range career goals and plans.

Characteristics of the Occupation

Here, too, three general questions appear to be relevant: 8

1. *What are the requirements and working conditions?* What 9
training and skills are needed for admission? What general per
sonal qualities—such as initiative, social competence, a par
ticular temperament, or physical endurance—are required?
What would the individual be doing? In what kind of setting?
Equally important, how do these requirements fit what the in
dividual has to offer and what he or she enjoys doing?

Here it may be emphasized that different positions within 10
a broad occupational category may vary greatly in work ac
tivities and conditions. For example, a clinical psychologist
working primarily with marital problems might engage in quite
different daily activities and live in quite a different world from
a physiological psychologist who is doing research on en
docrine function in rats. Even the requisite knowledge and
skills differ greatly, depending on the area of specialization and
the particular job within it.

2. *What does the occupation have to offer?* What rewards and 11
satisfactions can be expected in terms of income, social status,
and opportunities for advancement and personal growth? Are
the rewards and satisfactions the kind the individual wants?
Will the individual find the work interesting and personally
fulfilling? What can he or she expect to contribute? In the long
run, we are likely to find our work more meaningful and fulfill
ing if we feel that we are making a contribution to our chosen
field.

3. *What changes are likely to occur in the field?* Since today's 12
college students will be working beyond the year 2000 A.D., the
question of future trends in one's chosen occupational area is
a relevant one. With the accelerating rate of technological and
social change, major shifts in many occupations are taking
place even in relatively short periods of time. Thus, it is impor
tant that the individual not only gain a clear view of given oc
cupations as they now exist but also know about probable
changes in the near and distant future that might affect his or
her work.

Stages in Career Choice

An occupational choice may not be made until the indi- 13
vidual reaches late adolescence or early adulthood. But prior to
this time, many decisions have been made that have led toward
or away from given occupations. And long before the first job,
the individual has developed ideas about the function of work
and attitudes toward different kinds of work. Thus, career
choice is a developmental process: the groundwork for it has
been laid in many kinds of experiences long before the final,
explicit choice is made. Investigators have pointed to three
stages in career choice:

Stage I. Fantasy period. For most children this period ex- 14
tends until about age eleven. In this stage children do not relate
occupational choice to their intellectual and personal qualifica
tions or to realistic opportunities. Rather, they tend to make the
assumption that they can become whatever they want to

become—whether it be a police officer, a scientist, an astronaut, or a physician. Children often try out many occupational roles in their play, identifying with the occupation of their father or mother or other adults they know or have seen on television.

Stage II. Tentative period. From about eleven to seventeen years of age, young people recognize the need to decide sometime on a future occupation. Now they make tentative choices based on whatever awareness they have of their interests, abilities, and values as well as environmental opportunities. At first, compatible interests appear to be a primary consideration in career choice. Later they begin to consider ability and training prerequisites, and still later personal values become an important consideration. By the end of this period, they recognize that it is necessary to integrate interests, abilities, and values and to allow for the realities of environmental limitations and opportunities in making a tentative vocational choice.

Stage III. Realistic choice stage. From about the age of seventeen, young people try to work out a suitable occupational plan by translating their own desires into a real-life occupation. This process is often very difficult, especially for young people who find that their occupational dreams are unrealistic. At this stage, they often realize that it is necessary to compromise between their hopes and desires and reality. This stage, in turn, involves *exploration*, as young people acquire information and possibly work experience, *crystallization*, as they narrow their range of alternatives and prepare to make a career choice; and finally, *specification* with commitment to a given occupational goal.

Several investigators have also found that *negative choices* are of great importance. Often people are sure about what they do *not* want to do, while they are unclear about what they *do* want to do. Besides limiting the occupations from which choices are later made, negative choices also form points of reference against which new possibilities are evaluated. Thus, in a general sense, we narrow our field of choice over time. Again, however, caution is desirable since we may inadvertently rule out career possibilities on the basis of inadequate or inaccurate information.

Here it may be emphasized that family background and parental expectations as well as social class and ethnic factors may play key roles in an individual's choice of career. It may also be emphasized that career choice, like development, is not a finite process. People may be constantly reevaluating their work experiences or they may suddenly find that they are bored and unfulfilled, disheartened and saddened by a career that once gave them pleasure and excitement. Or perhaps a change in health may force a worker to seek another career, as when a surgeon develops arthritis, a dancer is crippled by bad knees, or a construction worker develops heart disease. Or a change in the economy or technology may eliminate jobs and force even successful and satisfied workers into other fields. Like everything else in our lives, career choice is subject to change.

15

16

17

18

COMPREHENSION

1. The main idea in this article is that
   a. in choosing the right occupation a person has to consider opportunities in a field
   b. a person has to know the obstacles in a particular field
   c. many occupations are oversupplied with workers
   d. both the characteristics of the individual and the characteristics of the job must be considered in choosing an occupation

2. The author of this article makes the point that assessment instruments developed by psychologists provide information that
   a. can be used to predict career preferences in the future
   b. clearly indicate what people want to do and become
   c. pertain only to the present
   d. are of no use at all to people who are trying to decide on a career

3. In choosing an occupation, an important consideration is
   a. how much the job pays
   b. how large the company is
   c. whether the employee must relocate
   d. probable changes that may occur in the occupation in the future

4. There are several key factors in an individual's choice of career. From among these, the author emphasizes
   a. family background, parental expectations, social class, and ethnic factors
   b. that career choice is a once-in-a-lifetime decision
   c. that a change in health need not mean a change in career
   d. that technology decreases the number of career options

5. The most difficult stage in the process of career choice is
   a. the fantasy stage
   b. the realistic choice stage
   c. the developmental stage
   d. the tentative stage

VOCABULARY

Directions: *The meaning of the following terms from selection 17 cannot be clearly determined from the context. Using the dictionary entries, select the appropriate definition of the term as it is used in the reading selection.*

1. assessment (par. 6)
   a. estimation
   b. evaluation
   c. assistant
   d. special payment

2. clinical (par. 10)
   a. one who works directly with patients
   b. one who objectively studies data
   c. emotional person
   d. analytical person

as·sess (ə-sĕs′) *tr.v.* **-sessed, -sessing, -sesses. 1.** To estimate the value of (property) for taxation. **2.** To set or determine the amount of (a tax, fine, or other payment). **3.** To charge (a person or property) with a tax, fine, or other special payment. **4.** To evaluate; appraise. —See Synonyms at **estimate.** [Middle English *assessen*, from Old French *assesser*, from Latin *assidere* (past participle *assessus*), "to sit beside," be an assistant judge : *ad-*, near to + *sedere*, to sit (see **sed-¹** in Appendix*).] —**as·sess′a·ble** *adj.*
as·sess·ment (ə-sĕs′mənt) *n.* **1.** The act of assessing. **2.** An amount assessed.

clin·i·cal (klĭn′ĭ-kəl) *adj.* **1.** Pertaining to or connected with a clinic. **2.** Of or pertaining to direct observation and treatment of patients. **3.** Analytical; highly objective; rigorously scientific: *clinical details.* **4.** Administered on a deathbed or sickbed: *a clinical sacrament.* —**clin′i·cal·ly** *adv.*

3. endocrine (par. 10)
   a. ductless gland system
   b. internal system
   c. secretion
   d. duct system

en·do·crine (ĕn′də-krĭn, -krēn′, -krĭn′) *adj.* Also **en·do·crin·ic** (-krĭn′ĭk), **en·doc·ri·nous** (ĕn-dŏk′rə-nəs). **1.** Secreting internally. **2.** Of or pertaining to any of the ductless or endocrine glands. —*n.* **1.** The internal secretion of a gland. **2.** An endocrine gland. [ENDO- + Greek *krīnein*, to separate, "secrete" (see **skeri-** in Appendix*).]

4. developmental (par. 13)
   a. happening
   b. growing and changing
   c. static
   d. grouping

de·vel·op·ment (dĭ-vĕl′əp-mənt) *n.* **1.** The act of developing. **2.** A developed state, condition, or form. **3.** Something that has been developed; a product or result of developing. **4.** An event, occurrence, or happening: *a development in the war.* **5.** A group of dwellings built by the same contractor. —**de·vel′op·men′tal** *adj.* —**de·vel′op·men′tal·ly** *adv.*

DISCUSSION

1. The author argues that a person must be aware of both the opportunities and the obstacles of a given career choice. Discuss the problems you have faced or are facing in your attempt to make a career choice.
2. Select at least one of the questions under "Characteristics of the Individual" and answer it with reference to your own career choice.
3. Coleman states that the realistic stage is a period of compromise between one's "hopes and desires and reality." Do you agree? Is compromise inevitable? What kinds of adjustments or compromises have you made, or are you making, in your own career choice?

Difficulty level: C

18. Down at the Cross

James Baldwin

White Americans find it as difficult as white people elsewhere do to divest themselves of the notion that they are in possession of some intrinsic value that black people need, or want. And this assumption—which, for example, makes the solution to the Negro problem depend on the speed with which Negroes accept and adopt white standards—is revealed in all kinds of striking ways, from Bobby Kennedy's assurance that a Negro can become President in forty years to the unfortunate tone of warm congratulation with which so many liberals address their Negro equals. It is the Negro, of course, who is presumed to have become equal—an achievement that not only proves the comforting fact that perseverance has no color but also overwhelmingly corroborates the white man's sense of his own value. Alas, this value can scarcely be corroborated in any other way; there is certainly little enough in the white man's public or private life that one should desire to imitate. White men, at the bottom of their hearts, know this. Therefore, a vast amount of the energy that goes into what we call the Negro problem is produced by the white man's profound desire not to be judged by those who are not white, not to be seen as he

1

is, and at the same time a vast amount of the white anguish is rooted in the white man's equally profound need to be seen as he is, to be released from the tyranny of his mirror. All of us know, whether or not we are able to admit it, that mirrors can only lie, that death by drowning is all that awaits one there. It is for this reason that love is so desperately sought and so cunningly avoided. Love takes off the masks that we fear we cannot live without and know we cannot live within. I use the word "love" here not merely in the personal sense but as a state of being, or a state of grace—not in the infantile American sense of being made happy but in the tough and universal sense of quest and daring and growth. And I submit, then, that the racial tensions that menace Americans today have little to do with real antipathy—on the contrary, indeed—and are involved only symbolically with color. These tensions are rooted in the very same depths as those from which love springs, or murder. The white man's unadmitted—and apparently, to him, unspeakable—private fears and longings are projected onto the Negro. The only way he can be released from the Negro's tyrannical power over him is to consent, in effect, to become black himself, to become a part of that suffering and dancing country that he now watches wistfully from the heights of his lonely power and, armed with spiritual traveller's checks, visits surreptitiously after dark. How can one respect, let alone adopt, the values of a people who do not, on any level whatever, live the way they say they do, or the way they say they should? I cannot accept the proposition that the four-hundred-year travail of the American Negro should result merely in his attainment of the present level of the American civilization. I am far from convinced that being released from the African witch doctor was worthwhile if I am now—in order to support the moral contradictions and the spiritual aridity of my life—expected to become dependent on the American psychiatrist. It is a bargain I refuse. The only thing white people have that black people need, or should want, is power—and no one holds power forever. White people cannot, in the generality, be taken as models of how to live. Rather, the white man is himself in sore need of new standards, which will release him from his confusion and place him once again in fruitful communion with the depths of his own being. And I repeat: The price of the liberation of the white people is the liberation of the blacks—the total liberation, in the cities, in the towns, before the law, and in the mind. Why, for example—especially knowing the family as I do—I should *want* to marry your sister is a great mystery to me. But your sister and I have every right to marry if we wish to, and no one has the right to stop us. If she cannot raise me to her level, perhaps I can raise her to mine.

In short, we, the black and the white, deeply need each other here if we are really to become a nation—if we are really, that is, to achieve our identity, our maturity, as men and women. To create one nation has proved to be a hideously difficult task; there is certainly no need now to create two, one black and one white. But white men with far more political power than that possessed by the Nation of Islam movement

2

have been advocating exactly this, in effect, for generations. If this sentiment is honored when it falls from the lips of Senator Byrd, then there is no reason it should not be honored when it falls from the lips of Malcolm X. And any Congressional committee wishing to investigate the latter must also be willing to investigate the former. They are expressing exactly the same sentiments and represent exactly the same danger. There is absolutely no reason to suppose that white people are better equipped to frame the laws by which I am to be governed than I am. It is entirely unacceptable that I should have no voice in the political affairs of my own country, for I am not a ward of America; I am one of the first Americans to arrive on these shores.

This past, the Negro's past, of rope, fire, torture, castration, infanticide, rape; death and humiliation; fear by day and night, fear as deep as the marrow of the bone; doubt that he was worthy of life, since everyone around him denied it; sorrow for his women, for his kinfolk, for his children, who needed his protection, and whom he could not protect; rage, hatred, and murder, hatred for white men so deep that it often turned against him and his own, and made all love, all trust, all joy impossible—this past, this endless struggle to achieve and reveal and confirm a human identity, human authority, yet contains, for all its horror, something very beautiful. I do not mean to be sentimental about suffering—enough is certainly as good as a feast—but people who cannot suffer can never grow up, can never discover who they are. That man who is forced each day to snatch his manhood, his identity, out of the fire of human cruelty that rages to destroy it knows, if he survives his effort, and even if he does not survive it, something about himself and human life that no school on earth—and, indeed, no church—can teach. He achieves his own authority, and that is unshakable. This is because, in order to save his life, he is forced to look beneath appearances, to take nothing for granted, to hear the meaning behind the words. If one is continually surviving the worst that life can bring, one eventually ceases to be controlled by a fear of what life can bring; whatever it brings must be borne. And at this level of experience one's bitterness begins to be palatable, and hatred becomes too heavy a sack to carry. The apprehension of life here so briefly and inadequately sketched has been the experience of generations of Negroes, and it helps to explain how they have endured and how they have been able to produce children of kindergarten age who can walk through mobs to get to school. It demands great force and great cunning continually to assault the mighty and indifferent fortress of white supremacy, as Negroes in this country have done so long. It demands great spiritual resilience not to hate the hater whose foot is on your neck, and an even greater miracle of perception and charity not to teach your child to hate. The Negro boys and girls who are facing mobs today come out of a long line of improbable aristocrats—the only genuine aristocrats this country has produced. I say "this country" because their frame of reference was totally American. They were hewing out of the mountain of white supremacy the stone of their individuality. I have great respect for that unsung

3

army of black men and women who trudged down back lanes and entered back doors, saying "Yes, sir" and "No, Ma'am" in order to acquire a new roof for the schoolhouse, new books, a new chemistry lab, more beds for the dormitories, more dormitories. They did not like saying "Yes, sir" and "No, Ma'am," but the country was in no hurry to educate Negroes, these black men and women knew that the job had to be done, and they put their pride in their pockets in order to do it. It is very hard to believe that they were in any way inferior to the white men and women who opened those back doors. It is very hard to believe that those men and women, raising their children, eating their greens, crying their curses, weeping their tears, singing their songs, making their love, as the sun rose, as the sun set, were in any way inferior to the white men and women who crept over to share these splendors after the sun went down. But we must avoid the European error; we must not suppose that, because the situation, the ways, the perceptions of black people so radically differed from those of whites, they were racially superior. I am proud of these people not because of their color but because of their intelligence and their spiritual force and their beauty. The country should be proud of them, too, but, alas, not many people in this country even know of their existence. And the reason for this ignorance is that a knowledge of the role these people played—and play—in American life would reveal more about America to Americans than Americans wish to know.

COMPREHENSION

1. The author says that the only thing the white man has that black people need is
   a. money
   b. jobs
   c. power
   d. professional training
2. For Baldwin the word "love" means
   a. a romantic relationship
   b. friendship and brotherhood
   c. a state of grace
   d. sentimental feelings
3. In order ". . . to become a nation . . ." Baldwin argues that
   a. blacks and whites must work independently of each other
   b. blacks must achieve a position superior to the whites
   c. whites and blacks must work together as equals
   d. blacks must control their own lives
4. Baldwin feels white people's discrimination against blacks is based on
   a. color
   b. language and dialect differences
   c. projection of fears and longings
   d. social class distinctions

5. Baldwin says that the suffering that blacks have experienced has
   a. provided strength and authority
   b. caused disputes among black families
   c. delayed the civil rights movement
   d. advanced discrimination

VOCABULARY

Directions: *The meaning of the following terms from selection 18 cannot be clearly determined from the context. Using the dictionary entries, select the appropriate definition of the term as it is used in the reading selection.*

1. divest (par. 1)
   a. to rid
   b. to strip
   c. to clothe
   d. to deprive

di·vest (di vest′, dī-), *v.t.* **1.** to strip of clothing, ornament, etc. **2.** to strip or deprive of anything; dispossess. **3.** to rid of or free from: *He divested himself of all responsibility for the decision.* **4.** *Law.* to take away (property, rights, etc.). [< ML *dīvest(īre)*] —**di·vest′i·ble,** *adj.* —**di·vest′i·ture,** *n.* —**Syn. 1.** unclothe, denude. **2.** See **strip**[1].

2. intrinsic (par. 1)
   a. difficult
   b. part of something
   c. fundamental
   d. mathematical

in·trin·sic (ĭn-trĭn′sĭk) or **in·trin·si·cal** (-sĭ-kəl) *adj.* Belonging to the essential nature of a thing; inherent: *the intrinsic difficulty of mathematics.* [Old French *intrinseque,* inner, from Late Latin *intrinsecus,* inward, from Latin, inwardly, on the inside : *intrā,* within + *secus,* alongside.] —**in·trin′si·cal·ly** *adv.*

3. corroborates (par. 1)
   a. confirms
   b. provides new evidence
   c. describes
   d. states

cor·rob·o·rate (kə-rŏb′ə-rāt′) *tr.v.* **-rat·ed, -rat·ing.** To support or confirm by new evidence; attest the truth or accuracy of: *His account corroborates the defendant's alibi.* [From Latin *corrōborāre* : *com-,* with + *rōborāre,* to strengthen, from *rōbur,* hard oak.] —**cor·rob′o·ra′tion** *n.* —**cor·rob′o·ra′tive** *adj.* —**cor·rob′o·ra′tor** *n.*

4. surreptitiously (par. 1)
   a. carefully
   b. timely
   c. completely
   d. secretly

sur·rep·ti·tious (sûr′əp-tĭsh′əs) *adj.* Secret and stealthy: *a surreptitious glance.* [Latin *surreptīcius,* from *surreptus,* past part. of *surripere,* to take away secretly : *sub-,* secretly + *rapere,* to seize.] —**sur′rep·ti′tious·ly** *adv.* —**sur′rep·ti′tious·ness** *n.*

5. travail (par. 1)
   a. childbirth
   b. hard work
   c. strength
   d. torment

tra·vail (trə-vāl′, trăv′āl′) *n.* **1.** Strenuous or laborious exertion; toil. **2.** Tribulation or agony; anguish. **3.** The labor of childbirth. —See Syns at **labor.** —*intr.v.* **1.** To toil painfully or strenuously; labor. **2.** To be in the labor of childbirth. [Middle English, from Old French, from *travailler,* to work hard, from Late Latin *tripālium,* an instrument of torture : *tri-,* three + *pālus,* stake.]

6. aridity (par. 1)
   a. dryness
   b. dullness
   c. deserted quality
   d. wastefulness

ar·id (ăr′ĭd) *adj.* **1.** Lacking moisture or rainfall; parched; dry: *an arid climate.* **2.** Lacking interest or feeling; lifeless; dull: *a long, arid story.* [French *aride,* from Latin *āridus,* from *ārēre,* to be dry or parched.] —**a·rid′i·ty** (ə-rĭd′ĭ-tē) or **ar′id·ness** *n.*

7. hideously (par. 2)
   a. revolting
   b. threatening
   c. insightful
   d. extremely

hid·e·ous (hĭd′ē-əs) *adj.* **1.** Physically repulsive; revolting; ugly. **2.** Repugnant to the moral sense; despicable; odious. [Middle English *hidous,* from Old French *hidous, hideus,* from *hi(s)de,* fear, horror, perhaps from Latin *hispidus,* rough, shaggy. See **ghers-** in Appendix.*] —**hid′e·ous·ly** *adj.* —**hid′e·ous·ness** *n.*

8. palatable (par. 3)
   a. tasty
   b. sensible
   c. agreeable
   d. problem solving

pal·at·a·ble (păl′ĭt-ə-bəl) *adj.* **1.** Acceptable to the taste; sufficiently agreeable in flavor to be eaten. **2.** Acceptable to the mind or sensibilities; agreeable: *a palatable solution to the problem.* [From **PALATE.**] —**pal′at·a·bil′i·ty, pal′at·a·ble·ness** *n.*

DISCUSSION

1. How would you describe the author's attitude toward the white man? Select two sentences from the first paragraph to illustrate your answer.
2. What reason(s) does Baldwin give for his belief that white men are no better equipped to "frame the laws" of the country than he is? (See paragraph 2.)
3. What does Baldwin think the white man needs to improve living conditions in America for everyone?

Unit Four
Informative Prose

In this unit we will describe features common to the various types of informative prose that you frequently read and write as a college student. Informative writing can best be described as writing that explains or presents information or ideas. A writer may explain an event, an idea, a procedure or process, a feeling or emotion, or an action. The purpose of informative writing is to communicate information and ideas.

Most of what you read and write in college, in everyday life, and on the job focuses on the communication of information by explanation. Textbooks, newspapers, magazines, contracts, letters, brochures, and catalogs are all written to inform the reader. Similarly, writing tasks such as research papers, essay exam answers, class assignments, letters, and job applications all focus on the communication of information.

Although there are many types of informative prose, the chapters in this unit will focus on those types most useful to you as a college student. The reading portions of the unit will be concerned with textbook selections, essays, and nonfiction articles. The writing sections will focus on writing an essay—organizing and developing your ideas. In Chapters 10 and 11 we will discuss the four essential elements of informative prose: the subject, unifying idea, supporting details, and transitions. In Chapter 12 we will discuss the overall organization of expository prose. You will see that most informative writing contains an introduction, a body, and a conclusion or summary.

Just as an effective paragraph is written about a particular topic, an effective article or selection is also written about one item or concept that is called the subject. Similarly, a well-written paragraph expresses a main idea, and an essay also develops a statement throughout that is called the unifying idea. Further, just as a paragraph's main idea is developed by supporting details, so is the unifying idea developed by details that support or explain it. Finally, both paragraphs and essays use signal words or transitions to connect ideas and show the direction of thought. These common elements might be diagrammed as shown on the following page.

Paragraphs		*Essays*
topic ◄———————	what the writing is about ——————►	subject
main idea ◄———————	make a general statement ——————►	unifying idea
supporting details ◄———	explain and support ——— ►	supporting statements
signal words/ transitions ◄———	connect and show direction ——► of thought	transitions

Not only do paragraphs and essays have common elements, they also have a parallel structure, or physical arrangement. In a paragraph the topic sentence states the idea that will be developed. In an essay, the introduction serves this function. The supporting sentences in a paragraph develop the main idea of a paragraph; in an essay, the body develops the unifying idea. In a paragraph the summary or concluding sentence ties the ideas together; a summary also brings an essay to a close. The parallel structure of paragraphs and essays can be diagrammed as follows:

Common Structural Parts

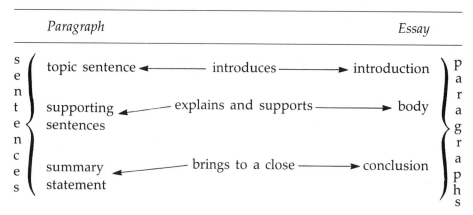

	Paragraph		*Essay*	
s e n t e n c e s	topic sentence ◄———	introduces ——►	introduction	p a r a g r a p h s
	supporting sentences ◄—	explains and supports ——►	body	
	summary statement ◄—	brings to a close ——►	conclusion	

Throughout this unit you will see how all the individual skills you have learned about reading and writing work together to enable you to read and write more effectively. In the reading sections of the chapters, you will learn how the five steps for effective reading—prereading, establishing a purpose, reading, reviewing, and reacting— allow you to understand informative prose. In the writing section of each chapter you will see how the five steps in the writing process— prewriting, composing, checking the content and organization, revising, and proofreading—can help you to write more effectively.

10. The Subject and Unifying Idea

Although varying widely in content and purpose, all informative prose has *four* common elements. First, there must be one general concept, called the *subject*. Second, any piece of informative writing must have a *unifying idea*—a statement of what the whole essay or selection is saying about the subject. Third, this unifying idea must be explained by the *supporting details*. Finally, these details must be connected by transitions—words or phrases, or sentences, that show relationships. You will learn to identify the subject and unifying idea as you read, and you will learn how to focus and develop them as you write.

RECOGNIZING THE SUBJECT

The subject is what the entire article or selection is about. Generally, you can think of it as the one person, place, object, or idea that is discussed throughout the piece of writing. The writer will not always state the subject explicitly, but it should be the first major piece of information you discover. Each paragraph in an article or selection in some way discusses or relates to the subject. To find the subject of a passage, ask yourself this question: What is the main thing that the author is concerned with throughout the selection? Now, read the following short selection and identify the subject.

> You see things vacationing on a motorcycle in a way that is completely different from any other. In a car you're always in a compartment, and because you're used to it you don't realize that through that car window everything you see is just more TV. You're a passive observer and it is all moving by you boringly in a frame.
> On a cycle the frame is gone. You're completely in contact with it all. You're *in* the scene, not just watching it anymore, and the sense of presence is overwhelming. That concrete whizzing by five inches below your foot is the real thing, the same stuff you walk on, it's right there, so blurred you can't focus on it, yet you can put your foot down and touch it anytime, and the whole thing, the whole experience, is never removed from immediate consciousness.[1]

In this passage, the subject is vacationing on a motorcycle. The selection is written to explain how riding on a motorcycle differs from traveling in other ways. Every sentence in these two paragraphs in some way describes the experience of traveling on a motorcycle.

The most effective way to quickly identify the subject of a selection is to preread it. In prereading, among other things, you read the title, the first paragraph, and the headings. The title of an article or selection might announce the subject or provide some clues about it. The first paragraph, which often serves as an introduction, usually states or suggests the subject. Each of these parts provides clues or direct statements about the subject. Now read the first paragraph of "Can Machines Think?" (page 288). As you read, notice how the subject of this selection is emphasized in the first paragraph.

You should have noticed that each sentence in the first paragraph was concerned with some aspect or feature of computers. This first paragraph, then, clearly establishes computers as the specific subject of the selection.

In longer selections, or in textbook chapters where the general subject is divided into more specific subjects, headings can be helpful in identifying the subjects of particular sections. For example, in an economics text, the heading "Gross National Product" clearly tells you that gross national product is the subject to be discussed in the section of the text that follows. You will find that headings deserve careful attention because they quickly tell you what the material is about. They help to focus your attention and tell you what to expect in the section. Newspapers and popular magazine articles, reference books, and journals, as well as certain types of essays, also use headings to label the subject.

RECOGNIZING THE UNIFYING IDEA

The unifying idea is a broad statement of what the entire piece of writing is about. You might think of it as an idea that brings together all the ideas expressed in the selection.

The unifying idea is the primary message about the subject of the entire passage. Every paragraph in the article or selection in some way proves, supports, explains, develops or gives an example of the unifying idea. For example, if the subject of a selection is "Winter," a unifying idea might be that "Winter is the worst season of the year."

To find the unifying idea, try to identify the one idea that all the paragraphs are about. Ask yourself this question: What idea do all the other ideas explain or support or relate to?

Here are some very simple examples of unifying ideas and supporting details. They are presented in outline form to help you see the relationship of ideas.

Example 1

SUBJECT: Winter

UNIFYING IDEA: Winter is the worst season of the year.

SUPPORTING DETAILS: 1. Snow and ice create transportation problems.
                       2. Outdoor activities are limited.
                       3. It gets dark too early.

Example 2

SUBJECT: Notetaking

UNIFYING IDEA: There are several reasons why taking lecture notes is important.

SUPPORTING DETAILS: 1. Your notes will be a written record of what is important to learn and study.
  2. Taking notes will help you concentrate.

Example 3

SUBJECT: National Speed Limit

UNIFYING IDEA: The establishment of a national speed limit of 55 mph is reasonable.

SUPPORTING DETAILS: 1. It limits gas consumption and alleviates the national fuel problem.
  2. It reduces the number of fatal collisions.
  3. It reduces the total number of accidents.

Notice, in each set of examples, that the progression of thought is from general to specific. The subject is a general idea, object, or concept; the unifying idea limits the subject by focusing on a particular aspect or feature of the subject. Then, the supporting details provide even more specific information about the unifying idea.

How to Identify the Unifying Idea

Basically, in identifying the unifying idea, you are trying to find the most important idea the writer is expressing about the subject. The unifying idea may be presented in several ways, depending on the type of material and the writer's style; it might be stated at the beginning, at the end, or unstated.

Directly Stated at Beginning

In many types of informative writing, the unifying idea is clearly stated at the beginning. Usually, in this case, it is presented in the first paragraph. In a long selection, however, the first paragraph may be very general and intended only to capture your interest; then you might find the unifying idea presented in the second paragraph. In the following short selection, notice that the unifying idea is directly stated in the first paragraph.

Most children in school fail.

For a great many, this failure is avowed and absolute. Close to forty percent of those who begin high school, drop out before they finish. For college, the figure is one in three.

Many others fail in fact if not in name. They complete their schooling only because we have agreed to push them up through the grades and out of the schools, whether they know anything or not. There are many more such children than we think. If we "raise our standards" much higher, as some would have us do, we will find out very soon just how many there are. Our classrooms will bulge with kids who can't pass the test to get into the next class.

But there is a more important sense in which almost all children fail: Except for a handful, who may or may not be good students, they fail to develop more than a tiny part of the tremendous capacity for learning, understanding, and creating with which they were born and of which they made full use during the first two or three years of their lives.?

The very first sentence of this selection presents the unifying idea: "Most children in school fail." Throughout the passage the author explains why children fail and what he means by failure. As you read you understand that the author feels children fail because they fail to develop their ability to think and learn.

Strongly Implied

In other types of writing, however, the unifying idea is strongly suggested or implied, but is not directly stated. In this case the important ideas in the selection add up to or lead up to a unifying idea, but there is no single sentence that clearly states what the author is trying to express. As you read the following selection notice how the writer leads you to answer the question of whether machines can think.

Can Machines Think?

David Dempsey and Philip G. Zimbardo

A computer is often called a "thinking machine," and in many ways it is just that. Computers perform difficult and time-saving mathematical computations, as well as problems in logic and reasoning. One model plays checkers (and beats the champions!). Still another "composes" music. Computers run other machines, answer questions, and guide astronauts on takeoff. Above all, they are infinitely faster than any brain ever known. Does all this mean that, functionally at least, computers "think" like human beings? [1]

Not quite. Yet the similarities are intriguing. Like the brain, the computer takes information (usually by "reading" a punched tape with instructions). It processes information with the object of providing new information. It has a *memory* and uses thinking strategies, and it communicates (through a print-out or cathode-ray tube). [2]

Critics of the claims made for computer intelligence point out several differences between machines and the human brain, saying that the so-called "intelligence" of a computer is only apparent, or simulative. To begin with, computers must be programmed (given instructions). Programming can only be done by a human being, or by another computer that has itself been programmed by people. Moreover, computers are single-minded and can only work on one problem or set of problems [3] at a time. To perform another type of operation requires another program.

And computers are far from infallible. The growing number of crimes by computer has shown this. A recent example is the Equity Funding Corporation scandal in Los Angeles, which involved the selling of fake insurance policies to other insurance companies. Many wondered why the computer's "audit track" had failed to detect the fraud, even though it was supposed to pick up any discrepancies in the company accounts. The answer, according to one investigator was simple. "Computers," he said, "can't smell." (The audit track itself had been rigged.)

This, indeed seems to be one of the computer's weaknesses. They have none of the curiosity that makes the human brain reach for higher levels of thought. And they lack weaknesses that might be to their advantage, like impatience and discouragement. Steps are being taken to correct this, however. One model (Simon, 1967) does get impatient (by selecting only the best alternatives found within a given time) and discouraged (it stops processing after a given number of failures).

Whatever the limitations of computers, it is difficult to imagine a modern technological society operating without them. As an aid to information processing they have no match. Whether they have a "mind" of their own is another matter.

Each of the paragraphs in this selection discusses a feature of computers. Together, these paragraphs "add up" or point toward a unifying idea. The first paragraph defines the computer as a thinking machine. Paragraph 2 points out similarities between computers and the human brain. In paragraph 3 the writer explains that computers must be programmed. Paragraph 4 describes mistakes that computers make that people do not. Paragraph 5 suggests that computers lack basic human qualities. The last paragraph states that despite their limitations computers are valuable for information processing, and our society cannot get along without them. However, the overall message—or unifying idea—is not directly stated. The ideas presented seem to lead or point toward this idea: Computers are valuable aids and can perform many tasks, but they still cannot equal human intelligence. Or, stated another way, the selection seems to suggest that machines can "think" only in a mechanical way according to the way they are programmed.

When reading material that seems to use this approach, it is particularly important to review what you have read, and you may need to reread certain portions of the selection. As you read, review, and reread, keep this question in mind: "What important idea does each of these paragraphs seem to be leading toward?" Your answer can serve as your statement of the unifying idea.

Unstated

In some forms of informative writing, the author does not lead you toward a realization of the unifying idea. There is no step-by-step progression of ideas that leads to a conclusion. This is particularly true of forms of descriptive writing in which the writer's purpose is to convey an impression rather than to state and develop a statement or communicate a specific message. You might think of the unifying idea for this type of writing as hidden or buried. As you read, you have to "uncover" the writer's meaning by carefully adding together specific pieces of the selection. You also have to be aware of the writer's tone and attitude toward the subject.

Identifying the Subject and Unifying Idea in Longer Selections

So far in this chapter, the selections used as examples have been fairly brief. However, in most reading situations you will be reading material that is much longer. Textbook chapters, or sections of chapters, and magazine and newspaper articles are all longer than the samples you have read in this chapter so far.

When reading longer selections, you will need to use a systematic approach to identifying the subject and central thought. The following section explains how you can use the same Five Steps to Effective Reading used throughout the text to help you identify the subject and central thought. As you read each step, test it out on the sample selection "Death with Dignity" that follows the directions:

1. *Preread the selection.* To become familiar with the overall content and organization of the selection before you begin reading it, look at:
    a. the title
    b. the footnote, to determine the source of the selection
    c. the first paragraph
    d. the headings
    e. the first sentence after each heading
    f. the last paragraph

    During your prereading, identify the subject of the selection and try to find clues about the unifying idea.

2. *Establish a purpose for reading.* Before beginning to read, decide two or three questions you want to be able to answer about the subject.

3. *Read the selection.* As you read, keep in mind the questions you asked and look for the answers. Also, look for the unifying idea of the selection.

4. *Review the selection.* Review the selection by rereading the title, first paragraph, headings, and last paragraph.

5. *Think about and react to what you have read.*

By prereading this sample selection you learn that Kübler-Ross's article is about the needs of people who are dying. The title "Death with Dignity" announces the subject of the essay, and the first paragraph further explains or clarifies this title. In this paragraph Kübler-Ross establishes her focus on death. She says she is, in fact, not concerned with death with dignity, but rather with living with dignity. This statement suggests that Kübler-Ross regards death as part of life or dying as the final stage of living. Thus you should suspect, at this point, that this concept of death is the unifying idea of the selection. From the heading "Need of the Patient for Hope" and the paragraph following you learn that this section of the article is concerned with two essential needs of fatally ill patients—the most important of which is hope, followed by love. The last paragraph suggests an alternative to the loneliness which has been described in the article.

From your prereading, you might have established the following purposes or questions to answer as you read:

1. What are the needs of dying people?
2. How can death be dignified?
3. Why is hope important?
4. What loneliness does Kübler-Ross refer to in the last paragraph?

Then, as you read the selection, you are able to confirm your expectation that the subject of the selection is death with dignity, and you discover that the unifying idea is that death is a part of life and that dying patients should be allowed to die in the comfortable environment that will meet their two most important needs—hope and reassurance of not being deserted.

Death with Dignity

Elisabeth Kübler-Ross

I do not like to talk about dying with dignity, but I would like to talk about living with dignity, and I think that makes a difference.

I have interviewed over 500 terminally ill patients and asked them to share with us what it is like to be dying, what kind of needs, fears, and fantasies those patients have, and, perhaps most important, it tells what kind of things can we do, by which I mean family members and members of the helping professions, to be more helpful.

We started this project not as a research project or anything planned, but as a chance happening. I think it became important that I was born and raised in Switzerland. In the old country—and I guess in the old times in this country, also—death was part of life, like birth is.

When I was a child, people used to be born at home and often died at home. Dying patients were not often institutionalized. This did not make dying easier for the dying patient, but I think most important of all, it helped the children and grandchildren to learn that death is part of life.

When I came to this country, I was very impressed that the children are not allowed to visit patients in hospitals or the mental institutions. Very seldom do you hear the laughter of

Statement of Dr. Elisabeth Kübler-Ross before the U.S. Senate Committee on Aging. Reprinted by permission.

children in nursing homes. And I have seen hundreds of people in this country who have never experienced a death in the family. What we have learned from interviewing over 500 dying patients—and I am not talking about dying children, who, by the way, die much easier than grownups—the majority of our patients want to die very badly at home. Yet, close to 80 percent of all patients interviewed died in an institution. Patients who can prepare themselves early and in a familiar comfortable environment for their impending death are better able to finish their unfinished business, to put their house in order, as they pass through the stages of dying, as I have outlined in my book, *On Death and Dying*.

Family members still now believe that it is better "not to tell" the patient. We found the opposite to be true. If we will listen to the patient and talk with them about their illness, they will proceed much quicker to the stage of acceptance, and not resignation. Eighty percent of our patients in nursing homes want to die very badly, but they are not in the stage of acceptance. They are in a stage of resignation, which is kind of a feeling of defeat "what's the use, I am tired of living."

NEED OF THE PATIENT FOR HOPE

Patients have two basic essential needs when they are informed that they have a potentially fatal illness: The biggest need is always to allow for hope. Hope is not the same as hope for cure treatment or prolongation of life. When a patient is dying, this hope will change to something that is not associated with cure treatment or prolongation of life.

To give you a practical example of how hope changes, like hope from the living to the hope of the dying: I visited a young mother with small children who had cancer. Each time I saw her, she said, "I hope those research laboratories work hard and I can get one of their new miracle drugs, and I get well." Naturally, I shared those hopes with her, though the probability was extremely slim.

One day I visited her, and she looked very different. She said, "Dr. Ross, a miracle happened." I said, "Did you get the new drugs?" She said, "No, I know now that these miracle drugs are not forthcoming, and I am no longer afraid." I asked her, "What is your hope now?" She said, "I hope my children are going to make it."

If we are not afraid to face and talk about dying, we would then say, "Do you feel like talking about it?"

As long as a patient is alive, he needs hope, but not the projection of our hope, which is usually a prolongation of life.

Besides the need for hope, patients need a reassurance that they will not be deserted, yet most of our patients who become beyond medical help feel deserted.

To give you a brief clinical example of what I mean by the loneliness of dying, I had a 28-year-old mother of three small children with liver disease. Because of her liver disease, she was going in and out of hepatic comas, and became frequently confused and psychotic.

Her husband could not take it any more. He had spent all his savings on doctor and hospital bills. He had these three little children. He had no homemaker, no help whatsoever. He was heavily in debt, and he never knew when he came home from work whether his wife was still functioning.

One day he said, "It would be better if you would live one single day and function as a housewife and a mother, rather than to prolong this misery any longer."

Unfortunately nobody helped this desperate husband and father, who tried unsuccessfully to provide for his family. The patient herself desperately looked for hope, which nobody gave her. She went to the hospital, where a young resident told her, "There is nothing else I can do for you."

She then went home, and in her desperation went to a faith healer, who told her that she was cured. She believed this, and stopped taking the medication, stopped taking the diet, and she again slipped into a coma.

Nobody helped this family. She was again admitted to the hospital. By then, the family had it. They just could not cope with it any more.

In the hospital, the same tragedy: The medical ward wanted to transfer her to the psychiatric ward and the latter did not want a dying patient and insisted that she be kept on a medical floor. They could not tolerate this woman who walked up and down the hallway talking about God's miracles, of the faith healer who cured her.

It became like a ping-pong game, and this is the tragedy of hospitalized patients who cause all these anxieties in us. We don't know what to say or do with them.

I told this woman that I would never talk with her about her illness or dying, and I would not desert her. "Let's only talk about the present." She became the best patient I ever had, but she was put in the last room at the end of a long hallway, farthest away from the nursing station.

Not one door closed, but two doors. She never had a visitor.

This woman, when I visited with her one day, sat on the edge of the bed with the telephone off the hook in her hands. I said, "What in the world are you doing?" She said, "Oh, just to hear a sound!" This is the loneliness of the dying patients that I am talking about.

Another time, she was lying on her bed smiling, with her arms stiff down the side of her body and I asked her, "What in the world are you smiling about?" She looked at me and said, "Don't you see these beautiful flowers that my husband surrounded me with?" Needless to say, there were no flowers.

It took me a while to appreciate that this woman realized that she just could not live without some expression of love and care, hopefully coming from her husband. In order to live, this woman had to develop a delusion of flowers, sent to her by her husband after her death.

This is the loneliness I am talking about. And these things would be preventable if we would not hospitalize all these patients, but if we could give the family some help at the beginning, if we could occasionally relieve them with homemakers, if we could send physicians and caseworkers to their homes, so that this last hospitalization can be prevented, and the dying patient can at least die in his own home, surrounded by the children, and also in the familiar environment that they have lived, and where they have been loved. But in order to do this, we have to give help not only to the dying patient but to such desperate husbands who try to make ends meet and just cannot make it alone.

Now look back or review the selection. You should notice that each idea presented in the selection in some way explains or supports the unifying idea. In this article you can see that each paragraph develops Kübler-Ross's unifying idea.

As you reacted to and thought about this article, you probably thought about your reactions to death or recalled the death of someone close to you. Relating the subject and unifying idea to your own experiences is a useful technique to help you react to and evaluate what you have read.

EXERCISE 10–1

Directions: *Choose* one *of the selections at the end of this unit and follow these steps:*

1. *Preread the selection.* Underline or highlight portions of the selection that you used in prereading. Identify the subject of the selection.

   SUBJECT: _____

2. *Establish a purpose for reading.* Using your prereading, write three questions you expect to be able to answer as you read.

   a. _____

   b. _____

   c. _____

3. *Read the selection.* As you read, try to find the answers to your questions, and write them in the space provided.

   a. _____

   b. _____

   c. _____

4. *Review the selection.* Review by rereading the title, first paragraph, headings (if available), and the last paragraph. Identify the unifying idea of the selection:

   UNIFYING IDEA: _____

5. *React to and think about what you read.* Identify the author's purpose and intended audience. In the writing section of this chapter, you will have a chance to write your ideas on this subject.

DEVELOPING THE SUBJECT AND UNIFYING IDEA

Sometimes understanding and completing reading assignments for some of your college courses can be a difficult task. Often it is difficult to see what a textbook writer is getting at, even though he or she has written in a well-planned and organized way. Sometimes you have to really concentrate in order to determine the unifying idea in a professional piece of writing. Imagine how frustrated you would be if that writer frequently strayed from the topic or presented the information in a poorly planned or disorganized way. Your readers experience similar problems when you do not focus clearly on your subject or fail to maintain a unifying idea throughout your writing.

In an effectively written paragraph the author should (1) focus on a specific topic, (2) clearly present one main idea, (3) support that idea, and (4) relate supporting details to one another. Similarly, a well-written essay, paper, or composition should be concerned with one subject, contain one unifying idea, and provide clarifying links between supporting paragraphs.

As you would expect, the techniques that you have developed for writing effective paragraphs also apply to the writing of essays. The same Five Steps to Effective Writing that you have been using throughout the text will also help you to organize and develop well-written essays. Throughout the rest of this chapter, and in the other chapters in this unit, you will see how these steps enable you to focus your subject, to state and develop a unifying idea, to support that idea, and to connect your ideas with transitions.

Focusing the Subject

One of the most challenging tasks in writing is to construct a unified message. In other words, there must be one idea that connects all the other parts of the essay. As you are writing you should remember that your purpose is to write so that your reader will understand your message. Your reader will appreciate a paper that is clear, concise, and coherent. Before you begin writing, always ask yourself this question: What is the one idea I want to discuss throughout this piece of writing?

Often you begin writing with a subject that is too broad to treat in an essay. Your first step is to narrow that subject into a topic that can be easily managed. Here's a good rule of thumb: The shorter the essay, the narrower the topic must be. If you are writing a twenty-page term paper your topic can be more general than if you are writing a two-page composition.

Narrowing a subject involves dividing your subject into smaller pieces. Often you will have to divide it more than once. If a piece of cake is too large to eat in one bite, you could cut it in half. But depending on the size of the original piece, it may still be too large, and you may have to divide it again. Similarly, depending on how broad your subject is, you may have to narrow or subdivide it more than once. For instance, suppose you had to narrow the subject of "crime" to a topic that could be managed in a two-page essay. You might narrow it as follows:

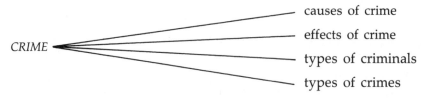

The subject of crime was broken down into four topics. However, each of these topics is still too broad to cover in a two-page paper, so further narrowing is needed. To do this, you would select one of the topics and treat it as you did the original subject, dividing it into several categories. If you chose types of crimes, you could narrow it as follows:

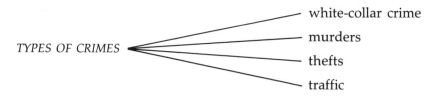

If necessary, you could narrow one of these topics further, as follows:

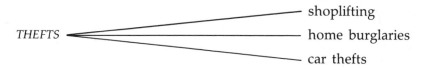

As you can see, a subject can be narrowed numerous times in order to produce a topic that is appropriate for your situation and purpose. Furthermore, a topic can also be made more specific to meet your needs.

Avoiding Common Problems in Focusing the Topic

There are several problems that students experience in a writing class and in other courses in which papers or essays are assigned. One problem is unfamiliarity with the subject; a second is lack of interest in the subject; a third is having nothing to say about the subject. At one time or another you have probably had to write about a subject that had little meaning for you for one or more of the above reasons.

An approach to handling these problems is actually a form of narrowing your subject. One way to overcome one of these problems is to try to make the subject mean something by connecting it to a topic you are interested in or know something about. Suppose you are asked to write about the changing American economy. At first this subject may seem boring, and you may feel that you don't know very much about the topic. Try to think of some feature of the economy that you do know something about or are interested in. For instance, are you interested in money? in getting a job? in getting a bank loan to pay tuition? in buying a car? If so, then you could focus the subject so that you can write about an aspect you are interested in. For instance, you might limit "a changing economy" to one of the following topics:

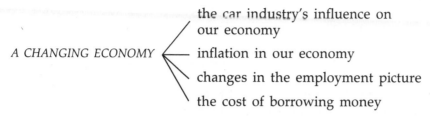

A CHANGING ECONOMY
- the car industry's influence on our economy
- inflation in our economy
- changes in the employment picture
- the cost of borrowing money

Each of these topics might provide a more interesting approach to the subject.

Occasionally you may be faced with a subject you know little or nothing about. When this happens it may be necessary to find out a little about the subject before you begin to narrow it. As a first step, check the dictionary definitions of terms related to the subject. Often this is enough to help you to start thinking about the subject. Or you might check an encyclopedia to find out how the subject is broken down into topics and subtopics.

Developing a Unifying Idea

Once you have narrowed your subject to a manageable topic, your next step is to generate ideas about that topic, and using a prewriting technique will help you accomplish this task.

Prewriting

As you will recall, you can develop ideas using free writing or by asking questions about the topic. Either technique will generate ideas, and from those ideas you will often find an emerging focus or cluster of ideas that supports a larger, more general idea. Especially in free writing, since there are no restrictions about the content or organization, you may find a thought or group of thoughts or ideas repeated; or you may see that several statements each seem to support a larger, more important idea.

Suppose you started a free-writing exercise on the topic of buying cars. Then, after you finished, you reread your writing and discovered, among others, the following statements:

Cars are expensive.
I have to borrow money to buy one.
I could borrow from my father.
The interest would be high.
It would take several years to pay it back.

Together, these statements seem to "add up" to or suggest a larger idea: buying a car is an expensive, long-range commitment. This statement could function as the unifying idea for a short essay.

The next step is to evaluate, revise, and test out this tentative unifying idea to be sure that it will serve as a base for producing a well-written essay. Certainly you do not want to take the time to write out a full rough draft only to realize when you have finished writing that it needs to be drastically changed. To avoid this inefficient use of your time, ask yourself the following questions:

1. Can this idea be fully explained and supported within the length of the paper I am writing?
2. Is the idea clear? Does it make a statement or assertion about my topic?
3. Do I have enough to say about this idea? (You might refer back to your free writing or questions to help answer this question. You should be generally familiar with the idea and be able to relate it to your experiences.)
4. Is this idea worth writing about? (Think about your audience. Would they want to read about this idea? Is it interesting and important enough to write about?)

Composing

Once you are satisfied with your unifying idea, the next step is to identify supporting ideas and write them into a rough draft. In the next chapter we will discuss specific techniques for writing these supporting ideas.

Checking the Content and Organization

Once you have written your rough draft you should again evaluate the effectiveness of your unifying statement. At this point you should see if it accurately reflects the ideas included in the essay. The most important question to ask is: Does each idea included in the essay in some way explain or support the unifying idea? If your answer is no for only one or two ideas, then your unifying idea is probably acceptable, and you only need to revise or omit the ideas that do not relate. However, if your answer is no for many ideas, then you need to revise and rewrite your unifying idea.

A second useful question is: Is my statement of the unifying idea as specific as possible? That is, does it give the reader as much information as possible about the ideas expressed in the essay? For example, suppose your essay is about the metric system, and you present several reasons why you feel the United States should not convert to the metric system. Which of the following unifying ideas would be most informative to your reader?

The United States should not convert to the metric system.

Due to the costs of conversion and the confusion that would result, the United States should not convert to the metric system.

Both statements accurately describe what will be discussed in the essay. However, the second statement is more specific and suggests to the reader a further direction or focus of the essay. The reader knows your two main objections to the conversion—the costs and the confusion.

Revising

As a part of your revision, then, rewrite your statement of the unifying idea to make it as informative as possible. Also, revise or leave out supporting ideas that do not directly relate.

Demonstration

So you can see exactly how a subject is focused and a unifying idea is developed, we will now work through each of the steps. Suppose an English instructor assigned a one page paper on a topic related to Dr. Elisabeth Kübler-Ross's article "Death with Dignity". One student began this assignment by choosing the general subject of terminal illness.

Narrowing the Subject

The writer first narrowed the broad subject of terminal illness into three broad topics.

TERMINAL ILLNESS: *Topics*
1. Effects on the family
2. The problem of knowing you'll die soon
3. Care of the terminally ill

The writer decided to write about the problem of knowing you'll die soon.

Developing a Unifying Idea

To develop ideas about the topic, this writer decided to do a free-writing exercise that focuses on the attitudes the writer developed as a result of reading the Kübler-Ross article. Here is what the student wrote:

The Problem of Knowing You'll Die Soon

I don't know what to write. I don't even know why I ~~selected~~ chose this topic. I keep thinking about the young woman in Dr. Kübler-Ross's article the one who made herself believe her husband had sent flowers. How awful. But I feel sorry for him too. I never really thought about dying or even being sick. I wonder what I'd do. I'd want to do everything; I'd definitely go to Egypt. If I knew I only had a little while to live, I'd want to see the Pyramids. I'd be really scared. I don't know what I believe about dying. I mean heaven and hell and all that. I know I'd never go to hell, but what if you just die and that's it. Like sometimes when you fall asleep without intending to. How would it be if it was like that—nothing. If I were in pain or couldn't get around, I'd be angry. What a waste. I think I'd want it to end fast then. This is a creepy assignment. I don't even want to think about death, especially my own. I would feel awful about my family. It's all so difficult — for everyone.

It would seem like you'd be cut off from everyone. When someone is dying no one wants to talk about it. Everyone thinks the person who's dying wouldn't want to talk about it. But I bet they would. It would be constantly on your mind. I don't think I could be brave about it. I'd be angry and scared and I'd want to talk. Boy is this hard, I don't know anything about dying. As if anybody does. That's one thing you do all by yourself and you never get to tell anyone about it. Well, not anybody who's alive. I've never known anyone with a long illness.

Notice that the writer was having difficulty with the subject matter. There are a lot of diversions, and the writer is even reluctant to explore her feelings on death. Finally, however, the writer pinpointed the problem—little or no experience with people who are dying. Coming to this awareness helped the writer realize that she had to develop a topic she could write about. Look at the second prewriting exercise, which shows how the writer further developed some of the ideas expressed in the prewriting exercise.

After reading the article by Dr. Kübler-Ross I realize that I don't know much about death and dying. No one in my family has died, which is unusual, I guess. I have all my grandparents and they're all healthy. I've never even seen a dead person. When I went to our neighbor's funeral, the coffin was closed. He died in a car accident. I've never known anyone with a terminal illness, so I really don't know much about it. I know how it feels to be lonely though. But I suppose you feel more than lonely when you're dying. The one thing I keep thinking about is that nobody talks about death. I've just realized that I've never really talked about death; I don't even think about it. I wonder if my grandparents do. They worry a lot about getting sick, especially about money and how much hospitals cost. Death seems to be a topic nobody discusses. I keep trying to think about how I could bring it up with my friends. They wouldn't want to talk about it. They'd think I was morbid. Besides I would be afraid to discuss it. Almost superstitious. It's like if you don't talk about it, it won't happen, but it might if you do. Now that I think about it, the same thing could happen to my grandparents (like the woman in the hospital). Because maybe none of us would be able to face them because we wouldn't know what to say. Even in religion classes we only talk about what happens after you've died. No one tells you about dying, what it's like and all that. I guess I always thought it was like going to sleep and never waking up. I would want to be with my parents or grandparents if they were dying just so they'd know I loved them. But I wonder if it would be okay to cry. Maybe that would upset them too much. That's the problem. Nobody knows how to act when someone is dying.

You can see that the writer freely expressed her realization that death is not a topic that comes up for discussion even though it is a very real aspect of human existence. In looking for the starting point for the development of a unifying idea, the writer selected the following sentences and then asked the four questions on page 298.

> The one thing I keep thinking about is that nobody talks about death. I've just realized that I've never really talked about death.

> Even in religion classes we only talk about what happens after you've died.

I would want to be with my parents or grandparents if they were dying, just so they'd know I loved them.

The writer felt that these sentences led to a unifying idea: Death is never discussed in our culture, so we don't know how to cope with it.

Composing: Rough Draft Sample

In the rough draft notice how the writer draws the main ideas and supporting details into a discussion that reflects the unifying idea developed in the free-writing exercise.

In her article "Death with Dignity" Dr. Elizabeth Kübler = Ross discusses the problem of people who are dying. She mentions how difficult it is both for the individual and the family. ~~One problem that occ~~ We never talk about death. We are not prepared to handle it. ~~Dr.~~

Dr. ^Kübler = Ross ~~says~~ said that most people who are ready to die have hope, but their hope is not for recovery. They accept the fact that they are dying and have hope for the future of their children. If we knew more about how they come to develop that hope we might be able to help people who are dying. If we understood why they have hope we might be able to help people who are dying to have that hope without having to suffer alone. In order to do this, though, we need to be more open about death.

People should not have to die alone in cold, lonely hospital rooms. They should be in a place where they are comfortable and peaceful. They should feel ~~cared~~ loved and cared for. They should not have to be in pain either. Most of all, they should be able to talk about their fears.

Probably the best place to begin teaching people to be more open about dying is in the church. All religions seem to discuss the problems of life after death and people are used to hearing about death. Churches could help people by educating them about dying.

More research has to be done on dying. We don't seem to know very much about it. No one can help people die ~~more comfortably~~ with dignity until ~~everyone~~ we know what to tell people about dying. If people such as Dr. E. Kübler-Ross continue with their work we can find out what death is all about. Then we can learn to cope with death and dying instead of pretending it ~~does~~ isn't happening.

Checking the Content and Organization

As part of this step the writer checked the effectiveness of the unifying statement. Most of the statements in the essay did support the unifying idea. However, she found that the unifying idea as stated in the rough draft needed to be developed throughout the essay. Transitions helped the essay to move from a discussion of ideas presented in the article written by Kübler-Ross to the writer's own attitudes about what should be done to help people through a terminal illness.

Revising

Compare the rough draft and the revision. Notice the changes in the progression of thought. Also, look carefully at the changes the writer made in the midst of writing sentences. These changes are important because they demonstrate that the writer is aware of the options or choices she can make in deciding how to express her ideas. This revision shows that numerous details were added, sentences were revised and combined, and organizational changes were made. You can also see that the writer often inserted a word or sentence after a paragraph or perhaps even the whole essay was completed.

In her article "Death with Dignity" Dr. Elizabeth Kübler-Ross discusses ~~how terminal illness affects the dying individual who is dying as well as the family members~~ the effects of terminal illness on ~~the relationship~~ the dying individual and on the family. In her studies Dr. ~~Ross~~ (Kübler-) discovered that people who are ready to die have hope, but their hope is not for recovery ~~or their own lives.~~ Instead their hope and attention centers on the people who will be left behind, usually their families.

If we knew more about how terminally ill people develop *that* a sense of hope and eventually accept the fact that they ~~will die~~ *are dying,* we might be able to help people ~~who~~ *to* die with dignity. People should not have to die alone in a hospital room because their families are too tired *to be with them.* The families should never have to feel that a person's death is just a relief *for everyone, including the person who is ill.* If we could help make death less frightening, ~~that~~ it would help both the dying person and the family.

One reason ~~of the reasons~~ why terminal illness causes so much grief is that people are afraid to talk about death. People who are terminally ill should be able to discuss their fears, but people never discuss death. All religions seem to discuss the problems of life after death, but the process of dying is never discussed. ⌐*It would be better if a dying person could be open about his or her fear of dying.* Churches could help people by educating them about dying. The church is the best place to begin because death is viewed as a stepping stone to another life. In that atmosphere the discussion ~~would~~ of death would be less frightening and might lead to hope.

Churches cannot begin educating people about dying until we know more about it. No one can ~~tell~~ help people die with dignity until we know what to tell people about dying. If people such as Dr. Elizabeth Kübler=Ross continue with their work, we can find out what would make dying a less frightening event. Then maybe we can learn to cope with death and dying instead of pretending it will never happen to us or *to* someone we love.

Look back to the prewriting exercises and follow the progression of thought. Notice how the student crossed out sentences and revised as she was writing. You should never be concerned with neatness until you are merely copying your paper over. Write your rough drafts on scrap paper, so you won't be tempted to hand in a rough draft as a final paper.

Proofreading

The following typed copy is how the paper looked when the writer handed it in to her English instructor. Probably if the writer had left the essay for a day or so, she might have made even further changes. Before reading through the final copy, read through the revision and circle any errors you see. Then read the final paper and see if you caught the same errors the writer found while proofreading.

In her article "Death with Dignity" Dr. Elisabeth Kübler-Ross discusses the effects of terminal illness on the dying individual and on the family. In her studies, Dr. Kübler-Ross discovered that people who are ready to die have hope, but their hope is not for recovery or their own lives. Instead, their hope and attention centers on the people who will be left behind, usually their families.

If we knew more about how terminally ill people develop that sense of hope and eventually accept the fact that they are dying, we might be able to help people to die with dignity. People should not have to die alone in a hospital room because their families are too tired to be with them. The families should never have to feel that a person's death is just a relief for everyone, including the person who is ill. If we could help make death less frightening, it would help both the dying person and the family.

One reason why terminal illness causes so much grief is that people are afraid to talk about death. People who are terminally ill should be able to discuss their fears, but people never discuss death. All religions seem to discuss the problems of life after death, but the process of dying is never discussed. It would be better if a dying person could be open about his or her fear of dying. Churches could help people by educating them about dying. The church is the best place to begin because death is viewed as a stepping stone to another life. In that atmosphere the discussion of death would be less frightening and might lead to hope.

Churches cannot begin educating people about dying until we know more about it. No one can help people die with dignity until we know what to tell people about dying. If people such as Dr. Elisabeth Kübler-Ross continue with their work, we can find out what would make dying a less frightening event. Then maybe we can learn to cope with death and dying instead of pretending it will never happen to us or someone we love.

The writing assignment you saw developed here was particularly difficult for the student because the instructor provided no guidelines. However, the student was successful in narrowing the subject, developing a unifying idea, and expanding that idea into an organized, acceptable paper.

EXERCISE 10–2

Directions: *Choose a reading selection from the end of this unit. If you have not yet read the selection, preread and read it, then write the title and subject here:*

TITLE: _____

SUBJECT: _____

Using the subject of the selection as a starting point, follow each of these steps:

1. *Prewriting.*
   a. Narrow the subject into three possible topics:

   _____

   _____

   _____

   b. Select one topic and use a five-minute free-writing exercise or write several questions that occur to you about the topic to generate ideas.
2. *Composing.* Select the most important ideas you see in your prewriting exercise. Develop these ideas into a paper consisting of an introduction, body, and conclusion. Include the details your reader will need in order to have a clear understanding of your purpose and message.
3. *Checking the Content and Organization.* Write an outline that shows the relationship between main ideas and supporting details. Then answer the following questions.
   a. What is the subject of your paper?

   _____

   _____

   b. What sentences in your paper specify the topic?

   _____

   _____

   c. What sentences help project the unifying idea?

   _____

   _____

   _____

4. *Revising.* Use the five questions on pages 26–27 to help you revise your paper. Answer each question and write a list of

changes you need to make. Next, look carefully at each paragraph and note the method of organization. Answer the following questions.

a. Which method of paragraph organization do you use most frequently?

_____

_____

b. Does that method work best in relating the unifying idea? Why?

_____

_____

_____

c. Write the main idea of each paragraph.

_____

_____

_____

_____

d. Is each main idea a supporting statement for the unifying idea?

_____

Rewrite any sentences and paragraphs that require improvement, then write a clean copy of the paper.

5. *Proofreading.* Consult your revised proofreading checklist from Chapter 9, page 251. Read through your paper carefully, placing a check in the proofreading checklist next to each item that you corrected in your paper. List the errors you corrected in the right column of the proofreading checklist. See if you have reduced the number of errors you have made in the past.

SUMMARY

In this chapter we discussed two elements that are important to many types of informative prose—the subject and unifying idea. The subject of an article or essay is the person, place, object, or idea that the entire piece of writing is about, whereas the unifying idea is a broad general statement of what the writer is saying about the subject. We also presented techniques for identifying the subject and unifying idea in reading and for developing the subject and unifying idea in writing.

PROOFREADING CHECKLIST

Essay Title _____

Date _____

TYPE	✔	ERROR	FREQUENCY	DESCRIPTION
GRAMMAR		Run-on Sentence Sentence Fragment Subject/Verb Agreement Verb Tense Pronoun Agreement		
MECHANICS		Capitalization Italics Abbreviation		
PUNCTUATION		, (Comma) ; (Semicolon) ' (Apostrophe) " (Quotation Marks) . (Period) ! (Exclamation Point) ? (Question Mark) : (Colon) — (Dash) ( ) (Parentheses) - (Hyphen)		

		ERROR	CORRECTION	
SPELLING ERRORS				

11. Supporting Details and Transitions

IDENTIFYING SUPPORTING DETAILS

As you have already learned, informative prose is structured around a unifying idea, or statement of what the whole article, selection, or chapter is about. Most or all of the paragraphs in such a piece of writing explain and develop the unifying idea. These paragraphs, then, consist of supporting details that back up and provide further information about the unifying idea.

Suppose you are glancing through a magazine article on "Decision Factors in Buying a Car," and you decide to read a section of the article titled "Compact Cars." This could be outlined as follows:

SUBJECT:	Compact Cars
UNIFYING IDEA:	Compact cars have numerous advantages
SUPPORTING DETAILS:	1. Small cars get 30 percent better gas mileage than luxury cars.
	2. When parking space is at a premium, compact cars often can fit into space where larger cars cannot.
	3. The original purchase price of a compact car is much less than larger cars.

You can see that this section of the article gives three advantages of compact cars over larger cars. Each advantage is a supporting detail. Of course, each detail itself would have been further explained by presenting several examples of the differences between specific cars. The second could have been developed through the use of statistics or examples. Then, the third might have been backed up by quoting the prices of specific makes of autos.

In most cases, a separate paragraph is written to present each supporting statement or detail. As a general rule of thumb, you should expect to find as many supporting statements as there are paragraphs. An exception to this rule occurs in longer passages or selections, in which the first paragraph serves as an introduction or lead-in to the selection, the final paragraph functions as a summary or conclusion, or both.

Generally, then, the information in a selection is organized into paragraphs, each of which has its own topic, main idea, supporting details, and organizational pattern. The main idea of each of these paragraphs relates to the unifying idea of the selection.

In the following selection, notice that the unifying idea is that radio stations employ many people other than those you hear on the air. As you read, try to identify the supporting statements.

The People You Never Hear

The radio world to most listeners may consist of the disc jockey, the newsperson, and the commentator; but the real world of radio is quite different. The "on the air" people may represent only about 10 to 15 percent of the total staff of most stations. In metro markets they may make up less than 10 percent. Who are the rest of the people?

Management personnel are at the top of the ladder. Each station has an owner or owners and a general manager (GM), who supervises all station activities. The GM's word is law and the decisions are final. Under the GM are the heads of the major departments.

Programming is the first department you might think of. The program director (PD) keeps track of air personnel, schedules shifts, and settles disputes involving the on-the-air staff. It is the PD's job to make sure that air personalities are slotted in at the proper times to elicit maximum audience response. If the ratings for the entire station are poor, the PD is likely to go.

Sales is often the most financially rewarding of all station jobs. Usually sales people have a guaranteed minimum "draw" of only a few hundred dollars per month, but they make up the difference by selling air time on commission. If they don't sell, they don't eat. There is usually a sales director or sales manager in charge who reports directly to the GM. In major markets there may be a few highly paid stars on the air, but at most stations it is the sales people who take home the most money.

Traffic is the department least known to the average radio listener. The traffic staff must schedule all the commercials. Only a fixed number are allowed each hour and competing products must not be placed back to back. It wouldn't be a good business practice to have a spot that urged you to "buy a Chevrolet today" played after one that told you "Ford has a better idea!" Traffic people make up the program logs, minute-by-minute projections of all commercials, IDs, promos, and other non-music materials. Air staff and engineers follow these logs exactly.

You should have seen that the supporting statements are:

1. Management personnel are necessary in a station's operation.
2. A programming department is necessary to schedule air time.
3. A sales staff is necessary to sell air time for commercials.
4. A traffic department is in charge of scheduling commercials.

Each paragraph in this selection supports the unifying idea by describing a department that works behind the scenes at a radio station.

The Organization of Supporting Statements

As you learned in Chapter 9, the details in a paragraph are not randomly arranged. Just as they have a particular order, supporting statements within a selection also have a pattern of arrangement. The same organization patterns that are used in paragraph development are also used in longer selections. For example, the details in a paragraph may be arranged chronologically; supporting statements in a selection may also follow a chronological pattern.

In addition to the common paragraph organization patterns presented in Chapter 9 (chronological order, statement-support, comparison-contrast, classification, cause-effect, definition, and description), several other common patterns are used in passages.

Question-Answer

Frequently, a writer may pose a question, often as a means of focusing the reader's attention, and then answer it in the remainder of a selection. A variation of this pattern is the statement of a problem followed by discussion of a solution. The following selection using the question-answer pattern appeared in *U.S. News and World Report* in an article on "How a President is Chosen."

Who Decides How Many Delegates Each State Should Have?
The apportionment rules for the Democratic convention were drawn up by the Democratic National Committee and are based half on population and half on the state's Democratic voting strength in the last three presidential elections. The Democrats this year are boosting the delegations in each state by 10 percent to insure space for party officials.

The Republican formula was adopted by the 1976 convention. Each state gets six delegates at large and three delegates for each congressional district in the state. Then it gets "bonus" at-large delegates if it elected a Republican governor, senator or at least half of its House delegation in 1976 or 1978. Still more bonus delegates are available if the Republican presidential candidate, Gerald R. Ford, carried the state in 1976.[1]

The first sentence of this selection states the basic question or problem. The rest answers and explains that question. This pattern is easily recognizable while reading because very early in the selection the question is directly stated or the problem is defined. If you notice this pattern in the beginning, you should read the rest of the selection to answer that question or solve that problem.

Order of Importance

A common method of arranging supporting statements is according to the order of their importance. A writer could present the strongest, most convincing statements early in the passage, then the next strongest, and end with the least important statements. On the other hand, a writer could lead up to his or her more important statements, stating the most important idea last.

You can often detect order of importance quite easily. Writers commonly use signal words to indicate the importance of supporting statements. Words like "primarily," "most important," "secondarily," or "finally" should be clues to you that this arrangement is being used. You will then easily recognize the main supporting ideas, since they often follow the signal words. For example, in the following passage, the author first presents the most important ("primary") reason to avoid sleeping pills then gives less important reasons.

> Difficulty in sleeping, often called insomnia, is a common problem experienced by most people on one occasion or another. It may be due to unfamiliar surroundings, excitement, stress, or depression. There are many remedies worth considering for occasional insomnia, but one remedy to be avoided, unless prescribed by a doctor, is sleeping pills.
>
> The primary reason to avoid sleeping pills is the possible harmful effects of the drugs they contain. Many sleeping pills contain barbiturates, which are addictive. Some pills also contain an antihistamine called methapyrilene that is under study to determine if it causes cancer.
>
> A second reason to avoid sleeping pills is that they promote drowsiness. If taken several days in succession, the pills cause a residue to build up in the bloodstream. This residue causes drowsiness during the day as well as at night.
>
> Finally, research evidence suggests that the pills have little long-term effectiveness in causing sleep. Other evidence suggests that some pills actually interfere with the natural mechanisms of sleep. As a result, sleep that occurs under the influence of sleeping pills may not be as restful as sleep that occurs naturally.

General to Particular/Particular to General

In organizing statements or paragraphs that support a central thought, writers may begin with general ideas and move gradually toward more specific or detailed statements. Also, a writer may choose the opposite approach, beginning with specifics and leading up to more inclusive statements.

In the following selection, about assumptions that can interfere with friendships or personal relationships, the author uses the general-to-specific pattern. The first paragraph contains a general explanation of the concept; the second gives an example of one person making an assumption.

Assumption

> Assuming that one knows the other person's feelings without checking is another common difficulty. It is easy to find in another person's behavior signs that will confirm almost any emotion one wishes to project onto that person, from anger to love. Reacting to the partner's perceived, rather than actual, emotions can set up cycles of misunderstanding and resentment.
>
> Consider, for example, a woman who calls a man friend "slim," which she considers an endearment. If he is

worried that his appearance is in fact too scrawny, he might dislike the nickname. Unless he speaks up and says so, however, she will sense only the tension in the air when she uses the name. This tension might be taken by her as a sign that he does not care for her or is withdrawing from her. Thus, keeping pain or dislike of something inside of oneself forces the other partner to make assumptions— often, inaccurate ones.[2]

The key to using this pattern lies in recognizing the general statements early in your reading. Since these statements may be found either in the first or last few paragraphs, prereading would pay off particularly well with this pattern. Once you are aware of the general ideas, it will be much easier to sort out those ideas which provide the major supporting details.

TRANSITIONS AS AN AID TO READING

In order for ideas and supporting statements to be easily understood, they must be connected. Each idea should lead to the next so that the reader can follow the direction and development of thought. To accomplish this, writers use a device called transitions. *Transitions* can be defined as words, phrases, or sentences that connect ideas, leading from one idea to another. In a sense, they bridge the gap between ideas. In Chapter 9, on paragraph organization, you learned that certain words and phrases can signal or suggest the relationship of ideas or help you identify the organizational pattern. Many of these words and phrases can also serve as transitions. For example, notice how the italicized word in this selection connects the ideas presented in the first paragraph with those in the second:

> Two myths about vitamins that are currently popular should be mentioned here. First, some people believe that vitamin C in sufficient doses can prevent the common cold. Based on the best research to date, it cannot. Nor can large doses of vitamin C cure colds. Such doses may produce a moderate lessening of the severity of cold symptoms, but the dose needed to achieve this modest effect is only about as much vitamin C as is found in two glasses of orange juice!
>
> *Another* myth is that vitamin E, taken in large doses, will enhance your sexual potency. There is no research basis in humans for this finding, and the evidence from animal data is weak. If taking vitamin E helps anyone's sexual performance, it will probably be simply because the person believed it would.[3]

Some students mistakenly skip over transitions because they think they do not contain crucial information. However, transitions help the reader to understand how ideas are related, and what direction of thought the writer will pursue next. When reading informative prose be sure to watch for tansitional words, phrases, and sentences.

1. *Transitional Words and Phrases.* Many of the same words that are used to connect details within a paragraph are used to connect supporting statements in paragraphs. Here is a list of some of the most common transitional words and phrases along with what they tell the reader.

Common transitional words/phrases	What they tell the reader
to the right, next to, in front, in the distance	relationship in space
in summary, in conclusion, therefore, thus, to sum up, in short, in brief	conclusion or summary
and, additionally, also, furthermore, moreover, likewise, similarly	continuation of the same train of thought
in other words, that is, in effect, again, to repeat	restatement of an idea
primarily, chiefly, secondarily, most important, equally important	importance of what is to follow
next, later, afterwards, before, while, then, concurrently, first, second	relationship in time
consequently, as a result, thus, therefore, then, hence	cause or effect
on the contrary, on the other hand, however, in contrast	a contrasting idea
for example, to illustrate, for instance, such as, specifically	an example

2. *Transitional Sentences.* You have just seen that paragraphs can be linked through the use of transitional words and phrases. However, depending on the complexity of the thoughts or the relationship of ideas, a word or phrase may not be sufficient. In this situation a writer may use a whole sentence or a part of a compound or complex sentence to make the transition. The transition may occur at the end of a paragraph, but more commonly it appears at the beginning of the next paragraph.

A transitional sentence connects or shows the relationship between two ideas. In the following example, discussing techniques for taking notes during a college lecture, the transition sentence is underlined:

Many instructors lecture from a carefully prepared outline of material they want the students to know. Later, when they make up a test on that material, they may refer back to their original outline in order to formulate appropriate test questions. In lecture notetaking, then, it is important to record accurately the instructor's main points and supporting information.

Accurate recording of information, however, is not sufficient for effective notetaking. Record the information in a format that easily shows the relative importance of ideas and establishes the organization of the lecture. The appropriate format will help you to review for a test in an organized way, and you will also remember the material more easily if it is organized in a specific pattern.

Here the transitional sentence tells the reader that the first idea (accurate recording) is not all that is necessary for effective notetaking. Notice that the transitional sentence repeats some of the key words from the first paragraph and supplies some additional information about them.

Precisely because they establish the connections between ideas, transitional words, phrases, and sentences are valuable aids in reading. Essentially, they function as signals or signposts that suggest direction of thought. Try to get in the habit of noticing transitions as you read. Further, when you notice a transition, be alert to the signal it gives you.

USING SUPPORTING DETAILS AND TRANSITIONS

The following selection illustrates how supporting details and transitions function in an article or selection. Preread, then read it; identify the unifying idea, and look for supporting statements. Also, be alert for transitions.

Body Language

Julius Fast

THE STARE THAT DEHUMANIZES

The cowpuncher sat his horse loosely and his fingers hovered above his gun while his eyes, ice cold, sent chills down the rustler's back.   1

A familiar situation? It happens in every Western novel, just as in every love story the heroine's eyes *melt* while the hero's eyes *burn* into hers. In literature, even the best literature, eyes are *steely, knowing, mocking, piercing, glowing,* and so on.   2

Are they really? Are they ever? Is there such a thing as a burning glance or a cold glance or a hurt glance? In truth there isn't. Far from being windows of the soul, the eyes are physiological dead ends, simply organs of sight and no more, differently colored in different people to be sure, but never really capable of expressing emotion in themselves.   3

And yet again and again we read and hear and even tell of the eyes being wise, knowing, good, bad, indifferent. Why is there such confusion? Can so many people be wrong? If the eyes do not show emotion, then why the vast literature, the stories and legends about them?   4

Of all parts of the human body that are used to transmit information, the eyes are the most important and can transmit the most subtle nuances. Does this contradict the fact that the eyes do not show emotion? Not really. While the eyeball itself shows nothing, the emotional impact of the eyes occurs because of their use and the use of the face around them. The reason they have so confounded observers is that by length of glance, by opening of eyelids by squinting and by a dozen little manipulations of the skin and eyes, almost any meaning can be sent out. 5

But the most important technique of eye management is the look, or the stare. With it we can often make or break another person. How? By giving him human or nonhuman status. 6

Simply, eye management in our society boils down to two facts. One, we do not stare at another human being. Two, staring is reserved for a non-person. We stare at art, at sculpture, at scenery. We go to the zoo and stare at the animals, the lions, the monkeys, the gorillas. We stare at them for as long as we please, as intimately as we please, but we do not stare at humans if we want to accord them human treatment. 7

We may use the same stare for the side-show freak, but we do not really consider him a human being. He is an object at which we have paid money to stare, and in the same way we may stare at an actor on a stage. The real man is masked too deeply behind his role for our stare to bother either him or us. However, the new theater that brings the actor down into the audience often gives us an uncomfortable feeling. By virtue of involving us, the audience, the actor suddenly loses his non-person status and staring at him becomes embarrassing to us. 8

If we wish pointedly to ignore someone, to treat him with an element of contempt, we can give him the same stare, the slightly unfocused look that does not really see him, the cutting stare of the socially elite. 9

Servants are often treated this way as are waiters, waitresses and children. However, this may be a mutually protective device. It allows the servants to function efficiently in their overlapping universe without too much interference from us, and it allows us to function comfortably without acknowledging the servant as a fellow human. The same is true of children and waiters. It would be an uncomfortable world if each time we were served by a waiter we had to introduce ourselves and indulge in social amenities. 10

A TIME FOR LOOKING

With unfamiliar human beings, when we acknowledge their humanness, we must avoid staring at them, and yet we must also avoid ignoring them. To make them into people rather than objects, we use a deliberate and polite inattention. We look at them long enough to make it quite clear that we see them, and then we immediately look away. We are saying, in body language, "I know you are there," and a moment later we add, "But I would not dream of intruding on your privacy." 11

The most important thing in such an exchange is that we do not catch the eye of the one whom we are recognizing as a person. We look at him without locking glances, and then we immediately look away. Recognition is not permitted. 12

There are different formulas for the exchange of glances depending on where the meeting takes place. If you pass someone in the street, you may eye the oncoming person till you are about eight feet apart, then you must look away as you pass. Before the eight-foot distance is reached, each will signal in which direction he will pass. This is done with a brief look in that direction. Each will veer slightly, and the passing is done smoothly. 13

For this passing encounter Dr. Erving Goffman in *Behavior in Public Places* says that the quick look and the lowering of the eyes is body language for, "I trust you. I am not afraid of you." 14

To strengthen this signal, you look directly at the other's face before looking away. 15

Sometimes the rules are hard to follow, particularly if one of the two people wears dark glasses. It becomes impossible to discover just what they are doing. Are they looking at you too long, too intently? Are they looking at you at all? The person wearing the glasses feels protected and assumes that he can stare without being noticed in his staring. However, this is a self-deception. To the other person, dark glasses seem to indicate that the wearer is always staring at him. 16

We often use this look-and-away technique when we meet famous people. We want to assure them that we are respecting their privacy, that we would not dream of staring at them. The same is true of the crippled or physically handicapped. We look briefly and then look away before the stare can be said to be a stare. It is the technique we use for any unusual situation where too long a stare would be embarrassing. When we see an interracial couple, we use this technique. We might use it when we see a man with an unusual beard, with extra long hair, with outlandish clothes, or a girl with a minimal mini-skirt may attract this look-and-away. 17

Of course, the opposite is also true. If we wish to put a person down, we may do so by staring longer than is acceptably polite. Instead of dropping our gazes when we lock glances, we continue to stare. The person who disapproves of interracial marriage or dating will stare rudely at the interracial couple. If he dislikes long hair, short dresses or beards, he may show it with a longer-than-acceptable stare. 18

THE AWKWARD EYES

The look-and-away stare is reminiscent of the problem we face in adolescence in terms of our hands. What do we do with them? Where do we hold them? Amateur actors are also made conscious of this. They are suddenly aware of their hands as awkward appendages that must somehow be used gracefully and naturally. 19

In the same way, in certain circumstances, we become aware of our glances as awkward appendages. Where shall we look? What shall we do with our eyes? 20

Two strangers seated across from each other in a railway 21
dining car have the option of introducing themselves and facing a meal of inconsequential and perhaps boring talk, or ignoring each other and desperately trying to avoid each other's
glance. Cornelia Otis Skinner, describing such a situation in an
essay, wrote, "They re-read the menu, they fool with the
cutlery, they inspect their own fingernails as if seeing them for
the first time. Comes the inevitable moment when glances
meet, but they meet only to shoot instantly away and out the
window for an intent view of the passing scene."

This same awkward eye dictates our looking behavior in 22
elevators and crowded buses and subway trains. When we get
on an elevator or train with a crowd we look briefly and then
look away at once without locking glances. We say, with our
look, "I see you. I do not know you, but you are a human and
I will not stare at you."

In the subway or bus where long rides in very close 23
circumstances are a necessity, we may be hard put to find some
way of not staring. We sneak glances, but look away before our
eyes can look. Or we look with an unfocused glance that misses
the eyes and settles on the head, the mouth, the body—for any
place but the eyes is an acceptable looking spot for the unfocused glance.

If our eyes do meet, we can sometimes mitigate the 24
message with a brief smile. The smile must not be too long or
too obvious. It must say. "I am sorry we have looked, but we
both know it was an accident."

In this selection, the unifying idea is stated in the first sentence of
the fifth paragraph. Although the idea is suggested earlier, here Fast
directly states that the eyes are the most important part of the body for
communication of information. Throughout the remainder of the selection, then, Fast explains and supports this statement. First he states that
the stare is the most important technique and that there are two basic
rules about staring: (1) People do not stare at another human being; and
(2) staring is reserved for a non-person. Each of these rules is explained
through the use of examples. Next, under "A Time for Looking" Fast
discusses the use of the "look-and-away" technique of acknowledging
another person. Then, throughout the rest of this section of the article,
the author explains this technique by providing explanation, reasons, and
examples. In the last section, "The Awkward Eyes," Fast discusses the
use of eyes in uncomfortable situations or close circumstances, in which
eye contact is almost inescapable.

You might outline Fast's article as follows:

UNIFYING IDEA: The eyes are the most important part of the body
for transmitting information.

STATEMENTS:
1. The use of the stare distinguishes those who are
treated as humans from those who are not.
2. The "look-and-away" technique acknowledges
another person.
3. The "awkward eye" indicates one's discomfort
with a situation or placement in a physically
close situation.

You have seen, then, that three key supporting details are provided as a means of explaining why or how the eyes communicate or transmit information. Now let's consider how Fast uses transitions to connect his ideas. You can see that he connected supporting statements as well as ideas that explain each of the supporting statements. The headings included also serve to divide or separate ideas and indicate what is to follow. Since Fast uses headings, fewer transitions are needed. Still, there are many transitions; here are a few examples:

Paragraph	Transition	Function/Aid to reading
6	but	change of thought
7	simply	restatement, in basic terms
8	We may use the same stare . . .	connects paragraphs 7 and 8
12	The important thing . . .	emphasis—an important idea will follow
17	We often use this look-and-away technique when . . .	examples
20	In the same way, . . .	comparison—a similar idea will follow

EXERCISE 11–1

Directions: *Read one of the selections at the end of this unit using these steps:*

1. *Prereading.* Preread the selection.
2. *Establish a Purpose.* Using what you learned from your prereading, write several questions you want to answer as you read.

_____

_____

_____

_____

3. *Read the selection.* Look for the answers to your questions as you read. Also look for the unifying idea and how supporting details explain this idea. Notice their function. Then respond to these questions:
   a. What was the unifying idea in the selection you read?

_____

_____

_____

_____

b. What were the most important supporting details in the selection? Outline them.

_____ _____ ___

_____

_____

_____

_____

c. What types of transitions did the author use? Go back through the selection and identify five transitional words, phrases, or sentences. List them and indicate what they tell you as a reader.

Transition	Aid to the reader
a. _____	_____
b. _____	_____
c. _____	_____
d. _____	_____
e. _____	_____

4. *Review.* Reread important parts of the selection.

5. *React.* Think about and react to what you read. You will have an opportunity to express your ideas about this subject in the writing exercise at the end of this chapter.

DEVELOPING SUPPORTING STATEMENTS AND TRANSITIONS

In the last chapter you concentrated on focusing the subject and developing the unifying idea in an essay. The next steps in writing an effective essay are to develop and organize the ideas that support your unifying idea and to connect those ideas using transitional words and phrases.

Think of the internal organization of a paragraph as a model that is repeated at a much broader level in a longer piece of writing. For example, one paragraph serves the same purpose in a long prose selection as a supporting detail does in a paragraph. The following diagram shows how paragraphs relate to the unifying idea.

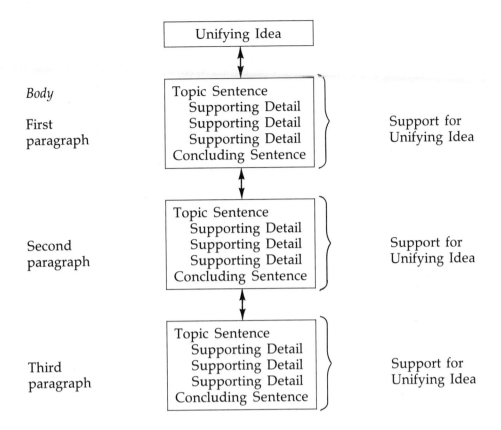

You can see that each paragraph in an essay relates directly to the unifying idea. The arrows in the diagram indicate that ideas are related. Later in this chapter you will see how transitions are used to tie these supporting statements together.

Developing Supporting Statements

Once you have narrowed and focused your subject and developed a unifying idea, the next step is to develop supporting ideas. Let's review the procedure you used to develop the unifying idea. You will see that these steps are also useful in selecting supporting ideas.

Prewriting

Prewriting, in addition to helping you develop a unifying idea, can also help you construct supporting statements. Reread your statements or questions and mark any ideas that seem to support your unifying idea. As you reread these ideas you will probably think of others that could be used. Be sure to jot these ideas down as they come to mind.

After rereading your prewriting exercise, if you do not find ideas that can be developed as support, you might do another prewriting exercise. Try to write any ideas or questions that come into mind about your unifying idea. If a second prewriting exercise does not help you develop supporting ideas, you should take another look at your unifying idea. It may need revision, or you may need to change it completely.

Composing: Writing Supporting Paragraphs

Once you have identified the facts and ideas supporting your unifying idea, the next step is to select appropriate supporting statements and to structure, revise, and organize them into supporting paragraphs.

The unifying idea determines your choice of supporting information. Only ideas that *directly* prove or explain the unifying idea can be included. Suppose your unifying idea is that sex education should not be taught in the public schools because it takes responsibilities away from parents. In writing supporting statements you should include only ideas that directly relate to this unifying idea. For example, although it may be true that sex education involves morals and values, it would be appropriate to include that idea in this essay only if you connect it to parental responsibility.

In writing supporting paragraphs you need to know three rules of thumb:

1. There must be a separate paragraph for each major supporting idea.
2. The topic sentence of each paragraph should state the major supporting point.
3. The remainder of the paragraph should explain and support the topic sentence. Indirectly, then, these sentences also support the unifying idea.

Composing: Organizing Supporting Statements

In arranging and developing supporting statements you should be concerned with two structures: (1) the sequence of the supporting paragraphs, and (2) the structure of ideas within each of the supporting paragraphs.

You have already learned to arrange details in a paragraph in specific types of organizational patterns. In an essay you will also arrange the supporting statements in a pattern, and you can use the same patterns for passages that you have already learned for paragraphs. The common organizational patterns of paragraphs are chronological, statement-support, comparison-contrast, classification, cause-effect, definition, and description. If none of these patterns seem appropriate, you could use one of the following more general methods of development.

1. *Questions-Answers.* As you know, a writer will often use a question to focus the reader's attention on a particular point. You can use a question to arouse your reader's attention, and then you can answer the question within the essay. However, the paragraphs that answer the question should be carefully structured. Try to divide the question into parts or organize the facts or ideas that answer the question in a systematic way.
2. *Order of Importance.* Another common method of arranging supporting statements is according to their order of importance. The most important ideas may be presented first, or the selection may begin with the less important ideas and lead up to the more important. Generally, if you want to use the clearest, most direct approach, you might begin by stating your most important idea first. However, if you want to leave your reader with your most important idea most immediately in mind when he or she finishes reading, then structure your ideas from least to most important.

3. *General to Particular/Particular to General.* As a reader you look for this organizational pattern in a piece of writing in order to help you understand the material better. As a writer you can begin with general statements or you can begin with very specific statements and end with general statements. This pattern is particularly useful when you are presenting a collection of facts or figures to support a statement. The important point to remember is to be consistent. Once you begin a pattern of organization, don't switch to the opposite pattern without making sure your reader will see that you have switched and understand your reason for doing so.

Checking the Content and Organization

Once you have written a rough draft of your essay, the next step is to reread it, checking for content and organization. To check content, you might ask yourself the following questions:

1. *Does each paragraph directly support the unifying idea?* Reread each paragraph and concentrate on the topic sentence. Does it directly prove or explain the unifying idea? If not, decide whether to eliminate it or how to revise it. Next, look at the supporting details. Does each detail explain or support the topic sentence? Again, revise or eliminate any sentences that do not explain or support the unifying idea.

2. *Are the supporting statements as specific as possible?* Reread each paragraph looking for statements that could be further explained. Also, look for ideas that may be unclear or misunderstood. It may help to imagine yourself in the position of the reader. As you read look for statements about which you might want further information or explanation.

3. *Are the supporting ideas organized in some way?* To help you see the organization of what you have written more clearly, it is useful to make a brief outline of your ideas. The outline will help you to see how your ideas are connected or whether they need to be rearranged.

Making Transitions

One feature of well-written essays is a certain clarity that effective use of transitions brings to them. Transitions enable the writer to proceed smoothly from idea to idea or from organizational pattern to organizational pattern. Let's go back to the format for a paragraph.

Topic Sentence
Supporting detail
    Secondary details
Supporting detail
    Secondary details
Concluding Sentence

Now imagine this same structure repeated throughout the structure of a longer piece of writing. It might resemble the following pattern.

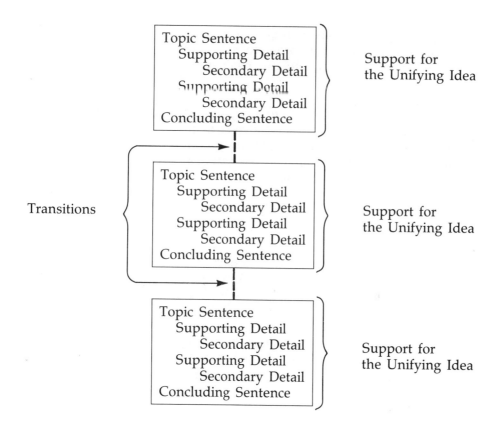

Notice that each paragraph is linked to the preceding one by a transition. Think of transitions as chains that connect ideas throughout a piece of writing. The transitions connect statements and paragraphs and form a unified essay. They must be included wherever a new idea is introduced, linking the new idea to the other thoughts.

Transitions in Sentences and Paragraphs

Transitions within sentences and between paragraphs make a tremendous difference in the tone and style of a piece of writing and lead to smooth changes in thought. Transitions occur in speech, but they are not as obvious; nor are they always accomplished in the same manner. In speech both the speaker and the listener depend on eye contact and body movements to aid transitions in thought. When a speaker wants to move from one idea to another, he or she may pause, change the volume of his or her voice, or use eye contact. In writing you do not have these aids to signal your change; you need to use words for this. Basically, there are three situations in which transitions are used: (1) to connect ideas within a sentence, (2) to connect sentences, or (3) to connect paragraphs.

You have already learned a great deal about how to connect ideas in sentences and paragraphs. In combining ideas within sentences, you learned how to use conjunctions to show the relationship between or among ideas. In writing paragraphs you learned how to use signal words to connect ideas and to provide the reader with clues to your organization or pattern of thought.

To recognize the importance of transitions within a paragraph, read the following paragraph, which is written without any transitions.

Usually I go on vacation with my parents. This year I decided to go with my friends. We went to the Bahamas. We wanted to snorkel and scuba dive. We chartered a sailboat. The charter included gourmet meals. We could help sail the boat, or we could just relax and enjoy the ride.

The paragraph becomes easier to read and makes more sense when transitional words and phrases are added. Look at the paragraph again and notice the italicized transitional words.

Usually I go on vacation with my parents, *but* this year I decided to go with my friends. We went to the Bahamas *since* we wanted to spend our days snorkeling and scuba diving. *Also*, we chartered a sailboat, *and* the charter included gourmet meals. *Furthermore*, we could help sail the boat if we wanted to, or we could just relax and enjoy the ride.

In essays it is still important to connect ideas within sentences and within paragraphs. However, in addition to these transitions, it is also necessary to connect the supporting paragraphs and to lead your reader from one main idea to another.

The main purpose of transitions within an essay is to lead the reader from paragraph to paragraph in a smooth, natural way. If you do not use transitions your reader may wonder: Why is the idea included? How does this fit in? What does this idea have to do with what was just said? What is the writer leading up to?

Transitional Words and Phrases

Often the presence or absence of a few connecting words and phrases can make the difference in whether ideas appear related or unrelated. It is easy for you to understand the relationships between your own ideas, but for a reader, the connections are not as obvious. Single words (*another, also, next, second, third*) are often sufficient to announce a change or shift to a new idea. In other situations phrases (*for example, in other words, to conclude*) suggest to the reader that a change in thought is about to occur. For a review of the common transitional or signal words and phrases and the change in thought that they suggest, see page 314.

Transitional Sentences

In some cases, a word or phrase is not sufficient to connect the ideas of one paragraph with those of another. Usually the greater the change in ideas, the greater the need for a transition. If you are discussing four personality characteristics of a person, words or phrases such as *another, a second characteristic,* or *finally,* might be all that is needed to move from one characteristic to another. However, if you have just finished discussing the four characteristics and are ready to move to the next paragraph in which you explain why, based on these traits, you like or dislike the person, then a stronger, clearer transition is needed. Often this is most effectively accomplished by beginning the new paragraph with a transitional sentence connecting the ideas in the previous paragraph or paragraphs to the new idea. For instance, a transitional sentence for a paragraph discussing personality characteristics might be: "Although Sam has these undesirable personality characteristics, I find that I enjoy his company."

EXERCISE 11-2

Directions: *Choose a reading from the end of this unit. If you have not yet read the selection, preread and read it, then write the title and subject of the reading:*

TITLE: _____

SUBJECT: _____

Using the subject of the selection as a starting point, follow each of these steps:

1. *Prewriting.*
   a. Narrow the subject into three possible topics:

   _____

   _____

   _____

   b. Select one topic and use a five-minute free-writing exercise or write several questions that occur to you about the topic to generate ideas.
2. *Composing.* Select the most important ideas you see in your prewriting exercise. Develop them into a paper consisting of an introduction, body, and conclusion. Include the details your reader will need in order to have a clear understanding of your purpose and message.
3. *Checking the Content and Organization.* Fill in the spaces in the model to help you check your organization. The model is only a guide; its primary purpose is to remind you to put all the pieces together. You can move the pieces around to suit your needs.

   Topic Sentence _____

   _____

   Supporting Detail _____

   _____. Transitional word or phrase +

   Supporting Detail _____

   _____

   Supporting Detail _____

Transitional word or phrase + Concluding Sentence _____

_____

_____ .

Transitional word or phrase + Topic Sentence _____

_____

_____

Supporting Detail _____

_____ .

Transitional word or phrase + Supporting Detail _____

_____

_____ .

Supporting Detail _____

Transitional word or phrase + Concluding Sentence _____

_____ .

Transitional word or phrase + Topic Sentence _____

_____ .

Supporting Detail _____

_____ .

Supporting Detail _____

_____

_____ .

Transitional word or phrase + Concluding Sentence _____

_____

_____

_____ .

4. *Revising.* Revise what you have written, rewording any sentences that are not clear or do not sound right. Make sure you have transitions and supporting statements.

PROOFREADING CHECKLIST

Essay Title _____

Date _____

TYPE	✔	ERROR	FREQUENCY	DESCRIPTION
GRAMMAR		Run-on Sentence Sentence Fragment Subject/Verb Agreement Verb Tense Pronoun Agreement		
MECHANICS		Capitalization Italics Abbreviation		
PUNCTUATION		, (Comma) ; (Semicolon) ' (Apostrophe) " (Quotation Marks) . (Period) ! (Exclamation Point) ? (Question Mark) : (Colon) — (Dash) ( ) (Parentheses) - (Hyphen)		

		ERROR	CORRECTION	
SPELLING ERRORS				

Ask a fellow student to read what you have written, paying special attention to transitions. Ask the student to underline all the transitions he or she notices. See if you both agree on where the transitions are made.

5. *Proofreading.* Proofread for mechanical errors, errors in spelling, punctuation, and grammar. Correct your errors. If you are unsure about spelling and punctuation, ask for another person's opinion. Place a check next to each item on the proofreading checklist that you correct. Describe each error in the column on the right.

SUMMARY

In this chapter we discussed the function of supporting details and transitions in informative prose. Supporting details are statements and ideas that in some way explain, prove, or support the unifying idea. They may be arranged in various patterns such as question-answer, order of importance, or general to particular/particular to general. Transitions are words, phrases, or sentences that connect ideas or lead from one idea to another. They help the reader understand the relationship or connection between ideas.

12. The Structure of Informative Prose

A wide range of printed materials can be classified as informative. This category includes anything that is written primarily to inform the reader or to present information. Movie reviews, business letters, newspaper articles, textbooks, magazine articles, "junk mail," research papers, technical reports, and catalogs are all considered informative prose, although they are very different in terms of audience, purpose, style, and content. Despite these differences there is an underlying structure or organization that is common to all prose. In the first portion of this chapter we will briefly discuss this basic structure and then focus on ways to organize and clarify it. In the writing portion of the chapter we will discuss the structure in detail and show how it can be used to write informative prose.

UNDERSTANDING THE STRUCTURE OF INFORMATIVE PROSE

In a very general sense, "informative prose" can refer to anything that is written, with the exception of poetry. However, in the reading portion of this chapter we will focus on materials (such as textbook selections and general information sources) that are most useful to college students. Rather than calling them informative prose, we will use *reading* and *selection* to mean a section taken from a larger piece of writing, such as a textbook chapter. *Article* will refer to any complete piece of writing such as a newspaper article.

Recognizing the Structure of Informative Prose

Although it varies widely in content and purpose, informative prose has some characteristic features. First is its overall structure. It usually follows the pattern of introduction-body-conclusion (or summary). That is, most articles or selections begin with an opening statement or paragraph (the introduction). The body, which states and develops the ideas to be expressed, follows. The selection or reading ends with a conclusion or summary, drawing together the ideas expressed in the body. Let's look at some techniques for reading these pieces.

Reading the Introduction

The primary purpose of an introduction is to announce what the reading selection will be about. Authors also use the introduction to capture the reader's interest, to connect the subject to an idea previously discussed, or to provide essential background information.

The introduction is important because it tells you what the selection will be about. It also gives you an idea of what to expect and starts you thinking about the subject.

Because the introduction announces the subject and sets the scene for the rest of the selection, you should read it as part of your prereading. As you read it, you should begin to anticipate what the selection will be about. You may begin to form ideas about how the author will approach the subject, how the ideas will be explained, or how the material in the body will be organized. The information contained in the introduction, along with the clues you get from the other parts of the selection that you check when prereading, will enable you to follow the author's thoughts more easily as you read the selection.

When reading an introduction, then, keep these questions in mind. They will focus your attention on the important information contained in the introduction.

1. If not identified in the title, what is the subject of the selection?
2. What is the unifying idea of the selection?
3. What is the writer's general approach and attitude toward the subject?
4. How will the ideas be arranged in the selection?
5. What background information does the writer present about the subject?

Now, refer to the selection on page 332. It includes portions of a chapter on "Marriages and Families" from a textbook titled *Well-Being: An Introduction to Health.* Eventually you will read the whole selection, but for now read *only* the first four paragraphs. They serve as an introduction to the chapter.

Now that you have read this introduction, let's see what types of information it provides about the chapter. Paragraph 1 presents the idea that there has been a change in how well marriages work. You should expect this idea to be developed throughout the chapter. In the second paragraph the writer asks questions that indicate specific topics to be explored in the chapter. Paragraph 3 introduces the topic of alternatives to marriage. However, in this introduction, Paragraph 4 is the most important. It provides you with a list of the topics the chapter will discuss and the order in which they will be presented. The first part of the chapter will discuss the following topics:

1. Why people marry
2. What traditional marriage is
3. How marriage has changed
4. Alternatives to marriage

Now reread the remaining sentences of Paragraph 4 and identify the three other major topics that this chapter discusses.

You should have identified the following topics: (1) choosing a marriage partner, (2) dynamics of a working marriage, and (3) marriages that do not work.

The authors of this sample introduction very carefully outlined the topics to be covered in the chapter. However, not all introductions are this straightforward. Some of the selections you will read in the rest of this chapter and in other chapters of this unit do not have introductions that clearly outline the topics to be discussed.

Reading the Body

The body of the selection presents and explains the ideas that the selection develops. The body of a short article may consist of only two or three paragraphs. The body of a textbook chapter, however, is long and usually divided into smaller parts or sections. Each section may have its own introduction, its own conclusion, or both. For example, the selection "Marriages and Families" is divided into four sections. Notice that the authors include an outline of these four sections at the beginning of the chapter. The four sections are:

Marriage and Its Alternatives
Choosing a Partner
Making Marriage Work
When Marriage Doesn't Work

In this chapter the author carefully introduces each section. Turn to the selection and read the two paragraphs (5 and 6) that introduce the section titled "Marriage and Its Alternatives." Notice that that section is further divided by headings. These headings are:

Why People Marry
Marriages and Families
Forces for Change
Alternatives Within Marriage
Alternatives to Marriage

Marriages and Families

John Dorfman, Sheila Kitzinger, and Herman Schuchman

Marriage and its alternatives
Why People Marry
Marriages and Families
Forces for Change
Alternatives Within Marriage
Alternatives to Marriage

Choosing a partner
Some Fundamental Considerations
Thin Ice: Some Questionable Foundations for Marriage

Making marriage work
Accepting Change
Communicating
Adjusting and Compromising

When marriage doesn't work
Looking Outside for Solutions
Divorce

Does marriage work any more? There is some evidence, in this country, to the contrary. At the turn of the century, the majority of marriages lasted until one of the persons died. Today, just over fifty percent of all U.S. marriages end in divorce. You may have heard people argue, or have argued yourself, that marriage is an outdated institution—restrictive, unstable, incapable of meeting the challenges of today's world.

At the same time, most of you reading this book either are, have been, or will be married at some point in your lives. You have your own ideas about what marriage can or should be and about why you do or do not want to be married. Where did you get your ideas about marriage? Do you consider your expectations fairly realistic? Those are among the questions we wish to explore in this chapter. Whether you personally endorse marriage or not, it remains important, a standard with which other forms of social relationships are compared.

Despite the existence of alternatives—singlehood, living together, and a variety of other, less conventional, arrangements—marriage remains extremely popular. It is estimated that more than ninety percent of the people in this country will be married at some point in their lives.

In this chapter we will begin by looking at some reasons why people marry, defining what marriage has traditionally been, looking at some ways in which it has changed, and discussing some of the alternatives to marriage. Next we will examine the process of choosing a marriage partner. We will then proceed to look at the dynamics of a working marriage and the positive coping mechanisms that partners can use to overcome the natural frictions that arise in any long-term relationship. Finally, we will examine some of the consequences when marriage does not work and some of the alternatives that people turn to when this situation arises.

MARRIAGE AND ITS ALTERNATIVES

Why marry, anyway? What is there about a ceremony, a certificate, a formal commitment, that is worth seeking out? Why cannot people simply live with whom they choose, for as long as the emotions of both dictate?

Those are good questions, and they are asked by an increasing number of people, both young and old. But the questions are not merely rhetorical; they have answers. There are advantages and disadvantages to marriage, just as there are to singlehood or any other choice an individual makes in organizing life. Choosing to marry does not guarantee the falling of a silken curtain and a free ride to happy-ever-after land. Neither, however, does avoiding marriage guarantee anything (not even spontaneity or freedom). The truth is that any major life-style choice works only as well as the people involved make it work.

Why People Marry

The continuing popularity of marriage is probably unrelated to a desire for sexual experience, which can increasingly be obtained outside marriage. Rather, it probably reflects an individual's desire to be number one in another person's eyes, to have that status formally symbolized, and to have a long-term companion who will provide emotional closeness and support.

People have a need for intimacy. We need to find someone to trust. We need to be accepted, to be loved, to be important to someone. We seek to gain warmth and closeness, to ward off loneliness, to structure our lives with a sense of purpose. All of these needs may contribute to our forming bonds with one particular person. As a way of strengthening, formalizing, or celebrating that bond, many of us turn to marriage. 8

The symbolic aspect of marriage has been criticized by some "If you really love each other," they ask, "why do you need a scrap of paper to prove it?" Of course, not everyone does. But people who do want that paper (and the ceremony, the ring, and perhaps the change of the woman's last name if both partners wish it) are acting in accordance with a long tradition of symbolism in our culture. Countries do not really need flags, nor do sports teams really require elaborate uniforms. Many of the symbols in our society recognize that people's identification and emotional response to things is intimately tied up with symbolism. When you were young, did you ever carve your initials and those of your boyfriend or girlfriend in a heart someplace? Did you ever go steady or think of going steady? These actions, like marriage, are a form of symbolism, a way of celebrating or strengthening a bond through announcing or formalizing it. 9

Marriage also provides a home base, a place to refuel oneself for the relationships and activities of a busy and taxing world. It is a place where hurts and unmet needs can be cared for, where people can be themselves, wearing no social mask (or hardly any) and feeling confident of being fully accepted. It provides a safe place to try out changes in oneself, to test old patterns and attitudes learned from family, and to consider or try out new patterns. It can be a safe place to argue, disagree, challenge, and be challenged. Most important, marriage can provide an opportunity to explore the deeper parts of oneself and of another person. 10

For many people, marriage marks the end of a hungry search for a partner which consumes vast amounts of energy during adolescence and early adulthood. In return for the satisfaction involved in having a confirmed partner, people often perceive themselves as giving up a measure of freedom. Perhaps it is not, in fact, quite that simple. Marriage may take away some freedoms. It may take away the freedom to have many sexual relationships, if that is a part of the marriage contract, as it is for most people. It takes away some control over one's own time, energy, money, and feelings. Living with, bonding with, another person means taking some of their needs into consideration and meeting them if you are to have your own needs met. But at the same time marriage may provide some freedoms and opportunities. It may, for example, offer the freedom to be oneself more fully, to take chances, to try things, with the knowledge that there is a warm and accepting person available to back you up regardless of what occurs. 11

Another important reason people marry is that they are expected to. Conditioning in this direction begins in the home 12 and is reinforced by school and by the media. Even in nursery school more than fifty percent of white girls say that they will marry and by the time they are twelve, ninety percent express that expectation. White boys are a bit less positive, but by the time they leave school, seventy-five percent are in favor of marriage for them. Black youngsters are not so certain: Between fourteen and seventeen years, when the white youngsters are getting interested in the idea, black youngsters are becoming less interested. By the time they leave school, only fifty percent of black young people think they will get married.

Regardless of the length of an article, chapter, or selection, the body of the material has its own organization. There must be a subject and a general idea that is discussed throughout the material. This idea is explained throughout the essay with supporting details connected by the use of transitional words and phrases. These four elements are important because together they express the basic content of the reading material.

Reading the body of a selection, article, or chapter is the third ("Read") step in the Steps to Effective Reading presented in Chapter 1. As you will recall, in this step you begin reading with your purposes for reading clearly fixed in mind. Then, you read to find the answers to these questions.

In addition to the specific purposes and questions you established from your prereading, other things you should look for as you read are:

1. How the author develops or supports the unifying idea.
2. What type (or types) of information is used to develop the unifying idea.
3. How the supporting details are organized.
4. How each paragraph relates to or supports the unifying idea.

Looking for these features will ensure that you are understanding what you are reading and will also improve your retention of the material.

Underlining As You Read

As you are reading the body, mark the location of important facts and ideas in the selection. Most students find it effective to underline or to use a highlighter pen to mark the sentences that express important ideas and facts. Others prefer to make marginal notes or to write summary outlines of the material. Regardless of the method you choose, it is useful to mark important ideas. Depending on your purpose for reading, the types of information you might mark include:

important background information
the unifying idea (make this stand out in some way)
supporting statements
facts you want to remember
names, dates, places
reasons, causes
key descriptive words
key similarities or differences
definitions

If you have marked these types of information as you read, you can use the markings in the Review step of the reading process. Rereading underlined material or notes is a well-proved method for increasing the amount you can remember from a given selection.

Reading the Summary or Conclusion

The primary purpose of the summary or conclusion is to draw together the ideas expressed in the body. It is also intended to enable the reader to see an overview of the content. The summary of a textbook chapter mentions only the most important ideas discussed in the chapter, whereas the last paragraph in a shorter article may summarize all the important ideas included in the body.

The following paragraph is a summary for "Marriages and Families."

Summary

This chapter discusses marriage, its alternatives, and its effectiveness. Reasons why people marry are discussed, defined, and ways in which it has changed are described. Alternatives to marriage are explored. The process of choosing a partner and the dynamics of a working marriage are examined. Finally, the consequences of marriages that do not work are discussed and alternatives that people turn to are considered.

Notice that this paragraph very briefly outlines both the organization and content of this textbook chapter. It mentions each of the four main divisions of the chapter and suggests what is considered in each.

The summary is important to read when you preread as well as when you finish reading. In prereading the summary provides an outline of topics covered in the article or chapter. When you read it later as part of the whole selection, it ties the ideas together and brings the article or selection to a close. When the summary or conclusion is read during the review process, it functions as a brief outline of the important ideas discussed.

The summary or conclusion is the writer's last chance to make a statement about the subject. Writers often take this opportunity to make a final concluding statement rather than to summarize what has already been said. That is, they draw together what has already been said to express an important new statement.

When reading a summary or conclusion, you might use the following questions as a guide:

1. What important ideas did the author summarize?
2. What final statements did the writer make about the subject?

Aids to Understanding Informative Prose

Writers of informative prose use numerous devices to clarify and organize their ideas and to assist the reader in understanding the content. These include titles, headings, and typographical aids. Each of these devices emphasizes important information or shows the organization of ideas.

Titles

Titles are usually labels that describe or indicate what the article, selection, or chapter is about. For example, a newspaper article title, "Fire Leaves Family Homeless," in the briefest possible way, describes what the article is about.

Headings

Headings are included in many types of expository prose. Newspaper and magazine articles, textbooks, reference books (such as encyclopedias), and nonfiction paperbacks often contain headings. Like titles, headings function as labels and indicate the general subject of the material that follows.

Many students ignore or skip over headings, not realizing that they are useful in prereading and reading, as well as in reviewing. Here is a list of headings from one section of "Marriages and Families." The section "Making Marriage Work" contains the following headings:

Accepting Change
Communicating
Adjusting and Compromising

When taken together, headings form an outline or list of topics covered in an article or selection. In prereading, the headings tell the reader what topics to expect to read about. In reading, headings announce a change of topic and make the organization of the material easier to follow. For review, headings provide an easy way for you to check your recall of content.

From the headings we just listed, you can see that this section of the chapter on "Marriages and Families" discusses three factors that help to make marriage work. The textbook chapter title, "Marriages and Families," clearly announces the two broad subjects covered by the chapter. Some students pay as little attention to titles as to headings, assuming they are not important because they only repeat what is said in the article or selection. Actually, titles, like headings, are important to both prereading and to reading. They often contain information or clues about the author's approach to the subject or about the organization of the material. For instance, a magazine article entitled "Coping With Bad Drivers Through Defensive Driving" not only tells you the subject of the article, coping with bad drivers, but also indicates how the author approaches the subject. The author's approach to coping with bad drivers is to prevent accidents by developing defensive driving techniques. Or, a chapter in a nonfiction book on tennis might be titled "Six Ways to Improve Your Backhand." From this title you suspect that the chapter will be organized into six sections, each of which will discuss one technique.

Although most titles are very descriptive and direct, some are used to catch your attention or to interest you in the article. For instance, the magazine article title "A Million Dollar Pleasure Machine" is written to interest you in the article. It makes you wonder, What kind of pleasure is the article about? What kind of pleasure can a machine produce? What kind of machine could cost a million dollars? Who uses it? In this case, if you began reading it, you would discover that the article was about a yacht.

Graphic Aids

Graphic aids refers to any changes in print or any added features to the printed page. They include such things as headings, italics, maps, pic tures, graphs, charts, and diagrams. Changes in print and the arrangement of words on a page alter the appearance of the page and help the reader to follow the organization of ideas

We have already discussed the most obvious change in type or print, the inclusion of headings. A second change in the appearance of words on a page occurs through the use of italics or slanted type. Words or phrases are printed in italics so they will stand out. Often new terms that are introduced and defined in the selection will be printed in italics.

The spacing, or arrangement of ideas on a page, or even within a paragraph, provides clues about the relative importance of ideas. For example, the listing of ideas is a common way to call a reader's attention to the information listed. When facts or ideas are numbered—for example, (1) scarcity of jobs, (2) inflation, and (3) high interest rates—you should realize that the writer is emphasizing them. The amount of space allowed between sections and between headings also provides clues to the organization and importance of ideas. Generally, the greater the amount of blank space allowed between paragraphs, headings, or sections, the greater the change in thought pattern and content.

Graphs, maps, charts, pictures, and diagrams are other important additions to a printed page. Each of these graphic aids in some way emphasizes an idea or concept. When you read, as well as when you preread, be sure to pay particular attention to them. The easiest way to determine what a map, graph, chart, picture, or diagram is emphasizing is to read the title, or legend. The legend usually identifies the topic that is graphically or visually displayed.

EXERCISE 12–1

Directions: *Choose one of the selections at the end of the unit. Read the selection using these steps.*

1. *Prereading.* Preread the selection, paying particular attention to the introduction and summary or conclusion. What types of typographical aids are used in the selection?

   _____

   _____

2. *Establishing a Purpose.* Using what you learned about the organization and content of the selection from prereading, write three questions that you want to answer as you read.

   a. _____

   b. _____

   c. _____

3. *Read the Selection.* Look for the answers to your purpose questions. As you read, underline important ideas you may want to refer to when writing about the subject of this selection. After you have finished reading the selection, answer the following questions:

a. What types of information are included in the introduction?

_____

_____

b. What types of information are contained in the summary or conclusion?

_____

_____

4. *Review.* Review the selection by rereading each of the following—the title, the introduction, typographical aids included in the body, your underlining, and the summary or conclusion.

5. *React.* Think about what you have read. The exercise at the end of the writing section of this chapter will give you an opportunity to express your ideas about the subject of the selection.

WRITING INFORMATIVE PROSE

As a reader, you have learned to expect a specific structure when you deal with informative prose, and you have seen that most writing of this type contains at least three main divisions: an introduction, a body or discussion, and a conclusion or summary. You have also seen how these divisions work together to clearly present the one unifying idea of a selection. When you write to inform your reader, you will find it best to employ this structure. First, introduce your reader to your topic; then develop or explain your topic; finally, draw your ideas together into a conclusion or summary. There is a recognizable pattern to this structure that will make writing a more organized activity, and it will make it easier for your reader to follow your thoughts.

Writing the Introduction

The basic purpose of an introduction to any piece of writing is to draw the reader's attention to the way you intend to inform him or her about the subject of your writing. A well-written introduction should identify the topic you are about to discuss, and it should also present your unifying idea about that topic. However, the introduction should also provide your reader with essential background information about the topic, and perhaps most important, it should capture the interest of the reader. This may sound like a lot to include in one or two paragraphs, but if you plan your introduction carefully, you can accomplish each of these objectives.

Have you ever been late to a movie and walked into it after it began? How did you feel? Most likely you felt somewhat confused or lost for a few minutes until you pieced things together. Your reader would experience a similar feeling if you began writing ideas and presenting facts and details without a context. Just as the beginning of a movie sets the scene and provides background information on the characters, the introduction of an essay establishes a setting or structure for the important ideas and details.

In order to identify and present your topic clearly and to state your unifying idea, you need to present a context, or frame of reference, for that idea. The context establishes the surrounding circumstances and ideas that relate to the unifying idea. It must gradually lead the reader to an awareness of the central issue or topic of the essay.

Essentially, the function of an introduction is to make a connection between the reader's knowledge and experience and the ideas expressed in the essay. Somehow you must connect your ideas to what the reader already knows or is interested in learning. Or you must make your topic interesting or appealing to your reader.

Besides drawing your reader into a topic, an introduction should also provide whatever background information your reader might require in order to understand your ideas. Often your introduction can also narrow a subject to a specific topic, including particular points of discussion you will present throughout the essay. For instance, suppose you were going to discuss the subject of monolingualism—the ability to speak only one language. Notice how the following introduction draws the reader into the subject, provides some background information, and, at the same time, points toward the ideas expressed about the topic.

> Do you think Americans are outdated and becoming obsolete? There is one area in which Americans have clearly taken the back seat. Americans have remained monolingual; the majority of Americans speak only *one* language. In many European countries, however, most people can speak two or three languages, including English. Americans' inability to communicate in languages other than their own has had serious effects on various aspects of American life, including economic development, cultural growth, and international politics.

This introduction catches the reader's interest by suggesting that Americans are outdated or obsolete; then it immediately narrows the subject to a particular point—monolingualism. Next, some background is provided on this subject, and a contrast is established between Americans and Europeans. Finally, the writer states the specific topic to be developed throughout the essay—that this feature has serious effects on American life.

Beyond drawing the reader's interest, identifying the subject, stating the unifying idea, and providing background information, the introduction may also suggest the organization of the essay. In the preceding example you learn that the essay will discuss the effects of monolingualism on Americans. However, you also learn the three major ways these effects will be classified or grouped: economic, cultural, and political. Also you can predict the order in which the effects will be discussed. You would expect them to be presented in the order in which they are mentioned in the introduction.

As you write an introduction, try to follow these steps:

1. Start by drawing your reader's interest and connecting your subject to his or her knowledge or experience.
2. Identify your subject and lead into a statement of your unifying idea.
3. Provide any background information that is necessary for the reader to understand your ideas.
4. If you outline the features, parts, or steps, or describe your general approach, include this information in the introduction in the same order in which you will present it in the body of the essay.

Writing the Body

The main part of an informative piece of writing is called the body. The body of an essay performs the same function as the supporting details within a paragraph, and it is the part of an essay that presents the discussion of your topic.

The unifying idea is the key to both the content and the organization of the body. In an essay the unifying idea should make a statement or assertion. The body of the essay, then, explains and supports this statement. The body's organization will depend on the nature and form of the unifying idea. Basically, the body of an essay can follow any of the patterns that are used to develop main ideas in paragraphs. Often, a combination of patterns can be used to support the unifying idea. For example, if the unifying idea states that an event has several effects, then the body would be organized to describe the effects. You would probably use a separate paragraph for each effect, and you could arrange them in one of two ways. You could present the effects in order, starting with the most immediate and ending with the most long-range effect; or you could arrange the effects in the order of their importance.

Here are a few suggestions for developing the body of your essay.

1. Try to have your unifying idea clearly in your mind.
2. Decide how you can explain the unifying example most effectively. Would definitions be appropriate? Would examples be effective? Should you use a comparison or a contrast?
3. Arrange supporting details in an organized pattern or sequence.
4. Use transitions to change from one supporting detail to another.
5. Provide more explanation or examples of key ideas.
6. In general, equally important ideas should receive equal treatment (same amount and type of explanation).
7. Be sure to support all general statements with facts, details, evidence, or examples.

The Conclusion or Summary

Students too frequently end their essays by simply stopping after their last piece of supporting information. This abrupt ending can leave the reader confused about the point of the essay or feeling that the message was incomplete. A good conclusion or summary can tie up the "loose ends" of an essay and put a finishing touch to your ideas.

Think of your conclusion or summary as your last chance to make your point in a clear and memorable fashion. There are really two directions you can take in writing the last paragraph or two of your essay. You can write a summary, simply restating the major points of the discussion, or you can write a conclusion, which presents a new idea that you have been leading up to throughout your essay.

Writing a Summary

You may wish to think of a summary as an outline expressed in paragraph form. As an outline lists the important points that relate to a particular topic, a summary should present the main points that relate to the subject and unifying idea of an essay. Further, just as an outline lists ideas in the order in which they are included in the piece of writing, a summary should also present ideas in the order in which they appeared in the body. In fact, when you write your summary, it may be useful to refer to the outline you prepared to check your content and organization.

A summary is intended to give your reader a brief review of your important ideas and is usually one paragraph long. Therefore, try to be selective in what you include, and make your statements brief and concise. Mention only the most important ideas that support your unifying idea.

A good way to check that you have written an effective summary is to reread it with the following question in mind:

If someone read *only* my summary, would he or she know what key ideas were covered in the essay?

If you cannot answer yes to this question, then your summary needs to be expanded to include more information.

As you write a summary, keep these suggestions in mind:

1. Limit your summary to one paragraph.
2. Restate your unifying idea.
3. Mention only the most important ideas that develop your unifying ideas.
4. Summarize the ideas in the order in which they appear in the body.
5. Make your statements brief and concise.

Writing a Conclusion

A conclusion goes beyond restating or outlining ideas already discussed in the body. Although it does tie the ideas together and brings the essay to a close, it does so in a different way than a summary. A conclusion offers the reader a final and often new approach to the topic and unifying idea. It often refers back to the introduction and connects the opening statements in the introduction with the concluding statements.

There are several ways that a conclusion can tie the essay together. It might suggest further directions for the study of a problem identified in the introduction; it might present changes needed in order to solve a problem suggested in the body; or it might make a striking statement for further thought. A conclusion might make a prediction based on facts presented in the body, offer a comment on the seriousness or importance of a particular issue, or give a strong final event or anecdote to emphasize the unifying idea without directly restating it.

To write an effective conclusion, you first should reread your introduction. Look for a "hook," or a way to refer back to ideas mentioned in the introduction. If you can revise your introduction so that it will provide this "hook," then do so. The following questions might be useful:

1. Reread your introduction. What does it promise the reader? Can you think of a final statement or comment on how the body fulfills that promise?
2. Reread the body. Are there any additional or different ideas or approaches that you might mention to the reader?
3. If your essay did not end where it did, what would be the next idea you would discuss? You might suggest that idea to your reader in your concluding statement.
4. Is there any advice or final comment you can make about the topic of your essay?
5. What might be the effects of the idea, change, procedure, or approach that you suggested in your essay?

You are probably wondering when you should use a summary statement and when a concluding statement is more appropriate. You might use the following rule of thumb: When your primary purpose is to present information, use a summary; when your purpose is to discuss ideas or involve your reader in a reaction to your ideas, use a conclusion. A summary carefully reviews the important ideas and ensures that your reader will understand and remember what you have said. A conclusion is designed to provoke thought. Once again, then, you can see that purpose shapes both your content and organization.

Applying the Structure to the Essay

In the reading section of this chapter you read the sample selection on "Marriages and Families." Consider the following writing assignment that was given to a class:

Where did you get your ideas about marriage? Write a brief discussion about your views on marriage and their source.

The following essay was written by a student to complete the writing assignment. Read it through, looking for the overall structure, topic, and unifying idea. After you have read it, we will analyze its effectiveness.

Sample Essay
  Marriage should be a partnership where both individuals share equal responsibility and resources. However, it should not keep either person from being self-sufficient. Marriage should also provide each partner with room for growth as well as a strong sense of security and support.
  These views on marriage have many sources. First, the idea of a partnership comes form my experience in my own family. My parents shared responsibilities, but my mother never had any control over the resources. She took care of the children and the home and even worked sometimes. My father had a good job, and he always made the decisions about money. I feel that both partners should have an equal say about how money is spent.

Next, my views on self-sufficiency in marriage were developed because my parents brought me up to take care of myself and not depend on other people. As a result of my parents' training, I would not want to marry someone who depended on me for everything. I think it's important for two people who live together to be able to survive alone either permanently or temporarily when it is necessary.

Finally, self-sufficiency is important, but two people have to love and need each other, too. Each partner should be able to develop his or her interests and talents without making life difficult for the other partner. The best example I have seen of such a situation is my sister's marriage. My sister is an artist, and she continues to have gallery shows in different cities even though she is married. Her husband is a teacher, and he is attending graduate school. They have different schedules and spend time apart, but they have a very close relationship.

Most of my views on marriages are the result of my own family life. I have chosen the best aspects of marriages that I know about, and then I have decided what I would add or change in my own life when I marry.

The Subject and Unifying Idea

Before analyzing the parts of this essay, let's briefly consider the topic and unifying ideas. First, consider the assignment. The first part of the assignment was stated in a question:

Where did you get your ideas about marriage?

Obviously the student had to focus on the source of her views about marriage, so the subject of this essay was partly provided by the constraints imposed by the assignment. Look at the description of the writer's task, which followed the question.

Write a brief discussion about your views on marriage and their sources.

The student had two requirements to fulfill. She had to state her views on marriage and then explain how she developed those views. The topic of the student's essay is the development of her views on what marriage should be, and the treatment of this topic was clearly necessary in order to meet the demands of the assignment.

Reread the essay. What idea is developed throughout the essay? You will find a statement that clearly articulates the unifying idea in the first sentence of the last paragraph.

Most of my views on marriage are the result of my own family life.

The unifying idea in the essay is the development of the student's views on marriage through personal observation within her family. She described both positive and negative aspects of marriages she was familiar with and explained how these aspects shaped attitudes about marriage.

As you can see, the purpose contributes to the formulation of the topic and the development of the unifying idea. The student probably could have stated the topic in the prewriting stage, but the unifying idea became evident only in the composing stage when she began seriously to consider the organization of ideas. Sometimes the unifying idea is immediately apparent, particularly when the purpose is very specific, and is developed even at the prewriting stage. However, it is not unusual for the unifying idea to become apparent in composing or as late as revision. You will notice that the unifying idea is closely connected to the organization of ideas, so as you check the organization make sure you also check to see that the unifying idea is apparent.

If you are in doubt, ask someone else to see if they notice a common thread of meaning. If your reader has difficulty moving from one paragraph to another, you may lack a unifying idea. If that is the case, go back to your prewriting exercises to see if you left out important ideas; you may have to expand your ideas.

In approaching this assignment you could do a free-writing exercise, make a list of views, or list some questions about marriage that might generate some ideas. You would then follow with the other steps in the writing process: composing, checking the content and organization, revising, and proofreading. But now, consider each part independently and look at how each contributes to the whole essay.

Introduction
Marriage should be a partnership where both individuals share equal responsibility and resources. However, it should not keep either person from being self-sufficient. Marriage should also provide each partner with room for growth as well as a strong sense of security and support.

In the introduction the writer defined her concept of marriage. She presents three strong statements of what makes a marriage. In the following paragraphs she develops each statement by adding supporting details that explain the views and their sources. She also uses transitions to connect the body of the paper. Look at the transitions (in italics) in these paragraphs:

First Paragraph of Body
These views on marriage have many sources. *First, the idea of a partnership comes from my experience in my own family.* My parents shared responsibilities, but my mother never had any control over the resources. She took care of the children and the home and even worked sometimes. My father had a good job, and he always made the decisions about money. I feel that both partners should have an equal say about how money is spent.

The writer uses the word "first" to call the reader's attention to the order of the ideas.

Second Paragraph of Body
Next, my views on self-sufficiency in marriage were developed because my parents brought me up to take care of myself and not depend on other people. As a result of my parents' training, I would not want to marry someone who depended on me for everything. I think it's important for two people

who live together to be able to survive alone either permanently or temporarily when it is necessary.

In this paragraph the writer uses the word "next" to introduce another point in the sequence of ideas.

Third Paragraph of Body
Finally, self-sufficiency is important, but two people have to love and need each other, too. Each partner should be able to develop his or her interests and talents without making life difficult for the other partner. The best example I have seen of such a situation is my sister's marriage. My sister is an artist, and she continues to have gallery shows in different cities even though she is married. Her husband is a teacher, and he is attending graduate school. They have different schedules and spend time apart, but they have a very close relationship.

In this paragraph the writer uses the word "finally" to introduce the last idea, but at the same time reaches back to the preceding paragraph to tie the discussion about self-sufficiency with the discussion of the elements of growth, security, and support in a marriage. She then describes the source of this view of marriage.

Conclusion
Most of my views on marriage are the result of my own family life. I have chosen the best aspects of marriages that I know about, and then I have decided what I would add or change in my own life when I marry.

The last paragraph provides a final statement that summarizes how the student developed her views on marriage. It also ties in all the key ideas that appeared in the essay.

Now let's look at another draft of the same essay. Here the student was asked to rewrite the essay so that the last paragraph was a concluding statement. Read the student's essay and notice, too, the reasons or explanations for some of the changes.

Introduction
My views on marriage are mostly the results of my own family life. My parents have a good marriage, but I would make some minor changes. My sister's marriage also provides a good model for me because her marriage combines the strengths of my parents' marriage with a stronger sense of sharing and cooperation.

This introduction does not define marriage or relate the writer's views, but it does describe existing situations that contribute to her views. Look at what would have happened if the second paragraph of the first sample writing assignment followed this introductory paragraph.

My views on marriage are mostly the results of my own family life. My parents have a good marriage, but I would make some minor changes. My sister's marriage also provides a good model for me because her marriage combines the strengths of my parents' marriage with a stronger sense of sharing and cooperation.

These views on marriage have many sources. First, the idea of a partnership comes from my experience in my own family. My parents shared responsibilities, but my mother never had any control over the resources. She took care of the children and the home and even worked sometimes. My father had a good job, and he always made the decisions about money. I feel that both partners should have an equal say about how money is spent.

These two paragraphs do not logically go together as they appear now, but the student realized that if the second paragraph were revised, it could follow the new introduction. Read the introduction with the revised paragraph that follows it.

My views on marriage are mostly the results of my own family life. My parents have a good marriage, but I would make some minor changes. My sister's marriage also provides a good model for me because her marriage combines the strength of my parents' marriage with a stronger sense of sharing and cooperation.

I view marriage as a partnership because my parents always shared responsibilities. In my own marriage, though, I would want to share resources as well as responsibilities. My mother took care of the children and the home and even worked sometimes, but my father always made the decisions about how the money was spent.

The next paragraph might consist of the following discussion.

My sister's marriage is a good marriage, too, but it is different. My sister is an artist, and she continues to have gallery shows in other cities. Her husband is a teacher, and he is also attending graduate school. They both contribute some of their earnings to manage their household, but they both keep some of their earnings to use independently. They cooperate with each other in managing their hectic schedules, and they maintain a close relationship even though they spend a lot of time apart.

Notice how the paragraphs are linked together. In the third paragraph the student wrote the following sentence: My sister's marriage is a good marriage, *too, but it is different*. The word "too" ties the discussion of the parents' marriage and the sister's marriage together; then the following clause, "but it is different," tells the reader to look for contrasts between the two marriages.

The conclusion in the revised essay introduces new ideas instead of summarizing the views that were presented:

My parents' marriage demonstrates the value of loyalty and support, and my sister's marriage shows what freedom and individuality contribute to a marriage. Marriage is affected by the traditions of the culture, and I think my sister's marriage reflects how my parents' marriage might have been if they had been born later. *Finally, though, if two people love each other and have similar views on life, I think they can work out a good marriage.*

The student introduces a list of desirable attitudes in a marriage—loyalty, support, freedom, and individuality. She also introduces a new idea by considering how marriage is affected by the culture and implies that the two marriages are, in a sense, products of their time. Her conclusion, though, is clearly marked by the word "finally." The two most important elements in a marriage are love and similar values.

These changes are not the only ones that could have been made. As you can see, a writer can choose to present ideas in a variety of ways. These examples were written by one writer, but the focus and organization are different. Both sample assignments fulfill the requirements of the assignment, but they are very different presentations of the same subject and unifying idea.

Checking the Effectiveness of Your Essay

Since you know what aids to look for as a reader you can assume that your audience will also look for the same elements. When you write you can evaluate the same parts of your essay to see if you have covered all the necessary parts. You might use the following list to check the effectiveness of your essay and to identify portions that need revision.

1. *The Title.* Does the title announce the general subject of the essay and give the reader some idea about your approach and your point of view—or attitudes—toward the subject? Your title should be interesting and to the point because it is the basis for the reader's first impression. If, for example, you are writing about a specific literary work and you simply use the title of the work as the title of your essay, provide the reader with a little information about what you have to say.

2. *The Introduction.* Does your first paragraph describe the topic and give the reader some idea about what you intend to say about it?

3. *The First Sentence of Each Paragraph.* Does the first sentence of each paragraph state what the paragraph is about? Does it connect the paragraph with the preceding one?

4. *The Remainder of Each Paragraph.* Do the other sentences in the paragraph contain details to support all your preceding statements?

5. *Transitions.* Do your transitions relate paragraphs to each other? Paragraphs in a paper should not stand alone. Are they connected with transitions?

6. *Last Sentence in a Paragraph.* Does the last sentence in a paragraph express a summary or concluding statement? A summary sentence restates what has been discussed in a paragraph. A concluding statement draws a conclusion or makes a final statement that is based on the discussion. Often it presents a base for further discussion or the presentation of a new idea in a paragraph that follows.

7. *The Last Paragraph.* Does the last paragraph consist of a summary, or restatement, or the ideas and facts that have been discussed in the essay? Does it create a final impression for the reader and clearly state your central thought in this paragraph? Or does the last paragraph function as a concluding statement, presenting the final conclusion that can be drawn about the ideas presented in the piece of writing?

EXERCISE 12–2

Directions: *Choose a reading from the end of this unit. If you have not yet read the selection, preread and read it, then write the title and subject here:*

TITLE: _____

SUBJECT: _____

Using the subject of the selection as a starting point, follow each of these steps:

1. *Prewriting.*
   a. Narrow the subject into three possible topics:

   _____

   _____

   _____

   b. Select one topic and use a five-minute free-writing exercise or write several questions that occur to you about the topic to generate ideas.
2. *Composing.* Select the most important ideas you see in your prewriting exercise. Develop these ideas into a paper consisting of an introduction, body, and conclusion. Include the details your reader will need in order to have a clear understanding of your purpose and message.
3. *Checking the Content and Organization.* Make a brief outline that shows the content and organization of your essay. Use the following outline as a model.

   I. Introduction

   _____   Briefly list the ideas that will be discussed in the intro-
   _____   duction.

   _____

   II. Body

   A. _____

   _____

   _____

   B. _____   List each main idea and its supporting details and label
   _____   it as paragraph A, B, C, etc.

   _____

C. _____

_____

_____

III. Conclusion

_____

_____

List the ideas that will be discussed in the conclusion and label your summary or concluding statement.

_____

_____

_____

4. *Revising.* Use the following revision checklist to help you revise your paper; then write a clean copy of the paper. Consult this checklist for each piece of writing you do in the future.

REVISION CHECKLIST

Unifying Idea

____ Read your first two sentences. Do they give a clear idea of the topic of your paper?

____ Is the unifying idea of your paper clearly expressed?

First Paragraph

____ Does your opening paragraph tell your reader what the whole essay is about? Is there a sentence that defines or states your purpose?

____ Does your first paragraph reveal who your audience is? If not, how can you change it so it will appeal to your audience?

____ Are there any generalizations? (Clue: a generalization frequently uses a pronoun.) Do you generalize using terms such as "everyone," "society," "people," and so forth?

Body

____ Does each paragraph support or explain your unifying idea? Have you provided adequate supporting details?

____ Are the paragraphs arranged in a logical sequence? Does one idea lead to the next?

____ Have you used transitions to connect your ideas?

Last Paragraph

____ How did you end the paper? Would your reader feel the topic needs further discussion?

Word Choice

____ Have you used a level of language appropriate for your audience?

____ Have you used specific, concrete, and descriptive words? Reread your paper looking for words that seem general, dull, or vague.

Sentence Structure

____ Have you used sentence patterns to combine ideas? Reread, looking for sentences that could be combined.

____ Have you used sentence patterns to show relationships among your ideas? Look at each sentence separately, then consider whether it could be combined with either the preceding or following sentence.

Paragraph Structure

____ Does each paragraph discuss a separate aspect of your topic?

____ Does each paragraph express a main idea that supports the unifying idea of the paper?

____ Have you provided facts, examples, definitions, or reasons to support the main idea of the paragraph?

____ Do the details answer the question who, what, why, where, or how about the topic?

____ In each paragraph organized? Will your thought pattern be apparent to your reader?

---

5. *Proofreading.* Read through your paper carefully, checking each item on the proofreading checklist. Correct each error and list it in the right column.

   Finally, construct a proofreading checklist that shows specifically what you need to check. The major categories are listed for you in the last page of this unit. Write in each type of error you have continued to make. Consult this checklist for each piece of writing you do in the future. Your list should be as long as it needed to be in Chapter 1 of this text.

SUMMARY

Informative prose refers to written materials that explain or present information. This chapter is concerned with its structure. Most informative prose follows the basic organizational pattern of introduction-body-conclusion (or summary) and has a subject and a unifying idea. In the chapter we discussed the functions of the introduction, body, and conclusion in both reading and writing. Readers use textual aids, including titles, headings, and graphic aids to help them understand ideas. Writers have many ways of presenting their ideas; their options become apparent if they analyze and question their own work. Writers should always keep purpose in mind to guide the presentation of subject and unifying idea.

PROOFREADING CHECKLIST				

Essay Title _____

Date _____

TYPE	✔	ERROR	FREQUENCY	DESCRIPTION
GRAMMAR		Run-on Sentence Sentence Fragment Subject/Verb Agreement Verb Tense Pronoun Agreement		
MECHANICS		Capitalization Italics Abbreviation		
PUNCTUATION		, (Comma) ; (Semicolon) ' (Apostrophe) " (Quotation Marks) . (Period) ! (Exclamation Point) ? (Question Mark) : (Colon) — (Dash) ( ) (Parentheses) - (Hyphen)		

		ERROR	CORRECTION	
SPELLING ERRORS				

Unit Four Reading Selections

Difficulty level: A

19. Sister Flowers

Maya Angelou

For nearly a year, I sopped around the house, the Store, the school and the church, like an old biscuit, dirty and inedible. Then I met, or rather got to know, the lady who threw me my first life line. 1

Mrs. Bertha Flowers was the aristocrat of Black Stamps. She had the grace of control to appear warm in the coldest weather, and on the Arkansas summer days it seemed she had a private breeze which swirled around, cooling her. She was thin without the taut look of wiry people, and her printed voile dresses and flowered hats were as right for her as denim overalls for a farmer. She was our side's answer to the richest white woman in town. 2

Her skin was a rich black that would have peeled like a plum if snagged, but then no one would have thought of getting close enough to Mrs. Flowers to ruffle her dress, let alone snag her skin. She didn't encourage familiarity. She wore gloves too. 3

I don't think I ever saw Mrs. Flowers laugh, but she smiled often. A slow widening of her thin black lips to show even, small white teeth, then the slow effortless closing. When she chose to smile on me, I always wanted to thank her. The action was so graceful and inclusively benign. 4

She was one of the few gentlewomen I have ever known, and has remained throughout my life the measure of what a human being can be. 5

Momma had a strange relationship with her. Most often when she passed on the road in front of the Store, she spoke to Momma in that soft yet carrying voice, "Good day, Mrs. Henderson." Momma responded with "How you, Sister Flowers?" 6

Mrs. Flowers didn't belong to our church, nor was she Momma's familiar. Why on earth did she insist on calling her Sister Flowers? Shame made me want to hide my face. Mrs. Flowers deserved better than to be called Sister. Then, Momma left out the verb. Why not ask. "How *are* you, *Mrs.* Flowers?" With the unbalanced passion of the young, I hated her for showing her ignorance to Mrs. Flowers. It didn't occur to me for many years that they were as alike as sisters, separated only by formal education. 7

Although I was upset, neither of the women was in the least shaken by what I thought an unceremonious greeting. Mrs. Flowers would continue her easy gait up the hill to her little bungalow, and Momma kept on shelling peas or doing whatever had brought her to the front porch. 8

Occasionally, though, Mrs. Flowers would drift off the road and down to the Store and Momma would say to me, "Sister, you go on and play." As I left I would hear the beginning of an intimate conversation. Momma persistently using the wrong verb, or none at all. 9

"Brother and Sister Wilcox is sho'ly the meanest—" "Is," Momma? "is"? Oh, please, not "is," Momma, for two or more. But they talked, and from the side of the building where I waited for the ground to open up and swallow me, I heard the soft-voiced Mrs. Flowers and the textured voice of my grandmother merging and melting. They were interrupted from time to time by giggles that must have come from Mrs. Flowers (Momma never giggled in her life). Then she was gone. 10

She appealed to me because she was like people I had never met personally. Like women in English novels who walked the moors (whatever they were) with their loyal dogs racing at a respectful distance. Like the women who sat in front of roaring fireplaces, drinking tea incessantly from silver trays full of scones and crumpets. Women who walked over the "heath" and read morocco-bound books and had two last names divided by a hyphen. It would be safe to say that she made me proud to be a Negro, just by being herself. 11

She acted just as refined as whitefolks in the movies and books and she was more beautiful, for none of them could have come near that warm color without looking gray by comparison. 12

I was fortunate that I never saw her in the company of powhitefolks. For since they tend to think of their whiteness as an evenizer, I'm certain that I would have had to hear her spoken to commonly as Bertha, and my image of her would have been shattered like the unmendable Humpty-Dumpty. 13

One summer afternoon, sweet-milk fresh in my memory, she stopped at the store to buy provisions. Another Negro woman of her health and age would have been expected to carry the paper sacks home in one hand, but Momma said, "Sister Flowers, I'll send Bailey up to your house with those things." 14

She smiled that slow dragging smile. "Thank you, Mrs. Henderson. I'd prefer Marguerite, though." My name was beautiful when she said it. "I've been meaning to talk to her, anyway." They gave each other age-group looks. 15

Momma said, "Well, that's all right then. Sister, go and change your dress. You going to Sister Flowers's." 16

The chifforobe was a maze. What on earth did one put on to go to Mrs. Flowers's house? I knew I shouldn't put on a Sunday dress. It might be sacrilegious. Certainly not a house dress, since I was already wearing a fresh one. I chose a school dress, naturally. It was formal without suggesting that going to Mrs. Flowers's house was equivalent to attending church. 17

I trusted myself back into the Store. 18

"Now, don't you look nice." I had chosen the right thing, 19
for once. . . .

There was a little path beside the rocky road, and Mrs. 20
Flowers walked in front swinging her arms and picking her
way over the stones.

She said, without turning her head, to me, "I hear you're 21
doing very good school work, Marguerite, but that it's all written. The teachers report that they have trouble getting you to
talk in class." We passed the triangular farm on our left and the
path widened to allow us to walk together. I hung back in the
separate unasked and unanswerable questions.

"Come and walk along with me, Marguerite." I couldn't 22
have refused even if I wanted to. She pronounced my name
so nicely. Or more correctly, she spoke each word with such
clarity that I was certain a foreigner who didn't understand
English could have understood her.

"Now no one is going to make you talk—possibly no one 23
can. But bear in mind, language is man's way of communicating with his fellow man and it is language alone which
separates him from the lower animals." That was a totally new
idea to me, and I would need time to think about it.

"Your grandmother says your read a lot. Every chance you 24
get. That's good, but not good enough. Words mean more than
what is set down on paper. It takes the human voice to infuse
them with the shades of deeper meaning."

I memorized the part about the human voice infusing 25
words. It seemed so valid and poetic.

She said she was going to give me some books and that 26
I not only must read them, I must read them aloud. She suggested that I try to make a sentence sound in as many different
ways as possible.

"I'll accept no excuse if you return a book to me that has 27
been badly handled." My imagination boggled at the punishment I would desire if in fact I did abuse a book of Mrs.
Flowers's. Death would be too kind and brief.

The odors in the house surprised me. Somehow I had 28
never connected Mrs. Flowers with food or eating or any other
common experience of common people. There must have been
an outhouse, too, but my mind never recorded it.

The sweet scent of vanilla had met us as she opened the 29
door.

"I made tea cookies this morning. You see, I had planned 30
to invite you for cookies and lemonade so we could have this
little chat. The lemonade is in the icebox."

It followed that Mrs. Flowers would have ice on an ordi- 31
nary day, when most families in our town bought ice late on
Saturdays only a few times during the summer to be used in
the wooden ice-cream freezers.

She took the bags from me and disappeared through the 32
kitchen door. I looked around the room that I had never in my
wildest fantasies imagined I would see. Browned photographs
leered or threatened from the walls and the white, freshly done
curtains pushed against themselves and against the wind. I
wanted to gobble up the room entire and take it to Bailey, who
would help me analyze and enjoy it.

"Have a seat, Marguerite. Over there by the table." She 33
carried a platter covered with a tea towel. Although she warned
that she hadn't tried her hand at baking sweets for some time,
I was certain that like everything else about her the cookies
would be perfect.

They were flat round wafers, slightly browned on the 34
edges and butter-yellow in the center. With the cold lemonade
they were sufficient for childhood's lifelong diet. Remembering
my manners, I took nice little lady-like bites off the edges. She
said she had made them expressly for me and that she had a
few in the kitchen that I could take home to my brother. So I
jammed one whole cake in my mouth and the rough crumbs
scratched the insides of my jaws, and if I hadn't had to
swallow, it would have been a dream come true.

As I ate she began the first of what we later called "my 35
lesson in living." She said that I must always be intolerant of
ignorance but understanding of illiteracy. That some people,
unable to go to school, were more educated and even more intelligent than college professors. She encouraged me to listen
carefully to what country people called mother wit. That in
those homely sayings was couched the collective wisdom of
generations.

When I finished the cookies she brushed off the table and 36
brought a thick, small book from the bookcase. I had read *A
Tale of Two Cities* and found it up to my standards as a romantic
novel. She opened the first page and I heard poetry for the first
time in my life.

It was the best of times and the worst of times . . ." Her 37
voice slid in and curved down through and over the words. She
was nearly singing. I wanted to look at the pages. Were they
the same that I had read? Or were there notes, music, lined on
the pages, as in a hymn book? Her sounds began cascading
gently. I knew from listening to a thousand preachers that she
was nearing the end of her reading, and I hadn't really heard,
heard to understand, a single word.

"How do you like that?" 38

It occurred to me that she expected a response. The sweet 39
vanilla flavor was still on my tongue and her reading was a
wonder in my ears. I had to speak.

I said, "Yes, ma'am." It was the least I could do, but it was 40
the most also.

"There's one more thing. Take this book of poems and 41
memorize one for me. Next time you pay me a visit, I want you
to recite."

I have tried often to search behind the sophistication of 42
years for the enchantment I so easily found in those gifts. The
essence escapes but the aura remains. To be allowed, no, in-
vited, into the private lives of strangers, and to share their joys
and fears, was a chance to exchange the Southern bitter worm-
wood for a cup of mead with Beowulf or a hot cup of tea and
milk with Oliver Twist. When I said aloud, "It is a far, far better
thing that I do, than I have ever done . . ." tears of love filled
my eyes at my selflessness.

On that first day, I ran down the hill and into the road 43
(few cars ever came along it) and had the good sense to stop
running before I reached the Store.

I was liked, and what a difference it made. I was respected 44 not as Mrs. Henderson's grandchild or Bailey's sister but for just being Marguerite Johnson.

Childhood's logic never asks to be proved (all conclusions 45 are absolute). I didn't question why Mrs. Flowers had singled me out for attention, nor did it occur to me that Momma might have asked her to give me a little talking to. All I cared about was that she had made tea cookies for *me* and read to *me* from her favorite book. It was enough to prove that she liked me.

COMPREHENSION

1. "Sister Flowers" is a story about
   a. a young girl's life in the ghetto
   b. the conflict between the rich and the poor in a small town
   c. the relationship between two older women
   d. how a young girl's life was influenced by her relationship with an older woman
2. Marguerite was embarrassed by her "Momma" because
   a. she was fat and sloppy
   b. she was a snob
   c. she spoke ungrammatical English
   d. she was uneducated
3. Sister Flowers was impressed by Marguerite because
   a. she was a good cook
   b. she read a lot and did well in school
   c. she was polite
   d. her family was rich
4. Sister Flowers and Marguerite's "Momma" were
   a. bitter enemies
   b. casual acquaintances
   c. good friends
   d. sisters
5. One of the important lessons that Marguerite learned from Sister Flowers was
   a. how to bake cookies
   b. how to keep house
   c. how to speak proper English
   d. how to read and recite poetry

VOCABULARY

Directions: *The meaning of the following terms from selection 19 cannot be clearly determined from the context. Using the dictionary entries, select the appropriate definition of the term as it is used in the reading selection.*

1. benign (par. 4)
   a. beneficial
   b. not malignant
   c. promoting well-being
   d. showing gentleness

be·nign (bĭ-nīn′) *adj.* **1.** Of a kind disposition: *a benign person.* **2.** Showing gentleness; kindly: *a benign embrace.* **3.** Tending to promote well-being; beneficial: *a benign climate.* **4.** *Pathol.* Not malignant: *a benign tumor.* —See Syns at **kind.** [Middle English *benigne*, from Old French, from Latin *benignus*, "well-born."] —**be·nign′ly** *adv.*

2. sacrilegious (par. 17)
   a. keeping sacred
   b. stealing
   c. making fun of something sacred
   d. keeping Sunday as a holy day
3. infuse (par. 24)
   a. to instill
   b. to steep
   c. to extract
   d. to boil
4. valid (par. 25)
   a. legal
   b. effective
   c. based on good
   d. based on evidence
5. aura (par. 42)
   a. particular quality
   b. mysterious
   c. characteristic
   d. personal

sac·ri·lege (săk'rə-lĭj) *n.* The profanation of something sacred. [Middle English, from Old French, from Latin *sacrilegium,* from *sacrilegus,* one who steals sacred things.] —**sac'ri·le'gious** (-lĭj'əs, -lē'jəs) *adj.* —**sac'ri·le'gious·ly** *adv.* —**sac'ri·le'gious·ness** *n.*

in·fuse (ĭn-fyōoz') *tr.v.* -**fused,** -**fus·ing.** 1. To fill; imbue; inspire: *The teacher infused the children with a great love of learning.* 2. To impart or instill: *The coach infused a feeling of pride in his men.* 3. To steep or soak without boiling in order to extract soluble elements: *infuse tea leaves.* [Middle English *infusen,* from Old French *infuser,* from Latin *infundere,* to pour in : *in-,* in + *fundere,* to pour.] —**in·fus'er** *n.*

val·id (văl'ĭd) *adj.* 1. Well-grounded; sound; supportable: *a valid objection.* 2. Producing the desired results; efficacious: *valid methods.* 3. Legally sound and effective; incontestable; binding: *a valid title.* 4. *Logic.* a. Containing premises from which the conclusion may logically be derived: *a valid argument.* b. Correctly inferred or deduced from a premise: *a valid conclusion.* 5. *Archaic.* Of sound health; robust.

au·ra (ôr'ə) *n.* 1. An invisible breath or emanation. 2. A distinctive air or quality that characterizes a person or thing: *a man with an aura of nobility and mystery.* [Middle English, from Latin, breeze, from Greek.]

DISCUSSION

1. The story is told by Marguerite. What impression does she create about her life in the first paragraph?
2. In what ways did Sister Flowers affect Marguerite's attitude toward herself?

Difficulty level: A

20. Soap Operas

Edward J. Whetmore

Though dozens of different daytime formats have been tried, daytime TV is still pretty much *soap operas* and *game shows.* The soaps were introduced from radio when daytime TV first began, deriving their name from the soap products that were often sponsors. The soap opera format was brought intact from radio and it's changed little over the years. Protagonists are put into conflict situations, usually involving close friends or relatives, and must make decisions to resolve those conflicts. Some soaps, like *The Guiding Light* and *The Edge of Night,* boast 20 or more years on daytime TV and a loyal audience.

The soap opera depends so much on human interaction that we may use the term to describe our own conflicts. ("Gee, my father isn't speaking to me, my sister is getting an abortion, and I'm flunking out of school. My life is really like a soap opera!") In reality, few lives are as troubled and confused as those on the soaps. As with much of TV, our real lives are dull by comparison.

Soap opera characters are carefully created for the mass audience. They are usually young (25-35), well dressed, and financially comfortable. Leading men are doctors and lawyers. Leading women are attractive and well manicured. Indoor sets are unusually large and boast wall-to-wall carpeting, plush drapes, and built in wet bars. Soap opera characters tend to be very sophisticated and do a lot of eating, drinking, and arguing.

Regular viewers can name all the characters in a given soap and describe their history in detail. The casual observer gets lost in the plot, which has more twists and turns than a mountain highway:

Let's see . . . John's son is getting married today to the woman who used to be his father's wife, who was recently divorced from the doctor who delivered his illegitimate daughter. That illegitimate daughter is really Bill's mother, Nell, whose father was a doctor where Bill was in medical school. We know that Bill never graduated but came to town and set up practice anyway. Things were going great until he and Nell got divorced, but then she found out she was his mother and. . . .

Unlike prime-time shows, soaps are often shot only a day or two before they are aired. This five-show-a-week schedule takes its toll on cast and crew. There is usually little budget for retakes, and sometimes missed cues and blown lines must be aired. It really keeps the cast on their toes. One advantage to the schedule is that the soap script may incorporate recent news events, while prime-time shows, shot as much as six months in advance, cannot.

Critics contend that all soaps are nauseatingly similar, but actually each is aimed at a special segment of the audience. Although 70 percent of that audience is women, there are different age groups. One hit among young viewers during the late 1970s was *The Young and the Restless*. It featured young characters and concentrated on presenting the latest fashions along with the plot.

Soap operas often set clothing and fashion trends. Most are taped in New York, and many fashion designers across the country keep an eye on the soaps to see what is happening. "What's in vogue in the soaps today will be in the shops tomorrow" is a standard saying.

Of more significance, soap operas are a fascinating study of audience-character relationships. There is no other media audience so involved with its programs and so devoted to its characters. When soap characters have an on-camera birthday, they can expect lots of cards from fans. If they are sick, thousands of viewers write and send get-well greetings. If a popular character "dies," viewers protest. And, unlike the prime-time audience, soap watchers tend to have a good handle on what they receive from their programs. The desire to believe in romantic love, the desire to see evil punished and virtue rewarded, and the desire to see others make mistakes are most often cited by the viewers themselves. Soap characters are usually good or evil, positive or negative, with well-defined personalities.

During *Mary Hartman, Mary Hartman's* airing in the mid- 10
1970s, many viewers found themselves hooked on the genre
for the first time. Norman Lear's self-described "slightly bent"
soap was different. Mary's grandfather (the "Fernwood
Flasher") was arrested for exhibitionism, sister Kathy went to
work in a massage parlor, and Mary was about to have an affair
with a local cop. For all of that, Mary retained her innocence;
she was always a victim of circumstance.

While *Mary Hartman, Mary Hartman* represented a depar- 11
ture from traditional soap format (for one thing, it was often
aired in the late evening rather than in the daytime), its real
significance may be in *how* it got on the air. Despite all of his
successes, Lear could not convince the three networks to give
Mary a chance. So he brought 50 independent TV station
managers from all over the country to Los Angeles for a quiet
dinner on his lawn. Afterwards he screened an episode of his
new soap and asked them to carry it, sweetening the pot by
offering it at budget rates.

Those who accepted were probably grateful. Within 12
weeks the show had doubled existing ratings for most stations
in its time period. It was the first time the major networks had
been successfully bypassed. New producers could take more
controversial shows directly to the stations, diminishing the
power of the networks to dictate what was popular. Dozens of
books and hundreds of articles have been written about this
problem, but it took Norman Lear's success to prove that the
network stranglehold could be broken. In the midst of it all was
a show from the most widely criticized genre on television.

COMPREHENSION

1. This article is mainly about
   a. how the major networks control programming
   b. the characteristics of soap operas
   c. why *Mary Hartman, Mary Hartman* was a success
   d. how audiences identify with soap opera characters
2. Individual soap operas
   a. are all alike
   b. are aimed at a special segment of the audience
   c. appeal to one age group
   d. appeal only to women
3. One advantage in the filming schedule of soap operas is
   a. fashionable clothes can be worn
   b. the budget can be kept low
   c. recent news events can be a part of the script
   d. soap operas can be shown live
4. Soap opera characters are
   a. well defined
   b. played by second-rate actors
   c. admired by the audience
   d. always well educated
5. According to the author, the real significance of Lear's success
   was that

a. a new audience for soaps evolved
b. *Mary Hartman, Mary Hartman* was not a traditional soap opera
c. *Mary Hartman, Mary Hartman* was broadcast by independent TV stations
d. the show doubled its ratings in a few weeks

VOCABULARY

Directions: *The meaning of the following terms from selection 20 cannot be clearly determined from the context. Using the dictionary entries, determine the appropriate definition of the term as it is used in the reading selection.*

1. protagonists (par. 1)
   a. leaders
   b. first combatants
   c. spokesmen
   d. leading characters

pro·tag·o·nist (prō tag′ə nist), *n.* **1.** the leading character or hero of a drama or other literary work. **2.** a leader of or spokesman for a movement, cause, etc. [< Gk *prōtagōnist(ḗs)* actor who plays the first part, lit., first combatant. See PROTO-, ANTAGONIST] —**pro·tag′o·nism,** *n.*

2. interaction (par. 2)
   a. correspondence
   b. reciprocal influence
   c. exchange
   d. intercourse

in·ter·act (in′tər akt′), *v.i.* to act one upon another. —**in′·ter·ac′tive,** *adj.*
in·ter·ac·tion (in′tər ak′shən), *n.* reciprocal action or influence. —**in′ter·ac′tion·al,** *adj.*

3. incorporate (par. 6)
   a. from a corporation
   b. integrate
   c. enbody
   d. include

in·cor·po·rate¹ (*v.* in kôr′pə rāt′; *adj.* in kôr′pə rit, -prit), *v.,* **-rat·ed, -rat·ing,** *adj.* —*v.t.* **1.** to form into a corporation. **2.** to form into a society or organization. **3.** to put or introduce into a body or mass as an integral part or parts. **4.** to take in or include as a part or parts, as the body or a mass does. **5.** to form or combine into one body or uniform substance, as ingredients. **6.** to embody. —*v.i.* **7.** to unite or combine so as to form one body. **8.** to form a corporation. —*adj.* **9.** incorporated, as a company. **10.** combined into one body, mass, or substance. **11.** *Archaic.* embodied. [ME < LL *incorporāt(us)* embodied. See IN-², CORPORATE] —**in·cor′po·ra′tive,** *adj.*

4. vogue (par. 8)
   a. fashion
   b. popular
   c. successful
   d. acceptable

vogue (vōg), *n.* **1.** the fashion, as at a particular time. **2.** a period of popular currency, acceptance, or favor; popularity: *The book had a great vogue.* [< MF: wave or course of success < OIt *voga* a rowing < *vogare* to row, sail < ?] —**Syn. 1.** mode. See **fashion.**

5. genre (par. 10)
   a. style of painting
   b. category of artistic work
   c. endeavor
   d. design

gen·re (zhän′rə; *Fr.* zhäN′Rə), *n., pl.* **-res** (-rəz; *Fr.* -Rə), *adj.* —*n.* **1.** genus; kind; sort; style. **2.** a class or category of artistic endeavor having a particular form, content, technique, or the like. **3.** *Fine Arts.* **a.** paintings in which scenes of everyday life form the subject matter. **b.** a realistic style of painting using such subject matter. —*adj.* **4.** *Fine Arts.* of or pertaining to genre. [< F: kind, sort; see GENDER¹]

6. exhibitionism (par. 10)
   a. showing off
   b. swaggering
   c. compulsive indecent exposure
   d. inappropriate behavior

ex·hi·bi·tion·ism (ek′sə bish′ə niz′əm), *n.* **1.** a tendency to behave in such a way as to attract attention. **2.** *Psychiatry.* a disorder characterized esp. by a compulsion to exhibit the genitals.

DISCUSSION

1. Why do you watch or not watch soap operas?
2. Consider the effects of soap operas on adolescents. Are they harmful?
3. Does the audience's involvement with individual soap opera characters limit an actor's career?

Difficulty level: A

21. A Fable for Tomorrow

Rachel Carson

There was once a town in the heart of America where all
life seemed to live in harmony with its surroundings. The town
lay in the midst of a checkerboard of prosperous farms, with
fields of grain and hillsides of orchards where, in spring, white
clouds of bloom drifted above the green fields. In autumn, oak
and maple and birch set up a blaze of color that flamed and
flickered across a backdrop of pines. Then foxes barked in the
hills and deer silently crossed the fields, half hidden in the
mists of the fall mornings. 1

Along the roads, laurel, viburnum, and alder, great ferns,
and wildflowers delighted the traveler's eye through much of
the year. Even in winter the roadsides were places of beauty,
where countless birds came to feed on the berries and on the
seed heads of the dried weeds rising above the snow. The
countryside was, in fact, famous for the abundance and variety
of its bird life, and when the flood of migrants was pouring
through in spring and fall people traveled from great distances
to observe them. Others came to fish the streams, which flowed
clear and cold out of the hills and contained shady pools where
trout lay. So it had been from the days many years ago, when
the first settlers raised their houses, sank their wells, and built
their barns. 2

Then a strange blight crept over the area and everything
began to change. Some evil spell had settled on the community: mysterious maladies swept the flocks of chickens; the cattle and sheep sickened and died. Everywhere was a shadow of
death. The farmers spoke of much illness among their families.
In the town the doctors had become more and more puzzled
by new kinds of sickness appearing among their patients.
There had been several sudden and unexplained deaths, not
only among adults, but even among children, who would be
stricken suddenly while at play and die within a few hours. 3

There was a strange stillness. The birds, for example—
where had they gone? Many people spoke of them, puzzled
and disturbed. The feeding stations in the backyards were
deserted. The few birds seen anywhere were moribund; they
trembled violently and could not fly. It was a spring without
voices. On the mornings that had once throbbed with the dawn
chorus of robins, catbirds, doves, jays, wrens, and scores of
other bird voices there was now no sound; only silence lay over
the fields and woods and marsh. 4

On the farms the hens brooded, but no chicks hatched.
The farmers complained that they were unable to raise any
pigs—the litters were small and the young survived only a few
days. The apple trees were coming into bloom but no bees
droned among the blossoms, so there was no pollination and
there would be no fruit. 5

The roadsides, once so attractive, were now lined with browned and withered vegetation as though swept by fire. These, too, were silent, deserted by all living things. Even the streams were now lifeless. Anglers no longer visited them, for all the fish had died. 6

In the gutters under the eaves and between the shingles of the roofs, a white granular powder still showed a few patches; some weeks before it had fallen like snow upon roofs and the lawns, the fields and streams. 7

No witchcraft, no enemy action had silenced the rebirth of new life in the stricken world. The people had done it themselves. 8

This town does not actually exist, but it might easily have a thousand counterparts in America or elsewhere in the world. I know of no community that has experienced all the misfortunes I describe. Yet every one of these disasters has actually happened somewhere, and many real communities have already suffered a substantial number of them. A grim specter has crept upon us almost unnoticed, and this imagined tragedy may easily become a stark reality we all shall know. 9

COMPREHENSION

1. This selection is mainly about
   a. the causes of pollution
   b. how beautiful towns in the midwest were at one time
   c. what happens when there is a blight
   d. the possible effects of environmental pollution
2. Each disaster mentioned in the selection
   a. has happened in some community
   b. might happen someplace in the world
   c. could only happen in a town or city
   d. occurred in the Midwest about three years ago
3. The author probably believes that
   a. everyone is responsible for controlling the environment
   b. no one can control pollution
   c. large corporations cannot be held responsible for keeping the environment pollution free
   d. it is highly unlikely that the events described in the article could happen in the future
4. Fruit would not grow because
   a. the trees didn't blossom
   b. it shriveled on the branches
   c. the tree lacked water
   d. there were no bees to pollinate the trees
5. The cause of the disaster in the community was probably
   a. witchcraft
   b. polluted water
   c. the white granular substance
   d. a contagious disease

VOCABULARY

Directions: *The meaning of the following terms from selection 21 cannot be clearly determined from the context. Using the dictionary entries, select the appropriate definition of the term as it is used in the reading selection.*

1. harmony (par. 1)
   a. combination
   b. integration
   c. agreement
   d. collation

2. abundance (par. 2)
   a. overflowing
   b. plentiful amount
   c. fullness
   d. affluence

3. blight (par. 3)
   a. injurious environmental condition
   b. decay
   c. frustration
   d. lack of prosperity

4. maladies (par. 3)
   a. undesirable behaviors
   b. ailments
   c. poor conditions
   d. unwholesome habits

5. moribund (par. 4)
   a. becoming obsolete
   b. aging
   c. sickly
   d. nearing death

6. brooded (par. 5)
   a. flocked
   b. sat on eggs
   c. hovered
   d. sulked

7. specter (par. 9)
   a. ghost
   b. threatening possibility
   c. apparition
   d. phantom

har·mo·ny (här′mə-nē) *n., pl.* **-nies.** **1.** Agreement in feeling, approach, action, disposition, or the like; sympathy; accord. **2.** The pleasing interaction or appropriate combination of the elements in a whole. **3.** *Music.* **a.** The study of the structure, progression, and relation of chords. **b.** The simultaneous combination of notes in a chord. **c.** The structure of a musical work or passage as considered from the point of view of its chordal characteristics and relationships. **4.** *Archaic.* Pleasing sounds; music. **5.** A collation of parallel passages from the Gospels, with a commentary demonstrating their consonance and explaining their discrepancies. —See Synonyms at **proportion.** [Middle English *armonie,* from Old French *(h)armonie,* from Latin *harmonia,* from Greek, agreement, harmony, means of joining, from *harmos,* joint. See **ar-** in Appendix.*]

a·bun·dance (ə-bŭn′dəns) *n.* Also **a·bun·dan·cy** (-dən-sē). **1.** A great quantity; plentiful amount. **2.** Fullness to overflowing: *"My thoughts . . . are from the abundance of my heart."* (De Quincey). **3.** Affluence; wealth.

blight (blīt) *n.* **1.** Any of several plant diseases that result in sudden dying of leaves, growing tips, or an entire plant. **2.** An environmental condition that injures or kills plants or animals, as air pollution. **3.** One that withers hopes or ambitions, impairs growth, or halts prosperity. **4.** The state or result of being blighted. —*v.* **blighted, blighting, blights.** —*tr.* **1.** To cause to decline or decay. **2.** To ruin; destroy. **3.** To frustrate: *a mishap that blighted his hopes.* —*intr.* To suffer blight. [Origin unknown.]

mal·a·dy (măl′ə-dē) *n., pl.* **-dies.** **1.** A disease, disorder, or ailment: *"There were many sick of a malady that would not be healed."* (J.R.R. Tolkien). **2.** Any unwholesome condition. [Middle English *maladie,* from Old French, from *malade,* sick, from Latin *male habitus,* "ill-kept," "in poor condition" : *male,* ill, from *malus,* bad (see **mel-**⁵ in Appendix*) + *habitus,* past participle of *habēre,* to have, keep (see **ghabh-** in Appendix*).]

mor·i·bund (môr′ə-bŭnd′, mŏr′-) *adj.* **1.** At the point of death; about to die. **2.** Approaching an end; obsolescent: *"a commendable instinct for hastening the demise of moribund words"* (New Yorker). [Latin *moribundus,* from *mori,* to die. See **mer-**² in Appendix.*] —**mor′i·bun′di·ty** *n.* —**mor′i·bund′ly** *adv.*

brood (brood) *n.* **1.** The young of certain animals, as birds or fish; especially, a group of young birds or fowl hatched at one time and cared for by the same mother. **2.** The children in one family. —See Synonyms at **flock.** —*v.* **brooded, brooding, broods.** —*tr.* **1.** To sit on or hatch (eggs). **2.** To protect (young) by or as if by covering with the wings. —*intr.* **1.** To sit on or hatch eggs. **2.** To hover envelopingly: *"that gentle heat that brooded on the waters"* (Thomas Browne). **3.** To ponder moodily; sulk. —*adj.* Kept for breeding: *a brood mare.* [Middle English *brood,* Old English *brōd.* See **bhreu-**² in Appendix.*] —**brood′ing·ly** *adv.*

spec·ter (spĕk′tər) *n.* Also *chiefly British* **spec·tre.** **1.** A ghost; phantom; apparition. **2.** A mental image; phantasm: *"floating spectres of long forgotten spelling books"* (Lewis Carroll). **3.** A foreboding. [French *spectre,* from Latin *spectrum,* appearance, image. See **spectrum.**]

DISCUSSION

1. Are you aware of a particular pollution problem in your community? Is it possible to eliminate the problem? If so, how? If not, what actions might alleviate the problem?

2. Would you be willing to give up the convenience provided by modern industry and technology in order to reduce environmental pollution? What do you think you would have to give up? How would it change your life?

3. Is pollution a moral issue? an economic issue? an international problem? Whose responsibility is it?

Difficulty level: B

22. The Sale

Morris K. Holland and Gerald Tarlow

Selling is persuading people to decide to buy your product. Deciding to buy many things today involves fairly heavy decisions. One way salesmen overcome resistance to making large decisions is to induce people first to make small decisions. This technique is called the "foot-in-the-door technique." 1

The foot-in-the-door technique has probably been used on you. A salesperson calls and asks you to answer a few questions for a "survey." An advertisement in the paper invites you to return a coupon for a free booklet. You are asked to accept a free sample. Or a car dealer asks you to come down to the showroom for a party. Once you have taken a small step, a larger step is more likely, once a salesperson has a "foot" in your door, your are more likely to open the door all the way. 2

In one study, a group of women were contacted by experimenters who explained that they were working for the Committee for Safe Driving. They asked the women to sign petitions urging the legislature to give more attention to driving safety, most of the women signed the petition. Later, the experimenters called again on these women—and another group who had not been previously contacted—and asked each of them to permit the Committee to put in their front yards a large, unattractive sign reading "Drive Carefully." The women who had previously been requested to sign the petition reacted much differently from the women who had not been approached. Over half of the women previously approached agreed to have the sign in their front yards, while less than a fifth of the women who had not been approached agreed to the request. Once a small favor (signing a petition) was granted, a much larger favor (displaying a large sign) was more likely to be granted. 3

The foot-in-the-door technique also was applied in a sales program aimed at selling a large inventory of curtains and upholstery material to retail shops: 4

The salesman visited the store of the retailer (the target audience) and asked for a small favor: whether he would display a small sign which simply said, "Coming soon, Pronti-Cort." Since nothing further was explained to the storekeeper, his curiosity was piqued, and it was maintained by customers who asked him what the sign meant.

A week later, the salesman returned and asked those retailers who did the small favor to do a larger one—to come with him to the wholesaler's showroom, at which time the meaning of the sign would be made clear. Most of the storekeepers agreed.

The larger favor (coming to the showroom) was granted more easily after the smaller favor (displaying a small sign) was granted. At the showroom, the storekeepers were shown the products and a sales pitch was made; the sales volume was three times the initial forecast. The foot-in-the-door technique had been successful.

Why should the foot-in-the-door technique work? How 5 does agreeing to a small request make you more vulnerable to a large request? You might think that after you've done someone a favor, you'd be less likely to do them another; in fact, the opposite is the case—you are more likely to do it. One explanation of this effect is that people are motivated to be consistent in thought and action. Consider the three possible thoughts:

(a) I like you.
(b) I dislike you.
(c) I have just done a favor for you.

Now, *a* and *c* are consistent, but *b* and *c* are inconsistent—it is not consistent for me to do you a favor if I don't like you. If I am motivated to be consistent, and if I have just done a favor for you, I am motivated to like you. In fact, I will probably like you more after I have done a favor for you than I did before the favor, because of my need for internal consistency between feeling and action. Because of my need to avoid cognitive inconsistency or *cognitive dissonance*, I also tend to avoid reading things that are incompatible with my beliefs; I selectively expose myself to information supporting my existing belief system.

Belief follows action: what you do affects what you 6 believe. Remarkably enough, if you say things that you don't believe you may begin to believe them. People who have been paid small sums to make public speeches arguing for positions contrary to their private beliefs wind up having beliefs more consonant with their public statements. This evidence supports *the principle of cognitive dissonance: when actions are not consistent with underlying attitudes, the attitudes tend to change so as to become more consistent with the actions.* That is, your actions change your beliefs.

COMPREHENSION

1. The selection is mainly about
    a. sales techniques used in advertising
    b. why people buy things
    c. how a sales technique is based on the principle of cognitive dissonance
    d. how your beliefs change
2. The author states that human behavior is
    a. controlled by past experience
    b. motivated by need
    c. motivated to be consistent
    d. often irrational
3. The "foot-in-the-door sales technique" involves
    a. agreeing to buy something you don't need
    b. overcoming resistance to large decisions by encouraging people to make small decisions first
    c. getting someone's attention before trying to sell the product
    d. using high-pressure tactics to sell a product
4. Women who signed petitions for safe driving were
    a. aware that they were part of an experiment
    b. more agreeable to the placement of signs in their yards than women who were not asked to sign the petition
    c. less agreeable to placement of signs in their yards than women who were not asked to sign
    d. annoyed when they learned that they were part of an experiment
5. The principle of cognitive dissonance means
    a. people have the need for consistency, and when faced with an inconsistency they make the necessary changes in attitude to achieve consistency with action
    b. people's actions are controlled by their beliefs
    c. actions and beliefs are always consistent
    d. behavior is controlled by actions

VOCABULARY

Directions: *The meaning of the following terms from selection 22 cannot be clearly determined from the context. Using the dictionary entries, select the appropriate definition of the term as it is used in the reading selection.*

1. induce (par. 1)
    a. to persuade
    b. to produce
    c. to establish
    d. to bring about

    in·duce (in dōōs′, -dyōōs′), *v.t.*, **-duced, -duc·ing. 1.** to influence or persuade, as to some action, state of mind, etc.: *Induce him to stay.* **2.** to bring about or cause: *sleep induced by drugs.* **3.** *Physics.* to produce (magnetism, charge, emf, or electric current) by induction. **4.** *Logic.* to assert or establish (a proposition) on the basis of observations of particular facts. [ME < L *indūce(re)* (to) lead or bring in, introduce = *in-* IN-² + *dūcere* to lead] —**in·duc′er,** *n.* —**in·duc′i·ble,** *adj.* —**Syn. 1.** actuate, prompt, incite, urge, spur. See **persuade.** —**Ant. 1.** dissuade.

2. upholstery (par. 4)
    a. place that sells furniture coverings
    b. draperies
    c. furniture
    d. furniture coverings

    up·hol·ster·y (up hōl′stə rē, ə pōl′-), *n., pl.* **-ster·ies. 1.** the material supplied by an upholsterer, as cushions or furniture coverings. **2.** the business of an upholsterer.

3. piqued (par. 4)
   a. irritated
   b. aroused
   c. affected
   d. resented
4. vulnerable (par. 5)
   a. hurt
   b. critical
   c. susceptible
   d. open to attack
5. consonant (par. 6)
   a. a speech sound
   b. in opposition to
   c. agreeable with
   d. obstruction

pique (pēk), v., **piqued, piqu·ing,** n. —v.t. **1.** to affect with sharp irritation and resentment, esp. by some wound to pride: *He piqued her by refusing her invitation.* **2.** to wound (the pride, vanity, etc.). **3.** to excite (interest, curiosity, etc.). **4.** to arouse an emotion or provoke to action: *to pique someone to answer a challenge.* **5.** *Archaic.* to pride (oneself) (usually fol. by *on* or *upon*). —v.i. **6.** to cause anger, resentment, or sharp irritation in someone. —n. **7.** a feeling of irritation or resentment, as from a wound to pride or self-esteem. **8.** *Obs.* a state of irritated feeling between persons. [< MF *pique* (n.), *piquer* (v.) < VL *piccare*; see PICKAX, PIQUÉ, PIKE²]

vul·ner·a·ble (vul′nər ə bəl), *adj.* **1.** capable of or susceptible to being wounded or hurt, as by a weapon. **2.** open to criticism, temptation, etc.: *an argument vulnerable to refutation; He has proved himself vulnerable to bribery.* **3.** (of a place) open to attack or assault. **4.** *Bridge.* having won one of the games of a rubber. [< LL *vulnerābil(is)* = L *vulnerā(re)* to wound + *-bilis* -BLE; see VULNERARY] —**vul′ner·a·bil′-i·ty, vul′ner·a·ble·ness,** n. —**vul′ner·a·bly,** adv.

con·so·nant (kon′sə nənt), n. **1.** *Phonet.* (in English articulation) a speech sound produced by occluding (p, b; t, d; k, g), diverting (m, n, ṉg), or obstructing (f, v; s, z, etc.) the flow of air from the lungs (opposed to *vowel*). **2.** a letter that represents a consonant sound. —*adj.* **3.** in agreement; agreeable; consistent (usually fol. by *to* or *with*): *behavior consonant with his character.* **4.** corresponding or harmonious in sound. **5.** *Music.* constituting a consonance. **6.** consonantal. [late ME *consona(u)nt* < L *consonant-* (s. of *consonāns,* prp. of *consonāre* to sound with or together)] —**con′so·nant·ly,** adv. —**Ant. 5.** dissonant.

DISCUSSION

1. Do you think the sales technique described in the essay is fair to the consumer? Give some reasons for your answer.
2. Were you ever persuaded to buy something you didn't need or want? Why did you buy the item? Or, if you didn't buy the item, what made you decide not to?
3. Consider this statement from the essay: "What you do affects what you believe.... If you say things you don't believe you may begin to believe them."

Difficulty level: B

23. Whales and Dolphins

David Attenborough

Whales and dolphins of course, are also warm-blooded, milk-producing mammals and they too have a long ancestry, with fossils dating back to the beginning of the great radiation of the mammals fifty million years ago. But could these immense animals really be descended from a tiny creature like a tupaia? It is difficult to believe, and yet the logic of the deduction is undeniable. Their ancestors must have entered the seat at a time when the only mammals in existence were the little insectivores. But their anatomy is now so extremely adapted to swimming that it gives no clue as to how the move into the sea was made. It may be that the two main groups of whales have different ancestries, those with teeth having come from insectivores by way of primitive carnivores and the rest, the baleen whales, being descended more directly.

The major differences between the whales and the early mammals are attributable to adaptations for the swimming life. The forelimbs have become paddles. The rear limbs have been lost altogether, though there are a few small bones buried deep in the whale's body to prove that the whale's ancestors really did, at one time, have back legs. Fur, that hallmark of the mammals, depends for its effect as an insulator on air trapped between the hairs. So it is of little use to a creature that never comes to dry land, and the whales have lost that too, though once again there are relics, a few bristles on the snout to demonstrate that they once had a coat. Insulation, however, is still needed and whales have developed blubber, a thick layer of fat beneath the skin that prevents their body heat from escaping even in the coldest seas.

3 The mammals' dependency on air for breathing must be considered a real handicap in water, but the whale has minimized the problem by breathing even more efficiently than most land-livers. Man only clears about 15% of the air in his lungs with a normal breath. The whale, in one of its roaring, spouting exhalations, gets rid of about 90% of its spent air. As a result it only has to take a breath at very long intevals. It also has in its muscles a particularly high concentration of a substance called myoglobin, that enables it to store oxygen. It is this constituent that gives whale meat its characteristic dark colour. With the help of these techniques, the fin-back whale, for example, can dive to a depth of 500 metres and swim for forty minutes without drawing breath.

4 One group of whales has specialized in feeding on tiny shrimp-like crustaceans, krill, which swarm in vast clouds in the sea. Just as teeth are of no value to mammals feeding on ants, so they are no use to those eating krill. So these whales, like ant-eaters, have lost their teeth. Instead they have baleen, sheets of horn, feathered at the edges, that hang down like stiff, parallel curtains from the roof of the mouth. The whale takes a huge mouthful of water in the middle of the shoal of krill, half-shuts its jaws and then expels the water by pressing its tongue forward so that the krill remains and can be swallowed. Sometimes it gathers the krill by slowly cruising where it is thickest. It also can concentrate a dispersed shoal by diving beneath it and then spiralling up, expelling bubbles as it goes, so that the krill is driven towards the centre of the spiral. Then the whale itself, jaws pointing upwards, rises in the centre and gathers them in one gulp.

5 On such a diet, the baleen whales have grown to an immense size. The blue whale, the biggest of all, grows to over 30 metres long and weighs as much as twenty-five bull elephants. There is a positive and advantage to a whale in being large. Maintaining body temperature is easier the bigger you are and the lower the ratio between your volume and surface area. This phenomenon had affected the dinosaurs but their dimensions were limited by the mechanical strength of bone. Above a certain weight, limbs would simply break. The whales are less hampered. The function of their bones is largely to give rigidity. Support for their bodies comes from the water. Nor does a life spent gently cruising after krill demand great agility. So the baleen whales have developed into the largest living creatures of any kind that have ever lived on earth, four times heavier than the largest known dinosaur.

6 The toothed whales feed on different prey. The largest of them, the squid-eating sperm whale, only attains half the size of the blue whale. The smaller ones, dolphins, porpoises and

killer whales, hunt both fish and squid and have become extremely fast swimmers, some reputedly being able to reach speeds of over 40 kph.

Moving at such speeds, navigation becomes critically important. Fish are helped by their lateral line system, but mammals lost that far back in their ancestry and the toothed whales have instead a system based on the sounds used by shrews and elaborated by bats, sonar. Dolphins produce the ultra-sound with larynx and maybe an organ in the front of the head, the melon. The frequencies they use are around 200,000 vibrations a second, which is comparable to those used by bats. With its aid, they can not only sense obstacles in their path, but identify from the quality of the echo, the nature of the objects ahead. Thic can be demonstrated easily enough for dolphins flourish in oceanaria and eagerly cooperate in training. Blindfolded dolphins demonstrate that they can, without difficulty, pick out particular shapes of floating rings and will swiftly swim through the water, with blindfolds on their eyes, and exultantly collect on their snout the one shape that they know will bring a reward.

Dolphins produce a great variety of other noises quite apart from ultra-sounds and there has been considerable speculation as to whether these sounds constitute a language. Some workers have said that if only we were clever enough, we would be able to understand what they say and even exchange complex messages with them. So far, we have identified some twenty different sounds that dolphins make. Some seem to serve to keep a school together when they are travelling at speed. Some appear to be warning cries, and some call-signs so that animals can recognize each other at a distance. But no one yet has demonstrated that dolphins put these sounds together to form the equivalent of the two-word sentence that can justifiably be regarded as the beginning of true language. Chimpanzees can do so. But dolphins, as far as we can tell, cannot.

The great whales also have voices. Humpbacks, one of the baleen whales, congregate every spring in Hawaii to give birth to their young and to mate. Some of them also sing. Their song consists of a sequence of yelps, growls, high-pitched squeals and long-drawn-out rumbles. And the whales declaim these songs hour after hour in extended stately recitals. They contain unchanging sequences of notes that have been called themes. Each theme may be repeated over and over again—the number of times varies but the order of the themes in a song is always the same in any one season. Typically, a complete song lasts for about ten minutes, but some have been recorded that continue for half an hour; and whales may sing, repeating their songs, virtually continuously for over twenty-four hours. Each whale has its own characteristic song but it composes it from themes which it shares with the rest of the whale community in Hawaii.

The whales stay in Hawaiian waters for several months, calving, mating and singing. Sometimes they lie on the surface, one immense flipper held vertically in the air. Sometimes they beat the water with it. Occasionally, one will leap clear of the surface, all fifty tons in the air, the ridging of its underside plain to see, and fall back with a gigantic surge and thunderous crash. It will breach in this way again and again.

Then within a few days, the deep blue bays and straits off 11 the Hawaiian islands are empty. The whales have gone. Humpbacks appear a few weeks later off Alaska. It is very likely that these are the Hawaiian animals but more studies will have to be made before we can be certain that they are.

Next spring, they reappear in Hawaii and once more begin 12 to sing. But this time they have new themes in their repertoire and have dropped many of the old ones. Sometimes the songs are so loud that the whole hull of your boat resonates and you can hear ethereal moans and cries coming mysteriously, as from nowhere. If you dive into the peerlessly blue water and swim down, you may, with luck, see the singer hanging in the water below you, a cobalt shape in the sapphire depths. The sound penetrates your body, making the air in your sinuses vibrate in sympathy, as though you were sitting within the widest pipe of the largest cathedral organ, and the whole of your tissues are soaked in sound.

We still do not know why whales sing. Man can identify 13 each individual whale by its song and if he can do so, then surely whales can do the same. Water transmits sound better than air so it may well be that sections of these songs, particularly those low vibrating notes, can be heard by other whales ten, twenty, even thirty miles away informing them of the whereabouts and activities of the whole whale community.

COMPREHENSION

1. This article is mainly about
   a. how some mammals have adapted to living in the water
   b. the feeding habits of whales
   c. the navigational system used by dolphins
   d. the various sizes of mammals that live in the water
2. The major difference between whales and the early mammals can be attributed to
   a. insulation
   b. dependency on air
   c. adaptations for swimming
   d. a substance called myoglobin
3. One advantage of the whale's size is that
   a. the creature has greater agility
   b. maintaining body temperature is easier
   c. it makes swimming easier
   d. the bones provide strong support
4. To navigate through the water dolphins use
   a. songs
   b. high-frequency sounds
   c. vision
   d. color

5. The songs of the whales
   a. are all the same
   b. probably have a communicative function
   c. consist only of high-pitched sounds
   d. never change from year to year

VOCABULARY

Directions: *The meaning of the following terms from selection 23 cannot be clearly determined from the context. Using the dictionary entries, select the appropriate definition of the term as it is used in the reading selection.*

1. insectivores (par. 1)
   a. primitive plant forms
   b. cold-blooded animals
   c. reptiles
   d. mammals that feed on insects

in·sec·ti·vore (ĭn-sĕk′tə-vôr′, -vōr′) *n.* **1.** Any of various mammals of the order Insectivora, characteristically feeding on insects, and including the shrews, moles, and hedgehogs. **2.** An organism that feeds on insects.

2. constituent (par. 3)
   a. fundamental law
   b. component
   c. voter in a district
   d. power

con·stit·u·ent (kən stĭch′ o͞o ənt), *adj.* **1.** serving to compose or make up a thing; component: *the constituent parts of a motor.* **2.** having power to frame or alter a political constitution or fundamental law, as distinguished from lawmaking power: *a constituent assembly.* —*n.* **3.** a constituent element, material, etc.; component. **4.** a person who authorizes another to act for him, as a voter in a Congressional district. **5.** *Gram.* an element considered as part of a construction. [< L *constituent*- (s. of *constituēns,* prp. of *constituere* to set up, found, constitute) = con- CON- + -stitu- (var. s. of *status* STATUS) + -ent- -ENT] —**con·stit′u·ent·ly,** *adv.* —**Syn.** 3. See **element.**

3. shoal (par. 4)
   a. school of fish
   b. school of whales
   c. shallow area
   d. sandbar

shoal¹ (shōl) *n.* **1.** A shallow place in a body of water. **2.** A sandbank or sandbar. —*intr.v.* To become shallow. —*tr.v.* To make shallow. —*adj.* Having little depth; shallow. [Middle English *sholde,* from Old English *sceald,* shallow.]

4. declaim (par. 9)
   a. sing loudly
   b. formally recite
   c. deliver quietly
   d. recite poetically

de·claim (dĭ-klām′) *tr.v.* **1.** To deliver formal recitation. **2.** To speak loudly and vehemently; inveigh: *declaimed against pollution of the lake.* —*tr.v.* To recite formally: *declaim a poem.* [Middle English *declamen,* from Latin *dēclāmāre.*] —**dec′la·ma′tion** *n.* —**de·claim′er** *n.*

5. ethereal (par. 11)
   a. exquisite
   b. upper regions of space
   c. loud
   d. heavenly

e·the·re·al (ĭ-thîr′ē-əl) *adj.* **1.** Highly refined and delicate; exquisite: *ethereal music.* **2.** Of or pertaining to heaven or the heavens; heavenly: *ethereal beings.* **3.** Of or pertaining to the upper regions of the earth's atmosphere or the space beyond. **4.** *Chem.* Of or pertaining to ether. [From Latin *aetherius,* from Greek *aitherios,* from *aithēr,* ether.] —**e·the′re·al·ly** *adv.*

DISCUSSION

1. What was the most surprising piece of information you learned from reading this article?
2. Does the fact that dolphins are mammals influence your attitudes toward the creatures in any way? Why?
3. If it is discovered that dolphins actually have a language, will your thinking about the relationship between man and animals change in any way?

Difficulty level: B

24. Being There—TV As Baby Sitter

Jerzy Kosinski

With the advent of television, for the first time in history, all aspects of animal and human life and death, of societal and individual behavior, have been condensed on the average to a 19-inch diagonal screen and a 30-minute time slot. Television, a unique medium, neither a reality nor art, has become a primary reality for many of us, particularly for our children who are growing up in front of it.

Imagine a child watching this little world within which children and adults, monsters and saints, Presidents and commoners, mice and lions, kissing lovers and dying soldiers, skyscrapers and dog houses, flowers and detergents, are all reduced to about the same size, mixed together, given the same dramatic importance, and set in the same screen to be looked at. Hour after hour, day after day, the child watches this crowded, frenetically changing world as he or she pleases, silent or talking, eating or playing. After 5,000 to 10,000 hours of watching by the time of entering first grade, what might be the outlook of such a child? What does it expect of the world? What can it expect?

Quite likely, it expects all things in life to be as equal as they have been on television: neither bad nor good, neither pleasant nor painful, neither real nor unreal, merely more or less absorbing, merely of clearer or less clear image. It is a world without rank. To such a child, the world is neither to be felt nor understood but to be looked upon; it is there to entertain its viewer. If it doesn't, one alters it by switching the channel.

In the little world of television, all is solved within its magic dramatic slots, seldom exceeding 30 minutes. In spite of the commercials, the wounded hero either rises or quickly dies, lovers marry or divorce, villains kill or are killed, addicts are cured, justice usually wins, and war ends. All problems are solved again this week, as they were last, and will be next week. Life on TV is, by the nature of the medium, primarily visual. This means single-faceted, revealed in a simple speech and through the obvious gesture. No matter how deep the mystery, complexity or ambiguity, the TV camera claims to have penetrated it while, in fact, scanning its surface.

Parents leave their children in front of the TV as baby sitter, because many assume that it is infinitely safer to watch the Sesame world of television than to walk in the world outside of their home. But is it?

Unlike television, the child grows older. One day it walks out of the TV room. Against his expectations, he's finally put in a classroom full of other children. A child who for years has been trained to control the little world brought to him by television by changing its channels when he didn't like it, and was accustomed to maintaining the same emotional distance between himself and the world televised for his amusement, is naturally threatened by the presence of real people and events he cannot control. Others push him around, make faces at him, encroach. There is nothing he can do to stop them and no existing remedy will alleviate his trauma. He begins to feel that this real world unjustly limits him; that it seldom offers alternative channels to turn to.

In this unpredictable, threatening in its complexities world of real life, there are no neatly ordered thirty-minute private slots. Here, in life, the child brought up only as a viewer must feel persecuted. Ironically, our industrial state offers few situations and conflicts that can be resolved in thirty minutes. But the teenager keeps expecting it; when they are not resolved, he grows impatient, oscillating between the adamant scream, "Now," and a disillusioned whimper "So what?" His psychological defenses retarded, he is easily depressed and beaten down. In this world of hierarchy, unemployment, and brutish competition, he is soon challenged and outranked by others. Now he believes he is defective; instead of coming of age, he's coming apart. This breeding of passive, nonverbal, weak and vulnerable beings knows few exceptions. The kids of the upper classes counteract TV by being involved with real events—real horses, real forests, real mountains—all things they have seen, touched, experienced. They have been given an opportunity to exist outside the television room. However, many middle-class children, and almost all from poor families, are more and more often at the mercy of five or six hours of television a day.

My own attitude toward television is neutral. The medium is here to stay. The danger is in the use we make of it. I'm involved with TV the way I am with the motor car. The motor car has been with us for over 60 years, but it is only recently that we learned its exhaust pollutes our very environment.

In today's atomized, disjointed technological society, with so little attention paid to the individual, men and women need more than ever the inner strength to carry them through the daily pressures. This strength should come from early exposure to life at its most real—its sudden pleasures, joys and abandonment; but also its violence, its lack of justice, indifference, its pain, illness, and death. There is subtlety to man's fate which lies beyond the thirteen channels.

COMPREHENSION

1. The main idea in this article is that
   a. television is bad for children
   b. television can breed passive, nonverbal, weak, and vulnerable teenagers
   c. upper-class children are not severely affected by television
   d. there is too much emphasis on violence in TV programming
2. When a child entering the first grade has experienced 5,000 to 10,000 hours of TV viewing one might expect the child
   a. to expect all things in life to be as equal as they have been on television
   b. to expect everything to be bad

c. to expect everything to be pleasant

d. to have a clear image of reality

3. One of the consequences of too much television is
   a. a child becomes aggressive and pushy
   b. a child maintains emotional distance from his classmates
   c. a child is threatened by the presence of real people and events he or she cannot control
   d. a child finds school a traumatic experience

4. By adolescence the child brought up as a viewer
   a. is often disillusioned
   b. is always depressed and beaten down
   c. may believe he or she is defective
   d. is physically underdeveloped

5. Kosinski feels that television viewing should be
   a. limited to programs that present a realistic view of life
   b. balanced with real life experiences
   c. restricted only for young children
   d. carefully studied by child psychologists

VOCABULARY

Directions: *The meaning of the following terms from selection 24 cannot be clearly determined from the context. Using the dictionary entries, select the appropriate definition of the term as it is used in the reading selection.*

1. advent (par. 1)
   a. coming into being
   b. birth of Christ
   c. second coming
   d. penitential period

ad·vent (ad′vent), *n.* **1.** arrival or coming into being: *the advent of spring.* **2.** (*usually cap.*) the coming of Christ into the world. **3.** (*cap.*) the penitential period beginning four Sundays before Christmas, commemorating this. **4.** (*usually cap.*) See **Second Coming.** [early ME < L *advent(us)* a coming to = *ad-* AD- + *ven-* (s. of *venīre* to come) + *-tus* suffix marking n. denoting action]

2. ambiguity (par. 4)
   a. expression
   b. uncertainty
   c. intention
   d. explicitness

am·bi·gu·i·ty (am′bə gyoo′i tē), *n., pl.* **-ties. 1.** doubtfulness or uncertainty in meaning or intention: *to speak with ambiguity.* **2.** the condition of admitting more than one meaning. **3.** an equivocal or ambiguous expression, term, etc. [late ME *ambiguite* < L *ambiguitāt-* (s. of *ambiguitās*) = *ambigu-* (see AMBIGUOUS) + *-itāt- -ITY*] —**Syn. 1.** vagueness. **2.** equivocation. —**Ant. 1.** explicitness.

3. alleviate (par. 6)
   a. relieve
   b. release
   c. endure
   d. make easier

al·le·vi·ate (ə lē′vē āt′), *v.t.,* **-at·ed, -at·ing.** to make easier to endure; lessen; mitigate: *to alleviate sorrow; to alleviate pain.* [< LL *alleviāt(us)* (ptp. of *alleviāre*) = *al-* AL- + *levi(s)* light, not heavy + *-ātus* -ATE¹] —**al·le′vi·a′-tor,** *n.* —**Syn.** lighten, diminish, abate, relieve, assuage.

4. encroach (par. 6)
   a. to limit
   b. to trespass on property
   c. to trespass on the rights of another
   d. to seize

en·croach (en krōch′), *v.i.* **1.** to advance beyond proper limits; make gradual inroads. **2.** to trespass upon the property, domain, or rights of another, esp. stealthily or by gradual advances. [ME *encroche(n)* < OF *encrochie(r)* (to) hook in, seize = *en-* EN-¹ + *croc* hook < Gmc; see CROOK] —**en·croach′er,** *n.* —**Syn. 1, 2.** See **trespass.**

5. subtlety (par. 9)
   a. skills to be learned
   b. ideas that are difficult to detect
   c. devious problems
   d. fine distinctions

sub·tle (sŭt′l) *adj.* **-tler, -tlest. 1. a.** So slight as to be difficult to detect. **b.** Not obvious; abstruse: *a subtle problem.* **2.** Able to make fine distinctions; keen: *a subtle mind.* **3. a.** Skillful; clever. **b.** Sly; devious. [Middle English *subtil,* thin, fine, clever, from Old French, from Latin *subtīlis,* thin, fine.] —**sub′tle·ness** *n.* —**sub′tly** *adv.*
sub·tle·ty (sŭt′l-tē) *n., pl.* **-ties. 1.** The quality of being subtle. **2.** Something subtle, esp. a fine distinction.

DISCUSSION

1. The author states that men and women today need inner strength to carry them through the daily pressures. What is inner strength? How does one acquire it?
2. Kids of the upper classes counteract TV by being involved in real events. Is there a way this could also be accomplished amoung children of the middle class and from poor families?
3. The article emphasizes that TV presents everything in thirty-minute segments where all problems are resolved. Can you think of creative ways to change TV programming both in content and time segments?

Difficulty level: C

25. Mythology

Edith Hamilton

Greek and Roman mythology is quite generally supposed   1
to show us the way the human race thought and felt untold ages ago. Through it, according to this view, we can retrace the path from civilized man who lives so far from nature, to man who lived in close companionship with nature; and the real interest of the myths is that they lead us back to a time when the world was young and people had a connection with the earth, with trees and seas and flowers and hills, unlike anything we ourselves can feel. When the stories were being shaped, we are given to understand, little distinction had as yet been made between the real and the unreal. The imagination was vividly alive and not checked by the reason, so that anyone in the woods might see through the trees a fleeing nymph, or bending over a clear pool to drink behold in the depths a naiad's face.

The prospect of traveling back to this delightful state of   2
things is held out by nearly every writer who touches upon classical mythology, above all the poets. In that infinitely remote time primitive man could

> Have sight of Proteus rising from the sea;
> Or hear old Triton blow his wreathèd horn.

And we for a moment can catch, through the myths he made, a glimpse of that strangely and beautifully animated world.

But a very brief consideration of the ways of uncivilized   3
people everywhere and in all ages is enough to prick that romantic bubble. Nothing is clearer than the fact that primitive man, whether in New Guinea today or eons ago in the prehistoric wilderness, is not and never has been a creature who peoples his world with bright fancies and lovely visions. Horrors lurked in the primeval forest, not nymphs and naiads. Terror lived there, with its close attendant, Magic, and its most common defense, Human Sacrifice. Mankind's chief hope of escaping the wrath of whatever divinities were then abroad lay

in some magical rite, senseless but powerful, or in some offering made at the cost of pain and grief.

This dark picture is worlds apart from the stories of classical mythology. The study of the way early man looked at his surroundings does not get much help from the Greeks. How briefly the anthropologists treat the Greek myths is noteworthy.

Of course the Greeks too had their roots in the primeval slime. Of course they too once lived a savage life, ugly and brutal. But what the myths show is how high they had risen above the ancient filth and fierceness by the time we have any knowledge of them. Only a few traces of that time are to be found in the stories.

We do not know when these stories were first told in their present shape; but whenever it was, primitive life had been left far behind. The myths as we have them are the creation of great poets. The first written record of Greece is the *Iliad*. Greek mythology begins with Homer, generally believed to be not earlier than a thousand years before Christ. The *Iliad* is, or contains, the oldest Greek literature; and it is written in a rich and subtle and beautiful language which must have had behind it centuries when men were striving to express themselves with clarity and beauty, an indisputable proof of civilization. The tales of Greek mythology do not throw any clear light upon what early mankind was like. They do throw an abundance of light upon what early Greeks were like—a matter, it would seem, of more importance to us, who are their descendants intellectually, artistically, and politically, too. Nothing we learn about them is alien to ourselves.

People often speak of "the Greek miracle." What the phrase tries to express is the new birth of the world with the awakening of Greece. "Old things are passed away; behold, all things are become new." Something like that happened in Greece. Why it happened, or when, we have no idea at all. We know only that in the earliest Greek poets a new point of view dawned, never dreamed of in the world before them, but never to leave the world after them. With the coming forward of Greece, mankind became the center of the universe, the most important thing in it. This was a revolution in thought. Human beings had counted for little heretofore. In Greece man first realized what mankind was.

The Greeks made their gods in their own image. That had entered the mind of man before. Until then, gods had had no semblance of reality. They were unlike all living things. In Egypt, a towering colossus, immobile, beyond the power of the imagination to endow with movement, as fixed in the stone as the tremendous temple columns, a representation of the human shape deliberately made unhuman. Or a rigid figure, a woman with a cat's head suggesting inflexible, inhuman cruelty. Or a monstrous mysterious sphinx, aloof from all that lives. In Mesopotamia, bas-reliefs of bestial shapes unlike any beast ever known, men with birds' heads and lions with bulls' heads and both with eagles' wings, creations of artists who were intent upon producing something never seen except in their own minds, the very consummation of unreality.

These and their like were what the pre-Greek world worshiped. One need only place beside them in imagination any Greek statue of a god, so normal and natural with all its beauty, to percieve what a new idea had come into the world. With its coming, the universe became rational.

Saint Paul said the invisible must be understood by the visible. That was not a Hebrew idea, it was Greek. In Greece alone in the ancient world people were preoccupied with the visible; they were finding the satisfaction of their desires in what was actually in the world around them. The sculptor watched the athletes contending in the games and he felt that nothing he could imagine would be as beautiful as those strong young bodies. So he made his statue of Apollo. The storyteller found Hermes among the people he passed in the street. He saw the god "like a young man at that age when youth is loveliest," as Homer says. Greek artists and poets realized how splendid a man could be, straight and swift and strong. He was the fulfillment of their search for beauty. They had no wish to create some fantasy shaped in their own minds. All the art and all the thought of Greece centered in human beings.

Human gods naturally made heaven a pleasantly familiar place. The Greeks felt at home in it. They knew just what the divine inhabitants did there, what they ate and drank and where they banqueted and how thay amused themselves. Of course they were to be feared; they were very powerful and very dangerous when angry. Still, with proper care a man could be quite fairly at ease with them. He was even perfectly free to laugh at them. Zeus, trying to hide his love affairs from his wife and invariably shown up, was a capital figure of fun. The Greeks enjoyed him and liked him all the better for it. Hera was that stock character of comedy, the typical jealous wife, and her ingenious tricks to discomfit her husband and punish her rival, far from displeasing the Greeks, entertained them as much as Hera's modern counterpart does us today. Such stories made for a friendly feeling. Laughter in the presence of an Egyptian sphinx or an Assyrian bird-beast was inconceivable; but it was perfectly natural in Olympus, and it made the gods companionable.

On earth, too, the deities were exceedingly and humanly attractive. In the form of lovely youths and maidens they peopled the woodland, the forest, the rivers, the sea, in harmony with the fair earth and the bright waters.

That is the miracle of Greek mythology—a humanized world, men freed from the paralyzing fear of an omnipotent Unknown. The terrifying incomprehensibilities which were worshiped elsewhere, and the fearsome spirits with which earth, air and sea swarmed, were banned from Greece. It may seem odd to say that the men who made the myths disliked the irrational and had a love for facts; but it is true, no matter how wildly fantastic some of the stories are. Anyone who reads them with attention discovers that even the most nonsensical take place in a world which is essentially rational and matter-of-fact. Hercules, whose life was one long combat against preposterous monsters, is always said to have had his home in the city of Thebes. The exact spot where Aphrodite was born of the foam could be visited by any ancient tourist; it was just offshore from the island of Cythera. The winged steed Pegasus, after skimming the air all day, went every night to a comfortable stable in Corinth. A familiar local habitation gave reality to all the mythical beings. If the mixture seems childish, consider how reassuring and how sensible the solid background is as compared with the Genie who comes from nowhere when Aladdin rubs the lamp and, his task accomplished, returns to nowhere.

The terrifying irrational has no place in classical mythology. Magic, so powerful in the world before and after Greece, is almost nonexistent. There are no men and only two women with dreadful, supernatural powers. The demoniac wizards and the hideous old witches who haunted Europe and America, too, up to quite recent years, play no part at all in the stories. Circe and Medea are the only witches and they are young and of surpassing beauty—delightful, not horrible. Astrology, which has flourished from the days of ancient Babylon down to today, is completely absent from classical Greece. There are many stories about the stars, but not a trace of the idea that they influence men's lives. Astronomy is what the Greek mind finally made out of the stars. Not a single story has a magical priest who is terribly to be feared because he knows ways of winning over the gods or alienating them. The priest is rarely seen and is never of importance. In the *Odyssey* when a priest and poet fall on their knees before *Odysseus*, praying him to spare their lives, the hero kills the priest without a thought, but saves the poet. Homer says that he felt awe to slay a man who had been taught his divine art by the gods. Not the priest, but the poet, had influence with heaven—and no one was ever afraid of a poet. Ghosts, too, which have played so large and so fearsome a part in other lands, never appear on earth in any Greek story. The Greeks were not afraid of the dead—"the piteous dead," the *Odyssey* calls them.

The world of Greek mythology was not a place of terror for the human spirit. It is true that the gods were disconcertingly incalculable. One could never tell where Zeus's thunderbolt would strike. Nevertheless, the whole divine company, with a very few and for the most part not important exceptions, were entrancingly beautiful with a human beauty, and nothing humanly beautiful is really terrifying. The early Greek mythologists transformed a world full of fear into a world full of beauty.

This bright picture has its dark spots. The change came about slowly and was never quite completed. The gods-become-human were for a long time a very slight improvement upon their worshipers. They were incomparably lovelier and more powerful, and they were of course immortal; but they often acted in a way no decent man or woman would. In the *Iliad* Hector is nobler by far than any of the heavenly beings, and Andromache infinitely to be preferred to Athena or Aphrodite. Hera from first to last is a goddess on a very low level of humanity. Almost every one of the radiant divinities

14

15

16

could act cruelly or contemptibly. A very limited sense of right and wrong prevailed in Homer's heaven, and for a long time after.

Other dark spots too stand out. There are traces of time when there were beast-gods. The satyrs are goat-men and the centaurs are half man, half horse. Hera is often called "cow-faced," as if the adjective had somehow stuck to her through all her changes from a divine cow to the very human queen of heaven. There are also stories which point back clearly to a time when there was human sacrifice. But what is astonishing is not that bits of savage belief were left here and there. The strange thing is that they are so few. 17

Of course the mythical monster is present in any number of shapes, 18

> Gorgons and hydras and chimaeras dire,

but they are there only to give the hero his meed of glory. What could a hero do in a world without them? They are always overcome by him. The great hero of mythology, Hercules, might be an allegory of Greece herself. He fought the monsters and freed the earth from them just as Greece freed the earth from the monstrous idea of the unhuman supreme over the human.

Greek mythology is largely made up of stories about gods and goddesses, but it must not be read as a kind of Greek Bible, an account of the Greek religion. According to the most modern idea, a real myth has nothing to do with religion. It is an explanation of something in nature: how, for instance, any and everything in the universe came into existence: men, animals, this or that tree or flower, the sun, the moon, the stars, storms, eruptions, earthquakes, all that is and all that happens. Thunder and lightning are caused when Zeus hurls his thunderbolt. A volcano erupts because a terrible creature is imprisoned in the mountain and every now and then struggles to get free. The Dipper, the constellation called also the Great Bear, does not set below the horizon because a goddess once was angry at it and decreed that it should never sink into the sea. Myths are early science, the result of men's first trying to explain what they saw around them. But there are many so-called myths which explain nothing at all. These tales are pure entertainment, the sort of thing people would tell each other on a long winter's evening. The story of Pygmalion and Galatea is an example; it has no conceivable connection with any event in nature. Neither has the Quest of the Golden Fleece, nor Orpheus and Eurydice, nor many another. This fact is now generally accepted; and we do not have to try to find in every mythological heroine the moon or the dawn and in every hero's life a sun myth. The stories are early literature as well as early science. 19

But religion is there, too. In the background, to be sure, but nevertheless plain to see. From Homer through the tragedians and even later, there is a deepening realization of what human beings need and what they must have in their gods. 20

Zeus the Thunderer was, it seems certain, once a rain-god. He was supreme even over the sun, because rocky Greece 21 needed rain more than sunshine and the God of Gods would be the one who could give the precious water of life to his worshipers. But Homer's Zeus is not a fact of nature. He is a person living in a world where civilization has made an entry, and of course he has a standard of right and wrong. It is not very high, certainly, and seems chiefly applicable to others, not to himself; but he does punish men who lie and break their oaths; he is angered by any ill treatment of the dead; and he pities and helps old Priam when he goes as a suppliant to Achilles. In the *Odyssey*, he has reached a higher level. The swineherd there says that the needy and the stranger are from Zeus and he who fails to help them sins against Zeus himself. Hesiod, not much later than the *Odyssey* if at all, says of a man who does evil to the suppliant and the stranger, or who wrongs orphan children, "with that man Zeus is angry."

Then Justice became Zeus's companion. That was a new 22 idea. The buccaneering chieftains in the *Iliad* did not want justice. They wanted to be able to take whatever they chose because they were strong and they wanted a god who was on the side of the strong. But Hesiod, who was a peasant living in a poor man's world, knew that the poor must have a just god. He wrote, "Fishes and beasts and fowls of the air devour one another. But to man, Zeus has given justice. Beside Zeus on his throne Justice has her seat." These passages show that the great and bitter needs of the helpless were reaching up to heaven and changing the god of the strong into the protector of the weak.

So, back of the stories of an amorous Zeus and a cowardly 23 Zeus and a ridiculous Zeus, we can catch sight of another Zeus coming into being, as men grew continually more conscious of what life demanded of them and what human beings needed in the god they worshiped. Gradually this Zeus displaced the others, until he occupied the whole scene. At last he became, in the words of Dio Chrysostom, who wrote during the second century A.D.: "Our Zeus, the giver of every good gift, the common father and saviour and guardian of mankind."

The *Odyssey* speaks of "the divine for which all men long," 24 and hundreds of years later Aristotle wrote, "Excellence, much labored for by the race of mortals." The Greeks from the earliest mythologists on had a perception of the divine and the excellent. Their longing for them was great enough to make them never give up laboring to see them clearly, until at last the thunder and lightning were changed into the Universal Father.

COMPREHENSION

1. The main idea in this selection is that
    a. Greek mythology should be read as a Greek Bible
    b. Greek mythology is only entertaining literature about imagined people and events
    c. Greek mythology describes the early scientific knowledge and literature of the early Greeks
    d. Greek mythology is valuable because it provides a broad view of early Greek lifestyle

2. At the time Greek mythology was created, the Greeks were
   a. uncivilized
   b. mostly concerned with astronomy
   c. artistically and intellectually sophisticated
   d. exploring the existence of one all-powerful God
3. The "Greek Miracle" actually refers to
   a. a revolution in which the Greeks took over all mankind
   b. a point of view in which mankind is the center of the universe
   c. the destruction of the old civilization
   d. a religion requiring worship of various animal figures
4. Greek gods and goddesses
   a. were faultless
   b. were given many human traits
   c. resembled Egyptian gods
   d. never appeared on earth
5. The changes in Zeus can be attributed to
   a. men growing more conscious of the demands of life and of what they needed in a god
   b. his wife Hera's jealousy
   c. Hesiod saying that the poor needed a god
   d. the fact that Zeus was displaced by other gods

VOCABULARY

Directions: *The following terms from selection 25 cannot be clearly determined from the context. Using the dictionary entries, select the appropriate definition of the term as it is used in the reading selection.*

1. nymph (par. 1)
   a. young insect
   b. insect that lives in the woods
   c. female spirit of the woods
   d. stage of insect development

   nymph (nĭmf) *n.* **1.** *Gk. & Rom. Myth.* One of the female spirits dwelling in woodlands and waters. **2.** A young, incompletely developed form of certain insects, such as the grasshopper or dragonfly, that goes through a series of gradual changes before reaching the adult stage.

2. naiad (par. 1)
   a. mayfly
   b. acquatic creature
   c. water nymph
   d. insect

   nai·ad (nā'əd, -ăd', nī'-) *n., pl.* **-ads** or **-a·des** (-ə-dēz'). **1.** *Gk. Myth.* One of the nymphs living in and presiding over brooks, springs, streams, and fountains. **2.** The aquatic nymph of certain insects, such as the mayfly.

3. primeval (par. 3)
   a. unseen
   b. original
   c. young
   d. unspoiled

   pri·me·val (prī-mē'vəl) *adj.* Belonging to the first or earliest age or ages; original. [From Latin *prīmaevus*, young : *prīmus*, first + *aevum*, age.] **—pri·me'val·ly** *adv.*

4. omnipotent (par. 13)
   a. forceful
   b. godlike
   c. lacking authority
   d. having unlimited power

   om·nip·o·tent (ŏm-nĭp'ə-tənt) *adj.* Having unlimited or universal power, authority, or force. **—***n.* **Omnipotent.** God. [Middle English, from Old French, from Latin *omnipotēns* : *omni-*, all + *potēns*, powerful.] **—om·nip'o·tence** *n.* **—om·nip'o·tent·ly** *adv.*

5. incomprehensibilities
   (par. 13)
   a. things that are not
      understood
   b. misunderstandings
   c. understandings
   d. ideas that are not
      respected

in·com·pre·hen·si·ble (ĭn-kŏm′prĭ-hĕn′sə-bəl, ĭn′kŏm-) *adj.* Incapable of being understood or comprehended. —**in·com′pre·hen′si·bil′i·ty** or **in·com′pre·hen′si·ble·ness** *n.* —**in·com′pre·hen′si·bly** *adv.*

DISCUSSION

1. The author states that "Myths are early science, the result of men's first trying to explain what they saw around them." What are some possible myths that might occur as a result of modern man's attempt to explain what they see around them?
2. Can you think of stories that you heard as a child that explained occurrences in nature, for example, thunder? lightning? Did they have any value for you?
3. Do you see any similarities between the way the Greeks viewed their gods and they way modern man is involved in religion?

Difficulty level: C

26. Extrasensory Perception

James Geiwitz

Many people, including some psychologists, believe that it is possible for someone to form a percept using information that is not sensory; instead, they believe, the information comes from the minds of others, from the future, or from events so far away they could not possibly be sensed directly. Such phenomena are grouped under the label of *extrasensory perception* or *ESP*.

There are three subcategories of ESP. *Telepathy*, in which the source of input is the thought of another person, has also been called mind reading. *Clairvoyance* is the perception of events without direct sensory input. An example would be a parent who unexpectedly visualizes the death of a daughter in an automobile accident 2000 miles away, just as it is actually happening. *Precognition* is the perception of a future event— "fortune-telling." We will focus here on the evidence for and against mental telepathy, since it is easiest to study and has been the target of most research. The evidence on clairvoyance and precognition is similar and leads to almost identical conclusions.

Early scientific studies of ESP used a special deck of 25 picture cards, 5 each of a star, a circle, a square, a cross, and waves. In a telepathy experiment, one subject (the transmitter) goes through the deck and thinks about each card in turn; another subject (the receiver) tries to guess which picture is being transmitted. With five different pictures to choose from, subjects will guess right once out of five times by pure chance, they will average five correct guesses in the pack of 25. Those who *consistently* make more than five correct choices out of 25 are presumed to be telepathic.

There have been several reports of telepathic subjects. J. B. Rhine, a psychologist who spent most of his career at Duke University, tested many subjects who made a combined total of over 85,000 guesses, with an average "hit rate" of 7 out of 25. Another psychologist—who was determined to prove that ESP was nonsense—tested one subject 74 times with the 25-card deck, a total of 1850 trials. This subject averaged 18 hits per 25 guesses.

Recent studies have used similar procedures. At UCLA, Thelma Moss placed transmitter-subjects in in emotional situations. In one, the subject viewed scenes of Nazi concentration camps while listening to harsh music; in another, he viewed slides of nude women to the accompaniment of *The Stripper*. The reveiver was to describe his feelings, thoughts, and images; he was also shown two slides, and he was asked to choose the one the transmitter had seen. For example, if the transmitter had seen the nudes, the receiver would be shown a nude and one other, say, a scene of a concentration camp. He has a 50:50 chance of guessing correctly, so he must do consistently better than 50 percent to be presumed telepathic. In 16 experiments of this type, the results were statistically significant in ten.

Telepathy is widely studied in the Soviet Union, not just to determine whether it exists but to find out how it works. In one investigation of an experienced pair of subjects, the transmitter was asked to visualize a boxing match with the sender. He imagined either a 15-second round or a 45-second round. These were to correspond to dots and dashes in Morse code so that words or names could be sent. In this manner, the four-letter name "Ivan" was successfully transmitted from Leningrad to Moscow. (The receiver did not like this study, however, because once the transmitter punched him so hard, he fell off his chair!) In another experiment, a third person, also a receiver, tried to "bug" the communication between the other two, to intercept it en route. According to reports, he was successful. (Perhaps this is the reason for Russian interest in ESP.)

Now, with such evidence for ESP, why do so few psychologists—only 5 percent by one survey—accept the validity of ESP? There are a number of reasons. First, several ESP experiments have serious flaws in experimental procedure. In some of the early studies, the ESP deck of cards was manufactured in such a way that a faint imprint of the symbol could be seen on the back. In most experiments, there were no checks on recording errors, and it is quite probable that researchers who believed in ESP made a few errors, unintentionally, in the direction of their hypothesis. A "match" between two pictures, a common operational definition of successful telepathy, is a subjective judgment that also can be influenced by a strong belief in ESP. There have been a few cases of deliberate fakery, usually by someone claiming to have psychic powers. Sometimes "poor" data—chance guessing—

were not included in the final tabulations on the ground that the subject was tired.

Another reason psychologists are reluctant to accept ESP 8 as a valid phenomenon is that attempts to repeat successful experiments have generally been unsuccessful. I have personally designed and executed at least six ESP experiments, with no luck. Such failures, of course, are rarely if ever published. Even proponents of ESP complain that the phenomena are "here now" and "gone later." Until ESP can be demonstrated regularly, it will be suspect.

Similarly, the evidence for ESP in "natural" settings is 9 highly selective. For every case of someone correctly predicting an earthquake, there are thousands of cases where someone is convinced that an earthquake is about to occur, and nothing happens. And often "hunches" that are credited to ESP can be traced to normal, though, not always conscious, sensory processes. If your best friend from high school phones you just as you were thinking about her, maybe it's because you both read the same article about your hometown in the evening paper.

Finally, we must consider what it would mean if ESP were 10 accepted as valid. It would challenge the basic assumptions of every theory in psychology and, indeed, in other fields such as biology and physics as well. Scientists do not accept such challenges lightly, not without strong reason. So far the experimental evidence for ESP is not strong enough, by any means, and thus psychologists remain skeptical.

COMPREHENSION

1. This article is mainly about
   a. how to develop ESP
   b. who has done the most research in ESP
   c. experiments that have been done to study mental telepathy
   d. why mental telepathy does not exist
2. Extrasensory perception means that percepts are formed from
   a. information that is not sensory
   b. events that are in the future
   c. events that are far away
   d. the minds of others
3. The major difference between research on ESP in the United States and the Soviet Union is that the Russians
   a. use Morse code to test for ESP
   b. bug their own experiments
   c. study how ESP works as well as whether it exists
   d. use more than one "receiver" in their experiments
4. The most important reason why most psychologists do not accept ESP as a valid phenomenon is because
   a. there have been a few cases of deliberate fakery
   b. the results of unsuccessful experiments are rarely published
   c. sometimes "poor" data were not included in the final tabulations
   d. attempts to repeat successful experiments have been unsuccessful

5. The most important outcome if ESP were accepted as valid would be that
   a. the Russians would know how ESP works
   b. the basic assumption of every theory in psychology, biology, and physics would be challenged
   c. it would be difficult to figure out whether hunches should be credited to ESP or normal sensory experiences
   d. the communication industry would be seriously challenged

VOCABULARY

Directions: *The meaning of the following terms from selection 26 cannot be clearly determined from the context. Using the dictionary entries, select the appropriate definition of the term as it is used in the reading selection.*

1. presumed (par. 5)
   a. dared
   b. absent of proof
   c. taken for granted
   d. took advantage of

2. correspond (par. 6)
   a. communicate
   b. match
   c. equal
   d. respond

3. validity (par. 7)
   a. authority
   b. existence
   c. soundness
   d. state of being

4. imprint (par. 7)
   a. mark
   b. effect
   c. printer's note
   d. result

5. hypothesis (par. 7)
   a. fact
   b. purpose
   c. investigation
   d. theory

6. skeptical (par. 10)
   a. unconvinced
   b. easily persuaded
   c. eager to answer questions
   d. holding fundamental beliefs

pre·sume (prĭ-zoom′) v. **-sumed, -sum·ing.** —tr.v. **1.** To take for granted; assume to be true in the absence of proof to the contrary: *I presume the bus will be on time.* **2.** To give reasonable evidence for assuming; appear to prove. **3.** To venture; dare: *Children should not presume to contradict their elders.* —intr.v. To act overconfidently; take liberties. —**phrasal verb. presume on** (or **upon**). To take uncalled-for advantage of: *She presumed on his good nature.* [Middle English *presumen,* from Old French *presumer,* from Late Latin *praesūmere,* to venture, from Latin, to assume : *prae-,* before + *sūmere,* to take.] —**pre·sum′a·ble** (-zoo′mə-bəl) *adj.* —**pre·sum′a·bly** *adv.* —**pre·sum′er** *n.*

cor·re·spond (kôr′ə-spŏnd′, kŏr′-) *intr.v.* **-spond·ed, -spond·ing, -sponds. 1.** To be in agreement, harmony, or conformity; be consistent or compatible. **2.** To be similar, parallel, equivalent, or equal in character, quantity, origin, structure, or function. Used with *to: English "navel" corresponds to Greek "omphalos."* **3.** To communicate by letter, usually over a period of time. —See Synonyms at **agree.** [Old French *correspondre,* from Medieval Latin *correspondēre : com-,* together, mutually + *respondēre,* RESPOND.]

val·id (văl′ĭd) *adj.* **1.** Well-grounded on evidence or fact; sound: *a valid objection.* **2.** Legally sound: *a valid passport.* [French *valide,* from Old French, from Latin *validus,* strong, effective, from *valēre,* to be strong.] —**va·lid′i·ty** (və-lĭd′ə-tē) or **va′lid·ness** *n.* —**va′lid·ly** *adv.*
   Syns: **valid, cogent, solid, sound** *adj.* Core meaning: Based on good judgment, reasoning, or evidence (*a valid argument*).

¹**im·print** \im-′print, ′im-ˌ\ *vt* **1** : to mark by or as if by pressure : IMPRESS **2** : to fix indelibly or permanently (as on the memory)
²**im·print** \′im-ˌprint\ *n* [MF *empreinte,* fr. fem. of *empreint,* pp. of *empreindre* to imprint, fr. L *imprimere*] : something imprinted or printed: as **a** : a mark or depression made by pressure <the fossil ~ of a dinosaur's foot> **b** : a publisher's name often with address and date of publication printed at the foot of a title page **c** : an indelible distinguishing effect or influence <their work bears a sort of regional ~ —Malcolm Cowley>

hy·poth·e·sis (hī-pŏth′ĭ-sĭs) *n., pl.* **-ses** (-sēz′). **1.** An explanation that accounts for a set of facts and that can be tested by further investigation; theory. **2.** Something that is taken to be true for the purpose of argument or investigation; assumption. [Late Latin, from Greek *hupothesis,* proposal, supposition, from *hupotithenai,* to propose : *hupo-,* under + *tithenai,* to place.]

skep·ti·cal (skep′ti kəl), *adj.* **1.** inclined to skepticism; having doubt. **2.** showing doubt: *a skeptical smile.* **3.** denying or questioning the tenets of a religion. **4.** (*cap.*) of or pertaining to Skeptics or Skepticism. Also, **sceptical.** —**skep′ti·cal·ly,** *adv.* —**Syn. 1.** skeptic. **3.** unbelieving.

DISCUSSION

1. What is your position on ESP? Do you accept or reject the existence of telepathy, clairvoyance, and precognition?
2. What is the significance in the focus of the Russian experiments? What are the implications of their focus?
3. Which experiment described in the article sounds most convincing to you? Why?

Difficulty level: C

27. Verbal Taboo

S. I. Hayakawa

In every language there seem to be certain "unmentionables"—words of such strong affective connotations that they cannot be used in polite discourse. In English, the first of these to come to mind are, of course, words dealing with excretion and sex. We ask movie ushers and filling-station attendants where the "lounge" or "rest room" is, although we have no intention of lounging or resting. "Powder room" is another euphemism for the same facility, also known as "toilet," which itself is an earlier euphemism. Indeed, it is impossible in polite society to state, without having to resort to babytalk or a medical vocabulary, what a "rest room" is for. (It is where you "wash your hands.")

Money is another subject about which communication is in some ways inhibited. It is all right to mention *sums* of money, such as "ten thousand dollars" or "two dollars and fifty cents." But it is considered in bad taste to inquire directly into other people's financial affairs, unless such an inquiry is really necessary in the course of business. When creditors send bills, they practically never mention money, although that is what they are writing about. There are many circumlocutions: "We beg to call your attention to what might be an oversight on your part." "We would appreciate your early attention to this matter." "May we look forward to an early remittance?"

The fear of death carries over, quite understandably in view of the widespread confusion of symbols with things symbolized, into fear of the *words* having to do with death. Many people, therefore, instead of saying "died," substitute such expressions as "passed away," "gone to his reward," "departed," and "gone west." In Japanese, the word for death, *"shi,"* happens to have the same pronunciation as the word for the number four. This coincidence results in many linguistically awkward situations, since people avoid *"shi"* in the discussion of numbers and prices, and use *"yon,"* a word of different origin, instead.

Words having to do with anatomy and sex—and words even vaguely suggesting anatomical or sexual matters—have, especially in American culture, remarkable affective connotations. Ladies of the last century could not bring themselves to say "breast" or "leg"—not even of chicken—so that the terms "white meat" and "dark meat" were substituted. It was thought inelegant to speak of "going to bed," and "to retire" was used instead. In rural America there are many euphemisms for the word "bull"; among them are "he cow," "cow critter," "male cow," "gentleman cow." But Americans are not alone in their delicacy about such matters. When D. H. Lawrence's first novel, *The White Peacock* (1911), was published, the author was widely and vigorously criticized for having used (in innocuous context) the word "stallion." "Our hearts are warm, our bellies are full," was changed to "Our hearts are warm, and we are full," in a 1962 presentation of the Rodgers and Hammerstein musical *Carousel* before the British Royal Family.

5 These verbal taboos, though sometimes amusing, also produce serious problems—since they prevent frank discussion of sexual matters. Social workers, with whom the writer has discussed this question, report that young people of junior high school and high school age who contract venereal disease, become pregnant out of wedlock, and get into other serious trouble of this kind, are almost always profoundly ignorant of the most elementary facts about sex and procreation. Their ignorance is apparently due to the fact that neither they nor their parents have a vocabulary in which to discuss such matters: the nontechincal vocabulary of sex is to them too coarse and shocking to be used, while the technical, medical vocabulary is unknown to them. The social workers find, therefore, that the first step in helping these young people is usually linguistic: they have to be taught a vocabulary in which they can talk about their problems before they can be helped further.

6 The stronger verbal taboos have, however, a genuine social value. When we are extremely angry and we feel the need of expressing our anger in violence, the uttering of these forbidden words provides us with a relatively harmless verbal substitute for going berserk and smashing furniture; that is, they act as a kind of safety valve in our moments of crisis.

7 It is difficult to explain why some words should have such powerful affective connotations while others with the same informative connotations do not. Some of our verbal reticences, especially the religious ones, have the authority of the Bible: "Thou shalt not take the name of the Lord thy God in vain; for the Lord will not hold him guiltless that taketh his name in vain" (Exodus 21:7). "Gee," "gee whiz," "gosh almighty," "gee whillikens," and "gosh darn" are ways of avoiding saying "Jesus," "God Almighty," and "God damn"; and carrying the biblical injunction one step further, we also avoid taking the name of the Devil in vain by means of such expressions as "the deuce," "the dickens," and "Old Nick." It appears that among all the people of the world, among the civilized as well as the primitive, there is a feeling that the names of the gods are too holy, and the names of evil spirits too terrifying, to be spoken lightly.

8 The primitive confusion of word with thing, of symbol with thing symbolized, manifests itself in some parts of the world in a belief that the name of a person is *part of* that person. To know someone's name, therefore, is to have power over

him. Because of this belief, it is customary among some peoples for children to be given at birth a "real name" known only to the parents and never used, as well as a nickname or public name to be called by in society. In this way the child is protected from being put in someone's power. The story of Rumplestiltskin is a European illustration of this belief in the power of names.

COMPREHENSION

1. This selection is primarily
   a. a definition of euphemism
   b. a discussion of the misuse of certain words in American English
   c. an explanation of our reluctance to use certain words in polite conversation
   d. an analysis of the social value of verbal taboos
2. Verbal taboos often produce serious problems because they
   a. encourage young people to use vulgar language
   b. tend to encourage promiscuity
   c. result in ignorance of sexual matters among the young
   d. interfere with freedom of speech
3. Strong verbal taboos have genuine social value because they
   a. reduce swearing and cursing
   b. encourage communication
   c. lead to violence
   d. act as a kind of safety valve in moments of crisis
4. The cause of verbal reticences such as the reluctance to use religious terms, can be eventually traced to
   a. fear
   b. primitive cultures
   c. guilt
   d. good taste
5. It is customary in some cultures to keep a child's name a secret because
   a. there is a confusion about the relationship between a word and an object or person
   b. demons may use it to trap him or her
   c. it is believed that knowing a person's name gives power over him or her
   d. the real name is never used in society anyway

VOCABULARY

Directions: *The meaning of the following terms from selection 27 cannot be clearly determined from the context. Using the dictionary entries, select the appropriate definition of the term as it is used in the reading selection.*

1. connotations (par. 1)
   a. secondary meanings
   b. logic
   c. comprehension
   d. intention

con·no·ta·tion (kon/ə tā/shən), *n.* **1.** an act or instance of connoting. **2.** the associated or secondary meaning of a word or expression; implication: A *possible connotation of "home" is "a place of warmth, comfort, and affection."* Cf. **denotation** (def. 1). **3.** *Logic.* the set of attributes constituting the meaning of a term; comprehension; intension. [< ML *connotā-tiōn-* (s. of *connotātiō*) = *connotāt(us)* (ptp. of *connotāre*; see CONNOTE, -ATE¹) + *-iōn-* -ION] —**con·no·ta·tive** (kon/ə tā/-tiv, kə nō/tə-), **con·no/tive,** *adj.* —**con/no·ta·tive·ly, con·no/tive·ly,** *adv.*

2. discourse (par. 1)
   a. formal discussion
   b. sermon
   c. treatise
   d. conversation
3. euphemism (par. 1)
   a. harsh statement
   b. substituted expression
   c. blunt statement
   d. offensive expression
4. circumlocutions (par. 2)
   a. around
   b. roundabout expressions
   c. indirect
   d. words
5. procreation (par. 5)
   a. generation
   b. offspring
   c. bring
   d. produce offspring
6. reticences (par. 7)
   a. silences
   b. reservations
   c. disposed
   d. reserved

dis·course (*n.* dis′kōrs, -kôrs, dis kōrs′, -kôrs′; *v.* dis-kōrs′, -kôrs′), *n., v.,* **-coursed, -cours·ing.** —*n.* **1.** communication of thought by words; talk; conversation. **2.** a formal discussion of a subject in speech or writing, as a dissertation, treatise, sermon, etc. —*v.i.* **3.** to communicate thoughts orally; talk; converse. **4.** to treat a subject formally in speech or writing. —*v.t.* **5.** to give forth (musical sounds). [ME *discours* (< ML *discursus*) (cp. by influence of ME *cours* course), LL: conversation, L: a running to and fro (n. use of ptp. of *discurrere*) = dis- DIS-¹ + *cursus* (see COURSE)] —**dis·cours′er,** *n.*

eu·phe·mism (yōō′fə miz′əm), *n.* **1.** the substitution of a mild, indirect, or vague expression for one thought to be offensive, harsh, or blunt. **2.** the expression so substituted: *"To pass away" is a euphemism for "to die."* [< Gk *euphēmism(ós)* the use of words of good omen = *eu-* EU- + *phēm(ē)* speaking, fame + *-ismos* -ISM] —**eu′phe·mist,** *n.* —**eu·phe·mis′tic, eu·phe·mis′ti·cal,** *adj.* —**eu·phe·mis′ti·cal·ly,** *adv.*

cir·cum·lo·cu·tion (sûr′kəm lō kyōō′shən), *n.* **1.** a roundabout or indirect way of speaking; the use of superfluous words. **2.** a roundabout expression. [< L *circumlocūtiōn-* (s. of *circumlocūtiō*). See CIRCUM-, LOCUTION] —**cir·cum·loc·u·to·ry** (sûr′kəm lok′yə tōr′ē, -tôr′ē), *adj.*

pro·cre·ate (prō′krē āt′), *v.,* **-at·ed, -at·ing.** —*v.t.* **1.** to beget or generate (offspring). **2.** to produce; bring into being. —*v.i.* **3.** to beget offspring. **4.** to produce; bring into being. [< L *prōcreāt(us),* ptp. of *prōcreāre* to breed] —**pro′cre·a′tion,** *n.* —**pro′cre·a′tive,** *adj.* —**pro′cre·a′tive·ness,** *n.* —**pro′cre·a′tor,** *n.*

ret·i·cent (ret′i sənt), *adj.* disposed to be silent; reserved. [< L *reticent-* (s. of *reticēns,* prp. of *reticēre* to be silent) = re- RE- + *tac(ēre)* (to) be silent + *-ent-* -ENT] —**ret′i·cence, ret′i·cen·cy,** *n.* —**ret′i·cent·ly,** *adv.*

DISCUSSION

1. Do you feel that in the "long run" verbal taboos are useful in society? Explain why or why not.
2. Do you use euphemism as a verbal substitute for the violent expression of anger? What euphemisms do you use? Why do they work for you?
3. The author states that verbal taboos often cause problems as, for example, in the discussion of sexual matters. What other problems do you think might arise as a result of verbal taboos?

Selections for Further Reading

28. Our Enemy, the Cat

Alan Devoe

We tie bright ribbons around their necks, and occasionally little tinkling bells, and we affect to think that they are as sweet and vapid as the coy name "kitty" by which we call them would imply. It is a curious illusion. For, purring beside our fireplaces and pattering along our back fences, we have got a wild beast as uncowed and uncorrupted as any under heaven.

It is five millenniums since we snared the wild horse and broke his spirit to our whim, and for centuries beyond counting we have been able to persuade the once-free dog to fawn and cringe and lick our hands. But a man must be singularly blind with vanity to fancy that in the three — ten? — thousand years during which we have harbored cats beneath our rooftrees, we have succeeded in reducing them to any such insipid estate. It is not a "pet" (that most degraded of creatures) that we have got in our house, whatever we may like to think. It is a wild beast; and there adheres to its sleek fur no smallest hint of the odor of humanity.

It would be a salutary thing if those who write our simpering verses and tales about "tabby-sit-by-the-fire" could bring themselves to see her honestly, to look into her life with eyes unblurred by wishful sentiment. It would be a good thing — to start at the beginning — to follow her abroad into the moonlight on one of those raw spring evenings when the first skunk-cabbages are thrusting their veined tips through the melting snow and when the loins of catdom are hot with lust.

The love-play of domestic creatures is mostly a rather comic thing, and loud are the superior guffaws of rustic humans to see the clumsy, fumbling antics that take place in the kennels and the stockpen. But the man had better not laugh who sees cats in their rut. He is looking upon something very like aboriginal passion, untainted by any of the overlaid refinements, suppressions, and modifications that have been acquired by most of mankind's beasts. The mating of cats has neither the pathetic clumsiness of dogs' nor the lumbering ponderousness of cattle's, but — conducted in a lonely secret place, away from human view — is marked by a quick concentrated intensity of lust that lies not far from the borderline of agony. The female, in the tense moment of the prelude, tears with her teeth at her mate's throat, and, as the climax of the creatures' frenzy comes, the lean silky-furred flanks quiver vibrantly as a taut wire. Then quietly, in the spring night, the two beasts go their ways.

It will be usually May before the kittens come; and that episode, too, will take place secretly, in its ancient feline fashion, where no maudlin human eye may see. Great is the pique in many a house when "pussy," with dragging belly and distended dugs, disappears one night—scorning the cushioned maternity-bed that has been prepared for her—and creeps on silent feet to the dankest cranny of the cellar, there in decent aloneness to void her blood and babies. She does not care, any more than a lynx does, or a puma, to be pried upon while she licks the birth-hoods from her squirming progeny and cleans away the membrane with her rough pink tongue.

A kitten is not a pretty thing at birth. For many days it is a wriggling mite of lumpy flesh and sinew, blind and unaware, making soft sucking noises with its wet, toothless mouth, and smelling of milk. Daily, hourly, the rough tongue of the tabby ministers to it in its helplessness, glossing the baby-fur with viscid spittle, licking away the uncontrolled dung, cleaning away the crumbly pellet of dried blood from its pointed ears. By that tenth or fourteenth day when its eyes wholly unseal, blue and weak in their newness, the infant cat is clean to immaculateness, and an inalienable fastidiousness is deep-lodged in its spirit.

It is now—when the kitten makes its first rushes and sallies from its birthplace, and, with extraordinary gymnastics of its chubby body, encounters chair-legs and human feet and other curious phenomena—that it elicits from man those particular expressions of gurgling delight which we reserve for very tiny fluffy creatures who act very comically. But the infant cat has no coy intent to be amusing. If he is comic, it is only because of the incongruity of so demure a look and so wild a heart. For in that furry head of his, grim and ancient urges are already dictating.

Hardly larger than a powder-puff, he crouches on the rug and watches a fleck of lint. His little blue eyes are bright, and presently his haunches tense and tremble. The tiny body shivers in an ague of excitement. He pounces, a little clumsily perhaps, and pinions the fleeting lint-fleck with his paws. In the fractional second of that lunge, the ten small needles of his claws have shot from their sheaths of flesh and muscle. It is a good game; but it is not an idle one. It is the kitten's introduction into the ancient ritual of the kill. Those queer little stiff-legged rushes and prancings are the heritage of an old death-dance, and those jerkings of his hind legs, as he rolls on his back, are the preparation for that day when—in desperate conflict with a bigger beast than himself—he will win the fight by the time-old feline technique of disembowelment. Even now, in his early infancy, he is wholly and inalienably a cat.

While he is still young he has already formulated his attitude toward the human race into whose midst he has been born. It is an attitude not easily described, but compounded of a great pride, a great reserve, a towering integrity. It is even to be fancied that there is something in it of a sort of bleak contempt. Solemnly the cat watches these great hulking two-legged creatures into whose strange tribe he has unaccountably quiet spirit—and in his feline heart is neither love nor gratitude. He learns to take the food which they give him, to relish the warmth and the comfort and the caresses which they can offer, but these proferments do not persuade his wild mistrustful heart to surrender itself. He will not sell himself, as a dog will, for a scrap of meat; he will not enter into an allegiance. He is unchangeably and incorruptibly a cat, and he will accommodate himself to the ways and spirit of mankind no more than the stern necessity of his unnatural environment requires.

Quietly he dozes by the fire or on a lap, and purrs in his happiness because he loves the heat. But let him choose to move, and if any human hand tries to restrain him for more than a moment he will struggle and unsheath his claws and lash out with a furious hate. Let a whip touch him and he will slink off in a sullen fury, uncowed and outraged and unrepenting. For the things which man gives to him are not so precious or essential that he will trade them for his birth-right, which is the right to be himself—a furred four-footed being of ancient lineage, loving silence and aloneness and the night, and esteeming the smell of rat's blood above any possible human excellence.

He may live for perhaps ten years; occasionally even for twenty. Year after year he drinks the daily milk that is put faithfully before him, dozes in laps whose contours please him, accepts with casual pleasure the rubbing of human fingers under his chin—and withdraws, in every significant hour of his life, as far away from human society as he is able. Far from the house, in a meadow or a woods if he can find one, he crouches immobile for hours, his lithe body flattened concealingly in the grass or ferns, and waits for prey.

With a single pounce he can break a rabbit's spine as though it were a brittle twig. When he has caught a tawny meadow-mouse or a mole, he has, too, the ancient cat-ecstasy of toying and playing with it, letting it die slowly, in a long agony, for his amusement. Sometimes, in a dim remembrance from the remote past of his race, he may bring home his kill; but mostly he returns to the house as neat and demure as when he left, with his chops licked clean of blood.

Immaculate, unobtrusive, deep withdrawn into himself, he passes through the long years of his enforced companionship with humanity. He takes from his masters (how absurd a word it is) however much they may care to give him; of himself he surrenders nothing. However often he be decked with ribbons and cuddled and petted and made much over, his cold pride never grows less, and his grave calm gaze—tinged perhaps with a gentle distaste—is never lighted by adoration. To the end he adores only his own gods, the gods of mating, of hunting, and of the lonely darkness.

One day, often with no forewarning whatever, he is gone from the house and never returns. He has felt the presaging shadow of death, and he goes to meet it in the old unchanging way of the wild—alone. A cat does not want to die with the smell of humanity in his nostrils and the noise of humanity in his delicate peaked ears. Unless death strikes very quickly and suddenly, he creeps away to where it is proper that a proud wild beast should die—not on one of man's rugs or cushions, but in a lonely quiet place, with his muzzle pressed against the cold earth.

29. Man and Animal: The City and the Hive

Susanne K. Langer

Despite man's zoological status, which I wholeheartedly accept, there is a deep gulf between the highest animal and the most primitive normal human being: a difference in mentality that is fundamental. It stems from the development of one new process in the human brain—a process that seems to be entirely peculiar to that brain: the use of *symbols for ideas*. By "symbols" I mean all kinds of signs that can be used and understood whether the things they refer to are there or not. The word "symbol" has, unfortunately, many different meanings for different people. Some people reserve it for mystic signs, like Rosicrucian symbols; some mean by it *significant images,* such as Keats' "Huge cloudy symbols of a high romance"; some use it quite the opposite way and speak of "mere symbols," meaning empty gestures, signs that have lost their meanings; and some, notably logicians, use the term for mathematical signs, marks that constitute a code, a brief, concise language. In their sense, ordinary words are symbols, too. Ordinary language is a symbolism.

When I say that the distinctive function of the human brain is the use of symbols, I mean any and all of these kinds. They are all different from signs that animals use. Animals interpret signs, too, but only as pointers to actual things and events, cues to action or expectation, threats and promises, landmarks and earmarks in the world. Human beings use such signs, too, but above all they use symbols—especially words —to think and talk about things that are neither present nor expected. The words convey *ideas,* that may or may not have counterparts in actuality. This power of thinking *about* things expresses itself in language, imagination, and speculation—the chief products of human mentality that animals do not share.

Language, the most versatile and indispensable of all symbolisms, has put its stamp on all our mental functions, so that I think they always differ from even their closest analogues in animal life. Language has invaded our feeling and dreaming and action, as well as our reasoning, which is really a product of it. The greatest change wrought by language is the increased scope of awareness in speech-gifted beings. An animal's awareness is always of things in its own place and life. In human awareness, the present, actual situation is often the least part. We have not only memories and expectations; we have *a past* in which we locate our memories, and *a future* that vastly overreaches our own anticipations. Our past is a story, our future a piece of imagination. Likewise our ambient is a place in a wider, symbolically conceived place, the universe. We live in *a world.*

This difference of mentality between man and animal seems to me to make a cleft between them almost as great as the division between animals and plants. There is continuity between the orders, but the division is real nevertheless. Human life differs radically from animal life. By virtue of our incomparably wider awareness of our power of envisagement of things and events beyond any actual perception, we have acquired needs and aims that animals do not have; and even the most savage human society, having to meet those needs and implement those aims, is not really comparable to any animal society. The two may have some analogous functions, but the essential structure must be different, because man and beast live differently in every way.

Probably the profoundest difference between human and animal needs is made by one piece of human awareness, one fact that is not present to animals, because it is never learned in any direct experience: that is our foreknowledge of death. The fact that we ourselves must die is not a simple and isolated fact. It is built on a wide survey of facts that discloses the structure of history as a succession of overlapping brief lives, the patterns of youth and age, growth and decline; and above all that, it is built on the logical insight that *one's own life is a case in point.* Only a creature that can think symbolically *about* life can conceive of its own death. Our knowledge of death is part of our knowledge of life.

What, then, do we—all of us—know about life?

Every life that we know is generated from other life. Each living thing springs from some other living thing or things. Its birth is a process of new individuation, in a life stream whose beginning we do not know.

Individuation is a word we do not often meet. We hear about individuality, sometimes spoken in praise, sometimes as an excuse for someone's being slightly crazy. We hear and read about "the individual," a being that is forever adjusting, like a problem child, to something called "society." But how does individuality arise? What makes an individual? A fundamental, biological process of *individuation*, that marks the life of every stock, plant or animal. Life is a series of individuations, and these can be of various sorts, and reach various degrees.

Most people would agree, offhand, that every creature lives its life and then dies. This might, indeed, be called a truism. But, like some other truisms, it is not true. The lowest forms of life, such as the amoebae, normally (that is, barring accidents) do not die. When they grow very large and might be expected to lay eggs, or in some other way raise a family, they do no such thing; they divide, and make two small ones ready to grow. Well now, where is the old one? It did not die. But it is gone. Its individuation was only an episode in the life of the stock, a phase, a transient form that changed again. Amoebae are individuated in space—they move and feed as independent, whole organisms—but in time they are not self-identical individuals. They do not generate young ones while they themselves grow old; they grow old and *become* young ones.

All the higher animals, however, are final individuations that end in death. They spring from a common stock, but they do not merge back into it. Each one is an end. Somewhere on its way toward death it usually produces a new life to succeed it, but its own story is finished by death.

That is our pattern, too. Each human individual is a culmination of an inestimably long line—its ancestry—and each is destined to die. The living stock is like a palm tree, a trunk composed of its own past leaves. Each leaf springs from the trunk, unfolds, grows, and dies off; its past is incorporated in the trunk, where new life has usually arisen from it. So there constantly are ends, but the stock lives on, and each leaf has that whole life behind it.

The momentous difference between us and our animal cousins is that they do not know they are going to die. Animals spend their lives avoiding death, until it gets them. They do not know it is going to. Neither do they know that they are a part of a greater life, but pass on the torch without knowing. Their aim, then, is simply to keep going, to function, to escape troubles, to live from moment to moment in an endless Now.

Our power of symbolic conception has given us each a glimpse of himself as one final individuation from the great human stock. We do not know when or what the end will be, but we know that there will be one. We also envisage a past and future, a stretch of time so vastly longer than any creature's memory, and a world so much richer than any world of sense, that it makes our time in that world seem infinitesimal. This is the price of the great gift of symbolism.

In the face of such uncomfortable prospects (probably conceived long before the dawn of any religious ideas), human beings have evolved aims different from those of any other creatures. Since we cannot have our fill of existence by going on and on, we want to have *as much life as possible* in our short span. If our individuation must be brief, we want to make it complete; so we are inspired to think, act, dream our desires, create things, express our ideas, and in all sorts of ways make up by concentration what we cannot have by length of days. We seek the greatest possible individuation, or development of personality. In doing this, we have set up a new demand, not for mere continuity of existence, but for *self-realization*. That is a uniquely human aim.

But obviously, the social structure could not arise on this principle alone. Vast numbers of individualists realizing themselves with a vengeance would not make up an ideal society. A small number might try it; there is a place, far away from here, called the Self-Realization Golden World Colony. But most of us have no golden world to colonize. You can only do that south of Los Angeles.

Seriously, however, an ideal is not disposed of by pointing out that it cannot be implemented under existing conditions. It may still be a true ideal; and if it is very important we may have to change the conditions, as we will have to for the ideal of world peace. If complete individuation were really the whole aim of human life, our society would be geared to it much more than it is. It is not the golden world that is wanting, but something else; the complete individualist is notoriously not the happy man, even if good fortune permits his antics.

The fact is that *the greatest possible individuation* is usually taken to mean, "as much as is possible without curtailing the rights of others." But that is not the real measure of how much is possible. The measure is provided in the individual himself, and is as fundamental as his knowledge of death. It is the other part of his insight into nature—his knowledge of life, of the great unbroken stream, the life of the stock from which its individuation stems.

One individual life, however rich, still looks infinitesimal; no matter how much self-realization is concentrated in it, it is a tiny atom—and we don't like to be tiny atoms, not even hydrogen atoms. We need more than fullness of personal life to counter our terrible knowledge of all it implies. And we have more; we have our history, our commitments made for us before we were born, our relatedness to the rest of mankind. The counterpart of individuation from the great life of the stock is our rootedness in that life, our involvement with the whole human race, past and present.

30. Pavlova

Agnes De Mille

Anna Pavlova! My life stops as I write that name. Across the daily preoccupation of lessons, lunch boxes, tooth brushings and quarrelings with Margaret flashed this bright, unworldly experience and burned in a single afternoon a path over which I could never retrace my steps. I had witnessed the power of beauty, and in some chamber of my heart I lost forever my irresponsibility. I was as clearly marked as though she had looked me in the face and called my name. For generations my father's family had loved and served the theater. All my life I had seen actors and actresses and had heard theater jargon at the dinner table and business talk of box-office grosses. I had thrilled at Father's projects and watched fascinated his picturesque occupations. I took a proprietary pride in the profitable and hasty growth of "The Industry." But nothing in his world or my uncle's prepared me for theater as I saw it that Saturday afternoon.

Since that day I have gained some knowledge in my trade and I recognize that her technique was limited; that her arabesques were not as pure or classically correct as Markova's, that her jumps and batterie were paltry, her turns not to be compared in strength and number with the strenuous durability of Baronova or Toumanova. I know that her scenery was designed by second-rate artists, her music was on a level with restaurant orchestrations, her company definitely inferior to all the standards we insist on today, and her choreography mostly hack. And yet I say that she was in her person the quintessence of theatrical excitement.

As her little bird body revealed itself on the scene, either immobile in trembling mystery or tense in the incredible arc which was her lift, her instep stretched ahead in an arch never before seen, the tiny bones of her hands in ceaseless vibration, her face radiant, diamonds glittering under her dark hair, her little waist encased in silk, the great tutu balancing, quickening and flashing over her beating, flashing, quivering legs, every man and woman sat forward, every pulse quickened. She never appeared to rest static, some part of her trembled, vibrated, beat like a heart. Before our dazzled eyes, she dashed with the sudden sweetness of a hummingbird in action too quick for understanding by our gross utilitarian standards, in action sensed rather than seen. The movie cameras of her day could not record her allegro. Her feet and hands photographed as a blur.

Bright little bird bones, delicate bird sinews! She was all fire and steel wire. There was not an ounce of spare flesh on her skeleton, and the life force used and used her body until she died of the fever of moving, gasping for breath, much too young.

She was small, about five feet. She wore a size one and a half slipper, but her feet and hands were large in proportion to her height. Her hand could cover her whole face. Her trunk was small and stripped of all anatomy but the ciphers of adolescence, her arms and legs relatively long, the neck extraordinarily long and mobile. All her gestures were liquid and possessed of an inner rhythm that flowed to inevitable completion with the finality of architecture or music. Her arms seemed to lift not from the elbow or the arm socket, but from the base of the spine. Her legs seemed to function from the waist. When she bent her head her whole spine moved and the motion was completed the length of the arm through the elongation of her slender hand and the quivering reaching fingers. I believe there has never been a foot like hers, slender, delicate and of such an astonishing aggressiveness when arched as to suggest the ultimate in human vitality. Without in any way being sensual, being, in fact, almost sexless, she suggested all exhilaration, gaiety and delight. She jumped, and we broke bonds with reality. We flew. We hung over the earth, spread in the air as we do in dreams, our hands turning in the air as in water—the strong forthright taut plunging leg balanced on the poised arc of the foot, the other leg stretched to the horizon like the wing of a bird. We lay balancing, quivering, turning, and all things were possible, even to us, the ordinary people.

I have seen two dancers as great or greater since, Alicia Markova and Margot Fonteyn, and many other women who have kicked higher, balanced longer or turned faster. These are poor substitutes for passion. In spite of her flimsy dances, the bald and blatant virtuosity, there was an intoxicated rapture, a focus of energy, Dionysian in its physical intensity, that I have never seen equaled by a performer in any theater of the world. Also she was the *first* of the truly great in our experience.

I sat with the blood beating in my throat. As I walked into the bright glare of the afternoon, my head ached and I could scarcely swallow. I didn't wish to cry. I certainly couldn't speak. I sat in a daze in the car oblivious to the grownups' ceaseless prattle. At home I climbed the stairs slowly to my bedroom and, shutting myself in, placed both hands on the brass rail at the foot of my bed, then rising laboriously to the tips of my white buttoned shoes I stumped the width of the bed and back again. My toes throbbed with pain, my knees shook, my legs quivered with weakness. I repeated the exercise. The blessed, relieving tears stuck at last on my lashes. Only by hurting my feet could I ease the pain in my throat.

Death came to Anna Pavlova in 1931, when she was fifty. She had not stopped touring for a single season. Her knees had sustained some damage, but she would not rest, and she was in a state of exhaustion when the train that was carrying her to Holland was wrecked. She ran out into the snow in her nightgown and insisted on helping the wounded. When she reached The Hague she had double pneumonia. Her last spoken words were, "Get the *Swan* dress ready."

Standing on Ninth Avenue under the El, I saw the headlines on the front page of the *New York Times*. It did not seem possible. She was in essence the denial of death. My own life was rooted to her in a deep spiritual sense and had been during the whole of my growing up. It mattered not that I had only spoken to her once and that my work lay in a different direction. She was the vision and the impulse and the goal.

31. The Quest for Extraterrestrial Intelligence

Carl Sagan

Through all of our history we have pondered the stars and mused whether humanity is unique or if, somewhere else in the dark of the night sky, there are other beings who contemplate and wonder as we do, fellow thinkers in the cosmos. Such beings might view themselves and the universe differently. Somewhere else there might be very exotic biologies and technologies and societies. In a cosmic setting vast and old beyond ordinary human understanding, we are a little lonely; and we ponder the ultimate significance, if any, of our tiny but exquisite blue planet. The search for extraterrestrial intelligence is the search for a generally acceptable cosmic context for the human species. In the deepest sense, the search for extraterrestrial intelligence is a search for ourselves.

In the last few years—in one-millionth the lifetime of our species on this planet—we have achieved an extraordinary technological capability which enables us to seek out unimaginably distant civilizations even if they are no more advanced than we. That capability is called radio astronomy and involves single radio telescopes, collections or arrays of radio telescopes, sensitive radio detectors, advanced computers for processing received data, and the imagination and skill of dedicated scientists. Radio astronomy has in the last decade opened a new window on the physical universe. It may also, if we are wise enough to make the effort, cast a profound light on the biological universe.

Some scientists working on the question of extraterrestrial intelligence, myself among them, have attempted to estimate the number of advanced technical civilizations—defined operationally as societies capable of radio astronomy—in the Milky Way Galaxy. Such estimates are little better than guesses. They require assigning numerical values to quantities such as the numbers and ages of stars; the abundance of planetary systems and the likelihood of the origin of life, which we know less well; and the probability of the evolution of intelligent life and the lifetime of technical civilizations, about which we know very little indeed.

When we do the arithmetic, the sorts of numbers we come up with are, characteristically, around a million technical civilizations. A million civilizations is a breathtakingly large number, and it is exhilarating to imagine the diversity, lifestyles and commerce of those million worlds. But the Milky Way Galaxy contains some 250 billion stars, and even with a million civilizations, less than one star in 200,000 would have a planet inhabited by an advanced civilization. Since we have little idea which stars are likely candidates, we will have to examine a very large number of them. Such considerations suggest that the quest for extraterrestrial intelligence may require a significant effort.

Despite claims about ancient astronauts and unidentified flying objects, there is no firm evidence for past visitations of the Earth by other civilizations. We are restricted to remote signaling and, of the long-distance techniques available to our technology, radio is by far the best. Radio telescopes are relatively inexpensive; radio signals travel at the speed of light, faster than which nothing can go; and the use of radio for communication is not a short-sighted or anthropocentric activity. Radio represents a large part of the electromagnetic spectrum, and any technical civilization anywhere in the Galaxy will have discovered radio early—just as in the last few centuries we have explored the entire electromagnetic spectrum from short gamma rays to very long radio waves. Advanced civilizations might very well use some other means of communication with their peers. But if they wish to communicate with backward or emerging civilizations, there are only a few obvious methods, the chief of which is radio.

The first serious attempt to listen for possible radio signals from other civilizations was carried out at the National Radio Astronomy Observatory in Greenbank, West Virginia, in 1959 and 1960. It was organized by Frank Drake, now at Cornell University, and was called Project Ozma, after the princess of the Land of Oz, a place very exotic, very distant and very difficult to reach. Drake examined two nearby stars, Epsilon Eridani and Tau Ceti, for a few weeks with negative results.

Positive results would have been astonishing because as we have seen, even rather optimistic estimates of the number of technical civilizations in the Galaxy imply that several hundred thousand stars must be examined in order to achieve success by random stellar selection.

Since Project Ozma, there have been six or eight other such programs, all at a rather modest level, in the United States, Canada and the Soviet Union. All results have been negative. The total number of individual stars examined to date in this way is less than a thousand. We have performed something like one tenth of one percent of the required effort.

However, there are signs that much more serious efforts may be mustered in the reasonably near future. All the observing programs to date have involved quite tiny amounts of time on large telescopes, or when large amounts of time have been committed, only very small radio telescopes could be used. A comprehensive examination of the problem was recently made by a NASA committee chaired by Philip Morrison of the Massachusetts Institute of Technology. The committee identified a wide range of options, including new (and expensive) giant ground-based and spaceborne radio telescopes. It also pointed out that major progress can be made at modest cost by the development of more sensitive radio receivers and of ingenious computerized data-processing systems. In the Soviet Union there is a state commission devoted to organizing a search for extraterrestrial intelligence, and the large RATAN-600 radio telescope in the Caucasus, recently completed, is devoted part-time to this effort. Hand in hand with the recent spectacular advances in radio technology, there has been a dramatic increase in the scientific and public respectability of the entire subject of extraterrestrial life. A clear sign of the new attitude is the Viking missions to Mars, which are to a significant extent dedicated to the search for life on another planet.

But along with the burgeoning dedication to a serious search, a slightly negative note has emerged which is nevertheless very interesting. A few scientists have lately asked a curious question: If extraterrestrial intelligence is abundant, why have we not already seen its manifestations? Think of the advances by our own technological civilization in the past ten thousand years and imagine such advances continued over millions or billions of years more. If only a tiny fraction of advanced civilizations are millions or billions of years more advanced than ours, why have they not produced artifacts, devices or even industrial pollution of such magnitude that we would have detected it? Why have they not restructured the entire Galaxy for their convenience?

Skeptics also ask why there is no clear evidence of extraterrestrial visits to Earth. We have already launched slow and modest interstellar spacecraft. A society more advanced than ours should be able to ply the spaces between the stars conveniently if not effortlessly. Over millions of years such societies should have established colonies, which might themselves launch interstellar expeditions. Why are they not here? The temptation is to deduce that there are at most a few advanced extraterrestrial civilizations—either because statistically we are one of the first technical civilizations to have emerged or because it is the fate of all such civilizations to destroy themselves before they are much further along than we.

It seems to me that such despair is quite premature. All such arguments depend on our correctly surmising the intentions of beings far more advanced than ourselves, and when examined more closely I think these arguments reveal a range of interesting human conceits. Why do we expect that it will be easy to recognize the manifestations of very advanced civilizations? Is our situation not closer to that of members of an isolated society in the Amazon basin, say, who lack the tools to detect the powerful international radio and television traffic that is all around them? Also, there is a wide range of incompletely understood phenomena in astronomy. Might the modulation of pulsars or the energy source of quasars, for example have a technological origin? Or perhaps there is a galactic ethic of noninterference with backward or emerging civilizations. Perhaps there is a waiting time before contact is considered appropriate, so as to give us a fair opportunity to destroy ourselves first, if we are so inclined. Perhaps all societies significantly more advanced than our own have achieved an effective personal immortality and lose the motivation for interstellar gallivanting, which may, for all we know, be a typical urge only of adolescent civilizations. Perhaps mature civilizations do not wish to pollute the cosmos. There is a very long list of such "perhapses," few of which we are in a position to evaluate with any degree of assurance.

The question of extraterrestrial civilizations seems to me entirely open. Personally, I think it far more difficult to understand a universe in which we are the only technological civilization, or one of a very few, than to conceive of a cosmos brimming over with intelligent life. Many aspects of the problem are, fortunately, amenable to experimental verification. We can search for planets of other stars, seek simple forms of life on such nearby planets as Mars, and perform more extensive laboratory studies on the chemistry of the origin of life. We can investigate more deeply the evolution of organisms and societies. The problem cries out for a long-term, open-minded, systematic search, with nature as the only arbiter of what is or is not likely.

If there are a million technical civilizations in the Milky Way Galaxy, the average separation between civilizations is about 300 light-years. Since a light-year is the distance that light travels in one year (a little under 6 trillion miles), this implies that the one-way transit time for an interstellar communication from the nearest civilization is some 300 years. The time for a query and a response would be 600 years. This is the reason that interstellar dialogues are much less likely—particularly around the time of first contact—than interstellar monologues. At first sight, it seems remarkably selfless that a civilization might broadcast radio messages with no hope of knowing, at least in the immediate future, whether they have been received and what the response to them might be. But human beings often perform very similar actions as, for example, burying time capsules to be recovered by future generations, or even writing books, composing music and creating art intended for posterity. A civilization that had been aided by the receipt of such a message in its past might wish similarly to benefit other emerging technical societies.

For a radio search program to succeed, the Earth must be among the intended beneficiaries. If the transmitting civilization were only slightly more advanced than we are, it would possess ample radio power for interstellar communication — so much, perhaps, that the broadcasting could be delegated to relatively small groups of radio hobbyists and partisans of primitive civilizations. If an entire planetary government or an alliance of worlds carried out the project, the broadcasters could transmit to a very large number of stars, so large that a message is likely to be beamed our way, even though there may be no reason to pay special attention to our region of the sky.

It is easy to see that communication is possible, even without any previous agreement or contact between transmitting and receiving civilizations. There is no difficulty in envisioning an interstellar radio message that unambiguously arises from intelligent life. A modulated signal (beep, beep-beep, beep-beep-beep ...) comprising the numbers 1, 2, 3, 5, 7, 11, 13, 17, 19, 23, 29, 31 — the first dozen prime numbers — could have only a biological origin. No prior agreement between civilizations and no precautions against Earth chauvinism are required to make this clear.

Such a message would be an announcement, or beacon, signal, indicating the presence of an advanced civilization but communicating very little about its nature. The beacon signal might also note a particular frequency where the main message is to be found, or might indicate that the principal message can be found at higher time resolution at the frequency of the beacon signal. The communication of quite complex information is not very difficult, even for civilizations with extremely different biologies and social conventions. Arithmetical statements can be transmitted, some true and some false, each followed by an appropriate coded word (in dahs and dits, for example), which would transmit the ideas of true and false, concepts that many people might guess would be extremely difficult to communicate in such a context.

But by far the most promising method is to send pictures. A repeated message that is the product of two prime numbers is clearly to be decoded as a two-dimensional array, or raster — that is, a picture. The product of three prime numbers might be a three-dimensional still picture or one frame of a two-dimensional motion picture. As an example of such a message, consider an array of zeros and ones which could be long and short beeps or tones on two adjacent frequencies, or tones of different amplitudes, or even signals with different radio polarizations. In 1974 such a message was transmitted to space from the 305-meter antenna at the Arecibo Observatory in Puerto Rico, which Cornell University runs for the National Science Foundation. The occasion was a ceremony marking the resurfacing of the Arecibo dish, the largest radio/radar telescope on the planet Earth. The signal was sent to a collection of stars called M13, a globular cluster comprising about a million separate suns which happened to be overhead at the time of the ceremony. Since M13 is 24,000 light-years away, the message will take 24,000 years to arrive there. If any responsive creature is listening, it will be 48,000 years before we receive a reply. The Arecibo message was clearly intended not as a serious attempt at interstellar communication, but rather as an indication of the remarkable advances in terrestrial radio technology.

The decoded message says something like this: "Here is how we count from one to ten. Here are the atomic numbers of five chemical elements—hydrogen, carbon, nitrogen, oxygen and phosphorus—that we think are interesting or important. Here are some ways to put these atoms together: the molecules adenine, thymine, guanine and cytosine, and a chain compound of alternating sugars and phosphates. These molecular building blocks are in turn put together to form a long molecule of DNA comprising about four billion links in the chain. The molecule is a double helix. In some way this molecule is important for the clumsy-looking creature at the center of the message. That creature is 14 radio wavelengths, or about 176 centimeters, high. There are about four billion of these creatures on the third planet from our star. There are nine planets altogether—four little ones on the inside, four big ones toward the outside and one little one at the extremity. This message is brought to you courtesy of a radio telescope 2,430 wavelengths, or 306 meters, in diameter. Yours truly."

With many similar pictorial messages, each consistent with and corroborating the others, it is very likely that almost unambiguous interstellar radio communication could be achieved even between two civilizations that have never met. Our immediate objective is not to send such messages because we are very young and backward; we wish to listen.

The detection of intelligent radio signals from the depths of space would approach in an experimental and scientifically rigorous manner many of the most profound questions that have concerned scientists and philosophers since prehistoric times. Such a signal would indicate that the origin of life is not an extraordinary, difficult or unlikely event. It would imply that, given billions of years for natural selection, simple forms of life evolve generally into complex and intelligent forms, as on Earth; and that such intelligent forms commonly produce an advanced technology, as has also occurred here. But it is not likely that the transmissions we receive will be from a society at our own level of technological advance. A society only a little more backward than ours will not radio astronomy at all. The most likely case is that the message will be from a civilization far in our technological future. Thus, even before we decode such a message, we will have gained an invaluable piece of knowledge: that it is possible to avoid the dangers of the period through which we are now passing.

There are some who look on our global problems here on Earth—at our vasts national antagonisms, our nuclear arsenals, our growing populations, the disparity between the poor and the affluent, shortages of food and resources, and our inadvertent alterations of the natural environment—and conclude that we live in a system that has suddenly become unstable, a system that is destined soon to collapse. There are others who believe that our problems are soluble, that humanity is still in its childhood, that one day soon we will grow up. The receipt of a single message from space would show that it is possible to live through such technological adolescence: the transmitting civilization, after all, has survived. Such knowledge, it seems to me, might be worth a great price.

Another likely consequence of an interstellar message is a strengthening of the bonds that join all human and other beings on our planet. The sure lesson of evolution is that organisms elsewhere must have separate evolutionary pathways; that their chemistry and biology and very likely their social organizations will be profoundly dissimilar to anything on Earth. We may well be able to communicate with them because we share a common universe—because the laws of physics and chemistry and the regularities of astronomy are universal. But they may always be, in the deepest sense, different. And in the face of this difference, the animosities that divide the peoples of the Earth may wither. The differences among human beings of separate races and nationalities, religious and sexes, are likely to be insignificant compared to the differences between all human and all extraterrestrial intelligent beings.

If the message comes by radio, both transmitting and receiving civilizations will have in common at least a knowledge of radio-physics. The commonality of the physical sciences is the reason that many scientists expect the messages from extraterrestrial civilizations to be decodable—probably in a slow and halting manner, but unambiguously nevertheless. No one is wise enough to predict in detail what the consequences of such a decoding will be, because no one is wise enough to understand beforehand what the nature of the message will be. Since the transmission is likely to be from a civilization far in advance of our own, stunning insights are possible in the physical, biological and social sciences, in the novel perspective of a quite different kind of intelligence. But decoding will probably be a task of years and decades.

Some have worried that a message from an advanced society might make us lose faith in our own, might deprive us of the initiative to make new discoveries if it seemed that others had made those discoveries already, or might have other negative consequences. This is rather like a student dropping out of school because his teachers and textbooks are more learned than he is. We are free to ignore an interstellar message if we find it offensive. If we choose not to respond, there is no way for the transmitting civilization to determine that its message was received and understood on the tiny distant planet Earth. The translation of a radio message from the depths of space, about which we can be as slow and cautious as we wish, seems to pose few dangers to mankind; instead, it holds the greatest promise of both practical and philosophical benefits.

In particular, it is possible that among the first contents of such a message may be detailed prescriptions for the avoidance of technological disaster, for a passage through adolescence to maturity. Perhaps the transmissions from advanced civilizations will describe which pathways of cultural evolution are likely to lead to the stability and longevity of an intelligent species, and which other paths lead to stagnation or degeneration or disaster. There is, of course, no guarantee that such would be the contents of an interstellar message, but it would be foolhardy to overlook the possibility. Perhaps there are straightforward solutions, still undiscovered on Earth, to problems of food shortages, population growth, energy supplies, dwindling resources, pollution and war.

While there will surely be differences among civilizations, there may well be laws of development of civilizations which cannot be glimpsed until information is available about the evolution of many civilizations. Because of our isolation from the rest of the cosmos, we have information on the evolution of only one civilization—our own. And the most important aspect of that evolution—the future—remains closed to us. Perhaps it is not likely, but it is certainly possible that the future of human civilization depends on the receipt and decoding of interstellar messages from extraterrestrial civilizations.

And what if we make a long-term, dedicated search for extraterrestrial intelligence and fail? Even then we surely will not have wasted our time. We will have developed an important technology, with applications to many other aspects of our own civilization. We will have added greatly to our knowledge of the physical universe. And we will have calibrated something of the importance and uniqueness of our species, our civilization and our planet. For if intelligent life is scarce or absent elsewhere, we will have learned something significant about the rarity and value of our culture and our biological patrimony, painstakingly extracted over 4.6 billion years of tortuous evolutionary history. Such a finding will stress, as perhaps nothing else can, our responsibilities to the dangers of our time: because the most likely explanation of negative results, after a comprehensive and resourceful search, is that societies commonly destroy themselves before they are advanced enough to establish a high-power radio-transmitting service. In an interesting sense, the organization of a search for interstellar radio messages, quite apart from the outcome, is likely to have a cohesive and constructive influence on the whole of the human predicament.

But we will not know the outcome of such a search, much less the contents of messages from interstellar civilizations, if we do not make a serious effort to listen for signals. It may be that civilizations are divided into two great classes: those that make such an effort, achieve contact and become new members of a loosely tied federation of galactic communities, and those that cannot or choose not to make such an effort, or who lack the imagination to try, and who in consequence soon decay and vanish.

It is difficult to think of another enterprise within our capability and at a relatively modest cost that holds as much promise for the future of humanity.

32. Women: A House Divided

Margaret Mead and Rhoda Metraux

How far ahead are you thinking?

As the demands for immediate changes in women's lives become more strident and angry, this a question every woman must ask herself and try to answer honestly. For the time span within which change is projected will make a great difference, I believe. Concentration on the very near future—a decade or two—will certainly bring about some very necessary reforms, but it will also obscure the basic issue—how women will face living in a world in which homemaking and childbearing are no longer the central focus of their lives. Change in our time can be only a step toward preparing our daughters and our daughters' daughters to think and act in new ways.

There are other questions as well.

Married or single, working or not working today, women must begin to think in terms of a basic choice: Public role and private role—which is the more important? In an emergency which would you sacrifice? If your child was sick or unhappy, would you leave him in someone else's care, as a man must do? If your husband's job took him to another country, would you give up a promising career to go with him? Would you go far away from friends and relatives for your career?

However important, responsible and fulfilling a woman's work may be, the answer is quite predictable. Most women put their families first. And few will think them wrong. This is the choice women have been brought up to make and men have been taught to expect. It is the unusual woman, the woman wholly committed to her career or an important goal, on whom criticism descends.

Up to the present the dilemma is one most women have managed to avoid. One way of doing it has been by defining their work as an adjunct to their personal lives. Even today, when over one third of the women living in husband-wife homes—about 15 million married women—are working, this remains true. The kinds of positions women hold and the money they are paid are, at least in part, a reflection of women's own definitions of the place of work in their lives and of the reciprocal belief among men that giving a woman a career job is a high risk.

Only a change in viewpoint will enable women to take full advantage of the opportunities they now are so ardently seeking.

Looking ahead, another question each woman must ask herself is: How do you feel about other women?

Two generations ago the few women who chose work over a home cared a great deal about feminine solidarity. Set apart from the women who stayed home and the men among whom they worked, they had need to count on one another. Today, I think, women place far less reliance on other women for friendship or companionship. The picture most women have of a wider world outside the home is one in which they will spend their days together with men. But will they?

Women students complain—and rightly so—that women are far underrepresented at the upper level of the academic, the professional and the business world. A principal demand of every feminist group is that women be given equal opportunity with men to rise to the top. But are they prepared for a world in which women are active at every level?

Given the choice of a man or a woman, how many girls today would elect to study under a woman? How many women in business would choose to work for another woman? How many wives today willingly trust another woman with the care of their children? How many women enthusiastically accept another woman as a companion for recreation?

Perhaps the most valuable aspect of the new women's protest groups is the rediscovery that women can think and work together and find common ground for action. However, the continual fracturing of these groups suggests that women as a group do not easily achieve working solidarity.

The point is not that we have to look forward to some new division of the sexes in social life or in the working world. The point is rather that women as individuals want to be treated as people—as full human beings. For the present men are the principal target; it is they who are accused of treating women as second-class citizens. For some they are "the enemy." But we shall become full human beings, I think, only when we ourselves can treat one another as full human beings, worthy of other women's trust and respect.

This must include, as well, a new regard for women's traditional occupations, within and outside the home. Otherwise there is a very real danger that we shall lose what is most precious in human life—the ability to give devoted and cherishing care to other human beings—just at the time in human history when it is most imperative that we learn how to expand our capacity for caring and to translate it into ways of protecting the earth itself.

Women are in a peculiar position today. On the one hand they downgrade the things they know best how to do. But on the other hand they are extremely unwilling to share with others the tasks they do in their homes. The truth is, women are trapped in their present conception of a home as a very private place from which everyone but their husbands and children are excluded. How much of a trap it is comes out in the only solution to conflict between home and work many wives and mothers have to offer: Why can't my husband stay home in an emergency? Take care of a sick child for a day? Wait for the plumber? It doesn't occur to them that this is no solution. It would only put a man, instead of a woman, in the position of relinquishing outside responsibilities.

Such a solution looks only to the past. As long as a woman's care for her family represented her major social responsibility, her greatest opportunity for achieving a measure of independence and self-expression lay in having a home in which she was the chief executive. This we have achieved. In most American homes there are no mothers-in-law, no daughters-in-law, no maiden aunts or dependent sisters. Even daughters often leave home as soon as they are grown. There are no servants with status. At most there may be a cleaning woman with her own (usually mistaken) ideas of where to set down the ashtrays or how to arrange a bouquet. And now wives and mothers, though they reign supreme, look down on homemaking tasks.

By denigrating the tasks that women have done for their families we also have demeaned all those who could replace us in our homes. On this crucial point women's freedom to choose what they will do and women's view of other women are joined.

Looking to the future, beyond the day when women long to leave their homes out of discontent, we can find a way to reverse this trend. For then making a home for one's own family or for the family of a woman who has made a different choice will also be a matter of choice. Some women will choose to become engineers and doctors and lawyers and physicists and biochemists. And some will prefer to care for homes and little children. Whether this is a possibility that can be realized depends essentially on women's attitudes *now* toward women's roles as homemakers and caretakers of people. Will a woman biochemist, for instance, learn a new willingness to share her homemaking role with another woman who is professionally trained as a homemaker?

As women's sense of their freedom to make choices grows, the importance of what women have done and been in the past will acquire a new visibility. For this reason women have a special responsibility to accord dignity to women's work, to recognize the fact that the fields of women's traditional activities involve high-level skills, not only drudgery, and to prize those who, given a chance to do so, learn them as professionals.

Some forms of so-called women's work, of course, already are highly professionalized. The time has come when homemaking too should move in this direction. It is quite possible that just as today young men are choosing to be teachers of small children—with the greatest future benefit to early-childhood education—so also eventually some men will choose other, formerly feminine, caretaking roles as a profession. In another generation it may well be that people will speak not only of "mothering" but also of "fathering" and "parenting" as special talents to be sought out and developed in many individuals.

Women's attitudes toward other women are no less important in the redefinition of women's relationships to men, in the development of new styles of work and in the openness each may have to the other's interpretations of phenomena. In the past, distrusting their own abilities and viewpoints, women have been overeager to accept men's judgments or they have been overresistant to any modification of their own judgments about social legislation, the handling of crime, priorities in national goals or the uses made of the earth's resources.

But in time, as men and women begin to work together as intellectual equals on the multiple problems of public life, women will have new insights to offer and new solutions to propose. Then the feminine preference for persons, for care taking and conservation, for intimacy of understanding *combined with* the masculine preference for working with things, for mastery and exploitation, for rational objectivity, can enrich our perceptions of the world. For women this will involve a change of scale; for men, a greater trust in intuitive—subjective—processes.

No one can possibly predict how long it will take for partnerships of this kind to come to fruition. Nor can one begin to guess what new viewpoints about human behavior and the nature of civilization will grow out of such new associations of men and women.

But I think it is safe to say that the outcome depends on women's willingness to work for immediate change within a framework of more than one generation. What women have to give is not heritable in the sense that it is built into the female organism. It is, instead, learning that has been passed on from mother to child for hundreds of generations. It can be lost by women who deny their past. It can be distorted by women who deny the realities of a changing world. It can be safely learned and modified by daughters who sense their mothers are moving imaginatively in the direction their children—sons and daughters—will take in making a new social reality, given time.

33. Shooting an Elephant

George Orwell

In Moulmein, in lower Burma, I was hated by large numbers of people—the only time in my life that I have been important enough for this to happen to me. I was subdivisional police officer of the town, and in an aimless, petty kind of way anti-European feeling was very bitter. No one had the guts to raise a riot, but if a European woman went through the bazaars alone somebody would probably spit betel juice over her dress. As a police officer I was an obvious target and was baited whenever it seemed safe to do so. When a nimble Burman tripped me up on the football field and the referee (another Burman) looked the other way, the crowd yelled with hideous laughter. This happened more than once. In the end the sneering yellow faces of young men that met me everywhere, the insults hooted after me when I was at a safe distance, got badly on my nerves. The young Buddhist priests were the worst of all. There were several thousands of them in the town and none of them seemed to have anything to do except stand on street corners and jeer at Europeans.

All this was perplexing and upsetting. For at that time I had already made up my mind that imperialism was an evil thing and the sooner I chucked up my job and got out of it the better. Theoretically—and secretly, of course—I was all for the Burmese and all against their oppressors, the British. As for the job I was doing, I hated it more bitterly than I can perhaps make clear. In a job like that you see the dirty work of Empire at close quarters. The wretched prisoners huddling in the stinking cages of the lock-ups, the gray, cowed faces of the long-term convicts, the scarred buttocks of the men who had been flogged with bamboos—all these oppressed me with an intolerable sense of guilt. But I could get nothing into perspective. I was young and ill educated and I had had to think out my problems in the utter silence that is imposed on every Englishman in the East. I did not even know that the British Empire is dying, still less did I know that it is a great deal better than the younger empires that are going to supplant it. All I knew was that I was stuck between my hatred of the empire I served and my rage against the evil-spirited little beasts who tried to make my job impossible. With one part of my mind I thought of the British Raj as an unbreakable tyranny, as something clamped down, in *saecula sacculorum*, upon the will of prostrate peoples; with another part I thought that the greatest joy in the world would be to drive a bayonet into a Buddhist priest's guts. Feelings like these are the normal by-products of imperialism; ask any Anglo-Indian official, if you catch him off duty.

One day something happened which in a roundabout way was enlightening. It was a tiny incident in itself, but it gave me a better glimpse than I had had before of the real nature of imperialism—the real motives for which despotic governments act. Early one morning the sub-inspector at a police station the other end of the town rang me up on the 'phone and said that an elephant was ravaging the bazaar. Would I please come and do something about it? I did not know what I could do, but I wanted to see what was happening and I got on to a pony and started out. I took my rifle, an old .44 Winchester and much too small to kill an elephant, but I thought the noise might be useful *in terrorem*. Various Burmans stopped me on the way and told me about the elephant's doings. It was not, of course, a wild elephant, but a tame one which had gone "must." It had been chained up, as tame elephants always are when their attack of "must" is due, but on the previous night it had broken its chain and escaped. Its mahout, the only person who could manage it when it was in that state, had set out in pursuit, but had taken the wrong direction and was now twelve hours' journey away, and in the morning the elephant had suddenly reappeared in the town. The Burmese population had no weapons and were quite helpless against it. It had already destroyed somebody's bamboo hut, killed a cow and raided some fruit-stalls and devoured the stock; also it had met the municipal rubbish van and, when the driver jumped out and took to his heels, had turned the van over and inflicted violences upon it.

The Burmese sub-inspector and some Indian constables were waiting for me in the quarter where the elephant had been seen. It was a very poor quarter, a labyrinth of squalid bamboo huts, thatched with palm-leaf, winding all over a steep hillside. I remember that it was a cloudy, stuffy morning at the beginning of the rains. We began questioning the people as to where the elephant had gone and, as usual, failed to get any definite information. That is invariably the case in the East; a story always sounds clear enough at a distance, but the nearer you get to the scene of events the vaguer it becomes. Some of the people said that the elephant had gone in one direction, some said that he had gone in another, some professed not even to have heard of any elephant. I had almost made up my mind that the whole story was a pack of lies, when we heard yells a little distance away. There was a loud, scandalized cry of "Go away, child! Go away this instant!" and an old woman with a switch in her hand came round the corner of a hut, violently shooing away a crowd of naked children. Some more women followed, clicking their tongues and exclaiming; evidently there was something that the children ought not to have seen. I rounded the hut and saw a man's dead body sprawling in the mud. He was an Indian, a black Dravidian coolie, almost naked, and he could not have been dead many minutes. The people said that the elephant had come suddenly upon him round the corner of the hut, caught him with its trunk, put its foot on his back and ground him into the earth. This was the rainy season and the ground was soft, and his face had scored a trench a foot deep and a couple of yards long. He was lying on his belly with arms crucified and head sharply twisted to one side. His face was coated with mud, the eyes wide open, the teeth bared and grinning with an expression of unendurable agony. (Never tell me, by the way, that the dead look peaceful. Most of the corpses I have seen looked devilish.) The friction of the great beast's foot had stripped the skin from his back as neatly as one skins a rabbit. As soon as I saw the dead man I sent an orderly to a friend's house nearby to borrow an elephant rifle. I had already sent back the pony, not wanting it to go mad with fright and throw me if it smelt the elephant.

The orderly came back in a few minutes with a rifle and five cartridges, and meanwhile some Burmans had arrived and told us that the elephant was in the paddy fields below, only a few hundred yards away. As I started forward practically the whole population of the quarter flocked out of the houses and followed me. They had seen the rifle and were all shouting excitedly that I was going to shoot the elephant. They had not shown much interest in the elephant when he was merely ravaging their homes, but it was different now that he was going to be shot. It was a bit of fun to them, as it would be to an English crowd; besides they wanted the meat. It made me vaguely uneasy. I had no intention of shooting the elephant—I had merely sent for the rifle to defend myself if necessary—and it was always unnerving to have a crowd following you. I marched down the hill, looking and feeling a fool, with the rifle over my shoulder and an ever-growing army of people jostling at my heels. At the bottom, when you got away from the huts, there was a metalled road and beyond that a miry waste of paddy fields a thousand yards across, not yet ploughed but soggy from the first rains and dotted with coarse grass. The elephant was standing eight yards from the road, his left side toward us. He took not the slightest notice of the crowd's approach. He was tearing up bunches of grass, beating them against his knees to clean them, and stuffing them into his mouth.

I had halted on the road. As soon as I saw the elephant I knew with perfect certainty that I ought not to shoot him. It is a serious matter to shoot a working elephant—it is comparable to destroying a huge and costly piece of machinery—and obviously one ought not to do it if it can possibly be avoided. And at that distance, peacefully eating, the elephant looked no more dangerous than a cow. I thought then and I think now that his attack of "must" was already passing off; in which case he would merely wander harmlessly about until the mahout came back and caught him. Moreover, I did not in the least want to shoot him. I decided that I would watch him for a little while to make sure that he did not turn savage again, and then go home.

But at that moment I glanced round at the crowd that had followed me. It was an immense crowd, two thousand at the least and growing every minute. It blocked the road for a long distance on either side. I looked at the sea of yellow faces above the garish clothes—faces all happy and excited over this bit of fun, all certain that the elephant was going to be shot. They were watching me as they would watch a conjurer about to perform a trick. They did not like me, but with the magical rifle in my hands I was momentarily worth watching. And suddenly I realized that I should have to shoot the elephant after all. The people expected it of me and I had got to do it; I could feel their two thousand wills pressing me forward, irresistibly. And it was at this moment, as I stood there with the rifle in my hands, that I first grasped the hollowness, the futility of the white man's dominion in the East. Here was I, the white man with his gun, standing in front of the unarmed native crowd—seemingly the leading actor of the piece; but in reality I was only an absurd puppet pushed to and fro by the will of those yellow faces behind. I perceived in this moment that when the white man turns tyrant it is his own freedom that he destroys. He becomes a sort of hollow, posing dummy, the conventionalized figure of a sahib. For it is the condition of his rule that he shall spend his life in trying to impress the "natives," and so in every crisis he has got to do what the "natives" expect of him. He wears a mask, and his face grows to fit it. I had got to shoot the elephant. I had committed myself to doing it when I sent for the rifle. A sahib has got to act like a sahib; he has got to appear resolute, to know his own mind and do definite things. To come all that way, rifle in hand, with two thousand people marching at my heels, and then to trail feebly away, having done nothing—no, that was impossible. The crowd would laugh at me. And my whole life, every white man's life in the East, was one long struggle not to be laughed at.

But I did not want to shoot the elephant. I watched him beating his bunch of grass against his knees with that preoccupied grandmotherly air that elephants have. It seemed to me that it would be murder to shoot him. At that age I was not squeamish about killing animals, but I had never shot an elephant and never wanted to. (Somehow it always seems worse to kill a *large* animal.) Besides, there was the beast's owner to be considered. Alive, the elephant was worth at least a hundred pounds; dead, he would only be worth the value of his tusks, five pounds, possibly. But I had got to act quickly. I turned to some experienced-looking Burmans who had been there when we arrived, and asked them how the elephant had been behaving. They all said the same thing: he took no notice of you if you left him alone, but he might charge if you went too close to him.

It was perfectly clear to me what I ought to do. I ought to walk up to within, say, twenty-five yards of the elephant and test his behavior. If he charged, I could shoot; if he took no notice of me, it would be safe to leave him until the mahout came back. But also I knew that I was going to do no such thing. I was a poor shot with a rifle and the ground was soft mud into which one would sink at every step. If the elephant charged and I missed him, I should have about as much chance as a toad under a steam-roller. But even then I was not thinking particularly of my own skin, only of the watchful yellow faces behind. For at that moment, with the crowd watching me, I was not afraid in the ordinary sense, as I would have been if I had been alone. A white man mustn't be frightened in front of "natives"; and so, in general, he isn't frightened. The sole thought in my mind was that if anything went wrong those two thousand Burmans would see me pursued, caught, trampled on, and reduced to a grinning corpse like that Indian up the hill. And if that happened it was quite probable that some of them would laugh. That would never do. There was only one alternative. I shoved the cartridges into the magazine and lay down on the road to get a better aim.

The crowd grew very still, and a deep, low, happy sigh, as of people who see the theater curtain go up at last, breathed from innumerable throats. They were going to have their bit of fun after all. The rifle was a beautiful German thing with cross-hair sights. I did not then know that in shooting an elephant one would shoot to cut an imaginary bar running from ear-hole to ear-hole. I ought, therefore, as the elephant was sideways on, to have aimed straight at his ear-hole; actually I aimed several inches in front of this, thinking the brain would be further forward.

When I pulled the trigger I did not hear the bang or feel the kick—one never does when a shot goes home—but I heard the devilish roar of glee that went up from the crowd. In that instant, in too short a time, one would have thought, even for the bullet to get there, a mysterious, terrible change had come over the elephant. He neither stirred nor fell, but every line of his body had altered. He looked suddenly stricken, shrunken, immensely old, as though the frightful impact of the bullet had paralyzed him without knocking him down. At last, after what seemed a long time—it might have been five seconds, I dare say—he sagged flabbily to his knees. His mouth slobbered. An enormous senility seemed to have settled upon him. One could have imagined him thousands of years old. I fired again into the same spot. At the second shot he did not collapse but climbed with desperate slowness to his feet and stood weakly upright, with legs sagging and head drooping. I fired a third time. That was the shot that did for him. You could see the agony of it jolt his whole body and knock the last remnant of strength from his legs. But in falling he seemed for a moment to rise, for as his hind legs collapsed beneath him he seemed to tower upward like a huge rock toppling, his trunk reaching skyward like a tree. He trumpeted, for the first and only time. And then down he came, his belly toward me, with a crash that seemed to shake the ground even where I lay.

I got up. The Burmans were already racing past me across the mud. It was obvious that the elephant would never rise again, but he was not dead. He was breathing very rhythmically with long rattling gasps, his great mound of a side painfully rising and falling. His mouth was wide open—I could see far down into caverns of pale pink throat. I waited a long time for him to die, but his breathing did not weaken. Finally I fired my two remaining shots into the spot where I thought his heart must be. The thick blood welled out of him like red velvet, but still he did not die. His body did not even jerk when the shots hit home, the tortured breathing continued without a pause. He was dying, very slowly and in great agony, but in some world remote from me where not even a bullet could damage him further. I felt that I had got to put an end to that dreadful noise. It seemed dreadful to see the great beast lying there, powerless to move and yet powerless to die, and not even to be able to finish him. I sent back for my small rifle and poured shot after shot into his heart and down his throat. They seemed to make no impression. The tortured gasps continued as steadily as the ticking of a clock.

In the end I could not stand it any longer and went away. I heard later that it took him half an hour to die. Burmans were bringing dahs and baskets even before I left, and I was told they had stripped his body almost to the bones by the afternoon.

Afterward, of course, there were endless discussions about the shooting of the elephant. The owner was furious, but he was only an Indian and could do nothing. Besides, legally I had done the right thing, for a mad elephant has to be killed, like a mad dog, if its owner fails to control it. Among the Europeans opinion was divided. The older men said I was right, the younger men said it was a damn shame to shoot an elephant for killing a coolie, because an elephant was worth more than any damn Coringhee coolie. And afterward I was very glad that the coolie had been killed; it put me legally in the right and it gave me a sufficient pretext for shooting the elephant. I often wondered whether any of the others grasped that I had done it solely to avoid looking a fool.

References

CHAPTER 2

1. Wyler, Rose. *Science*. Racine, Wisc.: Western Publishing Company, 1973, p. 42.
2. Beiser, Arthur. *The Earth*. New York: Time-Life Books, 1970, p. 35.
3. *World Book Encyclopedia*, Book A. Chicago: Field Enterprises, 1977, p. 14a.

CHAPTER 5

1. Aceves, Jospeh B. and H. Gill King. *Introduction to Anthropology*. Glenview, Ill.: Scott, Foresman, 1979, p. 9.
2. Aceves and King, p. 11.
3. DeFleur, Melvin, et al. *Sociology: Human Society*. Glenview, Ill.: Scott, Foresman, 1977, p. 33.
4. Hewitt, Paul G. *Conceptual Physics*, 3rd ed. Boston: Little, Brown, 1977, p. 33.
5. DeFleur, p. 36.
6. Perry, John and Erna Perry. *Face to Face*. Boston: Little, Brown, 1976, p. 146.
7. Perry and Perry, p. 146.
8. Perry and Perry, pp. 179–180.
9. Medinnus, Gene R. and Ronald C. Johnson. *Child & Adolescent Psychology*. New York: John Wiley, 1969, p. 23.
10. Medinnus and Johnson, p. 23.
11. Medinnus and Johnson, p. 124.
12. Medinnus and Johnson, p. 273.

CHAPTER 6

1. Dorfman, John, et al. *Well-Being: An Introduction to Health*. Glenview, Ill.: Scott, Foresman, 1980, p. 54.
2. Stevens, Leonard A. "Every Drop Counts" in Lee Jacobus, *Issues and Response*. Harcourt Brace & World, 1968, p. 312.
3. Thomas, Lewis. "Death in the Open" in Joyce S. Steward, *Contemporary College Reader*. Glenview, Ill.: Scott, Foresman, 1978, p. 328.
4. Chisholm, Shirley. "I'd Rather Be Black Than Female," in Joyce S. Steward, ed., *Contemporary College Reader*. Glenview, Ill.: Scott, Foresman, 1978, p. 333.
5. Meehan, James R., et al. *Clerical Office Procedures*. Cincinnati: South-Western Publishing Co., 1973, p. 327.
6. Hamilton, Edith. *Mythology*. New York: New American Library, 1942, p. 19.

7. Asimov, Isaac. "Social Science Fiction,"in Dick Allen, ed., *Science Fiction: The Future*. New York: Harcourt Brace Jovanovich, 1971, p. 263.
8. Hayakawa, S. I. *Language in Thought and Action*, 2nd ed. New York: Harcourt Brace & World, 1964, p. 11.
9. Fromkin, Victoria and Robert Rodman. *An Introduction to Language*, New York: Holt, Rinehart and Winston, 1974, p. 176.
10. Key, Wilson B. *Subliminal Seduction*. New York: New American Library, 1973, p. 108.
11. Robinson, Diana. "Recharging Yourself Through Meditation," in Randall Decker, ed., *Patterns of Exposition*. Boston: Little, Brown, 1978, pp. 167–168.
12. Baker, Sheridan. "Writing as Discovery," in Wilfred A. Ferrell and Nicholas A. Salerno, *Strategies in Prose*, 11th ed. New York: Holt, Rinehart and Winston, 1978, p. 97.
13. Hackerman, Norman. "Higher Education: Who Needs It?" in Wilfred A. Ferrell and Nicholas A. Salerno, *Strategies in Prose*, 11th ed. New York: Holt, Rinehart and Winston, 1978, pp. 105–106.

CHAPTER 7

1. Holland, Morris K. *Using Psychology*. Boston: Little, Brown, 1975, pp. 140–141.
2. Camus, Albert. "The Guest," in Caroline Shrodes et al., *Reading for Understanding*. New York: Macmillan, 1968, p. 247.
3. Ellison, Ralph. *Invisible Man*. New York: New American Library, 1952, p. 7.
4. Chekhov, Anton. "The Bet," in Caroline Shrodes et al., *Reading for Understanding*. New York: Macmillan, 1968, p. 85.
5. Fromkin and Rodman, p. 191.
6. Hunt, Morton. "Don't Trust Anyone Over Thirty," in Lee Jacobus, *Issues and Response*, New York: Harcourt Brace & World, 1968, p. 386.
7. Hynek, J. Allen. "Are Flying Saucers Real?" in Jacobus, p. 172.
8. Fox, Edward S., and Edward W. Wheatley. *Modern Marketing*. Glenview, Ill.: Scott, Foresman, 1978, p. 142.
9. Wold, Milo, and Edmund Cykler. "Enjoyment of the Arts—The Nature of the Aesthetic Experience," in Donald Van Ess, ed., *The Common Wealth of Arts and Man*. New York: Thomas V. Crowell, 1973, p. 13.

10. Van Ess, Donald. "Style Elements in Music," in Van Ess, p. 83.
11. Fogg, Walter L., and Peyton E. Richter, *Philosophy Looks to the Future*. Boston: Holbrook Press, 1974, p. 10
12. Knox, David. *Exploring Marriage and the Family*. Glenview, Ill.: Scott, Foresman, 1979, p. 261.
13. Anderson, Sherwood. *Winesburg, Ohio*. New York: Viking Press, 1960, p. 179.
14. Syfers, Judy. "Why I Want a Wife," *Ms. Magazine*, Spring 1972.
15. Passell, Peter. "How to Grow an Avocado," in Thomas Cooley, ed., *Norton Sampler*. New York: W. W. Norton, 1979, p. 86.
16. Rowlands, John J. "Lonely Place," in Steward, p. 23.
17. Fromkin and Rodman, p. 17.
18. Curtin, Sharon. "Aging in the Land of the Young," in Decker, pp. 212–213.
19. Plotz, Judith. "Is a Crime Against the Mind No Crime at All?" in Farrell and Salerno, p. 111.
20. Fitzgerald, F. Scott. "Winter Dreams," in Bert C. Bach and Gordon Browning, *Fiction for Composition*. Glenview, Ill.: Scott, Foresman, 1968, p. 211.

CHAPTER 8
1. Geiwitz, James. *Looking at Ourselves: An Invitation to Psychology*. Boston: Little, Brown, 1976, pp 112–113.

CHAPTER 9
1. Woolf, Virginia. "The Duchess and the Jeweler," in James B. Hall, *The Realm of Fiction: 61 Short Stories*. New York: McGraw-Hill, 1965, p. 28.
2. "ABC's of How a President is Chosen." *U.S. News and World Report*. Vol. 88 (February 18, 1980), p. 45.

3. Korda, Michael. *Power*. New York: Ballantine Books, 1975, p. 4.
4. DeMaupassant, Guy. "The Piece of String," in Hall, p. 53.
5. Fromkin and Rodman, p. 173
6. Hayakawa, p. 48.
7. Catton, Bruce. "Grant and Lee: A Study in Contrasts," in Jo Ray McCuen and A. C. Winkler, *Readings for Writers*, 2nd ed. New York: Harcourt Brace Jovanovich, 1977, p. 213.
8. McCarty, Marilu H. *Dollars and Sense*. 2nd ed. Glenview, Ill.: Scott, Foresman, 1979, p. 114.
9. Coleman, James C. *Contemporary Psychology and Effective Behavior*, 4th ed. Glenview, Ill.: Scott, Foresman, 1979, p. 22.
10. Coleman, p. 26.
11. Toynbee, Arnold. "Intellectual Suicide at Puberty," in Decker, p. 158.
12. Knox, p. 173.

CHAPTER 10
1. Pirsig, Robert M. *Zen and the Art of Motorcycle Maintenance*. New York: Bantam Books, 1974, p. 4.
2. Holt, John. *How Children Fail*. New York: Pitman Publishing Corp., 1964, p. xiii.

CHAPTER 11
1. Whetmore, Edward J. *MediaAmerica*. Belmont, Calif.: Wadsworth, 1979, pp. 104–105.
2. *U.S. News & World Report*. February 18, 1980, p. 48.
3. Dorfman, John, et al. *Well-Being: An Introduction to Health*. Glenview, Ill.: Scott, Foresman, 1980, p. 43.
4. Dorfman et al., p. 213.

Answer Key

UNIT ONE

Chapter 1

NONE

Chapter 2

NONE

Unit One Reading Selections

1. "The Secret Pleasures of Mismanaging Time"

Comprehension	Vocabulary
1. d	1. d
2. d	2. b
3. c	3. c
4. a	4. a
5. d	5. d
	6. d
	7. b

2. "The Other You"

Comprehension	Vocabulary
1. a	1. a
2. a	2. a
3. b	3. c
4. b	4. d
5. b	

3. "Fun from the Start"

Comprehension	Vocabulary
1. b	1. c
2. c	2. a
3. d	
4. b	
5. a	

4. "To Lie or Not to Lie"

Comprehension	Vocabulary
1. b	1. c
2. b	2. d
3. c	3. b
4. c	4. a
5. a	5. d
	6. a
	7. c
	8. b
	9. a
	10. d

5. "Mate Selection"

Comprehension	Vocabulary
1. c	1. b
2. d	2. b
3. c	3. d
4. c	4. a
5. b	5. d
	6. a
	7. c
	8. a
	9. a
	10. a

6. "Violence in Sports"

Comprehension	Vocabulary
1. d	1. c
2. a	2. a
3. c	3. d
4. d	4. a
5. b	5. a
	6. c

UNIT TWO

Chapter 3

EXERCISE 3–2
1. C
2. C
3. I
4. I
5. I
6. I
7. C
8. I
9. I
10. C
11. I
12. I
13. C
14. I
15. I

EXERCISE 3–3

Subject	Verb
1. I	read
2. lawn mower	broke
3. child	chewed and swallowed
4. Sue	answered
5. snack bar	closes
6. letters	bring

7. inflation,
   unemployment   have caused
8. fashions   have changed
9. decorators   use
10. creations   dramatize
11. drowning   is caused
12. English Channel   is
13. Aicurus   owned
14. Equinox   occurs
15. dances   are

EXERCISE 3-4

1. Gloria Nickerson lives/where
2. Senator voted/what
3. footprints led/where or which
4. Mardi Gras is/what
5. Sal got/why
6. we ached/when
7. I read/how
8. schedule allows/what
9. restaurants are increasing/where or which
10. Tofu is made/what
11. support has increased/why
12. rates are available/when
13. ponds are/where or what
14. researchers found/how
15. firms recruit/where or what

Chapter 4

EXERCISE 4-1

3. students were interested; others were bored
4. Miami and Fort Lauderdale are; I prefer
5. dessert is; I make
6. writers tend; they do not realize
7. selecting a college is; it is influenced
8. customers complained; restaurant continued
10. students think; you would need
11. photography is; it requires
13. marriage consists; both are influenced
15. computers have become; role has not been realized, understood, explored

Chapter 5

EXERCISE 5-1

1. I...concentrate.
2. Betty...jacket,
3. I...test.
4. the service...slow.
5. I...light.
6. they...products.
7. you...work.
8. she...set.
9. the committee...proposal.
10. it...die.
11. humankind...years.
12. the anthropological...form,
13. the basic...same.
14. they...air.
15. their...patterns.

EXERCISE 5-2

Independent Clause	Core Parts
1. paraphrase...words	you/should paraphrase or put
2. I...seaman,	I/found
3. women, seldom... careers.	women/reach
4. many...Penny's,	people/buy
5. most...marriage.	people/choose
6. we...world	we/are told
7. Americans... government	Americans tend
8. the manufacturing... stop	manufacturing/would not stop
9. they...information	they/are
10. the relationship... simple	relationship/was
those...found	those/travelled
those...back	those/bought and brought
and...enjoyed it	they or some/learned
11. Piaget's...areas	research/has touched
but...intelligence	all/have had
12. it...adjustment.	it/is

Unit Two Reading Selections

7. "Kids' Country"

Comprehension	Vocabulary
1. b	1. c
2. c	2. c
3. c	3. b
4. c	
5. b	

8. "Angels on a Pin"

Comprehension	Vocabulary
1. c	1. a
2. d	2. d
3. b	
4. c	
5. a	

9. "Thermography"

Comprehension	Vocabulary
1. c	1. d
2. b	2. b
3. a	3. a
4. b	
5. c	

10. "The New (and Still Hidden) Persuaders"

Comprehension	Vocabulary
1. a	1. c
2. d	2. b
3. b	3. c
4. d	4. d
5. b	5. a

11. "What You See Is the Real You"

Comprehension	Vocabulary	
1. d	1. c	6. b
2. a	2. b	7. d
3. b	3. a	8. a
4. d	4. b	9. a
5. a	5. b	

12. "The Unique Human Time Sense"

Comprehension	Vocabulary
1. c	1. a
2. d	2. c
3. c	3. b
4. d	4. a
5. a	

UNIT THREE

Chapter 6

EXERCISE 6–2
1. color
2. furniture
3. meat
4. household appliance
5. car
6. distance
7. relative
8. media
9. living expenses
10. leisure time activities
11. natural sciences
12. literature
13. basic needs
14. personality traits

EXERCISE 6–3
1. Festival of Lakes
2. dead animals
3. racial prejudice
4. Picturephone
5. Greek mythology
6. definitions of science fiction
7. written language
8. animal communication
9. embedding
10. meditation
11. writing as discovery
12. elitism in education

Chapter 7

EXERCISE 7–1
1. first sentence
2. first sentence
3. first sentence
4. second sentence
5. second sentence
6. first sentence
7. first sentence
8. first sentence
9. first sentence
10. first sentence
11. first sentence
12. first sentence

EXERCISE 7–2
1. The writer wants a wife who will meet the physical and emotional needs of himself and his family.
2. By following the author's directions, the pit of a Florida avocado will produce a houseplant.
3. There is a sharp contrast between a beach resort in summertime and the wintertime.
4. Different cultures hold a similar belief that a single being was responsible for creating their languages.
5. Characteristics of aging include both mental and physical changes that weaken and frustrate the individual.
6. Your physical position and condition may affect your ability to appreciate art or beauty.
7. Plagiarism is common among college students.
8. Various theories have been offered to explain the appeal of drama.
9. Dexter observed the fall of evening and went for a swim.

Chapter 8

EXERCISE 8–1
1. a, c, d
2. a, b, c, d
3. a, b
4. a, b
5. a, b
6. a, b, d
7. a, b, c, d
8. a, b, c
9. b, c, d
10. a, c
11. a, c, d
12. a, c

Chapter 9

EXERCISE 9–1
1. chronological order
2. contrast
3. description
4. statement-support
5. definition
6. cause-effect
7. contrast
8. cause-effect
9. statement-support
10. statement-support
11. cause-effect
12. contrast

Unit Three Reading Selections

13. "Dazzled in Disneyland"
Comprehension	Vocabulary
1. d	1. b
2. a	2. a
3. a	3. a
4. c	
5. c	

14. "The Thin Grey Line"
Comprehension	Vocabulary
1. b	1. c
2. c	2. b
3. d	3. d
4. b	4. c
5. b	

15. "The Peter Principle"
Comprehension	Vocabulary
1. c	1. c
2. c	2. b
3. c	3. a
4. a	4. d
5. b	

16. "Euphemism"
Comprehension	Vocabulary
1. c	1. b
2. c	2. a
3. b	3. a
4. d	4. d
5. b	5. b
	6. c
	7. d

17. "Occupational Choice and Adjustment"
Comprehension	Vocabulary
1. d	1. b
2. c	2. c
3. d	3. a
4. a	4. b
5. c	

18. "Down at the Cross"
Comprehension	Vocabulary
1. c	1. c
2. c	2. a
3. c	3. a
4. a	4. d
5. c	5. b
	6. b
	7. a
	8. c

UNIT FOUR
Chapter 10
NONE

Chapter 11
NONE

Chapter 12
NONE

Unit Four Reading Selections

19. "Sister Flowers"
Comprehension	Vocabulary
1. d	1. d
2. c	2. c
3. b	3. a
4. c	4. b
5. d	5. c

20. "Soap Operas"
Comprehension	Vocabulary
1. b	1. d
2. b	2. b
3. c	3. d
4. c	4. a
5. c	5. b
	6. c

21. "A Fable for Tomorrow"
Comprehension	Vocabulary
1. d	1. c
2. a	2. b
3. a	3. a
4. d	4. b
5. c	5. d
	6. b
	7. b

22. "The Sale"
Comprehension	Vocabulary
1. c	1. a
2. c	2. d
3. b	3. b
4. b	4. c
5. b	5. c

23. "Whales and Dolphins"
Comprehension	Vocabulary
1. a	1. d
2. c	2. b
3. b	3. a
4. b	4. a
5. b	5. b

24. "Being There—TV as Baby Sitter"

Comprehension	Vocabulary
1. b	1. a
2. a	2. b
3. c	3. c
4. c	4. a
5. b	5. d

25. "Mythology"

Comprehension	Vocabulary
1. c	1. c
2. d	2. c
3. b	3. b
4. b	4. d
5. a	5. a

26. "Extrasensory Perception"

Comprehension	Vocabulary
1. c	1. c
2. a	2. b
3. c	3. c
4. d	4. a
5. b	5. d
	6. a

27. "Verbal Taboo"

Comprehension	Vocabulary
1. c	1. a
2. c	2. d
3. d	3. b
4. b	4. b
5. c	5. d
	6. b

Index

Index